J. Churchill, Theodore Martin, S. T. Coleridge

Dramatic works of Friedrich Schiller

Wallenstein and Wilhelm Tell

J. Churchill, Theodore Martin, S. T. Coleridge

Dramatic works of Friedrich Schiller
Wallenstein and Wilhelm Tell

ISBN/EAN: 9783743377332

Manufactured in Europe, USA, Canada, Australia, Japa

Cover: Foto ©Thomas Meinert / pixelio.de

Manufactured and distributed by brebook publishing software (www.brebook.com)

J. Churchill, Theodore Martin, S. T. Coleridge

Dramatic works of Friedrich Schiller

DRAMATIC WORKS

OF

FRIEDRICH SCHILLER.

WALLENSTEIN AND WILHELM TELL.

Translated in the Original Metre.

BY

S. T. COLERIDGE, J. CHURCHILL,

AND

SIR THEODORE MARTIN, K.C.B., LL.D.

LONDON: GEORGE BELL & SONS, YORK STREET,
COVENT GARDEN.
1891.

PREFACE.

Of the dramatic works contained in the following volume,
the first—WALLENSTEIN'S CAMP—was translated by Mr.
James Churchill, and appeared originally in 'Fraser's
Magazine.'

The PICCOLOMINI and DEATH OF WALLENSTEIN, which
form the second and third parts of this great dramatic
trilogy, are reprinted from the admirable rendering of
S. T. Coleridge, completed by the addition of all those
passages which he had omitted, and by a restoration of
Schiller's own arrangement of the acts and scenes. It is
said, in defence of the variations which exist between the
German original and the version given by Coleridge, that
he translated from a prompter's copy in manuscript,
before the drama had been printed, and that Schiller
himself subsequently altered it, omitting some passages,
adding others, and even engrafting several of Coleridge's
adaptations. However this may be, the publishers consider it advisable to give every line of Coleridge's version,
without the least alteration (especially as it contains
more than one fine passage not to be found in the printed
editions of Schiller), and to add, in brackets, all those
portions (upwards of 250 lines) which have heretofore
been omitted. These are chiefly translated by Mr. G. F.
Richardson, the translator of the poems of Körner. They
will be found at pages 52, 53, 59, 79, 80, 83, 85, 95,
100, 109, 161, 164, 169, 187, 188, 189, 251, 253, and
280.

The translation of WILHELM TELL is by Sir Theodore
Martin, and though executed many years earlier, it will
not be found unworthy of the successful translator of
'Faust.'

CONTENTS.

WALLENSTEIN'S CAMP,

TRANSLATED BY JAMES CHURCHILL.

THE PICCOLOMINI,

AND

THE DEATH OF WALLENSTEIN,

BY S. T. COLERIDGE.

INCLUDING SCENES AND PASSAGES HITHERTO OMITTED.

———

" Upon the whole there can be no doubt that this trilogy forms, in its original tongue, one of the most splendid specimens of tragic art the world has witnessed ; and none at all, that the execution of the version from which we have quoted so largely, places Mr. Coleridge in the very first rank of poetical translators. He is, perhaps, the solitary example of a man of very great original genius submitting to *all* the labours, and reaping *all* the honours, of this species of literary exertion."—*Blackwood,* 1823.

The Camp of Wallenstein is an introduction to the celebrated tragedy of that name ; and, by its vivid portraiture of
the state of the General's army, gives the best clue to the
spell of his gigantic power.   The blind belief entertained in
the unfailing success of his arms, and in the supernatural
agencies by which that success is secured to him ; the unre-
strained indulgence of every passion, and utter disregard of
all law, save that of the camp ; a hard oppression of the peasantry and plunder of the country ; have all swollen the soldiery with an idea of interminable sway.   But, as we have
translated the whole, we shall leave these reckless marauders
to speak for themselves.

Of Schiller's opinion concerning the Camp, as a necessary
introduction to the tragedy, the following passage taken from
the Prologue to the first representation, will give a just idea
and may also serve as a motto to the work :—

> "Not He it is, who on the tragic scene
>   Will now appear—but in the fearless bands
> Whom his command alone could sway, and whom
> His spirit fired, you may his shadow see,
> Until the bashful Muse shall dare to bring
> Himself before you in a living form ;
> For power it was that bore his heart astray—
> His Camp, alone, elucidates his crime."

THE CAMP OF WALLENSTEIN.

DRAMATIS PERSONÆ.

Sergeant-Major, } of a regiment of	*Recruit.*
Trumpeter, } Terzky's carabineers.	*Citizen.*
Artilleryman.	*Peasant.*
Sharpshooters.	*Peasant Boy.*
Mounted Yagers, of Holk's corps.	*Capuchin.*
Dragoons, of Butler's regiment.	*Regimental Schoolmaster.*
Arquebusiers, of Tiefenbach's regiment.	*Sutler Woman.*
Cuirassier, of a Walloon regiment.	*Servant Girl.*
Cuirassier, of a Lombard regiment.	*Soldiers' Boys.*
Crouts.	*Musicians.*
Hulans.	

(SCENE—*The camp before Pilsen, in Bohemia.*)

SCENE 1.

*Sutlers' tents—in front, a Slop-shop.—Soldiers of all colours
and uniforms thronging about.—Tables all filled.—Crouts
and Hulans cooking at a fire.—Sutler-woman serving out
wine.—Soldier-boys throwing dice on a drum-head —Singing
heard from the tent.*

Enter a Peasant and his Son.

SON.

FATHER, I fear it will come to harm,
So let us be off from this soldier swarm ;
But boist'rous mates will ye find in the shoal—
'Twere better to bolt while our skins are whole.

FATHER.

How now, boy ! the fellows won't eat us, tho
They may be a little unruly, or so.
See, yonder, arriving a stranger train,
Fresh comers are they from the Saal and Mayn.
Much booty they bring of the rarest sort—
'Tis ours, if we cleverly drive our sport

B 2

A captain, who fell by his comrade's sword,
This pair of sure dice to me transferr'd ;
To-day I'll just give them a trial, to see
If their knack's as good as it used to be.
You must play the part of a pitiful devil,
For these roaring rogues, who so loosely revel,
Are easily smooth'd, and trick'd, and flatter'd,
And, free as it came, their gold is scatter'd.
But *we*—since by bushels our all is ta'en,
By spoonfuls must ladle it back again ;
And, if with their swords they slash so highly,
We must look sharp, boy, and *do* them slyly.
           [*Singing and shouting in the tent*
Hark, how they shout ! God help the day !
'Tis the peasant's hide for their sport must pay.
Eight months in our beds and stalls have they
Been swarming here, until far around
Not a bird or a beast is longer found,
And the peasant, to quiet his craving maw,
Has nothing now left but his bones to gnaw.
Ne'er were we crush'd with a heavier hand,
When the Saxon was lording it o'er the land :
And these are the Emperor's troops, they say !—

SON.

From the kitchen a couple are coming this way,
Not much shall we make by such blades as they

FATHER.

They're born Bohemian knaves—the two—
Belonging to Terzky's carabineers,
Who've lain in these quarters now for years
The worst are they of the worthless crew.
Strutting, swaggering, proud, and vain,
They seem to think they may well disdain
With the peasant a glass of his wine to drain
But, soft—to the left o' the fire I see
Three riflemen, who from the Tyrol should be
Emmerick, come, boy, to them will we—
Birds of this feather 'tis luck to find,
Whose trim's so spruce, and their purse well lined.
           They move towards the tent.

SCENE II.

The above—Sergeant-Major, Trumpeter, Hulan

TRUMPETER.

What would the boor?—Out, rascal, away!

PEASANT

Some victuals and drink, worthy masters, I pray,
For not a warm morsel we've tasted to day.

TRUMPETER.

Ay, guzzle and guttle—'tis always the way

HULAN (*with a glass*).

Not broken your fast!—there—drink, ye hound!
He leads the peasant to the tent—the others come forward.

SERGEANT (*to the Trumpeter*).

Think ye, they've done it without good ground?
Is it likely they double our pay to day,
Merely that we may be jolly and gay?

TRUMPETER.

Why, the duchess arrives to-day, we know,
And her daughter too—

BERGEANT.

Tush! that's mere shcw—
'Tis the troops collected from other lands
Who here at Pilsen have joined our bands—
We must do the best we can t' allure 'em,
With plentiful rations, and thus secure 'em,
Where such abundant fare they find,
A closer league with us to bind

TRUMPETER.

Yes!—there's something in the wind

SERGEANT.

The generals and commanders too—

TRUMPETER.

A rather ominous sight, 'tis true

SERGEANT.

Who're met together so thickly here—

TRUMPETER.

Have plenty of work on their hands, that's clear.

SERGEANT.

The whisp'ring and sending to and fro—

TRUMPETER.

Ay! Ay!

SERGEANT

The big-wig from Vienna, I trow,
Who since yesterday's seen to prowl about
In his golden chain of office there—
Something's at bottom of this, I'll swear.

TRUMPETER.

A bloodhound is he, beyond a doubt,
By whom the duke's to be hunted out

SERGEANT.

Mark ye well, man!—they doubt us now,
And they fear the duke's mysterious brow;
He hath clomb too high for *them*, and fain
Would they beat him down from his perch again

TRUMPETER.

But we will hold him still on high --
That all would think as you and I!

SERGEANT.

Our regiment, and the other four
Which Terzky leads—the bravest corps
Throughout the camp, are the General's own,
And have been trained to the trade by himself alone
The officers hold their command of him,
And are all his own, or for life, or limb

SCENE III.

*Enter Croat with a Necklace.—Sharpshooter following him.
The above.*

SHARPSHOOTER.

Croat, where stole you that necklace, say?
Get rid of it, man—for thee 'tis unmeet:
Come, take these pistols in change, I pray.

CROAT.

Nay, nay, Master Shooter, you're trying to cheat.

SHARPSHOOTER.

Then I'll give you this fine blue cap as well,
A Lottery prize which just I've won:
Look at the cut of it—quite the swell!

CROAT (*twirling the Necklace in the Sun*).

But this is of pearls and of garnets bright,
See, how it plays in the sunny light!

SHARPSHOOTER (*taking the Necklace*).

Well, I'll give you to boot, my own canteen—
I'm in love with this bauble's beautiful sheen

[*Looks at it*

TRUMPETER.

See, now!—how cleanly the Croat is *done:*
Snacks! Master Shooter, and *mum's* the word.

CROAT (*having put on the cap*).

I think your cap is a smartish one.

SHARPSHOOTER (*winking to the Trumpeter*).

'Tis a regular swop—as these gents have heard.

SCENE IV.

The above.—An Artilleryman.

ARTILLERYMAN (*to the Sergeant*).

How is it, I pray, brother Carabineer?
Shall we longer stay here, our fingers warming,
While the foe in the field around is swarming?

SERGEANT.

Art thou, indeed, in such hasty fret?
Why the roads, as I think, are scarce passable yet.

ARTILLERYMAN.

For me they are not—I'm snug enough here—
But a courier's come, our wits to waken
With the precious news that Ratisbon's taken.

TRUMPETER.

Ha! then we soon shall have work in hand.

SERGEANT.

Indeed! to protect the Bavarian's land,
Who hates the Duke, as we understand,
We won't put ourselves in a violent sweat.

ARTILLERYMAN.

Heyday!—you'll find you're a wiseacre yet.

SCENE V

The above.—Two Yagers.—Afterwards Sutler-woman, Soldier boy, Schoolmaster, Servant-girl.

FIRST YAGER
See ! see !
Here meet we a jovial company !

TRUMPETER.
Who can those green coats be, I wonder,
That strut so gay and sprucely yonder?

SERGEANT.
They're the Yagers of Holk—and the lace they wear,
I'll be sworn. was ne'er purchased at Leipzig fair

SUTLER-WOMAN (*bringing wine*).
Welcome, good sirs !

FIRST YAGER.
Zounds, how now ?
Gustel of Blasewitz here, I vow !

SUTLER-WOMAN
The same in sooth—and you, I know,
Are the lanky Peter of Itzeho :
Who at Glückstadt once, in a revelling night,
With the wags of our regiment, put to flight
All his father's shiners—then crown'd the fun—

FIRST YAGER.
By changing his pen for a rifle gun

SUTLER-WOMAN.
We're old acquaintance, then, 'tis clear

FIRST YAGER.
And to think we should meet in Bohemia here !

SUTLER-WOMAN.
Oh, here to-day—to-morrow yonder—
As the rude war-broom. in restless trace,
Scatters and sweeps us from place to place.
Meanwhile I've been doom'd far round to wander.

FIRST YAGER.
So one would think, by the look of your face

SUTLER-WOMAN.
Up the country I've rambled to Temsewar,
Whither I went with the baggage car.

When Mansfeld before us we chased away;
With the Duke near Stralsund next we lay,
Where trade went all to pot, I may say.
I jogged with the succours to Mantua;
And back again came, under Feria
Then, joining a Spanish regiment,
I took a short cut across to Ghent;
And now to Bohemia I'm come to get
Old scores paid off, that are standing yet,
If a helping hand by the Duke be lent—
And yonder you see my sutler's tent.

FIRST YAGER.

Well, all things seem in a flourishing way,
But what have you done with the Scotchman, say,
Who once in the camp was your constant flame?

SUTLER-WOMAN.

A villain, who trick'd me clean, that same!
He bolted, and took to himself. whate'er
I'd managed to scrape together, or spare,
Leaving me naught but the urchin there

SOLDIER-BOY (springing forward).
Mother, is it my papa you name?

FIRST YAGER.

Well, the Emperor now must father this elf,
For the army must ever recruit itself.

SCHOOLMASTER.

Forth to the school, ye rogue—d'ye hear?

FIRST YAGER.

He, too, of a narrow room has fear.

SERVANT GIRL (entering).
Aunt, they'll be off.

SUTLER-WOMAN.
I come apace.

FIRST YAGER.
What gypsy is that with the roguish face?

SUTLER-WOMAN.
My sister's child from the south, is she.

FIRST YAGER.
Ay, ay, a sweet little niece—I see.

SECOND YAGER (*holding the girl*),
Softly, my pretty one! stay with me

GIRL.
The customers wait, sir, and I must go.
                    [*Disengages herself, and exit.*

FIRST YAGER.
That maiden's a dainty morsel, I trow!
And her aunt—by Heav'n! I mind me well,
When the best of the regiment loved her so,
To blows for her beautiful face they fell.
What different folks one's doomed to know!
How time glides off with a ceaseless flow!
And what sights as yet we may live to see!
    (*To the Sergeant and Trumpeter.*)
Your health, good sirs, may we be free,
A seat beside you here to take?

Scene VI
The Yagers, Sergeant, and Trumpeter.

SERGEANT.
We thank ye—and room will gladly make
To Bohemia welcome.

FIRST YAGER.
                    Snug enough here!
In the land of the foe *our* quarters were queer

TRUMPETER.
You hav'n't the look on't—you're spruce to view.

SERGEANT.
Ay, faith, on the Saal, and in Meissen too,
Your praises are heard from the lips of few

SECOND YAGER.
Tush, man!—why, what the plague d'ye mean ;'
The Croat had swept the fields so clean,
There was little, or nothing, for us to glean

TRUMPETER.
Yet your pointed collar is clean and sightly,
And, then, your hose, that sit so tightly!
Your linen so fine, with the hat and feather
Make a show of the smartest altogether!

(To Sergeant.)
That fortune should upon younkers shine—
While nothing in your way comes, or mine

SERGEANT.

But then we're the Friedlander's regiment,
And, thus, may honour and homage claim.

FIRST YAGER.

For us, now, that's no great compliment,
We, also, bear the Friedlander's name.

SERGEANT.

True—you form part of the general mass.

FIRST YAGER.

And you, I suppose, are a separate class!
The difference lies in the coats we wear,
And I have no wish to change with you there!

SERGEANT.

Sir Yager, I can't but with pity melt,
When I think how much among boors you've dwelt
The clever knack and the proper tone,
Are caught by the General's side alone.

FIRST YAGER.

Then the lesson is wofully thrown away,—
How he hawks and spits, indeed, I may say
You've copied and caught in the cleverest way
But his spirit, his genius—oh, these I ween,
On your guard parade are but seldom seen.

SECOND YAGER.

Why, zounds! ask for us wherever you will,
Friedland's wild hunt is our title still!
Never shaming the name, all undaunted we go
Alike thro' the field of a friend, or a foe:
Through the rising stalk, or the yellow corn,
Well know they the blast of Holk's Yager horn
In the flash of an eye, we are far or near,
Swift as the deluge, or there or here—
As at midnight dark, when the flames outbreak
In the silent dwelling where none awake;
Vain is the hope in weapons or flight,
Nor order nor discipline thwart its might.
Then struggles the maid in our sinewy arms,
But war hath no pity, and scorns alarms.

Go ask—I speak not with boastful tongue—
In Bareuth, Westphalia, Voigtland, where'er
Our troop has traversed—go, ask them there—
Children and children's children long,
When hundreds and hundreds of years are o'er
Of Holk will tell and his Yager corps.

SERGEANT.

Why, hark!   Must a soldier then be made
By driving this riotous, roaring trade!
'Tis drilling that makes him, skill and sense—
Perception—thought—intelligence.

FIRST YAGER.

'Tis liberty makes him!—Here's a fuss!
That I should such twaddle as this discuss.
Was it for this, that I left the school?
That the scribbling desk, and the slavish rule,
And the narrow walls, that our spirits cramp,
Should be met with again in the midst of the camp?
No!—Idle and heedless, I'll take my way,
Hunting for novelty every day;
Trust to the moment with dauntless mind,
And give not a glance or before or behind.
For this to the Emperor I sold my hide,
That no other care I might have to bide.
Through the foe's fierce firing bid me ride,
Through fathomless Rhine, in his roaring flow,
Where ev'ry third man to the devil may go,
At no bar will you find me boggling there;
But, farther than this, 'tis my special prayer,
That I may not be bother'd with aught like care

SERGEANT.

If this be your wish, you needn't lack it,
'Tis granted to all with the soldier's jacket.

FIRST YAGER.

What a fuss and a bother, forsooth, was made
By that man-tormentor, Gustavus the Swede,
Whose camp was a church, where prayers were said
At morning réveille and evening tattoo;
And, whenever it chanced that we frisky grew,
A sermon himself from the saddle he'd read.

SERGEANT.

Ay, that was a man with the fear of God.

FIRST YAGER.

Girls he detested ; and, what's rather odd,
If caught with a wench, you in wedlock were tack'd—
I could stand it no longer, so off I pack'd.

SERGEANT.

Their discipline now has a trifle slack'd.

FIRST YAGER.

Well, next to the League I rode over; their men
Were must'ring in haste against Magdeburg then
Ha ! that was another guess sort of a thing !—
In frolic and fun we'd a glorious swing;
With gaming, and drinking, and girls at call,
I'faith, sirs, our sport was by no means small.
For Tilly knew how to command, that's plain ;
He held himself in, but gave us the rein ;
And, long as he hadn't the bother of paying,
" Live, and let live !" was the General's saying,
But fortune soon gave him the slip ; and ne'er,
Since the day of that villanous Leipzig affair,
Would aught go aright.   'Twas of little avail
That we tried, for our plans were sure to fail.
If now we drew nigh, and rapp'd at a door,
No greeting awaited, 'twas opened no more ;
From place to place we went sneaking about,
And found that their stock of respect was out
Then touch'd I the Saxon bounty, and thought
Their service with fortune must needs be fraught

SERGEANT.

You join'd 'em then just in the nick to share
Bohemia's plunder?

FIRST YAGER.

I'd small luck there
Strict discipline sternly ruled the day,
Nor dared we a foeman's force display
They set us to guard the imperial forts
And plagued us all with the farce of the courts
War they waged as a jest 'twere thought—
And but half a heart to the business brought

They would break with none; and thus 'twas plain,
Small honour 'mong them could a soldier gain.
So heartily sick in the end grew I,
That my mind was the desk again to try;
When suddenly, rattling near and far,
The Friedlander's drum was heard to war

SERGEANT.

And how long here may you mean to stay?

FIRST YAGER.

You jest, man.—So long as *he* bears the sway,
By my soul! not a thought of change have I
Where better than here could the soldier lie?
Here the true fashion of war is found,
And the cut of power's on all things round;
While the spirit, whereby the movement's given,
Mightily stirs, like the winds of heaven,
The meanest trooper in all the throng.
With a hearty step shall I tramp along;
On a burgher's neck as undaunted tread,
As our General does on the prince's head.
As 'twas in the times of old 'tis now,
The sword is the sceptre, and all must bow.
One crime alone can I understand,
And that's to oppose the word of command.
What's not forbidden, to do make bold,
And none will ask you what creed you hold.
Of just two things in this world I wot,
What belongs to the army, and what does not
To the banner alone is my service brought

SERGEANT

Thus, Yager, I like thee—thou speak'st, I vow,
With the tone of a Friedland trooper now

FIRST YAGER.

"Tis not as an office *he* holds command,
Or a power received from the Emperor's hand,
For the Emperor's service what should he care?
What better for him does the Emperor fare?
With the mighty power, he wields at will,
Has ever he shelter'd the land from ill?

No ; a soldier-kingdom he seeks to raise,
And for this would set the world in a blaze,
Daring to risk and to compass all——
TRUMPETER.
Hush—who shall such words as these let fall?
FIRST YAGER.
Whatever I think may be said by me,
For the General tells us, the word is free
SERGEANT.
True—that he said so I fully agree,
I was standing by. "The word is free—
The deed is dumb—obedience blind!"
His very words I can call to mind
FIRST YAGER.
I know not if these were his words or no,
But he said the thing, and 'tis even so,
SECOND YAGER.
Victory ne'er will his flag forsake,
Though she's apt from others a turn to take:
Old Tilly outlived his fame's decline,
But, under the banner of Wallenstein,
There am I certain that victory's mine!
Fortune is spell-bound to him, and must yield ·
Whoe'er under Friedland shall take the field
Is sure of a supernatural shield:
For, as all the world is aware full well,
The Duke has a devil in hire from hell
SERGEANT.
In truth that he's charm'd is past a doubt,
For we know how, at Lutzen's bloody affair,
Where firing was thickest, he still was there,
As coolly as might be, sirs, riding about
The hat on his head was shot thro' and thro',
In coat and boots the bullets that flew
Left traces full clear to all men's view ;
But none got so far as to scratch off his skin,
For the ointment of hell was too well rubb'd in
FIRST YAGER.
What wonder so strange can you all see there?
An elk-skin jacket he happens to wear,
And through it the bullets can make no way.

SERGEANT

Tis an ointment of witches' herbs, I say,
Kneaded and cook'd by unholy spell

TRUMPETER.

No doubt 'tis the work of the powers of hell

SERGEANT.

That he reads in the stars, we also hear.
Where the future he sees—distant or near—
But I know better the truth of the case ·
A little grey man, at the dead of night,
Through bolted doors to him will pace—
The sentinels oft have hailed the sight,
And something great was sure to be nigh,
When this little Grey Coat had glided by.

FIRST YAGER.

Ay, ay, he's sold himself to the devil,
Wherefore, my lads, let's feast and revel.

SCENE VII.

The above.—Recruit, Citizen, Dragoon.

(*The Recruit advances from the tent, wearing a tin cap on his
head, and carrying a wine flask.*)

RECRUIT.

To father and uncle pray make my bow,
And bid 'em good bye—I'm a soldier now.

FIRST YAGER.

See, yonder they're bringing us something new

CITIZEN.

O, Franz, remember, this day you'll rue

RECRUIT (*sings*).

The drum and the fife,
    War's rattling throng,
And a wandering life
    The world along!
Swift steed—and a hand
To curb and command—
With a blade by the side
We're off far and wide,

As jolly and free,
As the finch in its glee,
On thicket or tree,
Under Heaven's wide hollow—
Hurrah! for the Friedlander's banner I'll follow!

SECOND YAGER.

Foregad! a jolly companion, though.

[*They salute him.*

CITIZEN.

He comes of good kin; now pray let him go.

FIRST YAGER.

And *we* weren't found in the streets you must know

CITIZEN.

I tell you his wealth is a plentiful stock;
Just feel the fine stuff that he wears for a frock.

TRUMPETER.

The Emperor's coat is the best he can wear.

CITIZEN.

To a cap manufactory he is the heir.

SECOND YAGER.

The will of a man is his fortune alone

CITIZEN.

His grandmother's shop will soon be his own.

FIRST YAGER.

Pish! traffic in matches! who would do 't?

CITIZEN.

A wine-shop his godfather leaves, to boot,
A cellar with twenty casks of wine.

TRUMPETER.

These with his comrades he'll surely share

SECOND YAGER.

Hark ye, lad—be a camp-brother of mine

CITIZEN.

A bride he leaves sitting, in tears, apart

FIRST YAGER.

Good—that now's a proof of an iron heart

CITIZEN.

His grandmother's sure to die with sorrow

SECOND YAGER.

The better—for then he'll inherit to-morrow

SERGEANT (*advances gravely, and lays his hand on the Recruit's tin cap*).

The matter, no doubt, you have duly weighed,
And here a new man of yourself have made;
With hanger and helm, sir, you now belong
To a nobler and more distinguished throng.
Thus, a loftier spirit, 'twere well to uphold—

FIRST YAGER.

And, specially, never be sparing of gold.

SERGEANT.

In Fortune's ship, with an onward gale,
My friend, you have made up your mind to sail
The earth-ball is open before you—yet there
Nought's to be gained, but by those who dare.
Stupid and sluggish your citizen's found,
Like a dyer's dull jade, in his ceaseless round ·
While the soldier can be whatever he will,
For war o'er the earth is the watchword still.
Just look now at me, and the coat I wear,
You see that the Emperor's baton I bear—
And all good government, over the earth,
You must know from the baton alone has birth;
For the sceptre that's sway'd by the kingly hand
Is nought but a baton, we understand.
And he who has corporal's rank obtain'd,
Stands on the ladder where all's to be gained,
And you, like another, may mount to that height—

FIRST YAGER.

Provided you can but read and write.

SERGEANT.

Now, hark to an instance of this, from me,
And one, which I've lived myself to see:
There's Buttler, the chief of dragoons, why he,
Whose rank was not higher a whit than mine,
Some thirty years since, at Cologne on Rhine,
Is a Major-General now—because
He put himself forward and gained applause;

Filling the world with his martial fame,
While slept my merits without a name.
And ev'n the Friedlander's self—I've heard—
Our General and all commanding Lord,
Who now can do what he will at a word,
Had at first but a private squire's degree ;
In the goddess of war yet trusting free,
He rear'd the greatness, which now you see,
And, after the Emperor, next is he.
Who knows what more he may mean or get?
Slily.) For all-day's evening isn't come yet.

FIRST YAGER.

He was little at first, tho' now so great—
For, at Altorf, in student's gown, he play'd,
By your leave, the part of a roaring blade,
And rattled away at a queerish rate.
His fag he had well nigh kill'd by a blow,
And their Nur'mberg worships swore he should go
To jail for his pains,—if he liked it, or no.
'Twas a new-built nest to be christen'd by him,
Who first should be lodged.   Well, what was his whim?
Why, he sent his dog forward to lead the way,
And they call the jail from the dog to this day.
That was the game a brave fellow should play,
And of all the great deeds of the General, none
E'er tickled my fancy, like this one.

[*During this speech, the Second Yager has begun toying
with the Girl, who has been in waiting.*]

DRAGOON (*stepping between them*).

Comrade—give over this sport, I pray

SECOND YAGER.

Why, who the devil shall say me nay?

DRAGOON.

I've only to tell you the girl's my own

FIRST YAGER.

Such a morsel as this, for himself alone!—
Dragoon, why say, art thou crazy grown?

SECOND YAGER.

In the camp to be keeping a wench for one!
No! the light of a pretty girl's face must fall,
Like the beams of the sun to gladden us all. (*Kisses her.*)

c 2

DRAGOON (*tears her away*).
I tell you again, that it sha'n't be done.

FIRST YAGER.
The pipers are coming, lads! now for fun!

SECOND YAGER (*to Dragoon*).
I sha'n't be far off, should you look for me.

SERGEANT.
Peace, my good fellows!—a kiss goes free.

SCENE VIII.

Enter Miners, and play a Waltz—at first slowly, and after-
wards quicker.—The First Yager dances with the Girl, the
Sutler-woman with the Recruit.—The Girl springs away, and
the Yager, pursuing her, seizes hold of a Capuchin Friar
just entering.

CAPUCHIN.
Hurrah! halloo! tol, lol, de rol, le!
The fun's at its height! I'll not be away!
Is't an army of Christians that join in such works?
Or are we all turn'd Anabaptists and Turks?
Is the Sabbath a day for this sport in the land,
As tho' the great God had the gout in his hand,
And thus couldn't smite in the midst of your band?
Say, is this a time for your revelling shouts,
For your banquetings, feasts, and holiday bouts?
Quid hic statis otiosi? declare
Why, folding your arms, stand ye lazily there?
While the furies of war on the Danube now fare,
And Bavaria's bulwark is lying full low,
And Ratisbon's fast in the clutch of the foe.
Yet, the army lies here in Bohemia still,
And caring for nought, so their paunches they fill!
Bottles far rather than battles you'll get,
And your bills than your broad swords more readily wet;
With the wenches, I ween is, your dearest concern,
And you'd rather roast oxen than Oxenstiern.
In sackcloth and ashes while Christendom's grieving,
No thought has the soldier his guzzle of leaving.
'Tis a time of misery, groans, and tears!
Portentous the face of the heavens appears!

And forth from the clouds behold blood-red,
The Lord's war-mantle is downward spread—
While the comet is thrust as a threatening rod,
From the window of Heaven by the hand of God.
The world is but one vast house of woe,
The Ark of the Church stems a bloody flow,
The Holy Empire—God help the same!
Has wretchedly sunk to a hollow name.
The Rhine's gay stream has a gory gleam,
The cloister's nests are robbed by roysters;
The church-lands now are changed to lurch-lands;
Abbacies, and all other holy foundations
Now are but Robber-sees—rogues' habitations.
And thus is each once-blest German state,
Deep sunk in the doom of the desolate!
Whence comes all this? O, that will I tell—
It comes of your doings, of sin, and of hell;
Of the horrible, heathenish lives ye lead,
Soldiers and officers, all of a breed.
For sin is the magnet, on every hand,
That draws your steel throughout the land.
As the onion causes the tear to flow,
So Vice must ever be followed by Woe—
The W duly succeeds the V,
This is the order of A, B, C.
    Ubi erit victoriæ spes,
Si offenditur Deus? which says,
How, pray ye, shall victory e'er come to pass,
If thus you play truant from sermon and mass,
And do nothing but lazily loll o'er the glass?
The woman, we're told in the Testament,
Found the penny, in search whereof she went
Saul met with his father's asses again,
And Joseph his precious fraternal train,
But he, who 'mong soldiers shall hope to see
God's fear, or shame, or discipline—he
From his toil, beyond doubt, will baffled return,
Tho' a hundred lamps in the search he burn
To the wilderness preacher, th' Evangelist says,
The soldiers, too, throng'd to repent of their ways,
And had themselves christen'd in former days.

Quid faciemus nos ? they said:
Tow'rd Abraham's bosom what path must we tread?
  Et ait illis, and, said he,
Neminem concutiatis ;
From bother and wrongs leave your neighbours free.
Neque calumniam faciatis ;
And deal nor in slander nor lies, d'ye see ?
Contenti estote—content ye, pray,
Stipendiis vestris—with your pay—
And curse for ever each evil way.
    There is a command—thou shalt not utter
The name of the Lord thy God, in vain ;
But, where is it men most blasphemies mutter?
Why here, in Duke Friedland's head quarters, 'tis plain
If for every thunder!—and every blast!
Which blazing ye from your tongue-points cast,
The bells were but rung, in the country round,
Not a bellman, I ween, would there soon be found ;
And if for each and ev'ry unholy prayer
Which to vent from your jabbering jaws you dare,
From your noddles were pluck'd but the smallest hair,
Ev'ry crop would be smooth'd ere the sun went down,
Tho' at morn 'twere as bushy as Absalom's crown.
Now Joshua, methinks, was a soldier as well—
By the arm of King David the Philistine fell ;
But where do we find it written, I pray,
That they ever blasphemed in this villanous way?
One would think ye need stretch your jaws no more,
To cry, " God help us !" than " Zounds !" to roar.
But, by the liquor that's pour'd in the cask, we know
With what it will bubble and overflow.
    Again, it is written—thou shalt not steal,
And this you follow, i'faith ! to the letter,
For open faced robbery suits ye better.
Tho gripe of your vulture claws you fix
On all—and your wiles and rascally tricks
Make the gold unhid in our coffers now,
And the calf unsafe while yet in the cow—
Ye take both the egg and the hen, I vow.
Contenti estote—the preacher said ;
Which means—be content with your army bread.

But how should the slaves not from duty swerve
The mischief begins with the lord they serve
Just like the members so is the head.
I should like to know who can tell me *his* creed.

FIRST YAGER.

Sir Priest, 'gainst ourselves rail on as you will——
Of the General we warn you to breathe no ill

CAPUCHIN.

Ne custodias gregem meam!
An Ahab is he, and a Jerobeam.
Who the people from faith's unerring way,
To the worship of idols would turn astray

TRUMPETER *and* RECRUIT

Let us not hear that again, we pray.

CAPUCHIN.

Such a Bramarbas, whose iron tooth
Would seize all the strongholds of earth, forsooth!——
Did he not boast, with ungodly tongue,
That Stralsund must needs to his grasp be wrung,
Though to heaven itself with a chain 'twere strung?

TRUMPETER

Will none put a stop to his slanderous bawl?

CAPUCHIN.

A wizard he is!—and a sorcerer Saul!——
Holofernes!—a Jehu!—denying, we know,
Like St. Peter, his Master and Lord below;
And hence must he quail when the cock doth crow—

BOTH YAGERS

Now, parson, prepare; for thy doom is nigh.

CAPUCHIN.

A fox more cunning than Herod I trow—

TRUMPETER *and both* YAGERS (*pressing against him*).

Silence, again,—if thou wouldst not die!

CROATS (*interfering*).

Stick to it, father; we'll shield you, ne'er fear,
The close of your preachment now let's hear.

CAPUCHIN (*still louder*).

A Nebuchadnezzar, in towering pride!
And a vile and heretic sinner beside!

He calls himself rightly the stone of a wall;
For, faith! he's a stumbling-stone to us all.
And ne'er can the Emperor have peace indeed,
Till of Friedland himself the land is freed.

> [*During the last passage, which he pronounces in
> an elevated voice, he has been gradually retreat-
> ing, the Croats keeping the other Soldiers off*

Scene IX.

The above, without the Capuchin.

FIRST YAGER (*to the Sergeant*).

But, tell us, what meant he 'bout chanticleer,
Whose crowing the General dares not hear?
No doubt it was uttered in spite and scorn.

SERGEANT.

Listen—'tis not so untrue as 't appears :
For Friedland was rather mysteriously born,
And is 'specially troubled with ticklish ears
He can never suffer the mew of a cat :
And, when the cock crows, he starts thereat.

FIRST YAGER.

He's one and the same with the lion in that.

SERGEANT

Mouse-still must all around him creep,
Strict watch in this the sentinels keep,
For he ponders on matters most grave and deep.

> [*Voices in the Tent.   A Tumult.*

Seize the rascal! lay on! lay on!

PEASANT'S VOICE.

Help!—mercy!—help!

OTHERS.

Peace! peace! begone!

FIRST YAGER.

Deuce take me, but yonder the swords are out!

SECOND YAGER.

Then I must be off, and see what 'tis about.

> [*Yagers enter the Tent*

SUTLER-WOMAN (*comes forward*).

A scandalous villain!--a scurvy thief!

TRUMPETER.

Good hostess, the cause of this clamorous grief?

SUTLER-WOMAN.

A cut-purse!—a scoundrel! the villain I call.
That the like in my tent should ever befall!
I'm disgraced and undone with the officers all!

SERGEANT.

Well, coz, what is it?

SUTLER-WOMAN.

Why, what should it be?
But a peasant they've taken just now with me—
A rogue with false dice, to favour his play.

TRUMPETER.

See! they're bringing the boor and his son this way

SCENE X.

Soldiers dragging in the Peasant, bound.

FIRST YAGER.

He must hang!

SHARPSHOOTERS *and* DRAGOONS
To the provost come on!

SERGEANT

'Tis the latest order that forth has gone.

SUTLER-WOMAN.

In an hour I hope to behold him swinging!

SERGEANT.

Bad work bad wages will needs be bringing.

FIRST ARQUEBUSIER (*to the others*).

This comes of their desperation.   We
First ruin them out and out. d'ye see;
Which tempts them to steal, as it seems to me

TRUMPETER.

How now! the rascal's cause would you plead?
The cur!—the devil is in you indeed'

FIRST ARQUEBUSIER.

The boor is a man—as a body may say.

FIRST YAGER (*to the Trumpeter*).

Let 'em go!—they're of Tiefenbach's corps, the railers,
A glorious train of glovers and tailors!
At Brieg, in garrison, long they lay;
What should they know about camps, I pray?

SCENE XI

The above.—Cuirassiers.

FIRST CUIRASSIER.

Peace ! what's amiss with the boor, may I crave?

FIRST SHARPSHOOTER.

He has cheated at play, the cozening knave !

FIRST CUIRASSIER.

But say, has he cheated *you*, man, of aught?

FIRST SHARPSHOOTER.

Just clean'd me out—and not left me a groat.

FIRST CUIRASSIER.

And can you, who've the rank of a Friedland man,
So shamefully cast yourself away,
As to try your luck with a boor at play ?
Let him run off, so that run he can

[*The Peasant escapes, the others throng together.*

FIRST ARQUEBUSIER.

He makes short work—is of resolute mood—
And that with such fellows as these is good.
Who is he?—not of Bohemia, that's clear.

SUTLER-WOMAN.

He's a Walloon—and respect, I trow,
Is due to the Pappenheim cuirassier !

FIRST DRAGOON (*joining*).

Young Piccolomini leads them now,
Whom they chose as Colonel, of their own free might,
When Pappenheim fell in Lutzen's fi~ht.

FIRST ARQUEBUSIER.

Durst they, indeed, presume so far?

FIRST DRAGOON.

This regiment is something above the rest.
It has ever been foremost throughout the war,
And may manage its laws, as it pleases best ·
Besides, 'tis by Friedland himself carest.

FIRST CUIRASSIER (*to the Second*)

Is't so in truth, man? Who averr'd it?

SECOND CUIRASSIER.

From the lips of the Colonel himself I heard

FIRST CUIRASSIER.

The devil ! we're not their dogs, I ween !

FIRST YAGER.

How now, what's wrong?   You're swoln with spleen !

SECOND YAGER.

Is it anything, comrades, may us concern ?

FIRST CUIRASSIER.

Tis what none need be wondrous glad to learn.

The Soldiers press round him.

To the Netherlands they would lend us now—
Cuirassiers, Yagers, and Shooters away,
Eight thousand, in all, must march, they say.

SUTLER-WOMAN.

What ! what ! again the old wandering way—
I got back from Flanders but yesterday !

SECOND CUIRASSIER (*to the Dragoons*).

You of Buttler's corps must tramp with the rest

FIRST CUIRASSIER.

And we, the Walloons, must doubtless be gone.

SUTLER-WOMAN.

Why of all our squadrons these are the best.

FIRST CUIRASSIER.

To march where that Milanese fellow leads on.

FIRST YAGER.

The Infant ! that's queer enough in its way.

SECOND YAGER.

The Priest—then, egad ! there's the devil to pay

FIRST CUIRASSIER.

Shall we then leave the Friedlander's train,
Who so nobly his soldiers doth entertain—
And drag to the field with this fellow from Spain ?
A niggard whom we in our souls disdain !
That'll never go down—I'm off, I swear.

TRUMPETER.

Why, what the devil should we do there ?
We sold our blood to th' Emperor—ne'er
For this Spanish red hat a drop we'll spare!

SECOND YAGER.

On the Friedlander's word and credit alone
We ranged ourselves in the trooper line,
And, but for our love to Wallenstein,
Ferdinand ne'er had our service known.

FIRST DRAGOON.

Was it not Friedland that formed our force?
His fortune shall still be the star of our course

SERGEANT.

Silence, good comrades, to me give ear—
Talking does little to help us here.
Much farther in this I can see than you all,
And a trap has been laid in which we're to fall

FIRST YAGER.

List to the order-book! hush—be still!

SERGEANT.

But first, cousin Gustel, I pray thee fill
A glass of Melneck, as my stomach's but weak;
When I've tost it off, my mind I'll speak.

SUTLER-WOMAN.

Take it, good Sergeant. I quake for fear—
Think you that mischief is hidden here?

SERGEANT.

Look ye, my friends, 'tis fit and clear
That each should consider what's most near.
But as the General says, say I,
One should always the whole of a case descry.
We call ourselves all the Friedlander's troops;
The Burgher, on whom we're billeted, stoops
Our wants to supply, and cooks our soups.
His ox, or his horse, the Peasant must chain
To our baggage car, and may grumble in vain.
Just let a lance-corp'ral, with seven good men,
Tow'rd a village from far but come within ken,
You're sure he'll be prince of the place, and may
Cut what capers he will, with unquestion'd sway.
Why, zounds! lads, they heartily hate us all—
And would rather the devil should give them a call,
Than our yellow collars And why don't they fall

On us fairly at once, and get rid of our lumber?
They're more than our match in point of number,
And carry the cudgel as we do the sword.
Why can we laugh them to scorn ? By my word,
Because we make up here a terrible horde.

FIRST YAGER.

Ay, ay, in the mass lies the spell of our might,
And the Friedlander judged the matter aright,
When, some eight or nine years ago, he brought
The Emperor's army together. They thought
Twelve thousand enough for the Gen'ral. In vain—
Said he—such a force I can never maintain.
Sixty thousand I'll bring ye into the plain,
And they, I'll be sworn, wont of hunger die,
And thus were we Wallenstein's men, say I

SERGEANT

For example—cut one of my fingers off—
This little one, here, from my right hand doff.
Is the taking my finger, then, all you've done?
No, no, to the devil my hand is gone!
'Tis a stump—no more—and use has none.
The eight thousand horse they wish to disband,
May be but a finger of our army's hand.
But, when they're once gone—may we understand
We are but one-fifth the less? Oh, no—
By the Lord, the whole to the devil will go!
All terror, respect, and awe, will be o'er,
And the Peasant will swell his crest once more;
And the Board of Vienna will order us where
Our troops must be quartered, and how we must fare,
As of old, in the days of their beggarly care.
Yes—and how long it will be who can say
Ere the General himself they may take away?
For they don't much like him at court, I learn,
And then it's all up with the whole concern!
For who, to our pay, will be left to aid us?
And see that they keep the promise they made us.
Who has the energy—who the mind—
The flashing thought—and the fearless hand—
Together to bring, and thus fastly bind
The fragments that form our close-knit band

For example, Dragoon—just answer us now,
From which of the countries of earth art thou?

DRAGOON.

From distant Erin came I here.

SERGEANT (*to the two Cuirassiers*)
You're a Walloon, my friend, that's clear·
And you, an Italian, as all may hear

FIRST CUIRASSIER.

Who I may be, faith! I never could say·
In my infant years they stole me away.

SERGEANT.

And you, from what far land may you be.

FIRST ARQUEBUSIER.

I come from Buchau—on the Feder Sea.

SERGEANT.

Neighbour, and you?

SECOND ARQUEBUSIER.

I am a Swiss.

SERGEANT (*to the Second Yager*)
And Yager, let's hear where your country is?

SECOND YAGER.

Up above Wismar, my fathers dwell

SERGEANT (*pointing to the Trumpeter,*
And he's from Eger—and I as well:
And, now, my comrades, I ask you whether.
Would any one think, when looking at us,
That we, from the North and South, had thus
Been hitherward drifted and blown together?
Do we not seem as hewn from one mass?
Stand we not close against the foe
As tho' we were glued, or moulded so?
Like mill-work don't we move, d'ye think!
'Mong ourselves in the nick, at a word or wink
Who has thus cast us, here, all as one,
Now to be sever'd again by none?
Who? why, no other than Wallenstein!

FIRST YAGER.

In my life it ne'er was a thought of mine,
Whether we suited each other or not,
I let myself go with the rest of the lot.

FIRST CUIRASSIER.

I quite agree in the Sergeant's opinion—
They'd fain have an end of our camp dominion,
And trample the soldier down, that they
May govern alone in their own good way.
'Tis a conspiration—a plot, I say!

SUTLER-WOMAN.

A conspiration—God help the day!
Then my customers won't have cash to pay.

SERGEANT.

Why, faith, we shall all be bankrupts made:
The captains and generals, most of them, paid
The costs of the regiments with private cash,
And, wishing, 'bove all, to cut a dash,
Went a little beyond their means—but thought,
No doubt, that they thus had a bargain bought.
Now they'll be cheated, sirs, one and all,
Should our chief, our head, the General fall

SUTLER-WOMAN

Oh, Heav'n! this curse I never can brook!
Why, half of the army stands in my book.
Two hundred dollars I've trusted madly,
That Count Isolani, who pays so badly.

FIRST CUIRASSIER.

Well, comrades, let's fix on what's to be done—
Of the ways to save us, I see but one;
If we hold together we needn't fear;
So let us stand out as one man here;
And then they may order and send as they will
Fast planted we'll stick in Bohemia still.
We'll never give in—no, nor march an inch,
We stand on our honour, and must not flinch.

SECOND YAGER.

We're not to be driven the country about,
Let 'em come here, and they'll find it out

FIRST ARQUEBUSIER.

Good sirs, 'twere well to bethink ye still,
That such is the Emperor's sovereign will.

TRUMPETER.

Oh, as to the Emperor, we needn't be nice.

FIRST ARQUEBUSIER.

Let me not hear you say so twice

TRUMPETER.

Why 'tis even so—as I just have said

FIRST YAGER.

True, man—I've always heard 'em say,
'Tis Friedland, alone, you've here to obey

SERGEANT.

By our bargain with him it should be so,
Absolute power is his, you must know.
We've war, or peace, but as he may please,
Or gold or goods he has power to seize,
And hanging or pardon his will decrees.
Captains and colonels he makes—and he,
In short, by th' Imperial seal is free,
To hold all the marks of sovereignty

FIRST ARQUEBUSIER.

The Duke is high and of mighty will,
But yet must remain, for good or for ill,
Like us all, but the Emperor's servant still.

SERGEANT

Not like us all—I there disagree—
Friedland is quite independent and free,
The Bavarian is no more a Prince than he;
For, was I not by myself to see,
When on duty at Brandeis, how th' Emperor said,
He wished him to cover his princely head

FIRST ARQUEBUSIER.

That was because of the Mecklenburgh land,
Which he held in pawn from the Emperor's hand.

FIRST YAGER (*to the Sergeant*).

In the Emperor's presence, man! say you so?
That, beyond doubt, was a wonderful go!

SERGEANT (*feels in his pocket*).

If you question my word in what I have told,
I can give you something to grasp and hold.

[*Showing a coin*

Whose image and stamp d'ye here behold?

SUTLER-WOMAN.

Oh! that is a Wall   n's, sure!

SERGEANT-MAJOR.

Well, there, you have it—what doubt can rest?
Is he not Prince just as good as the best?
Coins he not money like Ferdinand?
Hath he not his own subjects and land?
Is he not called your Highness, I pray?
And why should he not have his soldiers in pay?

FIRST ARQUEBUSIER.

That no one has ever meant to gainsay;
But we're still at the Emperor's beck and call,
For his Majesty 'tis who pays us all.

TRUMPETER.

In your teeth I deny it—and will again—
His Majesty 'tis who pays us *not*,
For this forty weeks, say, what have we got
But a promise to pay, believed in vain?

FIRST ARQUEBUSIER.

What then! 'tis kept in safe hands, I suppose

FIRST CUIRASSIER.

Peace, good sirs, will you come to blows?
Have you a quarrel and squabble to know
If the Emperor be our master or no?
'Tis because of our rank, as his soldiers bravo,
That we scorn the lot of the herded slave;
And will not be driven from place to place,
As priests or puppies our path may trace.
And, tell me, is't not the Sovereign's gain,
If the soldiers their dignity well maintain?
Who but his soldiers give him the state
Of a mighty, wide-ruling potentate?
Make and preserve for him, far and near,
The voice which Christendom quakes to hear?
Well enough *they* may his yoke-chain bear,
Who feast on his favours, and daily share,
In golden chambers, his sumptuous fare.
We—we of his splendours have no part,
Nought but hard wearying toil and care,
And the pride that lives in a soldier's heart.

SECOND YAGER.

All great tyrants and kings have shown
Their wit, as I take it, in what they've done;

D

They've trampled all others with stern command,
But the soldier they've led with a gentle hand

FIRST CUIRASSIER.

The soldier his worth must understand;
Whoe'er doesn't nobly drive the trade,
'Twere best from the business far he'd staid.
If I cheerily set my life on a throw,
Something still better than life I'll know;
Or I'll stand to be slain for the paltry pelf,
As the Croat still does—and scorn myself.

BOTH YAGERS.

Yes—honour is dearer than life itself.

FIRST CUIRASSIER.

The sword is no plough nor delving tool,
He, who would till with it, is but a fool.
For us, neither grass nor grain doth grow,
Houseless the soldier is doomed to go,
A changeful wanderer over the earth,
Ne'er knowing the warmth of a home-lit hearth.
The city glances—he halts—not there—
Nor in village meadows, so green and fair;
The vintage and harvest wreath are twined
He sees, but must leave them far behind.
Then, tell me, what hath the soldier left,
If he's once of his self-esteem bereft?
Something he *must* have his own to call,
Or on slaughter and burnings at once he'll fall

FIRST ARQUEBUSIER.

God knows, 'tis a wretched life to live!

FIRST CUIRASSIER.

Yet one which I for no other would give
Look ye—far round in the world I've been,
And all of its different service seen.
The Venetian Republic—the Kings of Spain
And Naples I've served, and served in vain.
Fortune still frowned—and merchant and knight
Craftsman and Jesuit, have met my sight;
Yet, of all their jackets, not one have I known
To please me like this steel coat of my own.

FIRST ARQUEBUSIER.

Well—that now is what I can scarcely say

FIRST CUIRASSIER.

In the world, a man who would make his way.
Must plague and bestir himself night and day.
To honour and place, if he choose the road,
He must bend his back to the golden load.
And if home-delights should his fancy please,
With children and grandchildren round his knees,
Let him follow an honest trade in peace.
I've no taste for this kind of life—not I!
Free will I live, and as freely die.
No man's spoiler nor heir will I be—
But, throned on my nag, I will smile to see
The coil of the crowd that is under me.

FIRST YAGER.

Bravo!—that's as I've always done.

FIRST ARQUEBUSIER.

In truth, sirs, it may be far better fun
To trample thus over your neighbour's crown

FIRST CUIRASSIER.

Comrade, the times are bad of late—
The sword and the scales live separate.
But do not then blame that I've preferr'd,
Of the two, to lean, as I have, to the sword.
For mercy in war I will yield to none,
Tho' I never will stoop to be drumm'd upon

FIRST ARQUEBUSIER.

Who but the soldier the blame should bear
That the labouring poor so hardly fare?
The war with its plagues, which all have blasted,
Now sixteen years in the land hath lasted.

FIRST CUIRASSIER.

Why, brother, the blessed God above
Can't have from us all an equal love.
One prays for the sun, at which t'other will fret:
One is for dry weather—t'other for wet.
What you, now, regard as with misery rife,
Is to me the unclouded sun of life.

If 'tis at the cost of the burgher and boor,
I really am sorry that they must endure ;
But how can I help it? Here, you must know,
'Tis just like a cavalry charge 'gainst the foe :
The steeds loud snorting, and on they go !
Whoever may lie in the mid career—
Be it my brother or son so dear,
Should his dying groan my heart divide,
Yet over his body I needs must ride,
Nor pitying stop to drag him aside.

FIRST YAGER.

True—who ever asks how another may bide?

FIRST CUIRASSIER.

Thus, my lads, 'tis my counsel, while
On the soldier dame Fortune deigns to smile,
That we with both hands her bounty clasp,
For it mayn't be much longer left to our grasp.
Peace will be coming some over night,
And then there's an end of our martial might.
The soldier unhorsed, and fresh-mounted the boor.
Ere you can think it, 'twill be as before.
As yet we're together firm bound in the land,
The hilt is yet fast in the soldier's hand.
But let 'em divide us, and soon we shall find
Short commons is all that remains behind.

FIRST YAGER.

No, no, by the Lord ! *that* won't do for me.
Come, come, lads, let's all now, as one, agree.

SECOND YAGER.

Yes, let us resolve on what 'tis to be

FIRST ARQUEBUSIER.

To the Sutler-woman, drawing out his leather purse.)
Hostess, tell us how high you've scored.

SUTLER-WOMAN

Oh, 'tis unworthy a single word.   [*They settle*

TRUMPETER.

You do well, sirs, to take a farther walk,
Your company only disturbs our talk.

                              [*Exeunt Arquebusiers.*

FIRST CUIRASSIER

Plague take the fellows—they're brave, I know.

FIRST YAGER.

They hav'n't a soul 'bove a soapboiler's though.

SECOND YAGER.

We're now alone, so teach us who can
How best we may meet and mar their plan.

TRUMPETER.

How? Why, let's tell 'em we will not go!

FIRST CUIRASSIER.

Despising all discipline! no, my lads, no
Rather his corps let each of us seek,
And quietly then with his comrades speak,
That every soldier may clearly know,
It were not for his good so far to go;
For my Walloons to answer I'm free,
Every man of 'em thinks and acts with me.

SERGEANT.

The Terzky regiments, both horse and foot,
Will thus resolve, and will keep them to't.

SECOND CUIRASSIER (*joining the first*)

The Walloons and the Lombards, one inten:

FIRST YAGER

Freedom is Yagers' own element.

SECOND YAGER.

Freedom must ever with might entwine—
I live and will die by Wallenstein.

FIRST SHARPSHOOTER.

The Lorrainers go on with the strongest tide,
Where spirits are light and courage tried.

DRAGOON

An Irishman follows his fortune s star.

SECOND SHARPSHOOTER.

The Tyrolese for their sovereign war.

FIRST CUIRASSIER.

Then, comrades, let each of our corps agree
A *pro memoriâ* to sign—that we,
In spite of all force or fraud, will be

To the fortunes of Friedland firmly bound.
For in him is the soldier's father found.
This we will humbly present, when done,
To Piccolomini—I mean the son—
Who understands these kind of affairs,
And the Friedlander's highest favour shares ·
Besides, with the Emperor's self, they say
He holds a capital card to play.

SECOND YAGER.

Well, then, in this, let us all agree,
That the Colonel shall our spokesman be!

ALL (going).

Good! the Colonel shall our spokesman be

SERGEANT

Hold, sirs—just toss off a glass with me
To the health of Piccolomini.

SUTLER-WOMAN (brings a flask).

This shall not go to the list of scores,
I gladly give it—success be yours!

CUIRASSIER

The soldier shall sway!

BOTH YAGERS

The peasant shall pay!

DRAGOONS and SHARPSHOOTERS

The army shall flourishing stand!

TRUMPETER and SERGEANT.

And the Friedlander keep the command!

SECOND CUIRASSIER (sings).

Arouse ye, my comrades, to horse! to horse!
  To the field and to freedom we guide!
For there a man feels the pride of his force,
  And there is the heart of him tried.
No help to him there by another is shown,
He stands for himself and himself alone.

[The Soldiers from the back ground have come forward
  during the singing of this verse, and form the chorus
  Chorus.

No help to him there by another is shown,
He stands for himself and himself alone.

DRAGOON.

Now freedom hath fled from the world, we find
    But lords and their bondsmen vile :
And nothing holds sway in the breast of mankind
    Save falsehood and cowardly guile.
Who looks in death's face with a fearless brow
The soldier, alone, is the freeman now
                    Chorus.
Who looks in death's face with a fearless brow,
The soldier, alone, is the freeman now.

FIRST YAGER.

With the troubles of life he ne'er bothers his pate,
    And feels neither fear nor sorrow ;
But boldly rides onward to meet with his fate—
    He may meet it to-day, or to-morrow!
And, if to-morrow 'twill come, then, I say,
Drain we the cup of life's joy to-day !
                    Chorus.
And, if to-morrow 'twill come, then, I say,
Drain we the cup of life's joy to-day !
            [*The glasses are here refilled, and all drink.*

SERGEANT.

'Tis from heaven his jovial lot has birth ;
    Nor needs he to strive or toil.
The peasant may grope in the bowels of earth,
    And for treasure may greedily moil :
He digs and he delves through life for the pelf,
And digs till he grubs out a grave for himself.
                    Chorus.
He digs and he delves through life for the pelf,
And digs till he grubs out a grave for himself

FIRST YAGER.

The rider and lightning steed—a pair
    Of terrible guests. I ween !
From the bridal-hall as the torches glare,
    Unbidden they join the scene :
Nor gold, nor wooing, his passion prove ;
By storm he carries the prize of love .
                    Chorus.
Nor gold, nor wooing, his passion prove ;
By storm he carries the prize of love !

SECOND CUIRASSIER.

Why mourns the wench with so sorrowful face?
  Away, girl, the soldier must go!
No spot on the earth is his resting-place;
  And your *true* love he never can know.
Still onward driven by fate's rude wind,
He nowhere may leave his peace behind.

Chorus.

Still onward driven by fate's rude wind,
He nowhere may leave his peace behind.

FIRST YAGER

*He takes the two next to him by the hand—the others do the
same—and form a large semicircle.*

Then rouse ye, my comrades—to horse! to horse!
  In battle the breast doth swell!
Youth boils—the life cup foams in its force—
  Up! ere time can the dew dispel!
And deep be the stake, as the prize is high—
Who life would win, he must dare to die!

Chorus.

And deep be the stake, as the prize is high—
Who life would win, he must dare to die!

[*The Curtain falls before the Chorus has finished.*

THE PICCOLOMINI.

PREFACE.

THE two Dramas,—PICCOLOMINI, or the first part of WAL-
LENSTEIN, and the DEATH of WALLENSTEIN, are introduced
in the original manuscript by a Prelude in one Act, entitled
WALLENSTEIN'S CAMP. This is written in rhyme, and in
nine-syllable verse, in the same *lilting* metre (if that expression may be permitted) with the second Eclogue of Spenser's
Shepherd's Calendar.

This prelude possesses a sort of broad humour, and is not
deficient in character: but to have translated it into prose,
or into any other metre than that of the original, would have
given a false idea both of its style and purport; to have
translated it into the same metre would have been incom
patible with a faithful adherence to the sense of the German,
from the comparative poverty of our language in rhymes;
and it would have been unadvisable, from the incongruity of
those lax verses with the present taste of the English public
Schiller's intention seems to have been merely to have
prepared his reader for the Tragedies by a lively picture of
laxity of discipline, and the mutinous dispositions of Wallenstein's soldiery. It is not necessary as a preliminary
explanation. For these reasons it has been thought expedient
not to translate it.

The admirers of Schiller, who have abstracted their idea
of that author from the Robbers, and the Cabal and Love,
plays in which the main interest is produced by the excite-
ment of curiosity, and in which the curiosity is excited by
terrible and extraordinary incident, will not have perused
without some portion of disappointment the Dramas, which
it has been my employment to translate. They should, however, reflect that these are Historical Dramas, taken from
a popular German History; that we must, therefore, judge
of them in some measure with the feelings of Germans; or,
by analogy, with the interest excited in us by similar Dramas
in our own language. Few, I trust, would be rash or ignorant enough to compare Schiller with Shakspeare; yet,
merely as illustration, I would say, that we should proceed

to the perusal of Wallenstein, not from Lear or Othello, but
from Richard the Second, or the three parts of Henry the
Sixth. We scarcely expect rapidity in an Historical Drama,
and many prolix speeches are pardoned from characters,
whose names and actions have formed the most amusing tales
of our early life. On the other hand, there exist in these
plays more individual beauties, more passages whose excellence will bear reflection, than in the former productions of
Schiller. The description of the Astrological Tower, and
the reflections of the Young Lover, which follow it, form in
the original a fine poem ; and my translation must have been
wretched indeed, if it can have wholly overclouded the beauties of the scene in the first act of the first play, between
Questenberg, Max. and Octavio Piccolomini. If we except
the scene of the setting sun in the Robbers, I know of no
part in Schiller's Plays which equals the first scene of the
fifth act of the concluding play *. It would be unbecoming in
me to be more diffuse on this subject. A translator stands
connected with the original author by a certain law of sub
ordination, which makes it more decorous to point out excel
'ences than defects : indeed he is not likely to be a fair
judge of either The pleasure or disgust from his own
labour will mingle with the feelings that arise from an after
view of the original Even in the first perusal of a work in
any foreign language which we understand, we are apt to
attribute to it more excellence than it really possesses, from
our own pleasurable sense of difficulty overcome without
effort. Translation of poetry into poetry is difficult, because
the translator must give a brilliancy to his language without
that warmth of original conception, from which such brilliancy would follow of its own accord. But the translator of
a living author is encumbered with additional inconveniences.
If he render his original faithfully, as to the *sense* of each
passage, he must, necessarily, destroy a considerable portion
of the *spirit ;* if he endeavour to give a work executed according to laws of *compensation*, he subjects himself to
imputations of vanity, or misrepresentation. I have thought
it my duty to remain bound by the sense of my original
with as few exceptions as the nature of the languages ren·
dered possible.   S T. C.

* In this edition, Scene III. Act V.

THE PICCOLOMINI.

DRAMATIS PERSONÆ.

WALLENSTEIN, *Duke of Friedland, Generalissimo of the Imperial Forces in the Thirty Years' War.*

OCTAVIO PICCOLOMINI, *Lieutenant-General.*

MAX. PICCOLOMINI, *his Son, Colonel of a Regiment of Cuirassiers.*

COUNT TERZKY, *the Commander of several Regiments, and Brother-in-law of Wallenstein.*

ILLO, *Field-Marshal, Wallenstein's Confidant.*

ISOLANI, *General of the Croats.*

BUTLER, *an Irishman, Commander of a Regiment of Dragoons.*

TIEFENBACH,
DON MARADAS, } *Generals under*
GOETZ, } *Wallenstein.*
KOLATTO,

NEUMANN, *Captain of Cavalry, Aide-de-Camp to Terzky.*

VON QUESTENBERG, *the War sioner, Imperial Envoy.*

BAPTISTA SENI, *an Astrologer.*

DUCHESS OF FRIEDLAND, *Wife of Wallenstein.*

THEKLA, *her Daughter, Princess of Friedland.*

THE COUNTESS TERZKY, *Sister of the Duchess.*

A CORNET.

COLONELS *and* GENERALS (*several*).

PAGES *and* ATTENDANTS *belonging to Wallenstein.*

ATTENDANTS *and* HOBOISTS *belonging to Terzky.*

MASTER OF THE CELLAR *to Count Terzky.*

VALET DE CHAMBRE *of Count Piccolomini.*

ACT I.

SCENE I

An old Gothic Chamber in the Council House at Pilsen, decorated with Colours and other War Insignia

ILLO *with* BUTLER *and* ISOLANI

ILLO.

Ye have come too late—but ye are come ! The distance
Count Isolani, excuses your delay.

ISOLANI.

Add this too, that we come not empty-handed
At Donauwerth * it was reported to us,

---

* A town about twelve German miles N.E. of Ulm.

A Swedish caravan was on its way,
Transporting a rich cargo of provision,
Almost six hundred waggons.   This my Croats
Plunged down upon and seized, this weighty prize :—
We bring it hither——

ILIO.
Just in time to banquet
The illustrious company assembled here.

BUTLER.
'Tis all alive ! a stirring scene here !

ISOLANI.
Ay !
The very churches are all full of soldiers.
                    [*Casts his eye round.*
And in the Council-house too, I observe,
You're settled, quite at home !   Well, well ! we soldiers
Must shift and suit us in what way we can.

ILLO.
We have the colonels here of thirty regiments.
You'll find Count Terzky here, and Tiefenbach,
Kolatto, Goetz, Maradas, Hinnersam,
The Piccolomini, both son and father——
You'll meet with many an unexpected greeting
From many an old friend and acquaintance   Only
Galas is wanting still, and Altringer

BUTLER.
Expect not Galas

ILLO (*hesitating*).
How so ?   Do *you* know——

ISOLANI (*interrupting him*).
Max. Piccolomini here ?—O bring me to him.
I see him yet, ('tis now ten years ago,
We were engaged with Mansfeldt hard by Dessau,
I see the youth, in my mind's eye I see him,
Leap his black war-horse from the bridge adown,
And t'ward his father, then in extreme peril,
Beat up against the strong tide of the Elbe.
The down was scarce upon his chin !   I hear
He has made good the promise of his youth
And the full hero now is finish'd in him.

ILLO.

You'll see him yet ere evening.   He conducts
The Duchess Friedland hither, and the Princess *
From Cärnthen †.   We expect them here at noon.

BUTLER.

Both wife and daughter does the Duke call hither?
He crowds in visitants from all sides

ISOLANI.

                        Hm!
So much the better! I had framed my mind
To hear of nought but warlike circumstance.
Of marches, and attacks, and batteries;
And lo! the Duke provides, and something too
Of gentler sort, and lovely, should be present
To feast our eyes.

ILLO (*who has been standing in the attitude of meditation, to*
     BUTLER, *whom he leads a little on one side*).
And how came you to know
That the Count Galas joins us not?

BUTLER.

                        Because
He importuned *me* to remain behind.

ILLO (*with warmth*).
And you?—You hold out firmly!
                        [*Grasping his hand with affection*
                            Noble Butler!

BUTLER.

After the obligation which the Duke
Had laid so newly on me——

ILLO.

                    I had forgotten
A pleasant duty—Major-General,
I wish you joy!

ISOLANI.

            What, you mean, of his regiment?
I hear, too, that to make the gift still sweeter,
The Duke has given him the very same

---

* The Dukes in Germany being always reigning powers, their sons and
daughters are entitled Princes and Princesses.
† Carinthia.

In which he first saw service, and since then,
Work'd himself, step by step, through each preferment,
From the ranks upwards.   And verily, it gives
A precedent of hope, a spur of action
To the whole corps, if once in their remembrance
An old deserving soldier makes his way

BUTLER.

I am perplex'd and doubtful, whether or no
I dare accept this your congratulation.
The Emperor has not yet confirm'd the appointment.

ISOLANI.

Seize it, friend! Seize it! The hand which in that post
Placed you, is strong enough to keep you there,
Spite of the Emperor and his Ministers!

ILLO.

Ay, if we would but so consider it!—
If we would *all* of us consider it so!
The Emperor gives us nothing; from the Duke
Comes all—whate'er we hope, whate'er we have

ISOLANI (*to* ILLO).

My noble brother! did I tell you how
The Duke will satisfy my creditors?
Will be himself my banker for the future,
Make me once more a creditable man!—
And this is now the third time, think of that!
This kingly-minded man has rescued me
From absolute ruin, and restored my honour

ILLO.

O that his power but kept pace with his wishes!
Why, friend! he'd give the whole world to his soldiers.
But at Vienna, brother!—here's the grievance.—
What politic schemes do they not lay to shorten
His arm, and where they can, to clip his pinions.
Then these new dainty requisitions! these,
Which this same Questenberg brings hither!—

BUTLER.

Ay!

These requisitions of the Emperor,—
I too have heard about them; but I hope
The Duke will not draw back a single inch!

ILLO.

Not from his right most surely, unless first
—From office!

BUTLER (*shocked and confused*).

Know you *aught* then?   You alarm me.

ISOLANI (*at the same time with* BUTLER, *and in a
hurrying voice*).

We should be ruin'd, every one of us!

ILLO

No more!

Yonder I see *our worthy friend* * approaching
With the Lieutenant-General, Piccolomini.

BUTLER (*shaking his head significantly*)

I fear we shall not go hence as we came

SCENE II.

Enter OCTAVIO, PICCOLOMINI, *and* QUESTENBERG

OCTAVIO (*still in the distance*).

Ay! ay! more still! Still more new visitors!
Acknowledge, friend! that never was a camp,
Which held at once so many heads of heroes

[QUESTENBERG.

Let none approach a camp of Friedland's troops
Who dares to think unworthily of war;
E'en I myself had nigh forgot its evils
When I surveyed that lofty soul of order,
By which while it destroys the world,— itself
Maintains the greatness which itself created.]

OCTAVIO (*approaching nearer*).

Welcome, Count Isolani!

ISOLANI.

My noble brother!

Even now am I arrived; it had been else my duty—

OCTAVIO.

And Colonel Butler—trust me, I rejoice
Thus to renew acquaintance with a man
Whose worth and services I know and honour
See, see, my friend!

* Spoken with a sneer.

There might we place at once before our eyes
The sum of war's whole trade and mystery—
[*To* QUESTENBERG, *presenting* BUTLER
and ISOLANI *at the same time to him.*
These two the total sum—Strength and Dispatch.
QUESTENBERG (*to* OCTAVIO).
And lo! betwixt them both, experienced Prudence!

OCTAVIO (*presenting* QUESTENBERG *to* BUTLER *and* ISOLANI)
The Chamberlain and War-Commissioner Questenberg,
The bearer of the Emperor's behests,
The long-tried friend and patron of all soldiers,
We honour in this noble visitor.   [*Universal silence*
ILLO (*moving towards* QUESTENBERG).
'Tis not the first time, noble Minister,
You have shown our camp this honour.
QUESTENBERG
                              Once before
I stood beside these colours.
ILLO.
Perchance too you remember *where* that was
It was at Znäim * in Moravia, where
You did present yourself upon the part
Of the Emperor, to supplicate our Duke
That he would straight assume the chief command
QUESTENBERG.
To *supplicate?* Nay, bold General!
So far extended neither my commission
(At least to my own knowledge) nor my zeal
ILLO.
Well, well, then—to *compel* him, if you choose
I can remember me right well, Count Tilly
Had suffer'd rotal rout upon the Lech.
Bavaria lay all open to the enemy,
Whom there was nothing to delay from pressing
Onwards into the very heart of Austria
At that time you and Werdenberg appear'd
Before our General, storming him with prayers,
And menacing the Emperor's displeasure,
Unless he took compassion on this wretchedness.

* A town not far from the Mine-mountains, on the high road from Vienna
to Prague.

ISOLANI (*steps up to them*).
Yes, yes, 'tis comprehensible enough,
Wherefore with your commission of to-day
You were not all too willing to remember
Your former one.

QUESTENBERG.
Why not, Count Isolani?
No contradiction sure exists between them.
It was the urgent business of that time
To snatch Bavaria from her enemy's hand ;
And my commission of to-day instructs me
To free her from her good friends and protectors

ILLO.
A worthy office !   After with our blood
We have wrested this Bohemia from the Saxon
To be swept *out* of it is all our thanks,
The sole reward of all our hard-won victories.

QUESTENBERG.
Unless that wretched land be doomed to suffer
Only a change of evils, it must be
Freed from the scourge alike of friend or foe.

ILLO.
What?   'Twas a favourable year ; the boors
Can answer fresh demands already

QUESTENBERG.
Nay,
If *you* discourse of herds and meadow-grounds—

ISOLANI.
The war maintains the war.   Are the boors ruin'd?
The Emperor gains so many more new soldiers.

QUESTENBERG.
And is the poorer by even so many subjects

ISOLANI.
Poh! we are all his subjects

QUESTENBERG.
Yet with a difference, General ! The one fill
With profitable industry the purse,
The others are well skill'd to empty it.
The sword has made the Emperor poor ; the plough
Must reinvigorate his resources.

E

ISOLANI.

Sure!
Times are not yet so bad.   Methinks I see
[*Examining with his eye the dress and ornaments of*
QUESTENBERG.
Good store of gold that still remains uncoin'd.

QUESTENBERG.
Thank Heaven! that means have been found out to hide
Some little from the fingers of the Croats.

ILLO.
There! The Stawata and the Martinitz,
On whom the Emperor heaps his gifts and graces,
To the heart-burning of all good Bohemians—
Those minions of court favour, those court harpies,
Who fatten on the wrecks of citizens
Driven from their house and home—who reap no harvests
Save in the general calamity—
Who now, with kingly pomp, insult and mock
The desolation of their country—these,
Let these, and such as these, support the war,
The fatal war, which they alone enkindled!

BUTLER.
And those state-parasites, who have their feet
So constantly beneath the Emperor's table,
Who cannot let a benefice fall, but they
Snap at it with dogs' hunger—they, forsooth,
Would pare the soldier's bread and cross his reckoning!

ISOLANI.
My life long will it anger me to think,
How when I went to court seven years ago,
To see about new horses for our regiment,
How from one antechamber to another
They dragg'd me on, and left me by the hour
To kick my heels among a crowd of simpering
Feast-fatten'd slaves, as if I had come thither
A mendicant suitor for the crumbs of favour
That fall beneath their tables.   And, at last,
Whom should they send me but a capuchin!
Straight I began to muster up my sins
For absolution—but no such luck for *me!*

This was the man, this capuchin, with whom
I was to treat concerning the army horses ·
And I was forced at last to quit the field,
The business unaccomplish'd.   Afterwards
The Duke procured me in three days, what I
Could not obtain in thirty at Vienna.

QUESTENBERG.

Yes, yes! your travelling bills soon found their way to us!
Too well I know we have still accounts to settle.

ILLO

War is a violent trade: one cannot always
Finish one's work by soft means ; every trifle
Must not be blacken'd into sacrilege.
If we should wait till you, in solemn council,
With due deliberation had selected
The smallest out of four-and-twenty evils,
I' faith we should wait long—
"Dash! and through with it!"—That's the better watch-
    word.
Then after come what may come.   'Tis man's nature
To make the best of a bad thing once past.
A bitter and perplex'd " what shall I do? '
Is worse to man than worst necessity.

QUESTENBERG.

Ay, doubtless, it is true ; the Duke *does* spare us
The troublesome task of choosing.

BUTLER.

                              Yes, the Duke
Cares with a father's feelings for his troops:
But how the Emperor feels for us, we see

QUESTENBERG.

His cares and feelings all ranks share alike,
Nor will he offer one up to another.

ISOLANI.

And therefore thrusts he us into the deserts
As beasts of prey, that so he may preserve
His dear sheep fattening in his fields at home

QUESTENBERG (*with a sneer*).

Count! this comparison you make, not I

E 2

ILLO.

Why, were we all the Court supposes us
'Twere dangerous, sure, to give us liberty
                QUESTENBERG (*gravely*).
You have taken liberty—it was not given you
And therefore it becomes an urgent duty
To rein it in with curbs.
                        [ILLO.
Expect to find a restive steed in us.
                QUESTENBERG.
A better rider may be found to rule it.
                ILLO.
He only brooks the rider who has tamed him.
                QUESTENBERG
Ay, tame him once, and then a child may lead him.
                ILLO.
The child, we know, is found for him already
                QUESTENBERG.
Be duty, sir, your study, not a name
BUTLER (*who has stood aside with* PICCOLOMINI, *but with visible
        interest in the conversation, advances.*)
Sir President, the Emperor has in Germany
A splendid host assembled; in this kingdom
Full twenty thousand soldiers are cantooned,
With sixteen thousand in Silesia;
Ten regiments are posted on the Weser,
The Rhine, and Maine; in Swabia there are six,
And in Bavaria twelve, to face the Swedes;
Without including in th' account, the garrisons
Who on the frontiers hold the fortresses.
This vast and mighty host is all obedient
To Friedland's captains; and its brave commanders,
Bred in one school, and nurtured with one milk,
Are all excited by one heart and soul;
They are as strangers on the soil they tread,
The service is their only house and home.
No zeal inspires them for their country's cause,
For thousands like myself were born abroad;
Nor care they for the Emp'ror, for one half
Deserting other service fled to ours,

Indiff'rent what their banner, whether 'twere
The Double Eagle, Lily, or the Lion.
Yet one sole man can rein this fiery host
By equal rule, by equal love and fear;
Blending the many-nationed whole in one;
And like the lightning's fires securely led
Down the conducting rod, e'en thus his power
Rules all the mass, from guarded post to post,
From where the sentry hears the Baltic roar.
Or views the fertile vales of the Adige,
E'en to the body-guard, who holds his watch
Within the precincts of th' Imperial palace!

QUESTENBERG.

What's the short meaning of this long harangue?

BUTLER.

That the respect, the love, the confidence,
Which makes us willing subjects of Duke Friedland.
Are not to be transferr'd to the first comer
That Austria's Court may please to send to us
We have not yet so readily forgotten
How the command came into Friedland's hands
Was it, forsooth, the Emperor's majesty
That gave the army ready to his hand,
And only sought a leader for it? No.
The army then had no existence. He,
Friedland it was, who called it into being,
And gave it to his sovereign—but receiving
No army at his hand;—nor did the Empero
Give Wallenstein to us as General.—No,
It was from Wallenstein we first received
The Emperor as our master and our sov'reign;
And he, he only, binds us to our banners!]

OCTAVIO (*interposing and addressing* QUESTENBERG,
My noble friend,

This is no more than a remembrancing
That you are now in camp, and among warriors
The soldier's boldness constitutes his freedom.
Could he act daringly, unless he dared
Talk even so? One runs into the other.
The boldness of this worthy officer,
[*Pointing to* BUTLER,

Which now is but mistaken in its mark,
Preserved, when nought but boldness could preserve it
To the Emperor, his capital city, Prague,
In a most formidable mutiny
Of the whole garrison.   [*Military music at a distance*
Hah! here they come!

ILLO.

The sentries are saluting them: this signal
Announces the arrival of the Duchess.

OCTAVIO (*to* QUESTENBERG).

Then my son Max. too has returned.   'Twas he
Fetch'd and attended them from Cärnthen hither

ISOLANI (*to* ILLO).

Shall we not go in company to greet them?

ILLO.

Well, let us go—Ho! Colonel Butler, come. [*To* OCTAVIO
You'll not forget, that yet ere noon we meet
The noble Envoy at the General's palace.

[*Exeunt all but* QUESTENBERG *and* OCTAVIO

SCENE III.

QUESTENBERG *and* OCTAVIO.

QUESTENBERG (*with signs of aversion and astonishment*).

What have I not been forced to hear, Octavio!
What sentiments! what fierce, uncurb'd defiance!
And were this spirit universal—

OCTAVIO.

            Hm!

You are now acquainted with three-fourths of the army

QUESTENBERG.

Where must we seek then for a second host
To have the custody of this?   That Illo
Thinks worse, I fear me, than he speaks.   And then
'This Butler too—he cannot even conceal
The passionate workings of his ill intentions.

OCTAVIO.

Quickness of temper—irritated pride;
'Twas nothing more.   I cannot give up Butler.
I know a spell that will soon dispossess
The evil spirit in *him*

QUESTENBERG (*walking up and down in evident disquiet*)
                     Friend, friend!
O! this is worse, far worse, than we had suffer'd
Ourselves to dream of at Vienna.   There
We saw it only with a courtier's eyes,
Eyes dazzled by the splendour of the throne.
We had not seen the War-chief, the Commander,
The man all-powerful in his camp.   Here, here,
'Tis quite another thing.
Here is no Emperor more—the Duke is Emperor.
Alas, my friend! alas, my noble friend!
This walk which you have ta'en me through the camp
Strikes my hopes prostrate.

                    OCTAVIO.
                         Now you see yourself
Of what a perilous kind the office is,
Which you deliver to me from the Court.
The least suspicion of the General
Costs me my freedom and my life, and would
But hasten his most desperate enterprise

                    QUESTENBERG.
Where was our reason sleeping when we trusted
This madman with the sword, and placed such power
In such a hand?   I tell you, he'll refuse,
Flatly refuse, to obey the Imperial orders.
Friend, he *can* do't, and what he can, he will.
And then the impunity of his defiance—
Oh! what a proclamation of our weakness!

                    OCTAVIO.
D'ye think too, he has brought his wife and daughter
Without a purpose hither?   Here in camp!
And at the very point of time, in which
We're arming for the war?   That he has taken
These, the last pledges of his loyalty,
Away from out the Emperor's domains—
This is no doubtful token of the nearness
Of some eruption?

                    QUESTENBERG.
                         How shall we hold footing
Beneath this tempest, which collects itself

And threats us from all quarters? The enemy
Of the empire on our borders, now already
The master of the Danube, and still farther,
And farther still, extending every hour!
In our interior the alarum-bells
Of insurrection — peasantry in arms—
All orders discontented—and the army,
Just in the moment of our expectation
Of aidance from it—lo! this very army
Seduced, run wild, lost to all discipline,
Loosen'd, and rent asunder from the state
And from their sovereign, the blind instrument
Of the most daring of mankind, a weapon
Of fearful power, which at his will *he* wields!

OCTAVIO

Nay, nay, friend! let us not despair too soon
Men's words are ever bolder than their deeds;
And many a resolute, who now appears
Made up to all extremes, will, on a sudden,
Find in his breast a heart he wot not of,
Let but a single honest man speak out
The true name of his crime! Remember too,
We stand not yet so wholly unprotected.
Counts Altringer and Gallas have maintain'd
Their little army faithful to its duty,
And daily it becomes more numerous.
Nor can he take us by surprise: you know
I hold him all encompass'd by my listeners.
Whate'er he does, is mine, even while 'tis doing—
No step so small, but instantly I hear it;
Yea, his own mouth discloses it.

QUESTENBERG

'Tis quite
Incomprehensible, that he detects not
The foe so near!

OCTAVIO.

Beware, you do not think,
That I by lying arts, and complaisant
Hypocrisy, have skulked into his graces,
Or with the substance of smooth professions
Nourish his all-confiding friendship! No—

Compell'd alike by prudence, and that duty
Which we all owe our country, and our sovereign
To hide my genuine feelings from him, yet
Ne'er have I duped him with base counterfeits!

QUESTENBERG.

It is the visible ordinance of Heaven.

OCTAVIO.

I know not what it is that so attracts
And links him both to me and to my son.
Comrades and friends we always were—long habit,
Adventurous deeds performed in company,
And all those many and various incidents
Which store a soldier's memory with affections,
Had bound us long and early to each other—
Yet I can name the day, when all at once
His heart *rose* on me, and his confidence
Shot out into sudden growth.   It was the morning
Before the memorable fight at Lützen.
Urged by an ugly dream, I sought him out,
To press him to accept another charger.
At a distance from the tents, beneath a tree,
I found him in a sleep.   When I had waked him
And had related all my bodings to him,
Long time he stared upon me, like a man
Astounded: thereon fell upon my neck,
And manifested to me an emotion
That far outstripp'd the worth of that small service
Since then his confidence has follow'd me
With the same pace that mine has fled from him.

QUESTENBERG

You lead your son into the secret?

OCTAVIO.

No!

QUESTENBERG.

What! and not warn him either what bad hands
His lot has placed him in?

OCTAVIO.

I must perforce
Leave him in wardship to his innocence
His young and open soul—dissimulation

Is foreign to its habits?   Ignorance
Alone can keep alive the cheerful air,
The unembarrass'd sense and light free spirit,
That make the Duke secure.

QUESTENBERG (*anxiously*).

My honour'd friend! most highly do I deem
Of Colonel Piccolomini—yet—if——
Reflect a little——

OCTAVIO

I must venture it.
Hush!—There he comes!

SCENE IV

MAX. PICCOLOMINI, OCTAVIO PICCOLOMINI, QUESTENBERG

MAX.

Ha! there he is himself   Welcome, my father!
[*He embraces his father   As he turns round, he observes* QUESTENBERG, *and draws back with a cold
and reserved air.*
You are engaged, I see.   I'll not disturb you.

OCTAVIO.

How, Max.?   Look closer at this visitor.
Attention, Max., an old friend merits—Reverence
Belongs of right to the envoy of your sovereign.

MAX. (*drily*).

Von Questenberg!—Welcome—if you bring with you
Aught good to our head quarters.

QUESTENBERG (*seizing his hand*).

Nay, draw not
Your hand away, Count Piccolomini!
Not on mine own account alone I seized it,
And nothing common will I say therewith.
[*Taking the hands of both*
Octavio—Max. Piccolomini!
O saviour names, and full of happy omen!
Ne'er will her prosperous genius turn from Austria,
While two such stars, with blessed influences
Beaming protection, shine above her hosts.

MAX.

Heh!—Noble minister! You miss your part.
You came not here to act a panegyric.
You're sent, I know, to find fault and to scold us—
I must not be beforehand with my comrades.

OCTAVIO (*to* MAX.).

He comes from court, where people are not quite
So well contented with the Duke, as here.

MAX.

What now have they contrived to find out in him?
That he alone determines for himself
What he himself alone doth understand!
Well, therein he does right, and will persist in 't
Heaven never meant him for that passive thing
That can be struck and hammer'd out to suit
Another's taste and fancy. He'll not dance
To every tune of every minister·
It goes against his nature—he can't do it,
He is possess'd by a commanding spirit,
And his, too, is the station of command.
And well for us it is so! There exist
Few fit to rule themselves, but few that use
Their intellects intelligently. Then
Well for the whole, if there be found a man,
Who makes himself what nature destined him,
The pause, the central point, to thousand thousands—
Stands fixed and stately, like a firm-built column,
Where all may press with joy and confidence
Now such a man is Wallenstein; and if
Another better suits the court—no other
But such a one as he can serve the army

QUESTENBERG

The army? Doubtless!

[MAX

What delight t'observe
How he incites and strengthens all around him,
Infusing life and vigour. Every power
Seems as it were redoubled by his presence:
He draws forth every latent energy,
Showing to each his own peculiar talent,

Yet leaving all to be what nature made their,
And watching only that they be nought else
In the right place and time; and he has skill
To mould the powers of all to his own end.

QUESTENBERG.

But who denies his knowledge of mankind,
And skill to use it? Our complaint is this:—
That in the master he forgets the servant,
As if he claimed by birth his present honours

MAX.

And does he not so? Is he not endow'd
With every gift and power to carry out
The high intents of nature, and to win
A ruler's station by a ruler's talent?

QUESTENBERG.

So then it seems to rest with him alone
What is the worth of all mankind beside!

MAX.

Uncommon men require no common trust;
Give him but scope, and he will set the bounds

QUESTENBERG

The proof is yet to come.

MAX.

                          Thus are ye ever.
Ye shrink from every thing of depth, and think
Yourselves are only safe while ye're in shallows]

OCTAVIO (to QUESTENBERG).

'Twere best to yield with a good grace, my friend.
Of *him* there you'll make nothing.

MAX. *(continuing)*.

                                    In their fear
They call a spirit up, and when he comes,
Straight their flesh creeps and quivers, and they dread him
More than the ills for which they call'd him up..
The uncommon, the sublime, must seem and be
Like things of every day. But in the field,
Ay, *there* the *Present Being* makes itself felt,
The personal must command, the actual eye
Examine . If to be the chieftain asks

All that is great in nature, let it be
Likewise his privilege to move and act
In all the correspondences of greatness.
The oracle within him, that which *lives*,
He must invoke and question—not dead books,
Not ordinances, not mould-rotted papers.

OCTAVIO.

My son! of those old narrow ordinances
Let us not hold too lightly.   They are weights
Of priceless value, which oppress'd mankind
Tied to the volatile will of their oppressors.
For always formidable was the league
And partnership of free power with free will.
The way of ancient ordinance, though it winds,
Is yet no devious path.   Straight forward goes
The lightning's path, and straight the fearful path
Of the cannon ball.   Direct it flies, and rapid;
Shattering that it *may* reach, and shattering what it reaches,
My son! the road the human being travels,
That, on which BLESSING comes and goes, doth follow
The river's course, the valley's playful windings,
Curves round the corn field and the hill of vines,
Honouring the holy bounds of property!
And thus secure, though late, leads to its end

QUESTENBERG.

O hear your father, noble youth! hear *him*,
Who is at once the hero and the man.

OCTAVIO.

My son, the nursling of the camp spoke in thee!
A war of fifteen years
Hath been thy education and thy school.
Peace hast thou never witness'd!   There exists
An higher than the warrior's excellence.
In war itself war is no ultimate purpose.
The vast and sudden deeds of violence,
Adventures wild, and wonders of the moment,
These are not they, my son, that generate
The Calm, the Blissful, and the enduring Mighty!
Lo there! the soldier, rapid architect!
Builds his light town of canvas, and at once
The whole scene moves and bustles momently,

With arms, and neighing steeds, and mirth and quarrel
The motley market fills; the roads, the streams /
Are crowded with new freights; trade stirs and hurries
But on some morrow morn, all suddenly,
The tents drop down, the horde renews its march.
Dreary, and solitary as a church-yard
The meadow and down-trodden seed-plot lie,
And the year's harvest is gone utterly

MAX.

O let the Emperor make peace, my father!
Most gladly would I give the blood-stained laurel
For the first violet * of the leafless spring,
Pluck'd in those quiet fields where I have journey'd

OCTAVIO.

What ails thee? What so moves thee all at once?

MAX.

Peace have I ne'er beheld? I *have* beheld it.
From thence am I come hither: O! that sight,
It glimmers still before me, like some landscape
Left in the distance,—some delicious landscape!
My road conducted me through countries where
The war has not yet reach'd. Life, life, my father—
My venerable father, life has charms
Which *we* have ne'er experienced. We have been
But voyaging along its barren coasts,
Like some poor ever-roaming horde of pirates,
That, crowded in the rank and narrow ship,
House on the wild sea with wild usages,
Nor know aught of the main land, but the bays
Where safeliest they may venture a thieves' landing
Whate'er in the inland dales the land conceals
Of fair and exquisite, O! nothing, nothing,
Do we behold of that in our rude voyage.

OCTAVIO (*attentive, with an appearance of uneasiness.*)
And so your journey has revealed this to you?

* In the original,
    " Den blut'gen Lorbeer geb'ich hin mit Freuden
      Fürs erste Veilchen, das der März uns bringt,
      Das dürftige Pfand der neuverjüngten Erde."

MAX

'Twas the first leisure of my life.　O tell me,
What is the meed and purpose of the toil,
The painful toil which robb'd me of my youth,
Left me a heart unsoul'd and solitary,
A spirit uninform'd, unornamented!
For the camp's stir, and crowd, and ceaseless larum,
The neighing war-horse, the air-shattering trumpet,
The unvaried, still returning hour of duty,
Word of command, and exercise of arms—
There's nothing here, there's nothing in all this,
To satisfy the heart, the gasping heart!
Mere bustling nothingness, where the soul is not—
This cannot be the sole felicity,
These cannot be man's best and only pleasures!

OCTAVIO.

Much hast thou learnt, my son, in this short journey.

MAX.

O! day thrice lovely! when at length the soldier
Returns home into life; when he becomes
A fellow-man among his fellow-men.
The colours are unfurl'd, the cavalcade
Marshals, and now the buzz is hush'd, and hark!
Now the soft peace-march beats, home, brothers, home
The caps and helmets are all garlanded
With green boughs, the last plundering of the fields.
The city gates fly open of themselves,
They need no longer the petard to tear them.
The ramparts are all filled with men and women,
With peaceful men and women, that send onwards
Kisses and welcomings upon the air,
Which they make breezy with affectionate gestures
From all the towers rings out the merry peal,
The joyous vespers of a bloody day.
O happy man, O fortunate! for whom
The well-known door, the faithful arms are open,
The faithful tender arms with mute embracing.

QUESTENBERG (*apparently much affected*).
　　　　　　O that you should speak
Of such a distant, distant time, and not
Of the to-morrow, not of this to-day

MAX. (*turning round to him quick and vehement*)
Where lies the fault but on you in Vienna!
I will deal openly with you, Questenberg.
Just now, as first I saw you standing here,
(I'll own it to you freely,) indignation
Crowded and press'd my inmost soul together.
'Tis ye that hinder peace, *ye!*—and the warrior,
It is the warrior that must force it from you.
Ye fret the General's life out, blacken him,
Hold him up as a rebel, and Heaven knows
What else still worse, because he spares the Saxons,
And tries to awaken confidence in the enemy;
Which yet's the only way to peace: for if
War intermit not during war, *how* then
And *whence* can peace come? Your own plagues fall on you!
Even as I love what's virtuous, hate I you.
And here I make this vow, here pledge myself,
My blood shall spurt out for this Wallenstein,
And my heart drain off, drop by drop, ere ye
Shall revel and dance jubilee o'er his ruin.   [*Exit*

SCENE V.

QUESTENBERG, OCTAVIO PICCOLOMINI

QUESTENBERG.

Alas, alas! and stands it so?
                    [*Then in pressing and impatient tones*
What friend! and do we let him go away
In this delusion—let him go away?
Not call him back immediately, not open
His eyes upon the spot?

        OCTAVIO (*recovering himself out of a deep study*)
                    He has now open'd mine,
And I see more than pleases me

                QUESTENBERG
                            What is it?

            OCTAVIO.

Curse on this journey!

                QUESTENBERG.
                    But why so?   What is it?

OCTAVIO.

Come, come along, friend! I must follow up
The ominous track immediately. Mine eyes
Are open'd now, and I must use them. Come!
[Draws QUESTENBERG on with him.

QUESTENBERG.

What now? *Where* go you then?

OCTAVIO.

To her herself.

QUESTENBERG

To——

OCTAVIO (*interrupting him, and correcting himself*)

To the Duke. Come let us go—'Tis done, 'tis done,
I see the net that is thrown over him.
Oh! he returns not to me as he went

QUESTENBERG.

Nay, but explain yourself.

OCTAVIO.

And that I should not

Foresee it, not prevent this journey! Wherefore
Did I keep it from him?—You were in the right
I should have warn'd him! Now it is too late.

QUESTENBERG.

But *what's* too late? Bethink yourself, my friend,
That you are talking absolute riddles to me.

OCTAVIO (*more collected*).

Come! to the Duke's. 'Tis close upon the hour
Which he appointed you for audience. Come!
A curse, a threefold curse, upon this journey!
[He leads QUESTENBERG off

ACT II.

SCENE I.

*Changes to a spacious Chamber in the House of the Duke of
Friedland.—Servants employed in putting the tables and
chairs in order —During this enters* SENI, *like an old
Italian Doctor, in black, and clothed somewhat fantastically. He carries a white staff, with which he marks out
the quarters of the heavens.*

FIRST SERVANT.

Come—to it, lads, to it! Make an end of it. I hear the

F

sentry call out, 'Stand to your arms!" They will be here
in a minute

SECOND SERVANT.

Why were we not told before that the audience would be
held here? Nothing prepared—no orders—no instructions.

THIRD SERVANT.

Ay, and why was the balcony chamber countermanded, that
with the great worked carpet? There one can look about one

FIRST SERVANT.

Nay, that you must ask the mathematician there. He says
it is an unlucky chamber.

SECOND SERVANT.

Poh! stuff and nonsense! That's what I call a *hum*. A
chamber is a chamber; what much can the place signify in
the affair?

SENI (*with gravity*).

My son, there's *nothing* insignificant,
Nothing! But yet in every earthly thing
First and most principal is place and time.

FIRST SERVANT (*to the second*).

Say nothing to him, Nat. The Duke himself must let him
have his own will

SENI (*counts the chairs, half in a loud, half in a low voice, till*
he comes to eleven, which he repeats).
Eleven! an evil number! Set twelve chairs.
Twelve! twelve signs hath the zodiac: five and seven,
The holy numbers. include themselves in twelve.

SECOND SERVANT.

And what may you have to object against eleven? I should
like to know that now.

SENI.

Eleven is transgression; eleven oversteps
The ten commandments.

SECOND SERVANT.

That's good! and why do you call five a holy number?

SENI.

Five is the soul of man: for even as man
Is mingled up of good and evil, so
The five is the first number that's made up
Of even and odd.

SECOND SERVANT.

The foolish old coxcomb!

FIRST SERVANT.

Ay! let him alone though I like to hear him; there is
more in his words than can be seen at first sight.

THIRD SERVANT

Off, they come.

SECOND SERVANT

There! Out at the side-door

> [*They hurry off.* SENI *follows slowly. A Page
> brings the staff of command on a red cushion, and
> places it on the table near the Duke's chair. They
> are announced from without, and the wings of the
> door fly open.*

SCENE II.

WALLENSTEIN, DUCHESS

WALLENSTEIN

You went then through Vienna, were presented
To the Queen of Hungary?

DUCHESS.

                    Yes; and to the Empress too,
And by both Majesties were we admitted
To kiss the hand

WALLENSTEIN.

              And how was it received,
That I had sent for wife and daughter hither
To the camp, in winter-time?

DUCHESS.

              I did even that
Which you commission'd me to do. I told them,
You had determined on our daughter's marriage,
And wish'd, ere yet you went into the field,
To show the elected husband his betrothed.

WALLENSTEIN.

And did they guess the choice which I had made?

DUCHESS.

They only hoped and wish'd it may have fallen
Upon no foreign nor yet Lutheran noble.

WALLENSTEIN.

And you--what do *you* wish, Elizabeth?

DUCHESS.

Your will, you know, was always mine.

WALLENSTEIN (*after a pause*).

Well then--
And in all else, of what kind and complexion
Was your reception at the court?

[*The* DUCHESS *casts her eyes on the ground, and
remains silent*

Hide nothing from me.   How were you received?

DUCHESS.

O! my dear lord, all is not what it was.
A canker-worm, my lord, a canker-worm
Has stolen into the bud.

WALLENSTEIN.

Ay! is it so!
What, they were lax? they fail'd of the old respect?

DUCHESS.

Not of respect.   No honours were omitted,
No outward courtesy; but in the place
Of condescending, confidential kindness,
Familiar and endearing, there were given me
Only these honours and that solemn courtesy.
Ah! and the tenderness which was put on,
It was the guise of pity not of favour.
No! Albrecht's wife, Duke Albrecht's princely wife,
Count Harrach's noble daughter, should not *so*—
Not wholly so should she have been received.

WALLENSTEIN.

Yes, yes; they have ta'en offence.   My latest conduct
They rail'd at it, no doubt.

DUCHESS.

O that they had!
I have been long accustomed to defend you,
To heal and pacify distemper'd spirits.
No; no one rail'd at you.   They wrapp'd them up,
O Heaven! in such oppressive, solemn silence!—
Here is no every-day misunderstanding,
No transient pique, no cloud that passes over;

Something most luckless, most unhealable,
Has taken place. The Queen of Hungary
Used formerly to call me her dear aunt,
And ever at departure to embrace me—

WALLENSTEIN.

Now she omitted it?

DUCHESS (*wiping away her tears after a pause*).
She *did* embrace me,
But then first when I had already taken
My formal leave, and when the door already
Had closed upon me, then did she come out
In haste, as she had suddenly bethought herself,
And press'd me to her bosom, more with anguish
Than tenderness.

WALLENSTEIN (*seizes her hand soothingly*).
Nay, now collect yourself.
And what of Eggenberg and Lichtenstein,
And of our other friends there?—

DUCHESS *shaking her head*).
I saw none.

WALLENSTEIN.

The Ambassador from Spain, who once was wont
To plead so warmly for me?—

DUCHESS.
Silent, silent!

WALLENSTEIN.

These suns then are eclipsed for us.   Henceforward
Must we roll on, our own fire, our own light.

DUCHESS.

And were it—were it, my dear lord, in that
Which mov'd about the court in buzz and whisper,
But in the country let itself be heard
Aloud—in that which Father Lamormain
In sundry hints and——

WALLENSTEIN (*eagerly*).
Lamormain! what said *he?*

DUCHESS.

That you're accused of having daringly
O'erstepped the powers entrusted to you, charged

With traitorous contempt of the Emperor
And his supreme behests. The proud Bavarian,
He and the Spaniards stand up your accusers—
That there's a storm collecting over you
Of far more fearful menace than that former one
Which whirl'd you headlong down at Regensburg
And people talk, said he, of——Ah !—

[Stifling extreme emotion

WALLENSTEIN.

Proceed !

DUCHESS

I cannot utter it !

WALLENSTEIN
Proceed !

DUCHESS.

They talk——.

WALLENSTEIN

Well !

DUCHESS

Of a second——(catches her voice and hesitates).

WALLENSTEIN
Second——

DUCHESS

More disgraceful

——Dismission

WALLENSTEIN
Talk they ?
[Strides across the Chamber in vehement agitation.

O ! they force, they thrust me

With violence, against my own will, onward !

DUCHESS (presses near to him in entreaty).
O ! if there yet be time, my husband ! if
By giving way and by submission, this
Can be averted—my dear lord, give way !
Win down your proud heart to it ! Tell that heart,
It is your sovereign lord, your Emperor
Before whom you retreat. O let no longer
Low tricking malice blacken your good meaning
With abhorr'd venomous glosses. Stand you up

Shielded and helm'd and weapon'd with the truth,
And drive before you into uttermost shame
These slanderous liars! Few firm friends have we—
You know it!—The swift growth of our good fortune,
It hath but set us up a mark for hatred.
What are we, if the sovereign's grace and favour
Stand not before us!

SCENE III.

Enter the Countess TERZKY, *leading in her hand the Princess*
THEKLA, *richly adorned with Brilliants*

COUNTESS, THEKLA, WALLENSTEIN, DUCHESS

COUNTESS

How, sister! What, already upon business?

[*Observing the countenance of the* DUCHESS

And business of no pleasing kind I see,
Ere he has gladden'd at his child. The first
Moment belongs to joy Here, Friedland! father!
This is thy daughter

[THEKLA *approaches with a shy and timid air, and
bends herself as about to kiss his hand. He receives her in his arms, and remains standing for
some time lost in the feeling of her presence*

WALLENSTEIN.

Yes! pure and lovely hath hope risen on me .
I take her as the pledge of greater fortune

DUCHESS.

'Twas but a little child when you departed
To raise up that great army for the Emperor:
And after, at the close of the campaign,
When you returned home, out of Pomerania,
Your daughter was already in the convent,
Wherein she has remained till now

WALLENSTEIN.

                              The while
We in the field here gave our cares and toils
To make her great, and fight her a free way
To the loftiest earthly good; lo! mother Nature
Within the peaceful silent convent walls

Has done her part, and out of her free grace
Hath she bestow'd on the beloved child
The god-like; and now leads her thus adorn'd
To meet her splendid fortune, and my hope.

DUCHESS (*to* THEKLA).

Thou wouldst not now have recognised thy father,
Wouldst thou, my child?   She counted scarce eight years,
When last she saw your face.

THEKLA.

O yes, yes, mother!

At the first glance !—My father has not alter'd.
The form that stands before me falsifies
No feature of the image that hath lived
So long within me !

WALLENSTEIN.

The voice of my child !

[*Then after a pause*

I was indignant at my destiny,
That it denied me a man-child, to be
Heir of my name and of my prosperous fortune,
And re-illume my soon extinguish'd being
In a proud line of princes.
I wronged my destiny.   Here upon this head,
So lovely in its maiden bloom will I
Let fall the garland of a life of war.
Nor deem it lost, if only I can wreath it,
Transmuted to a regal ornament,
Around these beauteous brows.

[*He clasps her in his arms as* PICCOLOMINI *enters*

SCENE IV.

Enter MAX. PICCOLOMINI, *and some time after* COUNT TERZKY,
the others remaining as before.

COUNTESS.

There comes the Paladin who protected us

WALLENSTEIN.

Max. ! Welcome, ever welcome ! Always wert thou
The morning star of my best joys !

MAX.

My General——

WALLENSTEIN.

Till now it was the Emperor who rewarded thee,
I but the instrument   This day thou hast bound
The father to thee, Max ! the fortunate father,
And this debt Friedland's self must pay.

MAX.

                  My prince !
You made no common hurry to transfer it.
I come with shame : yea, not without a pang !
For scarce have I arrived here, scarce deliver'd
The mother and the daughter to your arms,
But there is brought to me from your equerry *
A splendid richly-plated hunting dress
So to remunerate me for my troubles—
Yes, yes, remunerate me ! Since a trouble
It must be, a mere office, not a favour
Which I leapt forward to receive, and which
I came with grateful heart to thank you for.
No! 'twas not so intended, that my business
Should be my highest best good fortune !

        [TERZKY *enters, and delivers letters to the* DUKE,
             which he breaks open hurriedly.

COUNTESS (*to* MAX.).

Remunerate your trouble ! For his joy
He makes you recompense. 'Tis not unfitting
For you, Count Piccolomini, to feel
So tenderly—my brother it beseems
To show himself for ever great and princely

THEKLA.

Then I too must have scruples of his love :
For his munificent hands did ornament me
Ere yet the father's heart had spoken to me.

---

* A reviewer in the *Literary Gazette* observes that, in these l'nes, Mr.
Coleridge has misapprehended the meaning of the word " zug," a team, trans-
lating it as "anzug," a suit of clothes. The following version, as a substitute,
I propose :—

    When from your stables there is brought to me
    A team of four most richly harnessed horses.
The term, however, is "jagd-zug," which may mean a "hunting equipage,"
or a "hunting stud ; " although Hilpert gives only "a team   four horses."

MAX

Yes; 'tis his nature ever to be giving
And making happy.
> [*He grasps the hand of the* DUCHESS *with still in
> creasing warmth.*

How my heart pours out
Its all of thanks to him! O! how I seem
To utter all things in the dear name—Friedland.
While I shall live, so long will I remain
The captive of this name: in it shall bloom
My every fortune, every lovely hope.
Inextricably as in some magic ring
In this name hath my destiny charm-bound me!

COUNTESS (*who during this time has been anxiously watching
the* DUKE, *and remarks that he is lost in thought over the
letters*).
My brother wishes us to leave him. Come.

WALLENSTEIN (*turns himself round quick, collects himself.
and speaks with cheerfulness to the* DUCHESS).
Once more I bid thee welcome to the camp,
Thou art the hostess of this court. You, Max.,
Will now again administer your old office,
While we perform the sovereign's business here.
> [MAX. PICCOLOMINI *offers the* DUCHESS *his arm; the
> COUNTESS *accompanies the* PRINCESS

TERZKY (*calling after him*).
Max , we depend on seeing you at the meeting

SCENE V.

WALLENSTEIN. COUNT TERZKY

WALLENSTEIN (*in deep thought, to himself*).
She has seen all things as they are—It is so
And squares completely with my other notices
They have determined finally in Vienna,
Have given me my successor already;
It is the King of Hungary, Ferdinand,
The Emperor's delicate son! he's now their saviour,
He's the new star that's rising now! Of us
They think themselves already fairly rid.

And as we were deceased, the heir already
Is entering on possession—Therefore—despatch!

> [*As he turns round he observes* TERZKY, *and gives
> him a letter.*

Count Altringer will have himself excused,
And Gallas too—I like not this!

TERZKY

     And if
Thou loiterest longer, all will fall away,
One following the other.

WALLENSTEIN

     Altringer
Is master of the Tyrol passes I must forthwith
Send some one to him, that he let not in
The Spaniards on me from the Milanese.
——Well, and the old Sesin, that ancient trader
In contraband negociations, he
Has shown himself again of late. What brings he
From the Count Thur?

TERZKY.

     The Count communicates
He has found out the Swedish Chancellor
At Halberstadt, where the convention's held,
Who says, you've tired him out, and that he'll have
No further dealings with you.

WALLENSTEIN.

     And why so?

TERZKY.

He says, you are never in earnest in your speeches;
That you decoy the Swedes—to make fools of them ·
Will league yourself with Saxony against them,
And at last make yourself a riddance of them
With a paltry sum of money

WALLENSTEIN.

     So then, doubtless,
Yes, doubtless, this same modest Swede expects
That I shall yield him some fair German tract
For his prey and booty, that ourselves at last
On our own soil and native territory

May be no longer our own lords and masters!
An excellent scheme! No, no! They must be off,
Off, off! away! *we* want no such neighbours.

TERZKY.

Nay, yield them up that dot, that speck of land—
It goes not from your portion.   If you win
The game, what matters it to you who pays it?

WALLENSTEIN.

Off with them, off! Thou understand'st not this
Never shall it be said of me, I parcell'd
My native land away, dismember'd Germany,
Betray'd it to a foreigner, in order
To come with stealthy tread, and filch away
My own share of the plunder—Never! never!
No foreign power shall strike root in the empire,
And least of all these Goths! these hunger-wolves!
Who send such envious, hot and greedy glances
Toward the rich blessings of our German lands!
I'll have their aid to cast and draw my nets,
But not a single fish of all the draught
Shall they come in for.

TERZKY.

                    You will deal, however,
More fairly with the Saxons? they lose patience
While you shift round and make so many curves.
Say, to what purpose all these masks?   Your friends
Are plunged in doubts, baffled, and led astray in you.
There's Oxenstiern, there's Arnheim—neither knows
What he should think of your procrastinations
And in the end I prove the liar; all
Passes through me.   I've not even your handwriting

WALLENSTEIN

I *never* give handwriting; and thou knowest it.

TERZKY

But how can it be *known* that you are in earnest,
If the act follows not upon the word?
You must yourself acknowledge, that in all
Your intercourses hitherto with the enemy,
You might have done with safety all you have done,

Had you meant nothing further than to gull him
For the Emperor's service.

WALLENSTEIN *(after a pause, during which he looks
                narrowly on* TERZKY).

       And from whence dost *thou* know
That I'm *not* gulling him for the Emperor's service?
Whence knowest thou that I'm not gulling all of you?
Dost thou know *me* so well? When made I thee
The intendant of my secret purposes?
I am not conscious that I ever open'd
My inmost thoughts to thee. The Emperor, it is true,
Hath dealt with me amiss; and if I *would*,
i could repay him with usurious interest
For the evil he hath done me. It delights me
To know my *power;* but whether I shall use it,
Of that, I should have thought that thou couldst speak
No wiser than thy fellows.

TERZKY.
So hast thou always played thy game with us.

                        [*Enter* ILLO.

SCENE VI.
ILLO, WALLENSTEIN, TERZKY.

WALLENSTEIN.
How stand affairs without? Are they prepared?

ILLO.
You'll find them in the very mood you wish
They know about the Emperor's requisitions,
And are tumultuous.

WALLENSTEIN.
        How hath Isolani
Declared himself?

ILLO.
        He's yours both soul and body,
Since you built up again his Faro-bank.

WALLENSTEIN.
And which way doth Kolatto bend? Hast thou
Made sure of Tiefenbach and Deodati?

ILLO.
What Piccolomini does, that they do too.

WALLENSTEIN.

You mean, then, I may venture somewhat with them?

ILLO.

—If you are assured of the Piccolomini.

WALLENSTEIN.

Not more assured of mine own self.

TERZKY.

And yet
I would you trusted not so much to Octavio,
The fox!

WALLENSTEIN.

Thou teachest me to know my man?
Sixteen campaigns I have made with that old warrior.
Besides, I have his horoscope ·
We both are born beneath the like stars—in short,

[*With an air of mystery*

To this belongs its own peculiar aspect,
If therefore thou canst warrant me the rest— —

ILLO

There is among them all but this one voice,
You *must* not lay down the command.   I hear
They mean to send a deputation to you.

WALLENSTEIN.

If I'm in aught to bind myself to *them*,
They too must bind themselves to me

ILLO.

Of course.

WALLENSTEIN.

Their words of honour they must give, their oaths,
Give them in writing to me, promising
Devotion to my service *unconditional*.

ILLO

Why not?

TERZKY

Devotion *unconditional?*
The exception of their duties towards Austria
They'll always place among the premises.
With this reserve——

WALLENSTEIN (*shaking his head.*)
All *unconditional*
No premises, no reserves.

ILLO

A thought has struck me
Does not Count Terzky give us a set banquet
This evening?

TERZKY

Yes; and all the Generals
Have been invited.

ILLO (*to* WALLENSTEIN).

Say, will you here fully
Commission me to use my own discretion?
I'll gain for you the Generals' word of honour,
Even as you wish.

WALLENSTEIN.

Gain me their signatures!
How you come by them, that is *your* concern.

ILLO.

And if I bring it to you, black on white.
That all the leaders who are present here
Give themselves up to you, without condition;
Say, will you *then—then* will you show yourself
In earnest, and with some decisive action
Try your fortune

WALLENSTEIN.

Get but the signatures!

[ILLO.

Think what thou dost, thou canst not execute
The Emperor's orders, nor reduce thine army,
Nor send the regiments to the Spaniards' aid,
Unless thou wouldst resign thy power for ever.
Think on the other hand—thou canst not spurn
The Emperor's high commands and solemn orders,
Nor longer temporize, nor seek evasion,
Wouldst thou avoid a rupture with the court.
Resolve then! Wilt thou *now* by one bold act
Anticipate their ends, or doubting still,
Await the extremity?

WALLENSTEIN.
                                    There's time before
The extremity arrives.]
                    ILLO.
                                    Seize, seize the hour,
Ere it slips from you.   Seldom comes the moment
In life, which is indeed sublime and weighty.
To make a great decision possible,
O! many things, all transient and all rapid,
Must meet at once : and, hardly, they thus met
May by that confluence be enforced to pause
Time long enough for wisdom, though too short,
Far, far too short a time for doubt and scruple !
This is that moment.   See, our army chieftains,
Our best, our noblest, are assembled round you
Their king like leader!   On your nod they wait.
The single threads, which here your prosperous fortune
Hath woven together in one potent web
Instinct with destiny, O let them not
Unravel of themselves.   If you permit
These chiefs to separate, so unanimous
Bring you them not a second time together.
'Tis the high tide that heaves the stranded ship,
And every individual's spirit waxes
In the great stream of multitudes.   Behold
They are still here, here still !   But soon the war
Bursts them once more asunder, and in small
Particular anxieties and interests
Scatters their spirit, and the sympathy
Of each man with the whole.   He, who to-day
Forgets himself, forced onward with the stream,
Will become sober, seeing but himself.
Feel only his own weakness, and with speed
Will face about, and march on in the old
High road of duty, the old broad-trodden road,
And seek but to make shelter in good plight.
                    WALLENSTEIN
The time is not yet come
                    TERZKY
                                    So you say always.
But *when* will it be time?

WALLENSTEIN
                    When I shall say it
ILLO

You'll wait upon the stars, and on their hours,
Till the earthly hour escapes you.   O, believe me,
In your own bosom are your destiny's stars.
Confidence in yourself, prompt resolution,
This is your Venus! and the sole maliguant,
The only one that harmeth you, is Doubt.

WALLENSTEIN.

Thou speakest as thou understand'st.   How oft
And many a time I've told thee, Jupiter,
That lustrous god, was setting at thy birth
Thy visual power subdues no mysteries;
Mole-eyed, thou mayest but burrow in the earth,
Blind as that subterrestrial, who with wan
Lead-colour'd shine lighted thee into life.
The common, the terrestrial, thou mayest see,
With serviceable cunning knit together
The nearest with the nearest; and therein
I trust thee and believe thee! but whate'er
Full of mysterious import Nature weaves,
And fashions in the depths—the spirit's ladder,
That from this gross and visible world of dust
Even to the starry world, with thousand rounds,
Builds itself up; on which the unseen powers
Move up and down on heavenly ministries—
The circles in the circles, that approach
The central sun with ever-narrowing orbit—
These see the glance alone, the unsealed eye,
Of Jupiter's glad children born in lustre.

          [*He walks across the Chamber, then returns, and
                standing still, proceeds*

The heavenly constellations make not merely
The day and nights, summer and spring, not merely
Signify to the husbandman the seasons
Of sowing and of harvest.   Human action,
That is the seed too of contingencies,
Strew'd on the dark land of futurity
In hopes to reconcile the powers of fate
Whence it behoves us to seek out the seed-time.

                                              G

To watch the stars. select their proper hours,
And trace with searching eye the heavenly houses,
Whether the enemy of growth and thriving
Hide himself not, malignant, in his corner.
Therefore permit me my own time   Meanwhile
Do you your part.   As yet I cannot say
What I shall do—only, give way I will not
Depose me too they shall not.   On these points
You may rely.

PAGE (*entering*).
My Lords, the Generals

WALLENSTEIN.
Let them come in

[TERZKY.
Shall all the chiefs be present?

WALLENSTEIN.
'Twere needless.   Both the Piccolomini
Maradas, Butler, Forgœtsch, Deodati,
Karaffa, Isolani—these may come.

[TERZKY *goes out with the* PAGE

WALLENSTEIN (*to* ILLO).
Hast thou ta'en heed that Questenberg was watched?
Had he no means of secret intercourse?

ILLO
I have watched him closely—and he spoke with none
But with Octavio.]

SCENE VII.

WALLENSTEIN, TERZKY, ILLO. — *To them enter* QUESTEN
BERG, OCTAVIO, *and* MAX PICCOLOMINI, BUTLER. Iso
LANI, MARADAS, *and three other Generals.* WALLEN-
STEIN *motions* QUESTENBERG, *who in consequence takes
the chair directly opposite to him; the others follow,
arranging themselves according to their rank. There
reigns a momentary silence.*

WALLENSTEIN.
               I have understood.
'Tis true, the sum and import, Questenberg,
Of your instructions.   I have weighed them well,
And formed my final. absolute resolve :

Yet it seems fitting, that the Generals
Should hear the will of the Emperor from your mouth
May't please you then to open your commission
Before these noble Chieftains ?

QUESTENBERG
                              I am ready
To obey you; but will first entreat your Highness,
And all these noble Chieftains, to consider,
The Imperial dignity and sovereign right
Speaks from my mouth, and not my own presumption

WALLENSTEIN.
We excuse all preface.

QUESTENBERG.
                         When his Majesty
The Emperor to his courageous armies
Presented in the person of Duke Friedland
A most experienced and renown'd commander,
He did it in glad hope and confidence
To give thereby to the fortune of the war
A rapid and auspicious change.   The onset
Was favourable to his royal wishes.
Bohemia was delivered from the Saxons,
The Swede's career of conquest check'd !   These lands
Began to draw breath freely as Duke Friedland
From all the streams of Germany forced hither
The scattered armies of the enemy ;
Hither invoked as round one magic circle
The Rhinegrave, Bernhard, Banner, Oxenstiern,
Yea, and that never-conquer'd King himself;
Here finally, before the eye of Nürnberg,
The fearful game of battle to decide.

WALLENSTEIN.
To the point, so please you.

[QUESTENBERG.
                         A new spirit
At once proclaimed to us the new commander.
No longer strove blind rage with rage more blind ;
But in th' enlighten'd field of skill was shown
How fortitude can triumph over boldness,
And scientific art outweary courage.

                                    G 2

In vain they tempt him to the fight, he only
Entrenches him still deeper in his hold,
As if to build an everlasting fortress.
At length grown desperate, now, the king resolves
To storm the camp and lead his wasted legions,
Who daily fall by famine and by plague,
To quicker deaths than hunger and disease.
Through lines of barricades behind whose fence
Death lurks within a thousand mouths of fire,
He yet unconquer'd strives to storm his way.
There was attack, and there resistance, such
As mortal eye had never seen before :
Repulsed at last the king withdrew his troops
From this so murd'rous field, and not a foot
Of ground was gain'd by all that fearful slaughter.

WALLENSTEIN.

Pray spare us these recitals from gazettes,
Which we ourselves beheld with deepest horror]

QUESTENBERG.

In Nürnberg's camp the Swedish monarch left
His fame—in Lützen's plains his life.   But who
Stood not astounded, when victorious Friedland
After this day of triumph, this proud day,
March'd toward Bohemia with the speed of flight,
And vanish'd from the theatre of war ?
While the young Weimar hero * forced his way
Into Franconia, to the Danube, like
Some delving winter-stream, which, where it rushes
Makes its own channel ; with such sudden speed
He marched, and now at once 'fore Regensburg
Stood to the affright of all good Catholic Christians
Then did Bavaria's well-deserving Prince
Entreat swift aidance in his extreme need ;
The Emperor sends seven horsemen to Duke Friedland.
Seven horsemen couriers sends he with the entreaty :
He superadds his own, and supplicates
Where as the sovereign lord he can command
In vain his supplication !   At this moment
The Duke hears only his old hate and grudge,

---

* Bernhard of Saxe-Weimar, who succeeded Gustavus in command.

Barters the general good to gratify
Private revenge—and so falls Regensburg.

WALLENSTEIN.

Max., to what period of the war alludes he?
My recollection fails me here.

MAX.

He means
When we were in Silesia.

WALLENSTEIN

Ay! is it so!
But what had we to do *there?*

MAX.

To beat out
The Swedes and Saxons from the province.

WALLENSTEIN

True;
In that description which the Minister gave,
I seemed to have forgotten the whole war.
[*To* QUESTENBERG

Well, but proceed a little.

QUESTENBERG.

[We hoped upon the Oder to regain
What on the Danube shamefully was lost.
We looked for deeds of all-astounding grandeur
Upon a theatre of war, on which
A Friedland led in person to the field,
And the famed rival of the great Gustavus
Had but a Thurn and Arnheim to oppose him!
Yet the encounter of their mighty hosts
Served but to feast and entertain each other.
Our country groaned beneath the woes of war,
Yet nought but peace prevail'd in Friedland's camp!

WALLENSTEIN.

Full many a bloody strife is fought in vain,
Because its youthful general needs a vict'ry.
But 'tis the privilege of th' old commander
To spare the cost of fighting useless battles
Merely to show that he knows how to conquer.
It would have little help'd my fame to boast
Of conquest o'er an Arnheim; but far more

Would my forbearance have avail'd my country,
Had I succeeded to dissolve th alliance
Existing 'twixt the Saxon and the Swede

QUESTENBERG.

But you did not succeed, and so commenced
The fearful strife anew.   And here at length,]
Beside the river Oder did the Duke
Assert his ancient fame   Upon the fields
Of Steinau did the Swedes lay down their arms.
Subdued without a blow   And here, with others,
The righteousness of Heaven to his avenger
Deliver'd that long-practised stirrer-up
Of insurrection, that curse-laden torch
And kindler of this war, Matthias Thurn
But he had fallen into magnanimous hands ;
Instead of punishment he found reward,
And with rich presents did the Duke dismiss
The arch-foe of his Emperor.

WALLENSTEIN (laughs).
I know,
I know you had already in Vienna
Your windows and your balconies forestall'd
To see him on the executioner's cart.
I might have lost the battle, lost it too
With infamy, and still retain'd your graces—
But, to have cheated them of a spectacle,
Oh ! that the good folks of Vienna never,
No, never can forgive me !

QUESTENBERG
So Silesia
Was freed, and all things loudly called the Duke
Into Bavaria, now press'd hard on all sides.
And he did put his troops in motion : slowly,
Quite at his ease, and by the longest road
He traverses Bohemia ; but ere ever
He hath once seen the enemy, faces round,
Breaks up the march, and takes to winter quarters.

WALLENSTEIN.
The troops were pitiably destitute
Of every necessary, every comfort,

The winter came.   What thinks his Majesty
His troops are made of?   Ar'n't we men? subjected
Like other men to wet, and cold, and all
The circumstances of necessity?
O miserable lot of the poor soldier!
Wherever he comes in, all flee before him,
And when he goes away, the general curse
Follows him on his route.   All must be seized.
Nothing is given him.   And compell'd to seize
From every man, he's every man's abhorrence.
Behold, here stand my Generals.   Karaffa
Count Deodati! Butler! Tell this man
How long the soldier's pay is in arrears.

BUTLER

Already a full year.

WALLENSTEIN.

                    And 'tis the hire
That constitutes the hireling's name and duties,
The soldier's *pay* is the soldier's *covenant* *.

QUESTENBERG.

Ah! this is a far other tone from that,
In which the Duke spoke eight, nine years ago

WALLENSTEIN.

Yes! 'tis my fault, I know it: I myself
Have spoilt the Emperor by indulging him.
Nine years ago, during the Danish war,
I raised him up a force, a mighty force,
Forty or fifty thousand men, that cost him
Of his own purse no doit.   Through Saxony
The fury goddess of the war march'd on,
E'en to the surf-rocks of the Baltic, bearing
The terrors of his name·   That was a time!
In the whole Imperial realm no name like mine

* The original is not translatable into English:
                    ——Und sein Sold
          Muss dem *Soldaten* werden, darnach heisst er.
It might perhaps have been thus rendered:
          And that for which he sold his services,
          The soldier must receive—
but a false or doubtful etymology is no more than a dull pun.

Honour'd with festival and celebration—
And Albrecht Wallenstein, it was the title
Of the third jewel in his crown!
But at the Diet, when the Princes met
At Regensburg, there, there the whole broke out,
There 'twas laid open, there it was made known,
Out of what money-bag I had paid the host.
And what were now my thanks, what had I now.
That I, a faithful servant of the Sovereign,
Had loaded on myself the people's curses,
And let the Princes of the empire pay
The expenses of this war, that aggrandizes
The Emperor alone. What thanks had I!
What? I was offer'd up to their complaints
Dismiss'd, degraded!

QUESTENBERG.

But your Highness knowe
What little freedom he possess'd of action
In that disastrous diet.

WALLENSTEIN.

Death and hell!
I had that which could have procured him freedom
No! since 'twas proved so inauspicious to me
To serve the Emperor at the empire's cost.
I have been taught far other trains of thinking
Of the empire, and the diet of the empire.
From the Emperor, doubtless, I received this staff
But now I hold it as the empire's general—
For the common weal, the universal interest,
And no more for that one man's aggrandizement!
But to the point. What is it that's desired of me?

QUESTENBERG.

First, his Imperial Majesty hath will'd
That without pretexts of delay the army
Evacuate Bohemia.

WALLENSTEIN

In this season?
And to what quarter wills the Emperor
That we direct our course?

QUESTENBERG
To the enemy

His Majesty resolves, that Regensburg
Be purified from the enemy ere Easter,
That Lutheranism may be no longer preach'd
In that cathedral, nor heretical
Defilement desecrate the celebration
Of that pure festival.

WALLENSTEIN.
My generals,

Can this be realized?

ILLO.
'Tis not possible.

BUTLER.

It can't be realized.

QUESTENBERG
The Emperor

Already hath commanded colonel Suys
To advance towards Bavaria.

WALLENSTEIN
What did Suys?

QUESTENBERG

That which his duty prompted. He advanced

WALLENSTEIN.

What! he advanced? And I, his general,
Had given him orders, peremptory orders,
Not to desert his station! Stands it thus
With my authority? Is this the obedience
Due to my office, which being thrown aside.
No war can be conducted? Chieftains, speak.
You be the judges, generals! What deserves
That officer who, of his oath neglectful,
Is guilty of contempt of orders?

ILLO.
Death.

WALLENSTEIN (raising his voice, as all but ILLO had remained
silent and seemingly scrupulous).
Count Piccolomini! what has he deserved?

MAX. PICCOLOMINI (*after a long pause*).
According to the letter of the law,
Death.

ISOLANI.
Death.

BUTLER.
Death, by the laws of war.
[QUESTENBERG *rises from his seat,* WALLENSTEIN *follows*
all the rest rise.

WALLENSTEIN.
To this the law condemns him, and not I.
And if I show him favour, 'twill arise
From the reverence that I owe my Emperor.

QUESTENBERG.
If *so*, I can say nothing further—*here !*

WALLENSTEIN.
I accepted the command but on conditions :
And this the first, that to the diminution
Of my authority no human being,
Not even the Emperor's self, should be entitled
To do aught, or to say aught, with the army
If I stand warranter of the *event*,
Placing my honour and my head in pledge,
Needs must I have full mastery in all
The means thereto. What render'd this Gustavus
Resistless, and unconquer'd upon earth ?
This—that he was the monarch in his army !
A monarch, one who is indeed a monarch,
Was never yet subdued but by his equal.
But to the point ! The best is yet to come
Attend now, generals !

QUESTENBERG.
The Prince Cardinal
Begins his route at the approach of spring
From the Milanese ; and leads a Spanish army
Through Germany into the Netherlands.
That he may march secure and unimpeded,
'Tis the Emperor's will you grant him a detachment
Of eight horse-regiments from the army here

WALLENSTEIN.

Yes, yes! I understand!—Eight regiments! Well,
Right well concerted, father Lamormain!
Eight thousand horse! Yes, yes! 'tis as it should be!
I see it coming.

QUESTENBERG.

There is nothing coming.
All stands in front: the counsel of state-prudence,
The dictate of necessity!

WALLENSTEIN.

What then?
What, my Lord Envoy? May I not be suffer'd
To understand, that folks are tired of seeing
The sword's hilt in *my* grasp; and that your court
Snatch eagerly at this pretence, and use
The Spanish title, to drain off my forces,
To lead into the empire a new army
Unsubjected to my control? To throw me
Plumply aside,—I am still too powerful for you
To venture that. My stipulation runs,
That all the Imperial forces shall obey me
Where'er the German is the native language.
Of Spanish troops and of Prince Cardinals
That take their route as visitors, through the empire,
There stands no syllable in my stipulation.
No syllable! And so the politic court
Steals in on tiptoe. and creeps round behind it:
First makes me weaker, then to be dispensed with,
Till it dares strike at length a bolder blow
And make short work with me.
What need of all these crooked ways, Lord Envoy?
Straight-forward, man! his compact with me pinches
The Emperor. He would that I moved off!—
Well!—I will gratify nim!
          [*Here there commences an agitation among the Generals,
              which increases continually.*
It grieves me for my noble officers' sakes!
I see not yet, by what means they will come at
The moneys thay have advanced, or how obtain
The recompense their services demand.

Still a new leader brings new claimants forward,
And prior merit superannuates quickly.
There serve here many foreigners in the army,
And were the man in all else brave and gallant,
I was not wont to make nice scrutiny
After his pedigree or catechism.
This will be otherwise, i' the time to come.
Well—me no longer it concerns.   [*He seats himself*

MAX. PICCOLOMINI.

Forbid it, Heaven, that it should come to this!
Our troops will swell in dreadful fermentation—
The Emperor is abused—it cannot be.

ISOLANI.

It cannot be; all goes to instant wreck.

WALLENSTEIN.

Thou hast said truly, faithful Isolani!
What *we* with toil and foresight have built up,
Will go to wreck—all go to instant wreck.
What then? Another chieftain is soon found,
Another army likewise (who dares doubt it?)
Will flock from all sides to the Emperor,
At the first beat of his recruiting drum.
      [*During this speech,* ISOLANI, TERZKY, ILLO, *and* MARA-
         DAS *talk confusedly with great agitation.*

MAX. PICCOLOMINI (*busily and passionately going from one to
            another, and soothing them*).

Hear, my commander! Hear me, generals!
Let me conjure you, Duke! Determine nothing,
Till we have met and represented to you
Our joint remonstrances.—Nay, calmer! Friends!
I hope all may yet be set right again.

TERZKY.

Away! let us away! in the antechamber
Find we the others.   [*They*

BUTLER (*to* QUESTENBERG).

                  If good counsel gain
Due audience from your wisdom, my Lord Envoy!
You will be cautious how you show yourself.

In public for some hours to come—or hardly
Will that gold key protect you from mal-treatment.
                                        [*Commotions heard from without*

WALLENSTEIN.

A salutary counsel——Thou, Octavio!
Wilt answer for the safety of our guest
Farewell, Von Questenberg!
                              [QUESTENBERG *is about to speak*
                              Nay, not a word.
Not one word more of that detested subject!
You have perform'd your duty—We know how
To separate the office from the man.
    [*As* QUESTENBERG *is going off with* OCTAVIO, GOETZ
      TIEFENBACH, KOLATTO, *press in; several other Generals*
      following them.

GOETZ.

Where's he who means to rob us of our general?

TIEFENBACH (*at the same time*).

What are we forced to hear? That thou wilt leave us?

KOLATTO (*at the same time*).

We will live with thee, we will die with thee.

WALLENSTEIN (*with stateliness, and pointing to* ILLO).

There! the Field-Marshal knows our will.   [*Exit.*
    [*While all are going off the stage, the curtain drops.*

ACT III.

SCENE I.

A small Chamber.

ILLO *and* TERZKY.

TERZKY.

Now for this evening's business! How intend you
To manage with the generals at the banquet?

ILLO.

Attend! We frame a formal declaration,
Wherein we to the Duke consign ourselves
Collectively, to be and to remain
His both with life and limb, and not to spare
The last drop of our blood for *him*, provided

So doing we infringe no oath or duty
We may be under to the Emperor.—Mark!
This reservation we expressly make
In a particular clause, and save the conscience.
Now hear! this formula so framed and worded
Will be presented to them for perusal
Before the banquet. No one will find in it
Cause of offence or scruple.   Hear now further!
After the feast, when now the vap'ring wine
Opens the heart, and shuts the eyes, we let
A counterfeited paper, in the which
This one particular clause has been left out,
Go round for signatures.

TERZKY.

                    How! think you then
That they'll believe themselves bound by an oath,
Which we have trick'd them into by a juggle?

ILLO.

We shall have caught and caged them!   Let them then
Beat their wings bare against the wires, and rave
Loud as they may against our treachery;
At court their signatures will be believed
Far more than their most holy affirmations.
Traitors they are, and must be; therefore wisely
Will make a virtue of necessity

TERZKY.

Well, well, it shall content me; let but something
Be *done*, let only some decisive blow
Set us in motion.

ILLO.

Besides, 'tis of subordinate importance
How, or how far, we may thereby propel
The generals. 'Tis enough that we persuade
The Duke that they are his.—Let him but act
In his determined mood, as if he had them,
And he *will* have them.   Where he plunges in,
He makes a whirlpool, and all stream down to it.

TERZKY.

His policy is such a labyrinth,
That many a time when I have thought myself

Close at his side, he's gone at once, and left me
Ignorant of the ground where I was standing.
He lends the enemy his ear, permits me
To write to them, to Arnheim; to Sesina
Himself comes forward blank and undisguised:
Talks with us by the hour about his plans.
And when I think I have him—off at once—
He has slipp'd from me, and appears as if
He had no scheme, but to retain his place.

ILLO.

He give up his old plans! I'll tell you, friend:
His soul is occupied with nothing else,
Even in his sleep—They are his thoughts, his dreams.
That day by day he questions for this purpose
The motions of the planets——

TERZKY.

                              Ay! you know
This night, that is now coming, he with Seni
Shuts himself up in the astrological tower
To make joint observations—for I hear
It is to be a night of weight and crisis;
And something great, and of long expectation,
Takes place in heav'n.

                    [ILLO.
                    O that it might take place
On earth! The generals are full of zeal,
And would with ease be led to any thing,
Rather than lose their chief. Observe, too, that
We have at last a fair excuse before us,
To form a close alliance 'gainst the court,
Yet innocent its title, bearing simply
That we support him only in command.
But in the ardour of pursuit thou know'st
Men soon forget the goal from which they started.
The object I've in view is that the Prince
Shall either find them, or *believe* them ready
For every hazard. Opportunity
Will tempt him on. Be the great step once taken,
Which at Vienna's Court can ne'er be pardon'd,
The force of circumstance will lead him onward
The farther still and farther 'Tis the choice

That makes him undecisive;—come but need,
And all his powers and wisdom will come with it.

TERZKY.

'Tis this alone the enemy awaits
To change their chief and join their force with ours.]

ILLO.

Come! be we bold and make despatch.   The work
In this next day or two must thrive and grow
More than it has for years.   And let but only
Things first turn up auspicious here below—
Mark what I say—the right stars, too, will show themselves.
Come to the generals.   All is in the glow,
And must be beaten while 'tis malleable.

TERZKY.

Do you go thither, Illo.   I must stay
And wait here for the Countess Terzky.   Know
That we, too, are not idle.   Break one string,
A second is in readiness

ILLO.
            Yes! yes!
I saw your lady smile with such sly meaning.
What's in the wind?

TERZKY.
            A secret.   Hush! she comes.
                              [*Exit* ILLO

SCENE II.
(*The* COUNTESS *steps out from a Closet.*
COUNT *and* COUNTESS TERZKY.

TERZKY.

Well—is she coming? I can keep him back
No longer.

COUNTESS.
            She will be here instantly,
You only send him.

TERZKY.
                  I am not quite certain
I must confess it, Countess, whether or not
We are earning the Duke's thanks hereby.   You know,
No ray has broke out from him on this point.
You have o'erruled me, and yourself know best
How far you dare proceed.

COUNTESS.

I take it on me.

[*Talking to herself while she is advancing.*

Here's no need of full powers and commissions—
My cloudy Duke! we understand each other—
And without words.   What, could I not unriddle,
Wherefore the daughter should be sent for hither,
Why first *he*, and no other, should be chosen
To fetch her hither?   This sham of betrothing her
To a bridegroom *, whom no one knows—No! no!—
This may blind others! I see through thee, Brother!
But it beseems thee not, to draw a card
At such a game.   Not yet!—It all remains
Mutely delivered up to my finessing——
Well—thou shalt not have been deceived, Duke Friedland—
In her who is thy sister.——

SERVANT. *(enters).*

The Commanders!   [*Exit.*

TERZKY *(to the* COUNTESS).

Take care you heat his fancy and affections—
Possess him with a reverie, and send him,
Absent and dreaming to the banquet; that
He may not boggle at the signature.

COUNTESS.

Take you care of your guests!—Go, send him hither.

TERZKY.

All rests upon his undersigning

COUNTESS *(interrupting him).*

Go to your guests! Go——

ILLO *(comes back).*

Where art staying, Terzky?
The house is full, and all expecting you.

TERZKY

Instantly! instantly!   [*To the* COUNTESS.

And let him not
Stay here too long.   It might awake suspicion
In the old man——

* In Germany, after honourable addresses have been paid and formally
accepted, the lovers are called Bride and Bridegroom, even though the marriage should not take place till years afterwards.

COUNTESS

A truce with your precautions!

[*Exeunt* TERZKY *and* ILLO.

SCENE III.

COUNTESS, MAX. PICCOLOMINI.

MAX (*peeping in on the stage slily*).
Aunt Terzky! may I venture?
[*Advances to the middle of the stage, and looks around
him with uneasiness.*

She's not here!

Where is she?

COUNTESS.

Look but somewhat narrowly
In yonder corner, lest perhaps she lie
Conceal'd behind that screen.

MAX.

There lie her gloves!
[*Snatches at them, but the* COUNTESS *takes them herself.*
You unkind Lady! You refuse me this—
You make it an amusement to torment me.

COUNTESS.

And this the thanks you give me for my trouble?

MAX.

O, if you felt the oppression at *my* heart!
Since we've been here, so to constrain myself—
With such poor stealth to hazard words and glances—
These, these are not my habits!

COUNTESS.

You have still
Many new habits to acquire, young friend!
But on this proof of your obedient temper
I must continue to insist; and only
On this condition can I play the agent
For your concerns.

MAX.

But wherefore comes she not?

Where is she?

COUNTESS

Into *my* hands you must place it
Whole and entire.   Whom could you find, indeed,
More zealously affected to your interest?
No soul on earth must know it—not your father
He must not, above all.

MAX.

Alas! what danger?
Here is no face on which I might concentre
All the enraptured soul stirs up within me.
O Lady! tell me, is all changed around me?
Or is it only I?
I find myself,
As among strangers!   Not a trace is left
Of all my former wishes, former joys.
Where has it vanish'd to?   There was a time
When even, methought, with such a world as this.
I was not discontented.   Now how flat!
How stale!   No life, no bloom, no flavour in it!
My comrades are intolerable to me.
My father—Even to him I can say nothing.
My arms, my military duties—O!
They are such wearying toys!

COUNTESS.

But, gentle friend!
I must entreat it of your condescension,
You would be pleased to sink your eye, and favour
With one short glance or two this poor stale world,
Where even now much, and of much moment,
Is on the eve of its completion.

MAX.

Something,
I can't but know is going forward round me.
I see it gathering, crowding, driving on,
In wild uncustomary movements.   Well,
In due time, doubtless, it will reach even me
Where think you I have been, dear Lady?   Nay
No raillery.   The turmoil of the camp,
The spring-tide of acquaintance rolling in,
The pointless jest, the empty conversation,

Oppress'd and stifled me.   I gasp'd for air—
I could not breathe—I was constrain'd to fly,
To seek a silence out for my full heart;
And a pure spot wherein to feel my happiness
No smiling, Countess!   In the church was I.
There is a cloister here " To the heaven's gate," *
Thither I went, there found myself alone.
Over the altar hung a holy mother;
A wretched painting 'twas, yet 'twas the friend
That I was seeking in this moment.   Ah,
How oft have I beheld that glorious form
In splendour, 'mid ecstatic worshippers;
Yet, still it moved me not! and now at once
Was my devotion cloudless as my love.

COUNTESS
Enjoy your fortune and felicity!
Forget the world around you.   Meantime, friendship
Shall keep strict vigils for you, anxious, active.
Only be manageable when that friendship
Points you the road to full accomplishment.

[MAX.
But where abides she then ?   Oh golden time
Of travel, when each morning sun united
And but the coming night divided us;
Then ran no sand, then struck no hour for us,
And Time, in our excess of happiness,
Seemed on its course eternal to stand still.
Oh, he hath fallen from out his heaven of bliss
Who can descend to count the changing hours,
No clock strikes ever for the happy !]

COUNTESS.
How long is it since you declared your passion?

MAX.
This morning did I hazard the first word.

COUNTESS.
This morning the first time in twenty days?

---

* I am doubtful whether this be the dedication of the cloister, or the name
of one of the city gates, near which it stood.   I have translated it in the
former sense; but fearful of having made some blunder, I add the original.—
Es ist ein Kloster hier *zur Himmelspforte.*

MAX.

'Twas at that hunting-castle, betwixt here
And Nepomuck, where *you* had join'd us, and—
That was the last relay of the whole journey;
In a balcony we were standing mute,
And gazing out upon the dreary field:
Before us the dragoons were riding onward,
The safe-guard which the Duke had sent us—heavy
The inquietude of parting lay upon me,
And trembling ventured I at length these words:
This all reminds me, noble maiden, that
To-day I must take leave of my good fortune
A few hours more, and you will find a father,
Will see yourself surrounded by new friends,
And I henceforth shall be but as a stranger,
Lost in the many—" Speak with my aunt Terzky!"
With hurrying voice she interrupted me.
She falter'd.   I beheld a glowing red
Possess her beautiful cheeks, and from the ground
Raised slowly up her eye met mine—no longer
Did I control myself.

> [*The Princess* THEKLA *appears at the door, and re-
> mains standing, observed by the* COUNTESS, *but not by*
> PICCOLOMINI.

                                With instant boldness
I caught her in my arms, my lips touch'd hers;
There was a rustling in the room close by;
It parted us—'Twas you.   What since has happen'd,
You know.

COUNTESS (*after a pause, with a stolen glance at* THEKLA).
                And is it your excess of modesty;
Or are you so incurious, that you do not
Ask me too of my secret?

                    MAX
                Of *your* secret?

                    COUNTESS.

Why, yes!   When in the instant after you
I stepp'd into the room, and found my niece there.
What she in this first moment of the heart
Ta'en with surprise—

                MAX. (*with eagerness*).
                Well?

SCENE IV.

THEKLA (*hurries forward*), COUNTESS. MAX. PICCOLOMINI.

THEKLA (*to the* COUNTESS).

    Spare yourself the trouble:
That hears he better from myself.

MAX. (*stepping backward*).

      My Princess!
What have you let her hear me say, aunt Terzky?

THEKLA (*to the* COUNTESS).

Has he been here long?

COUNTESS.

     Yes; and soon must go.
Where have *you* stay'd so long?

THEKLA.

     Alas! my mother
Wept so again! and I—I see her suffer,
Yet cannot keep myself from being happy.

MAX.

Now once again I have courage to look on you.
To-day at noon I could not.
The dazzle of the jewels that play'd round you
Hid the beloved from me.

THEKLA.

     Then you saw me
With your eye only—and not with your heart?

MAX.

This morning, when I found you in the circle
Of all your kindred, in your father's arms,
Beheld myself an alien in this circle,
O! what an impulse felt I in that moment
To fall upon his neck, to call him *father!*
But his stern eye o'erpower'd the swelling passion,
It dared not but be silent. And those brilliants,
That like a crown of stars enwreathed your brows,
They scared me too! O wherefore, wherefore should he
At the first meeting spread as 'twere the ban
Of excommunication round you,—wherefore
Dress up the angel as for sacrifice.

And cast upon the light and joyous heart
The mournful burthen of *his* station?   Fitly
May love dare woo for love ; but such a splendour
Might none but monarchs venture to approach.

THEKLA

Hush! not a word more of this mummery ;
You see how soon the burthen is thrown off.

[*To the* COUNTESS.

He is not in spirits.   Wherefore is he not?
'Tis you, aunt, that have made him all so gloomy !
He had quite another nature on the journey—
So calm, so bright, so joyous eloquent.   [*To* MAX
It was my wish to see you always so,
And never otherwise !

MAX.

You find yourself
In your great father's arms, beloved lady !
All in a new world, which does homage to you,
And which, were't only by its novelty
Delights your eye.

THEKLA.

Yes ; I confess to you
That many things delight me here : this camp,
This motley stage of warriors, which renews
So manifold the image of my fancy,
And binds to life, binds to reality,
What hitherto had but been present to me
As a sweet dream !

MAX.

Alas ! not so to me.
It makes a dream of my reality.
Upon some island in the ethereal heights
I've lived for these last days.   This mass of men
Forces me down to earth.   It is a bridge
That, reconducting to my former life,
Divides me and my heaven.

THEKLA.

The game of life
Looks cheerful, when one carries in one's heart

The unalienable treasure. 'Tis a game,
Which having once review'd, I turn more joyous
Back to my deeper and appropriate bliss.
        [*Breaking off, and in a sportive tone.*
I- this short time that I've been present here,
What new unheard-of things have I not seen ,
And yet they all must give place to the wonder
Which this mysterious castle guards.

COUNTESS (recollecting).

                    And what
Can this be then?   Methought I was acquainted
With all the dusky corners of this house.

THEKLA (smiling).

Ay, but the road thereto is watch'd by spirits,
Two griffins still stand sentry at the door.

COUNTESS (laughs).

The astrological tower!—How happens it
That this same sanctuary, whose access
Is to all others so impracticable,
Opens before you even at your approach?

THEKLA.

A dwarfish old man with a friendly face
And snow-white hairs, whose gracious services
Were mine at first sight, open'd me the doors.

MAX.

That is the Duke's astrologer, old Seni.

THEKLA.

He question'd me on many points ; for instance,
When I was born, what month, and on what day,
Whether by day or in the night.

COUNTESS.

                    He wish'd
To erect a figure for your horoscope.

THEKLA.

My hand too he examined, shook his head
With much sad meaning, and the lines, methought,
Did not square over truly with his wishes

COUNTESS.

Well, Princess, and what found you in this tower?
My highest privilege has been to snatch
A side-glance, and away!

THEKLA.

It was a strange
Sensation that came o'er me, when at first
From the broad sunshine I stepp'd in; and now
The narrowing line of daylight, that ran after
The closing door, was gone; and all about me
'Twas pale and dusky night, with many shadows
Fantastically cast.   Here six or seven
Colossal statues, and all kings, stood round me
In a half-circle.   Each one in his hand
A sceptre bore, and on his head a star;
And in the tower no other light was there
But from these stars · all seem'd to come from them.
"These are the planets," said that low old man,
"They govern worldly fates, and for that cause
Are imaged here as kings.   He farthest from you.
Spiteful, and cold, an old man melancholy,
With bent and yellow forehead, he is Saturn.
He opposite, the king with the red light,
An arm'd man for the battle, that is Mars;
And both these bring but little luck to man."
But at his side a lovely lady stood,
The star upon her head was soft and bright,
Oh that was Venus, the bright star of joy.
And the left hand, lo! Mercury, with wings
Quite in the middle glitter'd silver bright
A cheerful man, and with a monarch's mien;
And this was Jupiter, my father's star:
And at his side I saw the Sun and Moon.

MAX

O never rudely will I blame his faith
In the might of stars and angels.   'Tis not merely
The human being's Pride that peoples space
With life and mystical predominance;
Since likewise for the stricken heart of Love
This visible nature, and this common world,

Is all too narrow; yea, a deeper import
Lurks in the legend told my infant years
Than lies upon that truth, we live to learn
For fable is Love's world, his home, his birth-place;
Delightedly dwells he 'mong fays and talismans,
And spirits; and delightedly believes
Divinities, being himself divine
The intelligible forms of ancient poets,
The fair humanities of old religion,
The Power, the Beauty, and the Majesty,
That had her haunts in dale, or piny mountain,
Or forest by slow stream, or pebbly spring,
Or chasms, and wat'ry depths; all these have vanish'd.
They live no longer in the faith of reason!
But still the heart doth need a language, still
Doth the old instinct bring back the old names,
And to yon starry world they now are gone,
Spirits or gods, that used to share this earth
With man as with their friend *; and to the lover
Yonder they move, from yonder visible sky
Shoot influence down: and even at this day
'Tis Jupiter who brings whate'er is great,
And Venus who brings everything that's fair!

THEKLA

And if this be the science of the stars,
I too, with glad and zealous industry,
Will learn acquaintance with this cheerful faith.
It is a gentle and affectionate thought,
That in immeasurable heights above us,
At our first birth, the wreath of love was woven,
With sparkling stars for flowers.

COUNTESS

                  Not only roses
But thorns too hath the heaven, and well for you
Leave they your wreath of love inviolate:
What Venus twined, the bearer of glad fortune,
The sullen orb of Mars soon tears to pieces.

---

    * No more of talk, where god or angel guest
    With man, as with his friend familiar, used
    To sit indulgent.   *Paradise Lost*, B. IX.

MAX.

Soon will his gloomy empire reach its close.
Blest be the General's zeal : into the laurel
Will he inweave the olive-branch, presenting
Peace to the shouting nations.   Then no wish
Will have remain'd for his great heart !   Enough
Has he perform'd for glory, and can now
Live for himself and his.   To his domains
Will he retire ; he has a stately seat
Of fairest view at Gitschin ; Reichenberg,
And Friedland Castle, both lie pleasantly—
Even to the foot of the huge mountains here
Stretches the chase and covers of his forests :
His ruling passion, to create the splendid,
He can indulge without restraint ; can give
A princely patronage to every art,
And to all worth a Sovereign's protection.
Can build, can plant, can watch the starry courses——

COUNTESS.

Yet I would have you look, and look again,
Before you lay aside your arms, young friend !
A gentle bride, as she is, is well worth it,
That you should woo and win her with the sword.

MAX.

O, that the sword could win her !

COUNTESS.

What was that ?
Did you hear nothing?   Seem'd as if I heard
Tumult and iarum in the banquet-room.

[*Exit* COUNTES

SCENE V.

THEKLA *and* MAX. PICCOLOMINI

THEKLA (*as soon as the Countess is out of sight, in a quick low
voice to* PICCOLOMINI.
Don't trust them !   They are false !

MAX

Impossible !

THEKLA

Trust no one here but me.   I saw at once.
They had a *purpose.*

MAX.

     Purpose! but what purpose?
And how can we be instrumental to it?

THEKLA.

I know no more than you; but yet believe me:
There's some design in this! to make us happy,
To realize our union—trust me, love!
They but pretend to wish it.

MAX.

     But these Terzkys---
Why use we them at all?   Why not your mother?
Excellent creature! she deserves from us
A full and filial confidence.

THEKLA.

     She doth love you,
Doth rate you high before all others—but—
But such a secret—she would never have
The courage to conceal it from my father.
For her own peace of mind we must preserve it
A secret from her too.

MAX.

    Why any secret?
I love not secrets.   Mark what I will do.
I'll throw me at your father's feet—let *him*
Decide upon my fortunes!   He is true,
He wears no mask—he hates all crooked ways—
He is so good, so noble!

THEKLA (*falls on his neck*).
    That are you!

MAX.

You knew him only since this morn! but I
Have lived ten years already in his presence.
And who knows whether in this very moment
He is not merely waiting for us both
To own our loves, in order to unite us?
You are silent!—
You look at me with such a hopelessness!
What have you to object against your father?

THEKLA.

I?   Nothing.   Only he's so occupied—
He has no leisure time to think about

The happiness of us two   [*Taking his hand tenderly*
      Follow me !
Let us not place too great a faith in men.
These Terzkys—we will still be grateful to them
For every kindness, but not trust them further
Than they deserve;—and in all else rely—
On our own hearts !

MAX.

O ! shall we *e'er* be happy ?

THEKLA.

Are we not happy now ? Art thou not mine ?
Am I not thine ? There lives within my soul
A lofty courage—'tis love gives it me !
I ought to be less open — ought to hide
My heart more from thee—so decorum dictates :
But where in this place couldst thou seek for truth
If in my mouth thou didst not find it ?
[We now have met, then let us hold each other
Clasp'd in a lasting and a firm embrace.
Believe me this was more than their intent.
Then be our loves like some blest relic kept
Within the deep recesses of the heart.
From Heav'n alone the love has been bestow'd,
To Heav'n alone our gratitude is due
It can work wonders for us still.]

Scene VI.

To them enters the COUNTESS TERZKY.

COUNTESS (*in a pressing manner*).
          Come, come !

My husband sends me for you.—It is now
The latest moment.
   [*They not appearing to attend to what she says, she step*
    between them.

Part you !

THEKLA.

O, not yet !

It has been scarce a moment.

COUNTESS.
Ay! Then time
Flies swiftly with your Highness, Princess niece!

MAX
There is no hurry, aunt

COUNTESS
Away! away!
The folks begin to miss you.   Twice already
His father has ask'd for him.

THEKLA.
Ha! his father.

COUNTESS.
You understand *that*, niece!

THEKLA.
Why needs he
To go at all to that society?
'Tis not his proper company   They may
Be worthy men, but he's too young for them
In brief, he suits not such society.

COUNTESS.
You mean, you'd rather keep him wholly here?

THEKLA (*with energy*).
Yes! you have hit it, aunt! That is my meaning.
Leave him here wholly! Tell the company——

COUNTESS.
What! have you lost your senses, niece?
Count, you remember the conditions.   Come!

MAX. (*to* THEKLA).
Lady, I must obey.   Farewell, dear lady!
        [THEKLA *turns away from him with a quick motion*
What say you then, dear lady?

THEKLA (*without looking at him*).
Nothing.   Go!

MAX.
Can I, when you are angry——
        [*He draws up to her, their eyes meet, she stands silent
        a moment, then throws herself into his arms; he
        presses her fast to his heart*

COUNTESS

Off! Heavens! if any one should come!
Hark! What's that noise! It comes this way.—Off!

[MAX. *tears himself away out of her arms, and goes
The* COUNTESS *accompanies him.* THEKLA *follows
him with her eyes at first, walks restlessly across
the room, then stops, and remains standing, lost in
thought. A guitar lies on the table. she seizes it
as by a sudden emotion, and after she has played
awhile an irregular and melancholy symphony,
she falls gradually into the music and sings*

SCENE VII.

THEKLA (*plays and sings*).

The cloud doth gather, the greenwood roar,
The damsel paces along the shore;
The billows, they tumble with might, with might;
And she flings out her voice to the darksome night;
　　Her bosom is swelling with sorrow;
The world it is empty, the heart will die,
There's nothing to wish for beneath the sky:
Thou Holy One, call thy child away!
I've lived and loved, and that was to-day;
　　Make ready my grave-clothes to-morrow *

---

* I found it not in my power to translate this song with *literal* fidelity,
preserving at the same time the Alcaic movement, and have therefore added
the original, with a prose translation. Some of my readers may be more fortunate.

THEKLA (*spielt und singt*).

Der Eichwald brauset, die Wolken ziehn,
Das Mägdlein wandelt an Ufers Grün;
Es bricht sich die Welle mit Macht, mit Mach
Und sie singt hinaus in die finstre Nacht,
　　Das Auge von Weinen getrübet:
Das Herz is gestorben, die Welt ist leer,
Und weiter giebt sie dem Wunsche nichts mehr.
Du Heilige, rufe dein Kind zurück,
Ich habe genossen das irdische Glück,
　　Ich habe gelebt und geliebet.

LITERAL TRANSLATION.

THEKLA (*plays and sings*).

The oak-forest bellows, the clouds gather, the damsel walks to and fro on
the green of the shore; the wave breaks with might, with might, and she

SCENE VIII.

COUNTESS (*returns*), THEKLA.

COUNTESS.

Fie, lady niece! to throw yourself upon him
Like a poor gift to one who cares not for it,
And so must be flung after him!   For you,
Duke Friedland's only child, I should have thought,
It had been more beseeming to have shown yourself
More chary of your person.

THEKLA (*rising*).
And what mean you?

COUNTESS.

I mean, niece, that you should not have forgotten
Who *you* are, and who he is.   But perchance
That never once occurr'd to you.

THEKLA.
What then?

COUNTESS.

That you're daughter of the Prince Duke Friedland.

THEKLA.
Well, and what farther?

COUNTESS.
What? a pretty question!

sings out into the dark night, her eye discoloured with weeping: the heart
is dead, the world is empty, and further gives it nothing more to the wish.
Thou Holy One, call thy child home.   I have enjoyed the happiness of this
world, I have lived and have loved.

I cannot but add here an imitation of this song, with which my friend,
Charles Lamb, has favoured me, and which appears to me to have caught
the happiest manner of our old ballads.

> The clouds are blackening, the storms threat'ning,
>   The cavern doth mutter, the greenwood moan!
> Billows are breaking, the damsel's heart aching,
>   Thus in the dark night she singeth alone,
>   Her eye upward roving:
> The world is empty, the heart is dead surely,
>   In this world plainly all seemeth amiss;
> To thy heaven, Holy One, take home thy little one,
>   I have partaken of all earth's bliss,
>   Both living and loving.

THEKLA.

He was *born* that which we have but *become*.
He's of an ancient Lombard family,
Son of a reigning princess.

COUNTESS

Are you dreaming?
Talking in sleep? An excellent jest, forsooth!
We shall no doubt right courteously *entreat* him
To honour with his hand the richest heiress
In Europe.

THEKLA.

That will not be necessary.

COUNTESS.

Methinks 'twere well, though, not to run the hazard

THEKLA.

His father loves him; Count Octavio
Will interpose no difficulty——

COUNTESS.

His!

His father! *His!* But yours, niece, what of **yours?**

THEKLA.

Why I begin to think you fear his father.
So anxiously you hide it from the man!
His father, *his*, I mean.

COUNTESS (*looks at her as scrutinising*).

Niece, you are *false*.

THEKLA.

Are you then wounded? O, be friends with me!

COUNTESS.

You hold your game for won already. Do not
Triumph too soon!

THEKLA (*interrupting her, and attempting to soothe her*).

Nay now, be friends with me.

COUNTESS.

It is not yet so far gone.

THEKLA.

I believe you.

COUNTESS.

Did you suppose your father had laid out
His most important life in toils of war,

Denied himself each quiet earthly bliss,
Had banish'd slumber from his tent, devoted
His noble head to care, and for this only,
To make a happier pair of you? At length
To draw you from your convent, and conduct
In easy triumph to your arms the man
That chanced to please your eyes! All this, methinks,
He might have purchased at a cheaper rate

THEKLA.

That which he did not plant for me might yet
Bear me fair fruitage of its own accord.
And if my friendly and affectionate fate,
Out of his fearful and enormous being,
Will but prepare the joys of life for me—

COUNTESS.

Thou seest it with a lovelorn maiden's eyes
Cast thine eye round, bethink thee who thou all
Into no house of joyance hast thou stepp'd,
For no espousals dost thou find the walls
Deck'd out, no guests the nuptial garland wearing
Here is no splendour but of arms. Or think'st thou
That all these thousands are here congregated
To lead up the long dances at thy wedding!
Thou see'st thy father's forehead full of thought,
Thy mother's eye in tears: upon the balance
Lies the great destiny of all our house.
Leave now the puny wish, the girlish feeling,
O thrust it far behind thee! Give thou proof,
Thou'rt the daughter of the Mighty—*his*
Who where he moves creates the wonderful
Not to herself the woman must belong,
Annex'd and bound to alien destinies.
But she performs the best part, she the wisest
Who can transmute the alien into self,
Meet and disarm necessity by choice;
And what must be, take freely to her heart,
And bear and foster it with mother's love.

THEKLA.

Such ever was my lesson in the convent.
I had no loves, no wishes, knew myself

Only as his—his daughter—his, the Mighty!
His fame, the echo of whose blast drove to me
From the far distance, waken'd in my soul
No other thought than this—I am appointed
To offer myself up in passiveness to him.

CENTER>
COUNTESS.

That *is* thy fate.　Mould thou thy wishes to it.
I and thy mother gave thee the example.

THEKLA.

My fate hath shown me *him*, to whom behoves it
That I should offer up myself.　In gladness
Him will I follow.

COUNTESS.

　　　　　Not thy fate hath shown him
Thy heart, say rather--'twas thy heart, my child!

THEKLA.

Fate hath no voice but the heart's impulses.
I am all his! *His* present—*his* alone,
Is this new life, which lives in me? He hath
A right to his own creature.　What was I
Ere his fair love infused a soul into me?

COUNTESS.

Thou wouldst oppose thy father then, should he
Have otherwise determined with thy person?

[THEKLA *remains silent.　The* COUNTESS *continues,*
Thou mean'st to force him to thy liking?—Child,
His name is Friedland.

THEKLA.

　　　　　My name too is Friedland
He shall have found a genuine daughter in me.

COUNTESS.

What! he has vanquish'd all impediment,
And in the wilful mood of his own daughter
Shall a new struggle rise for him?　Child! child!
As yet thou hast seen thy father's smiles alone;
The eye of his rage thou hast not seen.　Dear child
I will not frighten thee.　To that extreme,
I trust, it ne'er shall come.　His will is yet
Unknown to me: 'tis possible his aims
May have the same direction as thy wish.

But this can never, never be his will,
That thou, the daughter of his haughty fortunes,
Should'st e'er demean thee as a love-sick maiden ·
And like some poor cost-nothing, fling thyself
Toward the man, who, *if* that high prize ever
Be destined to await him, yet, with sacrifices
The highest love can bring, must pay for it.

> [*Exit* COUNTESS.

SCENE IX.

THEKLA (*who during the last speech had been standing evi-
dently lost in her reflections*).

I thank thee for the hint.   It turns
My sad presentiment to certainty.
And it is so !—Not one friend have we here,
Not one true heart! we've nothing but ourselves!
O she said rightly—no auspicious signs
Beam on this covenant of our affections.
This is no theatre, where hope abides :
The dull thick noise of war alone stirs here ;
And Love himself, as he were arm'd in steel,
Steps forth, and girds him for the strife of death.

> [*Music from the banquet-room is heard.*

There's a dark spirit walking in our house,
And swiftly will the Destiny close on us.
It drove me hither from my calm asylum,
It mocks my soul with charming witchery,
It lures me forward in a seraph's shape,
I see it near, I see it nearer floating,
It draws, it pulls me with a god-like power—
And lo! the abyss—and thither am I moving—
I have no power within me not to move !

> [*The music from the banquet-room becomes louder*

O when a house is doom'd in fire to perish,
Many and dark Heaven drives his clouds together,
Yea, shoots his lightnings down from sunny heights,
Flames burst from out the subterraneous chasms,
* And fiends and angels, mingling in their fury,
Sling fire-brands at the burning edifice.   [*Exit* THEKLA

---

* There are few who will not have taste enough to laugh at the two con-

ACT IV.

SCENE I.

*A large Saloon lighted up with festal Splendour; in the midst
of it, and in the centre of the Stage, a Table richly set out,
at which eight Generals are sitting, among whom are* OCTAVIO
PICCOLOMINI, TERZKY, *and* MARADAS. *Right and left of
this, but farther back, two other Tables, at each of which six
persons are placed. The Middle Door, which is standing
open, gives to the prospect a fourth Table with the same number of persons. More forward stands the sideboard. The
whole front of the Stage is kept open for the Pages and
Servants in waiting. All is in motion. The Band of Music
belonging to* TERZKY'S *Regiment march across the Stage,
and draw up round the Tables. Before they are quite off
from the front of the Stage,* MAX. PICCOLOMINI *appears,*
TERZKY *advances towards him with a paper,* ISOLANI *comes
up to meet him with a Beaker or Service-cup.*

TERZKY, ISOLANI, MAX. PICCOLOMINI.

ISOLANI.

Here, brother, what we love! Why, where hast been?
Off to thy place—quick! Terzky here has given
The mother's holiday wine up to free booty.
Here it goes on as at the Heidelberg castle.
Already hast thou lost the best. They're giving
At yonder table ducal crowns in shares;
There's Sternberg's lands and chattels are put **up,**
With Eggenberg's, Stawata's, Lichtenstein's,
And all the great Bohemian feodalities.
Be nimble, lad! and something may turn up
For thee—who knows? off—to thy place! quick! march!

TIEFENBACH *and* GOETZ (*call out from the second and third
tables*).

Count Piccolomini!

TERZKY.

Stop, ye shall have him in an instant.—Read

cluding lines of this soliloquy; and still fewer, I would fain hope, who woul
not have been more disposed to shudder, had I given a *faithful* translation.
For the readers of German I have added the original:

Blind-wüthend schleudert selbst der Gott der Freud>
Den Pechkranz in das brennende Gebäude.

This oath here, whether as 'tis here set forth,
The wording satisfies you.   They've all read it,
Each in his turn, and each one will subscribe
His individual signature.

MAX (reads).

" Ingratis servire nefas."

ISOLANI.

That sounds to my ears very much like **Latin,**
And being interpreted, pray what may't mean?

TERZKY.

No honest man will serve a thankless master

MAX.

" Inasmuch as our supreme Commander, the illustrious
Duke of Friedland, in consequence of the manifold affronts
and grievances which he has received, had expressed his
determination to quit the Emperor, but on our unanimous
entreaty has graciously consented to remain still with the
army, and not to part from us without our approbation
thereof, so we, collectively and *each in particular,* in the
stead of an oath personally taken, do hereby oblige ourselves—likewise by him honourably and faithfully to hold,
and in nowise whatsoever from him to part, and to be ready
to shed for his interests the last drop of our blood, so far,
namely, as *our oath to the Emperor will permit it. (These
last words are repeated by* ISOLANI.)   In testimony of which
we subscribe our names."

TERZKY.

Now!—are you willing to subscribe this paper?

ISOLANI.

Why should he not? All officers of honour
Can do it, ay, must do it —Pen and ink here!

TERZKY.

Nay, let it rest till after meal.

ISOLANI (drawing MAX. along).
Come, Max.
[Both seat themselves at their table.

SCENE II.

TERZKY, NEUMANN.

TERZKY (*beckons to* NEUMANN, *who is waiting at the side-table
and steps forward with him to the edge of the stage*).
Have you the copy with you. Neumann?   Give it
It may be changed for the other?

NEUMANN.
                              I have copied it
Letter by letter, line by line : no eye
Would e'er discover other difference,
Save only the omission of that clause,
According to your Excellency's order.

TERZKY.
Right! lay it yonder, and away with this—
It has performed its business—to the fire with it—
    [NEUMANN *lays the copy on the table, and steps back
        again to the side-table.*

SCENE III.

ILLO (*comes out from the second Chamber*), TERZKY.

ILLO.
How goes it with young Piccolomini!

TERZKY.
All right, I think   He has started no objection

ILLO.
He is the only one I fear about—
He and his father.   Have an eye on both !

TERZKY.
How looks it at your table : you forget not
To keep them warm and stirring?

ILLO
                              O, quite cordial.
They are quite cordial in the scheme.   We have them
And 'tis as I predicted too.   Already
It is the talk, not merely to maintain
The Duke in station.   " Since we're once for all
Together and unanimous, why not,"
Says Montecuculi, " ay, why not onward.
And make conditions with the Emperor

There in his own Vienna?" Trust me, Count,
Were it not for these said Piccolomini,
We might have spared ourselves the cheat.

TERZKY.

And Butler?
How goes it there? Hush!

SCENE IV

To them enter BUTLER *from the second table.*

BUTLER.

Don't disturb yourselves.
Field-Marshal, I have understood you perfectly.
Good luck be to the scheme; and as to me,
[*With an air of mystery*
You may depend upon me.

ILLO (*with viracity*).

May we, Butler?

BUTLER

With or without the clause, all one to me!
You understand me? My fidelity
The Duke may put to any proof—I'm with him!
Tell him so! I'm the Emperor's officer,
As long as 'tis his pleasure to remain
The Emperor's general! and Friedland's servant,
As soon as it shall please him to become
His own lord

TERZKY.

You would make a good exchange
No stern economist, no Ferdinand,
Is he to whom you plight your services.

BUTLER (*with a haughty look*).

I do not put up my fidelity
To sale, Count Terzky! Half a year ago
I would not have advised you to have made me
An overture to that, to which I now
Offer myself of my own free accord.—
But that is past! and to the Duke, Field Marshal,
I bring myself together with my regiment.
And mark you, 'tis my humour to believe,
The example which I give will not remain
Without an influence.

ILLO.

Who is ignorant,
That the whole army look to Colonel Butler,
As to a light that moves before them?

BUTLER.

Ey?

Then I repent me not of that fidelity
Which for the length of forty years I held,
If in my sixtieth year my good old name
Can purchase for me a revenge so full.
Start not at what I say, sir Generals!
My real motives—they concern not you.
And you yourselves, I trust, could not expect
That this your game had crook'd *my* judgment—**or**
That fickleness, quick blood, or such like cause,
Has driven the old man from the track of **honour**,
Which he so long had trodden. Come, my **friends**!
I'm not thereto determined with less firmness,
Because I know and have looked steadily
At that on which I have determined.

ILLO.

Say,
And speak roundly, what are we to deem you?

BUTLER.

A friend! I give you here my hand! I'm yours
With all I have. Not only men, but money
Will the Duke want.—Go, tell him, sirs!
I've earn'd and laid up somewhat in his service,
I lend it him; and is he my survivor,
It has been already long ago bequeathed him.
He is my heir. For me, I stand alone
Here in the world; nought know I of the feeling
That binds the husband to a wife and children.
My name dies with me, my existence ends.

ILLO.

'Tis not your money that he needs—a heart
Like yours weighs tons of gold down, weighs down **millions**!

BUTLER.

I came a simple soldier's boy from Ireland
To Prague—and with a master, whom I buried.

From lowest stable duty I climb'd up,
Such was the fate of war, to this high rank,
The plaything of a whimsical good fortune.
And Wallenstein too is a child of luck ;
I love a fortune that is like my own.

ILLO.

All powerful souls have kindred with each other.

BUTLER.

This is an awful moment ! to the brave
To the determined, an auspicious moment.
The Prince of Weimar arms, upon the Maine,
To found a mighty dukedom   He of Halberstadt,
That Mansfeldt, wanted but a longer life
To have mark'd out with his good sword a lordship
That should reward his courage.   Who of these
Equals our Friedland?   There is nothing, nothing
So high, but he may set the ladder to it!

TERZKY

That's spoken like a man !

BUTLER

Do you secure the Spaniard and Italian—
I'll be your warrant for the Scotchman Lesly.
Come, to the company !

TERZKY.

Where is the master of the cellar?   Ho!
Let the best wines come up.   Ho! cheerly, boy !
Luck comes to-day, so give her hearty welcome.

[Excunt, each to his table.

SCENE V.

The MASTER OF THE CELLAR, advancing with NEUMANN,
Servants passing backwards and forwards.

MASTER OF THE CELLAR.

The best wine! O, if my old mistress, his lady mother,
could but see these wild goings on, she would turn herself
round in her grave. Yes, yes, sir officer! 'tis all down the
hill with this noble house! no end, no moderation! And
this marriage with the Duke's sister a splendid connexion, a
very splendid connexion! but I will tell you, sir officer, it
looks no good.

NEUMANN.

Heaven forbid! Why, at this very moment the whole prospect is in bud and blossom!

MASTER OF THE CELLAR.

You think so?—Well, well! much may be said on that head

FIRST SERVANT (comes).

Burgundy for the fourth table.

MASTER OF THE CELLAR.

Now, sir lieutenant, if this an't the seventieth flask—

FIRST SERVANT.

Why, the reason is, that German lord, Tiefenbach, sits at that table.

MASTER OF THE CELLAR (continuing his discourse to
NEUMANN).

They are soaring too high. They would rival kings and electors in their pomp and splendour; and wherever the Duke leaps, not a minute does my gracious master, the Count, loiter on the brink—(to the Servants).—What do you stand there listening for? I will let you know you have legs presently Off! see to the tables, see to the flasks! Look there! Count Palfi has an empty glass before him!

RUNNER (comes).

The great service-cup is wanted, sir; that rich gold cup with the Bohemian arms on it. The Count says you know which it is

MASTER OF THE CELLAR.

Ay! that was made for Frederick's coronation by the artist William—there was not such another prize in the whole booty at Prague.

RUNNER.

The same!—a health is to go round in him

MASTER OF THE CELLAR (shaking his head while he fetches
and rinses the cups).

This will be something for the tale-bearers—this goes to Vienna.

NEUMANN.

Permit me to look at it.—Well, this is a cup indeed! How heavy! as well it may be, being all gold.—And what neat things are embossed on it! how natural and elegant they look!—There, on the first quarter, let me see. That proud

Amazon there on horseback, she that is taking a leap over the
crosier and mitres, and carries on a wand a hat together with
a banner, on which there's a goblet represented. Can you
tell me what all this signifies?

MASTER OF THE CELLAR.

The woman you see there on horseback, is the Free Election of the Bohemian Crown.   That is signified by the round
hat, and by that fiery steed on which she is riding.   The hat
is the pride of man; for he who cannot keep his hat on before
kings and emperors is no free man.

NEUMANN.

But what is the cup there on the banner?

MASTER OF THE CELLAR.

The cup signifies the freedom of the Bohemian Church,
as it was in our forefathers' times.   Our forefathers in the
wars of the Hussites forced from the Pope this noble privilege ; for the Pope, you know, will not grant the cup to any
layman.   Your true Moravian values nothing beyond the cup;
it is his costly jewel, and has cost the Bohemians their precious blood in many and many a battle.

NEUMANN.

And what says that chart that hangs in the air there, over
it all?

MASTER OF THE CELLAR.

That signifies the Bohemian letter-royal, which we forced
from the Emperor Rudolph—a precious, never to be enough
valued parchment, that secures to the new church the old privileges of free ringing and open psalmody   But since he of
Steiermark has ruled over us, that is at an end ; and after the
battle at Prague, in which Count Palatine Frederick lost crown
and empire, our faith hangs upon the pulpit and the altar—
and our brethren look at their homes over their shoulders;
but the letter-royal the Emperor himself cut to pieces with
his scissors.

NEUMANN.

Why, my good Master of the Cellar! you are deep read in
the chronicles of your country?

MASTER OF THE CELLAR.

So were my forefathers, and for that reason were they minstrels, and served under Procopius and Ziska.   Peace be with

their ashes! Well, well! they fought for a good cause though
—There! carry it up!

NEUMANN.

Stay! let me but look at this second quarter. Look *there!*
That is, when at Prague Castle the Imperial counsellors, Mai
tinitz, and Stawata, were hurled down head over heels. 'Tis
even so! there stands Count Thur who commands it.

[Runner *takes the service-cup and goes off with it.*

MASTER OF THE CELLAR.

O let me never more hear of that day. It was the three-
and-twentieth of May, in the year of our Lord one thousand
six hundred and eighteen. It seems to me as it were but
yesterday—from that unlucky day it all began, all the heart-
aches of the country Since that day it is now sixteen years,
and there has never once been peace on the earth

[*Health drunk aloud at the second table.*

The Prince of Weimar! Hurra!

[*At the third and fourth table*

Long live Prince William! Long live Duke Bernard!
Hurra!   [*Music strikes up*

FIRST SERVANT.

Hear 'em! Hear 'em! What an uproar!

SECOND SERVANT (*comes in running*).

Did you hear? They have drunk the Prince of Weimar's
health

THIRD SERVANT.

The Swedish Chief Commander!

FIRST SERVANT (*speaking at the same time*).

The Lutheran!

SECOND SERVANT.

Just before, when Count Deodati gave out the Emperor's
health, they were all as mum as a nibbling mouse.

MASTER OF THE CELLAR.

Po, po! When the wine goes in strange things come out.
A good servant hears, and hears not!—You should be nothing
but eyes and feet, except when you are called to.

SECOND SERVANT.

[*To the* Runner, *to whom he gives secretly a flask of
wine, keeping his eye on the* Master of the Cellar,
standing between him and the Runner.

Quick, Thomas! before the Master of the Cellar runs this

way—'tis a flask of Frontignac!—Snapped it up at the third table—Canst go off with it?

RUNNER (*hides it in his pocket*).
All right!   [*Exit the* Second Servant

THIRD SERVANT (*aside to the* First).
Be on the hark, Jack! that we may have right plenty to tell to Father Quivoga.—He will give us right plenty of abso lution in return for it.

FIRST SERVANT.
For that very purpose I am always having something to do behind Illo's chair —He is the man for speeches to make you stare with!

MASTER OF THE CELLAR (*to* NEUMANN).
Who, pray, may that swarthy man be, he with the cross, that is chatting so confidently with Esterhats?

NEUMANN.
Ay! he too is one of those to whom they confide too much He calls himself Maradas, a Spaniard is he.

MASTER OF THE CELLAR (*impatiently*).
Spaniard! Spaniard!— I tell you, friend, nothing good comes of those Spaniards. All these outlandish fellows are little better than rogues.

NEUMANN.
Fy, fy! you should not say so, friend. There are among them our very best generals, and those on whom the Duke at this moment relies the most.

MASTER OF THE CELLAR.
[*Taking the flask out of the* Runner's *pocket.*
My son, it will be broken to pieces in your pocket
[TERZKY *hurries in, fetches away the Paper and calls to a Servant for Pen and Ink, and goes to the back of the Stage.*

MASTER OF THE CELLAR (*to the* Servants).
The Lieutenant-General stands up.—Be on the watch —
Now! They break up.—Off and move back the forms.
[*They rise at all the Tables, the Servants hurry off the front of the Stage to the Tables; part of the guests come forward.*

Scene VI.

OCTAVIO PICCOLOMINI *enters in conversation with* MARADAS, *and both place themselves quite on the edge of the Stage on one side of the Proscenium. On the side directly opposite,* MAX. PICCOLOMINI, *by himself, lost in thought, and taking no part in any thing that is going forward. The middle space between both, but rather more distant from the edge of the Stage, is filled up by* BUTLER, ISOLANI, GOETZ, TIEFEN-BACH. *and* KOLATTO.

ISOLANI (*while the Company is coming forward*).
Good night, good night, Kolatto! Good night, Lieutenant General!—I should rather say, good morning.

GOETZ (*to* TIEFENBACH).
Noble brother! (*making the usual compliment after meals*).

TIEFENBACH.
Ay! 'twas a royal feast indeed.

GOETZ.
Yes, my Lady Countess understands these matters. Her mother-in-law. Heaven rest her soul, taught her!—Ah! tha was a housewife for you!

TIEFENBACH.
There was not her like in all Bohemia for setting out a table

OCTAVIO (*aside to* MARADAS).
Do me the favour to talk to me—talk of what you will—or of nothing. Only preserve the appearance at least of talking. I would not wish to stand by myself, and yet I conjecture that there will be goings on here worthy of our attentive observation. (*He continues to fix his eye on the whole follow-ing scene.*)

ISOLANI (*on the point of going*).
Lights! lights!

TERZKY (*advances with the Paper to* ISOLANI)
Noble brother; two minutes longer!—Here is something to subscribe.

ISOLANI.
Subscribe as much as you like—but you must excuse me from reading it.

TERZKY.

There is no need. It is the oath which you have already read.—Only a few marks of your pen!

[ISOLANI *hands over the Paper to* OCTAVIO *respectfully*

TERZKY.

Nay, nay, first come first served. There is no precedence here. [OCTAVIO *runs over the Paper with apparent indifference.* TERZKY *watches him at some distance.*

GOETZ (*to* TERZKY).

Noble Count! with your permission—good night.

TERZKY.

Where's the hurry? Come one other composing draught. (*To the* Servants).—Ho!

GOETZ.

Excuse me—a nt able.

TERZKY

A thimble-full!

GOETZ.

Excuse me.

TIEFENBACH (*s.'s down*).

Pardon me, nobles!—This standing does not agree with me.

TERZKY.

Consult only your own convenience, General'

TIEFENBACH.

Clear at head, sound in stomach—only my legs won't carry me any longer

ISOLANI (*pointing at his corpulence*).

Poor legs! how *should* they! Such an unmerciful load:
[OCTAVIO *subscribes his name, and reaches over the Paper to* TERZKY, *who gives it to* ISOLANI; *and he goes to the table to sign his name.*

TIEFENBACH.

'Twas that war in Pomerania that first brought it on. Out in all weathers—ice and snow—no help for it. I shall never get the better of it all the days of my life

GOETZ.

Why. in simple verity, your Swede makes no nice inquiries about the season

TERZKY (*observing* ISOLANI, *whose hand trembles excessively so*
          that he can scarce direct his pen).

Have you had that ugly complaint long, noble brother?—
Dispatch it.

ISOLANI.

The sins of youth! I have already tried the chalybeate
waters. Well—I must bear it.

[TERZKY *gives the Paper to* MARADAS; *he steps to*
the table to subscribe.

OCTAVIO (*advancing to* BUTLER).

You are not over fond of the orgies of Bacchus, Colonel!
I have observed it. You would, I think, find yourself more
to your liking in the uproar of a battle, than of a feast.

BUTLER.

I must confess, 'tis not in my way.

OCTAVIO (*stepping nearer to him friendlily*).

Nor in mine either, I can assure you; and I am not a
little glad, my much honoured Colonel Butler, that we agree
so well in our opinions. A half dozen good friends at most,
at a small round table, a glass of genuine Tokay, open hearts,
and a rational conversation—that's my taste!

BUTLER.

And mine too, when it can be had.

[*The paper comes to* TIEFENBACH, *who glances over*
it at the same time with GOETZ *and* KOLATTO.
MARADAS *in the mean time returns to* OCTAVIO
All this takes place, the conversation with BUTLER
proceeding uninterrupted.

OCTAVIO (*introducing* MARADAS *to* BUTLER).

Don Balthasar Maradas! likewise a man of our stamp, and
long ago your admirer.   [BUTLER *bows*

OCTAVIO (*continuing*).

You are a stranger here—'twas but yesterday you arrived
—you are ignorant of the ways and means here. 'Tis a
wretched place—I know, at our age, one loves to be snug and
quiet. What if you moved your lodgings?—Come, be my
visitor. (BUTLER *makes a low bow*) Nay, without compli
ment!—For a friend like you, I have still a corner remaining.

K

BUTLER (*coldly*).

Your obliged humble servant, my Lord Lieutenant-General

[*The paper comes to* BUTLER, *who goes to the table
to subscribe it. The front of the stage is vacant,
so that both the* PICCOLOMINIS, *each on the side
where he had been from the commencement of the
scene, remain alone.*

OCTAVIO (*after having some time watched his son in silence,
advances somewhat nearer to him*

You were long absent from us, friend!

MAX.

I——urgent business detained me.

OCTAVIO.

And, I observe, you are still absent!

MAX.

You know this crowd and bustle always makes me silent.

OCTAVIO (*advancing still nearer*).

May I be permitted to ask what the business was that
detained you? *Terzky* knows it without asking?

MAX.

What does Terzky know?

OCTAVIO.

He was the only one who did not miss you.

ISOLANI (*who has been attending to them for some distance
steps up*)

Well done, father! Rout out his baggage! Beat up his
quarters! there is something there that should not be.

TERZKY (*with the paper*).

Is there none wanting? Have the whole subscribed?

OCTAVIO.

All

TERZKY (*calling aloud*).

Ho! Who subscribes?

BUTLER (*to* TERZKY).

Count the names. There ought to be just thirty.

TERZKY.

Here is a cross

TIEFENBACH.

That's my mark.

ISOLANI.

He cannot write; but his cross is a good cross, and is
honoured by Jews as well as Christians.

OCTAVIO (*presses on to* MAX.).

Come, general! let us go.　It is late.

TERZKY.

One Piccolomini only has signed.

ISOLANI (*pointing to* MAX.).

Look! that is your man, that statue there, who has had
neither eye, ear, nor tongue for us the whole evening.

[MAX. *receives the paper from* TERZKY, *which he looks
upon vacantly.*

SCENE VII.

To these enter ILLO *from the inner room.　He has in his
hand a golden service-cup, and is extremely distempered with
drinking;* GOETZ *and* BUTLER *follow him, endeavouring to
keep him back*

ILLO.

What do you want?　Let me go

GOETZ *and* BUTLER.

Drink no more, Illo! For Heaven's sake, drink no more.

ILLO (*goes up to* OCTAVIO, *and shakes him cordially by the
hand, and then drinks*).

Octavio! I bring this to you! Let all grudge be drowned
in this friendly bowl! I know well enough, ye never loved
me—Devil take me!—and I never loved you!—I am always
even with people in that way!　Let what's past be past—
that is, you understand—forgotten!　I esteem you infinitely
(*Embracing him repeatedly*).　You have not a dearer friend
on earth than I—but that you know.　The fellow that cries
rogue to you calls me villain—and I'll strangle him!—my
dear friend!

TERZKY (*whispering to him*).

Art in thy senses?　For Heaven's sake, Illo, think where
you are!

ILLO (*aloud*).

What do you mean?—There are none but friends here, are
there? (*Looks round the whole circle with a jolly and tri
umphant air.*)　Not a sneaker amongst us, thank Heaven!

TERZKY (*to* BUTLER, *eagerly*).

Take him off with you, force him off, I entreat you, Butler!

BUTLER (*to* ILLO).

Field Marshal! a word with you. (*Leads him to the sideboard*)

ILLO (*cordially*).

A thousand for one; Fill—Fill it once more up to the brim. To this gallant man's health!

ISOLANI (*to* MAX. *who all the while has been staring on the paper with fixed but vacant eyes*).

Slow and sure my noble brother!—Hast *parsed* it all yet? Some words yet to go through?—Ha?

MAX. (*waking as from a dream*).

What am I to do?

TERZKY, *and at the same time* ISOLANI.

Sign your name. (OCTAVIO *directs his eyes on him with intense anxiety*)

MAX. (*returns the paper*).

Let it stay till to-morrow. It is *business* —to-day I am not sufficiently collected. Send it to me to-morrow.

TERZKY.

Nay, collect yourself a little.

ISOLANI.

Awake man! awake!—Come, thy signature, and have done with it! What! Thou art the youngest in the whole company, and would be wiser than all of us together? Look there! thy father has signed—we have all signed.

TERZKY (*to* OCTAVIO).

Use your influence. Instruct him.

OCTAVIO.

My son is at the age of discretion.

ILLO (*leaves the service-cup on the sideboard*).

What's the dispute?

TERZKY.

He declines subscribing the paper

MAX.

I say, it may as well stay till to-morrow.

ILLO.

It cannot stay. We have all subscribed to it—and so must you.—You must subscribe.

MAX.

Illo, good night!

ILLO.

No! You come not off so! The Duke shall learn who are his friends. (*All collect round* ILLO *and* MAX.)

MAX.

What my sentiments are towards the Duke, the Duke knows. every one knows—what need of this wild stuff?

ILLO.

This is the thanks the Duke gets for his partiality to Ita lians and foreigners. Us Bohemians he holds for little better than dullards—nothing pleases him but what's outlandish.

TERZKY (*in extreme embarrassment, to the Commanders, whc at* ILLO's *words give a sudden start as preparing to resen: them.*)

It is the wine that speaks, and not his reason. Attend nc: to him, I entreat you.

ISOLANI (*with a bitter laugh*).

Wine invents nothing : it only *tattles*.

ILLO.

He who is not with me is against me. Your tender con sciences! Unless they can slip out by a back-door, by a puny proviso—

TERZKY (*interrupting him*).

He is stark mad—don't listen to him!

ILLO (*raising his voice to the highest pitch*).

Unless they can slip out by a *proviso*. What of the pro viso? The devil take this proviso!

MAX. (*has his attention roused, and looks again into the paper*).

What is there here then of such perilous import? You make me curious—I must look closer at it.

TERZKY (*in a low voice to* ILLO).

What are you doing, Illo? You are ruining us.

TIEFENBACH (*to* KOLATTO).

Ay, ay! I observed, that before we sat down to supper. it was read differently.

GOETZ.

Why, I seemed to think so too.

ISOLANI.

What do I care for that? Where there stand other names, mine can stand too.

TIEFENBACH.

Before supper there *was* a certain proviso therein, or short clause, concerning our duties to the Emperor.

BUTLER (*to one of the Commanders*).

For shame, for shame! Bethink you. What is the main business here? The question now is, whether we shall keep our General, or let him retire. One must not take these things too nicely, and over-scrupulously.

ISOLANI (*to one of the Generals*).

Did the Duke make any of these provisos when he gave you your regiment?

TERZKY (*to* GOETZ).

Or when he gave you the office of army-purveyancer, which brings you in yearly a thousand pistoles!

ILLO.

He is a rascal who makes us out to be rogues. If there be any one that wants satisfaction, let him say so,—I am his man.

TIEFENBACH

Softly, softly! 'Twas but a word or two.

MAX. (*having read the paper gives it back*).

Till to-morrow therefore!

ILLO (*stammering with rage and fury, loses all command over himself, and presents the paper to* MAX. *with one hand, and his sword in the other*).

Subscribe—Judas!

ISOLANI.

Out upon you, Illo!

OCTAVIO, TERZKY, BUTLER (*all together*)
Down with the sword!

MAX. (*rushes on him suddenly and disarms him, then to* COUNT TERZKY).

Take him off to bed.

> [Max. *leaves the stage.*—ILLO *cursing and raving is held back by some of the Officers, and amidst a universal confusion the Curtain drops.*

ACT V

SCENE I.

A Chamber in PICCOLOMINI'S *Mansion.—It is Night*

OCTAVIO PICCOLOMINI.   *A* Valet de Chambre *with Lights*

OCTAVIO.

——And when my son comes in, conduct him hither.
What is the hour?

VALET.

'Tis on the point of morning

OCTAVIO.

Set down the light.   We mean not to undress.
You may retire to sleep.

[*Exit* Valet.   OCTAVIO *paces, musing, across the chamber;* MAX. PICCOLOMINI *enters unobserved, and looks
at his father for some moments in silence*

MAX.

Art thou offended with me? Heaven knows
That odious business was no fault of mine.
'Tis true, indeed, I saw thy signature,
What *thou* hadst sanction'd, should not, it might seem,
Have come amiss to me.   But—'tis my nature—
Thou know'st that in such matters I must follow
My own light, not another's.

OCTAVIO (*goes up to him and embraces him*)
Follow it,
O follow it still further, my best son!
To-night, dear boy! it hath more faithfully
Guided thee than the example of thy father

MAX.

Declare thyself less darkly.

OCTAVIO
I will do so;
For after what has taken place this night,
There must remain no secrets 'twixt us two.

[*Both seat themselves.*

Max Piccolomini! what thinkest thou of
The oath that was sent round for signatures?

MAX

I hold it for a thing of harmless import.
Although I love not these set declarations

OCTAVIO.

And on no other ground hast thou refused
The signature they fain had wrested from thee?

MAX.

It was a serious business——I was absent—
The affair itself seem'd not so urgent to me.

OCTAVIO.

Be open, Max. Thou hadst then no suspicion?

MAX.

Suspicion! what suspicion? Not the least.

OCTAVIO.

Thank thy good angel, Piccolomini:
He drew thee back unconscious from the abyss.

MAX.

I know not what thou meanest.

OCTAVIO.

I will tell thee.

Fain would they have extorted from thee, son,
The sanction of thy name to villany;
Yes, with a single flourish of thy pen,
Made thee renounce thy duty and thy honour!

MAX. (rises).

Octavio!

OCTAVIO.

Patience! Seat yourself. Much yet
Hast thou to hear from me, friend!—hast for years
Lived in incomprehensible illusion.
Before thine eyes is Treason drawing out
As black a web as e'er was spun for venom:
A power of hell o'erclouds thy understanding.
I dare no longer stand in silence—dare
No longer see thee wandering on in darkness,
Nor pluck the bandage from thine eyes.

MAX.

My father!

Yet, ere thou speakest, a moment's pause of thought!
If your disclosures should appear to be
Conjectures only—and almost I fear
They will be nothing further—spare them! I
Am not in that collected mood at present,
That I could listen to them quietly

OCTAVIO.

The deeper cause thou hast to hate this light,
The more impatient cause have I, my son,
To force it on thee.   To the innocence
And wisdom of thy heart I could have trusted thee
With calm assurance—but I see the net
Preparing—and it is thy heart itself
Alarms me for thine innocence—that secret,
       [*Fixing his eyes stedfastly on his son's face*
Which thou concealest, forces *mine* from me.
    [MAX. *attempts to answer, but hesitates, and casts his*
      eyes to the ground embarrassed.

OCTAVIO (*after a pause*).

Know, then, they are duping thee!—a most foul game
With thee and with us all—nay, hear me calmly—
The Duke even now is playing.   He assumes
The mask, as if he would forsake the army;
And in this moment makes he preparations
That army from the Emperor to *steal*,
And carry it over to the enemy!

MAX.

That low Priest's legend I know well, but did not
Expect to hear it from thy mouth.

OCTAVIO.

              That mouth,
From which thou hearest it at this present moment,
Doth warrant thee that it is no Priest's legend.

MAX

How mere a maniac they supposed the Duke;
What, he can meditate?—the Duke?—can dream
That he can lure away full thirty thousand
Tried troops and true, all honourable soldiers,
More than a thousand noblemen among them,
From oaths, from duty, from their honour lure them,
And make them all unanimous to do
A deed that brands them scoundrels?

OCTAVIO

              Such a deed,
With such a front of infamy, the Duke
No way desires—what he requires of us

Bears a far gentler appellation. Nothing
He wishes, but to give the Empire peace.
And so, because the Emperor hates this peace,
Therefore the Duke—the Duke will force him to it.
All parts of the Empire will he pacify,
And for his trouble will retain in payment
(What he has already in his gripe)—Bohemia!

MAX.

Has he, Octavio, merited of us,
That we—that we should think so vilely of him?

OCTAVIO.

What *we would* think is not the question here,
The affair speaks for itself—and clearest proofs!
Hear me, my son—'tis not unknown to thee,
In what ill credit with the Court we stand.
But little dost thou know, or guess, what tricks,
What base intrigues, what lying artifices,
Have been employed—for this sole end—to sow
Mutiny in the camp! All bands are loosed—
Loosed all the bands, that link the officer
To his liege Emperor, all that bind the soldier
Affectionately to the citizen
Lawless he stands, and threateningly beleaguers
The state he's bound to guard   To such a height
'Tis swoln, that at this hour the Emperor
Before his armies—his own armies—trembles;
Yea, in his capital, his palace, fears
The traitors' poniards, and is meditating
To hurry off and hide his tender offspring——
Not from the Swedes, not from the Lutherans—No.
From his own troops to hide and hurry them!

MAX.

Cease, cease! thou torturest, shatterest me   I know
That oft we tremble at an empty terror;
But the false phantasm brings a real misery.

OCTAVIO

It is no phantasm. An intestine war,
Of all the most unnatural and cruel,
Will burst out into flames, if instantly
We do not fly and stifle it. The Generals

Are many of them long ago won over;
The subalterns are vacillating—whole
Regiments and garrisons are vacillating.
To foreigners our strongholds are entrusted;
To that suspected Schafgotch is the whole
Force of Silesia given up: to Terzky
Five regiments, foot and horse—to Isolani,
To Illo, Kinsky, Butler, the best troops.

MAX.

Likewise to both of us.

OCTAVIO.

     Because the Duke
Believes he has secured us—means to lure us
Still further on by splendid promises.
To me he portions forth the princedoms, Glatz
And Sagan; and too plain I see the bait
With which he doubts not but to catch thee

MAX.

          No! no!
I tell thee—no!

OCTAVIO.

    O open yet thine eyes!
And to what purpose think'st thou he has called
Hither to Pilsen?—to avail himself
Of our advice?—O when did Friedland ever
Need our advice?—Be calm, and listen to me
To sell ourselves are we called hither, and
Decline we that—to be his hostages.
Therefore doth noble Gallas stand aloof;
Thy father, too, thou wouldst not have seen here,
If higher duties had not held him fetter'd

MAX.

He makes no secret of it—needs make none—
That we're called hither for his sake—he owns it
He needs our aidance to maintain himself—
He did so much for us; and 'tis but fair
That we, too, should do somewhat now for him.

OCTAVIO.

And know'st thou what it is which we must do?
That Illo's drunken mood betray'd it to thee.

Bethink thyself—what hast thou heard, what seen?
The counterfeited paper—the omission
Of that particular clause, so full of meaning,
Does it not prove, that they would bind us down
To nothing good?

MAX.

That counterfeited paper
Appears to me no other than a trick
Of Illo's own device.   These underhand
Traders in great men's interests ever use
To urge and hurry all things to the extreme.
They see the Duke at variance with the Court,
And fondly think to serve him, when they widen
The breach irreparably.   Trust me, father,
The Duke knows nothing of all this.

OCTAVIO.

It grieves me
That I must dash to earth, that I must shatter
A faith so specious; but I may not spare thee!
For this is not a time for tenderness.
Thou must take measures, speedy ones—must act.
I therefore will confess to thee, that all
Which I've entrusted to thee now—that all
Which seems to thee so unbelievable,
That—yes, I will tell thee—(a pause)—Max.! I had it all
From his own mouth—from the Duke's mouth I had it.

MAX (in excessive agitation)

No!—no!—never!

OCTAVIO.

Himself confided to me
What I, 'tis true, had long before discovered
By other means—himself confided to me,
That 'twas his settled plan to join the Swedes;
And, at the head of the united armies,
Compel the Emperor——

MAX

He is passionate,
The Court has stung him—he is sore all over
With injuries and affronts; and in a moment
Of irritation, what if he, for once,
Forgot himself?   He's an impetuous man.

OCTAVIO

Nay, in cold blood he did confess this to me
And having construed my astonishment
Into a scruple of his power, he showed me
His written evidences—showed me letters,
Both from the Saxon and the Swede, that gave
Promise of aidance, and defined the amount.

MAX.

It cannot be!—can *not* be!—*can* not be!
Dost thou not see, it cannot!
Thou wouldst of necessity have shown him
Such horror, such deep loathing—that or he
Had taken thee for his better genius, or
Thou stood'st not now a living man before me—

OCTAVIO.

I have laid open my objections to him,
Dissuaded him with pressing earnestness;
But my *abhorrence*, the full sentiment
Of my *whole* heart—that I have still kept sacred
To my own consciousness.

MAX.

　　　　　And *thou* hast been
So treacherous? That looks not like my father!
I trusted not thy words, when thou didst tell me
Evil of him; much less can I *now* do it,
That thou calumniatest thy own self.

OCTAVIO.

I did not thrust myself into his secrecy.

MAX.

Uprightness merited his confidence.

OCTAVIO

He was no longer worthy of sincerity

MAX.

Dissimulation, sure, was still less worthy
Of thee, Octavio!

OCTAVIO

　　　　Gave I him a cause
To entertain a scruple of my honour?

MAX

That he did not evinced his confidence

OCTAVIO

Dear son, it is not always possible
Still to preserve that infant purity
Which the voice teaches in our inmost heart,
Still in alarm, for ever on the watch
Against the wiles of wicked men : e'en Virtue
Will sometimes bear away her outward robes
Soiled in the wrestle with Iniquity.
This is the curse of every evil deed,
That, propagating still, it brings forth evil.
I do not cheat my better soul with sophisms ;
I but perform my orders ; the Emperor
Prescribes my conduct to me.   Dearest boy,
Far better were it, doubtless, if we all
Obey'd the heart at all times ; but so doing.
In this our present sojourn with bad men,
We must abandon many an honest object.
'Tis now our call to serve the Emperor ;
By what means he can best be served—the heart
May whisper what it will—this is our call !

MAX

It seems a thing appointed, that to-day
I should not comprehend, not understand thee
The Duke, thou say'st, did honestly pour out
His heart to thee, but for an evil purpose :
And thou dishonestly hast cheated him
For a good purpose !   Silence, I entreat thee—
My friend, thou stealest not from me—
Let me not lose my father !

OCTAVIO (*suppressing resentment*).

As yet thou know'st not all, my son.   I have
Yet somewhat to disclose to thee.   [*After a pause.*
          Duke Friedland
Hath made his preparations.   He relies
Upon his stars.   He deems us unprovided,
And thinks to fall upon us by surprise.
Yea, in his dream of hope, he grasps already
The golden circle in his hand.   He errs,
We, too, have been in action—he but grasps
His evil fate, most evil, most mysterious !

MAX.

O nothing rash, my sire! By all that's good
Let me invoke thee—no precipitation!

OCTAVIO.

With light tread stole he on his evil way,
And light of tread hath Vengeance stole on after him
Unseen she stands already, dark behind him—
But one step more—he shudders in her grasp!
Thou hast seen Questenberg with me. As yet
Thou know'st but his ostensible commission:
He brought with him a *private* one, my son!
And that was for me only.

MAX.

May I know it?

OCTAVIO (*seizes the patent*).

Max.!

[*A pause.*

——In this disclosure place I in thy hands
The Empire's welfare and thy father's life:
Dear to thy inmost heart is Wallenstein:
A powerful tie of love, of veneration.
Hath knit thee to him from thy earliest youth.
Thou nourishest the *wish*,—O let me still
Anticipate thy loitering confidence!
The *hope* thou nourishest to knit thyself
Yet closer to him——

MAX.

Father——

OCTAVIO.

O, my son!
I trust thy heart undoubtingly. But am I
Equally sure of thy collectedness?
Wilt thou be able, with calm countenance,
To enter this man's presence, when that I
Have trusted to thee his whole fate?

MAX.

According
As thou dost trust me, father, with his crime.

[OCTAVIO *takes a paper out of his escrutoire,*
and gives it to him

MAX.

What! how! a full Imperial patent!

OCTAVIO.

Read it

MAX. (*just glances on it*).

Duke Friedland sentenced and condemn'd!

OCTAVIO.

Even so.

MAX. (*throws down the paper*).

O this is too much! O unhappy error!

OCTAVIO.

Read on. Collect thyself.

MAX (*after he has read further, with a look of affright and astonishment on his father*).

How! what! Thou! thou!

OCTAVIO.

But for the present moment, till the King
Of Hungary may safely join the army,
Is the command assign'd to me.

MAX.

And think'st thou,
Dost thou believe, that thou wilt tear it from him?
O never hope it!—Father! father! father!
An inauspicious office is enjoin'd thee.
This paper here—this! and wilt thou enforce it?
The mighty in the middle of his host,
Surrounded by his thousands, him wouldst thou
Disarm—degrade! Thou art lost, both thou and all of us.

OCTAVIO.

What hazard I incur thereby, I know
In the great hand of God I stand. The Almighty
Will cover with his shield the Imperial house,
And shatter, in his wrath, the work of darkness.
The Emperor hath true servants still; and even
Here in the camp, there are enough brave men
Who for the good cause will fight gallantly.
The faithful have been warn'd—the dangerous
Are closely watch'd. I wait but the first step,
And then immediately—

MAX
What! on suspicion?
Immediately?

OCTAVIO.
　　The Emperor is no tyrant.
The deed alone he'll punish, not the wish.
The Duke hath yet his destiny in his power.
Let him but leave the treason uncompleted,
He will be silently displaced from office,
And make way to his Emperor's royal son
An honourable exile to his castles
Will be a benefaction to him rather
Than punishment.　But the first open step—

MAX.
What callest thou such a step?　A wicked step
Ne'er will he take; but thou mightest easily,
Yea, thou hast done it, misinterpret him

OCTAVIO.
Nay, howsoever punishable were
Duke Friedland's purposes, yet still the steps
Which he hath taken openly, permit
A mild construction.　It is my intention
To leave this paper wholly unenforced
Till some act is committed which convicts him
Of high treason, without doubt or plea,
And that shall sentence him

MAX.
　　　　But who the judge?

OCTAVIO.
Thyself

MAX.
　　For ever, then, this paper will lie idle.

OCTAVIO.
Too soon, I fear, its powers must all be proved.
After the counter promise of this evening.
It cannot be but he must deem himself
Secure of the majority with *us;*
And of the army's general sentiment
He hath a pleasing proof in that petition,

Which thou delivered'st to him from the regiments.
Add this too—I have letters that the Rhinegrave
Hath changed his route, and travels by forced marches
To the Bohemian forests.   What this purports
Remains unknown ; and, to confirm suspicion,
This night a Swedish nobleman arrived here.

MAX.

I have thy word.   Thou'lt not proceed to action
Before thou hast convinced me—me myself.

OCTAVIO.

Is it possible?   Still, after all thou know'st,
Canst thou believe still in his innocence ?

MAX. (with enthusiasm).

Thy judgment may mistake ; my heart can not.
[Moderates his voice and manner.
These reasons might expound thy spirit or mine ;
But they expound not Friedland—I have faith :
For as he knits his fortunes to the stars,
Even so doth he resemble them in secret,
Wonderful, still inexplicable courses !
Trust me, they do him wrong.   All will be solved.
These smokes at once will kindle into flame—
The edges of this black and stormy cloud
Will brighten suddenly, and we shall view
The Unapproachable glide out in splendour.

OCTAVIO.

I will await it.

SCENE II

OCTAVIO and MAX. as before.   To them the Valet of the
Chamber

OCTAVIO.

How now, then ?

VALET.
A despatch is at the door.

OCTAVIO.

So early ?   From whom comes he then ?   Who is it?

VALET

That he refused to tell me.

OCTAVIO.

Lead him in
And, hark you—let it not transpire.

[*Exit Valet ; the Cornet steps in.*

OCTAVIO.

Ha! Cornet—is it you? and from Count Gallas?
Give me your letters

CORNET.

The Lieutenant-General
Trusted it not to letters.

OCTAVIO.

And what is it?

CORNET.

He bade me tell you—Dare I speak openly here?

OCTAVIO

My son knows all

CORNET.

We have him

OCTAVIO.

Whom?

CORNET

Sesina,
The old negociator.

OCTAVIO (*eagerly*).

And you have him?

CORNET.

In the Bohemian Forest Captain Mohrbrand
Found and secured him yester morning early .
He was proceeding then to Regensburg,
And on him were despatches for the Swede

OCTAVIO.

And the despatches——

CORNET

The Lieutenant-General
Sent them that instant to Vienna, and
The prisoner with them.

OCTAVIO.

This is, indeed, a tiding!
That fellow is a precious casket to us,
Enclosing weighty things.—Was much found on him?

CORNET.
I think, six packets, with Count Terzky's arms.

OCTAVIO.
Nrne in the Duke's own hand?

CORNET.
Not that I know

OCTAVIO
And old Sesina?

CORNET
He was sorely frighten'd,
When it was told him he must to Vienna
But the Count Altringer bade him take heart,
Would he but make a full and free confession

OCTAVIO.
Is Altringer then with your Lord? I heard
That he lay sick at Linz.

CORNET.
These three days past
He's with my master, the Lieutenant-General,
At Frauenburg.   Already have they sixty
Small companies together, chosen men;
Respectfully they greet you with assurances,
That they are only waiting your commands

OCTAVIO.
In a few days may great events take place.
And when must you return?

CORNET.
I wait your orders.

OCTAVIO.
Remain till evening.
Cornet signifies his assent and obeisance, and is going.
No one saw you—ha?

CORNET.
No living creature.   Through the cloister wicket
The Capuchins, as usual, let me in.

OCTAVIO.
Go, rest your limbs, and keep yourself conceal'd.
I hold it probable, that yet ere evening
I shall despatch you   The development

Of this affair approaches: ere the day,
That even now is dawning in the heaven,
Ere this eventful day hath set, the lot
That must decide our fortunes will be drawn.

[*Exit* Cornet.

Scene III.

Octavio *and* Max. Piccolomini.

OCTAVIO.

Well—and what now, son? All will soon be clear;
For all, I'm certain, went through that Sesina.

MAX. (*who through the whole of the foregoing scene has
been in a violent and visible struggle of feelings, at length
starts as one resolved.*)
I will procure me light a shorter way.
Farewell.

OCTAVIO.
Where now?—Remain here.

MAX.
To the Duke.

OCTAVIO (*alarmed*).
What——

MAX (*returning*).
If thou hast believed that I shall act
A part in this thy play—— Thou hast
Miscalculated on me grievously.
My way must be straight on. True with the tongue,
False with the heart—I may not, cannot be:
Nor can I suffer that a man should trust me—
As his friend trust me—and then lull my conscience
With such low pleas as these:—" I ask him not—
He did it all at his own hazard—and
My *mouth* has never lied to him."—No, no!
What a friend takes me for, that I must be.
—I'll to the Duke; ere yet this day is ended
Will I demand of him that he do save
His good name from the world, and with one stride
Break through and rend this fine-spun web of yours.
He can, he will!—*I* still am his believer
Yet I'll not pledge myself, but that those letters

May furnish you, perchance, with proofs against him.
How far may not this Terzky have proceeded—
What may not he himself too have permitted
Himself to do, to snare the enemy,
The laws of war excusing? Nothing, save
His own mouth shall convict him—nothing less!
And face to face will I go question him.

OCTAVIO

Thou wilt?

MAX.

I will, as sure as this heart beats.

OCTAVIO.

I have, indeed, miscalculated on thee.
I calculated on a prudent son,
Who would have bless'd the hand beneficent
That pluck'd him back from the abyss—and lo!
A fascinated being I discover,
Whom his two eyes befool, whom passion wilders,
Whom not the broadest light of noon can heal.
Go, question him!—Be mad enough, I pray thee.
The purpose of thy father, of thy Emperor,
Go, give it up free booty!—Force me, drive me
To an open breach before the time. And now
Now that a miracle of Heaven had guarded
My secret purpose even to this hour,
And laid to sleep Suspicion's piercing eyes,
Let me have lived to see that mine own son,
With frantic enterprise, annihilates
My toilsome labours and state-policy.

MAX.

Ay—this state policy? O how I curse it!
You will some time, with your state-policy,
Compel him to the measure: it may happen,
Because ye are *determined* that he is guilty,
Guilty ye'll *make* him. All retreat cut off,
You close up every outlet, hem him in
Narrower and narrower, till at length ye force him—
Yes, *ye*, ye *force* him, in his desperation,
To set fire to his prison. Father! father!
That never can end well it cannot—will not!

And let it be decided as it may,
I see with boding heart the near approach
Of an ill-starr'd, unblest catastrophe.
For this great Monarch-spirit, if he fall,
Will drag a world into the ruin with him.
And as a ship (that midway on the ocean
Takes fire) at once, and with a thunder-burst
Explodes, and with itself shoots out its crew
In smoke and ruin betwixt sea and heaven!
So will he, falling, draw down in his fall
All us, who're fix'd and mortised to his fortune
Deem of it what thou wilt; but pardon me,
That I must bear me on in my own way
All must remain pure betwixt him and me:
And, ere the daylight dawns, it must be known
Which I must lose—my father, or my friend.

               [During his exit the curtain drops.

THE
DEATH OF WALLENSTEIN.

DRAMATIS PERSONÆ.

WALLENSTEIN, *Duke of Friedland, Generalissimo of the Imperial Forces in the Thirty Years' War.*

DUCHESS OF FRIEDLAND, *Wife of Wallenstein.*

THEKLA, *her Daughter, Princess of Friedland.*

The COUNTESS TERZKY, *Sister of the Duchess.*

LADY NEUBRUNN.

OCTAVIO PICCOLOMINI, *Lieutenant-General.*

MAX. PICCOLOMINI, *his Son, Colonel of a Regiment of Cuirassiers.*

COUNT TERZKY, *the Commander of several Regiments, and Brother-in-law of Wallenstein.*

ILLO, *Field Marshal, Wallenstein's Confidant.*

ISOLANI, *General of the Croats.*

BUTLER, *an Irishman, Commander of a Regiment of Dragoons.*

GORDON, *Governor of Egra.*

MAJOR GERALDIN.

CAPTAIN DEVEREUX.

CAPTAIN MACDONALD.

AN ADJUTANT.

NEUMANN, *Captain of Cavalry, Aide-de-camp to Terzky.*

COLONEL WRANGEL, *Envoy from the Swedes.*

ROSENBURG, *Master of Horse.*

SWEDISH CAPTAIN.

SENI.

BURGOMASTER *of Egra.*

ANSPESSADE *of the Cuirassiers.*

GROOM OF THE CHAMBER, } *Belonging to*

A PAGE, } *the Duke.*

Cuirassiers, Dragoons, Servants.

ACT I.
SCENE I.

A Room fitted up for astrological labours, and provided with celestial Charts, with Globes, Telescopes, Quadrants, and other mathematical Instruments —Seven Colossal Figures, representing the Planets, each with a transparent Star of a different colour on its head, stand in a semicircle in the background, so that Mars and Saturn are nearest the eye —The remainder of the Scene, and its disposition, is given in the Fourth Scene of the Second Act.—There must be a Curtain over the Figures, which may be dropped, and conceal them on occasions.

[*In the Fifth Scene of this Act it must be dropped; but in the Seventh Scene, it must be again drawn up wholly or in part.*]

WALLENSTEIN *at a black Table, on which a Speculum Astrologicum is described with Chalk.* SENI *is taking Observations through a window.*

WALLENSTEIN.

All well—and now let it be ended, Seni. Come,
The dawn commences, and Mars rules the hour
We must give o'er the operation.   Come,
We know enough.

SENI.

Your Highness must permit me
Just to contemplate Venus.   She's now rising:
Like as a sun, so shines she in the east.

WALLENSTEIN.

She is at present in her perigee,
And now shoots down her strongest influences.
                    [*Contemplating the figure on the table.*
Auspicious aspect! fateful in conjunction,
At length the mighty three corradiate;
And the two stars of blessing, Jupiter
And Venus, take between them the malignant
Slily-malicious Mars, and thus compel
Into *my* service that old mischief-founder:
For long he viewed me hostilely, and ever
With beam oblique, or perpendicular,
Now in the Quartile, now in the Secundan,
Shot his red lightnings at my stars, disturbing
Their blessed influences and sweet aspects.
Now they have conquer'd the old enemy,
And bring him in the heavens a prisoner to me.

SENI (*who has come down from the window*).

And in a corner house, your Highness—think of that !
That makes each influence of double strength.

WALLENSTEIN.

And sun and moon, too, in the Sextile aspect,
The soft light with the vehement—so I love it
Sol is the heart, Luna the head of heaven,
Bold be the plan, fiery the execution.

SENI.

And both the mighty Lumina by no
Maleficus *affronted*.   Lo! Saturnus,
Innocuous, powerless. in cadente Domo.

WALLENSTEIN.

The empire of Saturnus is gone by;
Lord of the secret birth of things is he;

Within the lap of earth, and in the depths
Of the imagination dominates ;
And his are all things that eschew the light.
The time is o'er of brooding and contrivance,
For Jupiter, the lustrous, lordeth now,
And the dark work, complete of preparation,
He draws by force into the realm of light.
Now must we hasten on to action, ere
The scheme, and most auspicious positure
Parts o'er my head, and takes once more its flight,
For the heavens journey still, and sojourn not.

> [*There are knocks at the door.*

There's some one knocking there.   See who it is.

TERZKY (*from without*).

Open, and let me in.

WALLENSTEIN.

Ay—'tis Terzky.
What is there of such urgence?   We are busy.

TERZKY (*from without*).

Lay all aside at present, I entreat you.
It suffers no delaying.

WALLENSTEIN.

Open, Seni!

[*While* SENI *opens the door for* TERZKY, WALLENSTEIN
draws the curtain over the figures.

SCENE II.

WALLENSTEIN.   COUNT TERZKY

TERZKY (*enters*).

Hast thou already heard it?   He is taken.
Vallas has given him up to the Emperor.

> [SENI *draws off the black table, and exit.*

WALLENSTEIN (*to* TERZKY).

Who has been taken?   Who is given up?

TERZKY

The man who knows our secrets, who knows every
Negociation with the Swede and Saxon,
Through whose hands all and every thing has pass'd——

WALLENSTEIN (*drawing back*).

Nay, not Sesina?—Say, No!   I entreat thee.

TERZKY.

All on his road for Regensburg to the Swede
He was plunged down upon by Gallas' agent.
Who had been long in ambush, lurking for him.
There must have been found on him my whole packet
To Thur. to Kinsky, to Oxenstiern, to Arnheim:
All this is in their hands; they have now an insight
Into the whole—our measures and our motives.

SCENE III.

To them enters ILLO.

ILLO (*to* TERZKY).

Has he heard it?

TERZKY.

He has heard it.

ILLO (*to* WALLENSTEIN).

Thinkest thou still
To make thy peace with the Emperor, to regain
His confidence? E'en were it now thy wish
To abandon all thy plans, yet still they know
What thou hast wish'd: then forwards thou must press:
Retreat is now no longer in thy power.

TERZKY

They have documents against us, and in hands,
Which show beyond all power of contradiction—

WALLENSTEIN.

Of my handwriting—no iota. Thee
I punish for thy lies

ILLO.

And thou believest,
That what this man, and what thy sister's husband,
Did in thy name, will not stand on thy reck'ning?
His word must pass for thy word with the Swede,
And not with those that hate thee at Vienna?

TERZKY

In wr't'ng thou gavest nothing—But bethink thee.
How far thou venturedst by word of mouth
With this Sesina! And will he be silent?
If he can save himself by yielding up
Thy secret purposes, will he retain them?

ILLO

Thyself dost not conceive it possible ;
And since they now have evidence authentic
How far thou hast already gone, speak!—tell us,
What art thou waiting for? Thou canst no longer
Keep thy command; and beyond hope of rescue
Thou'rt lost, if thou resign'st it.

WALLENSTEIN.

                    In the army
Lies my security. The army will not
Abandon me.   Whatever they may know,
The power is mine, and they must gulp it down—
And if I give them caution for my fealty,
They must be satisfied, at least appear so.

ILLO.

The army, Duke, *is* thine now—for this moment—
'Tis thine : but think with terror on the slow,
The quiet power of time.   From open violence
The attachment of thy soldiery secures thee
To-day—to-morrow: but grant'st thou them a respite,
Unheard, unseen, they'll undermine that love
On which thou now dost feel so firm a footing,
With wily theft will draw away from thee
One after the other——

WALLENSTEIN.
              'Tis a cursed accident!

ILLO.

Oh! I will call it a most blessed one,
If it work on thee as it ought to do,
Hurry thee on to action—to decision.
The Swedish General——

WALLENSTEIN.
                    He's arrived! Know'st thou
What his commission is——

ILLO.
              To thee alone
Will he entrust the purpose of his coming.

WALLENSTEIN.
A cursed, cursed accident! Yes, yes,
Sesina knows too much, and won't be silent

TERZKY.

He's a Bohemian fugitive and rebel,
His neck is forfeit.   Can he save himself
At thy cost, think you he will scruple it?
And if they put him to the torture, will he,
Will *he*, that dastardling, have strength enough——

WALLENSTEIN (*lost in thought*).

Their confidence is lost, irreparably!
And I may act which way I will, I shall
Be and remain for ever in their thought
A traitor to my country.   How sincerely
Soever I return back to my duty,
It will no longer help me——

ILLO.

                Ruin thee,
That it will do!   Not thy fidelity,
Thy weakness will be deemed the sole occasion—

WALLENSTEIN (*pacing up and down in extreme agitation*)

What! I must realize it now in earnest,
Because I toy'd too freely with the thought!
Accursed he who dallies with a devil!
And must I—I *must* realize it now—
Now, while I have the power, it *must* take place?

ILLO.

Now—now—ere they can ward and parry it!

WALLENSTEIN (*looking at the paper of signatures*).

I have the Generals' word—a written promise!
Max. Piccolomini stands not here—how's that?

TERZKY.

It was——he fancied——

ILLO.

              Mere self-willedness.
There needed no such thing 'twixt him and you.

WALLENSTEIN.

He is quite right; there needed no such thing.
The regiments, too, deny to march for Flanders—
Have sent me in a paper of remonstrance
And openly resist the Imperial orders.
The first step to revolt's already taken.

ILLO.

Believe me, thou wilt find it far more easy
To lead them over to the enemy
Than to the Spaniard.

WALLENSTEIN.

I will hear, however,
What the Swede has to say to me

ILLO (*eagerly to* TERZKY).

Go, call him
He stands without the door in waiting.

WALLENSTEIN.

Stay!
Stay but a little.   It hath taken me
All by surprise; it came too quick upon me;
'Tis wholly novel, that an accident,
With its dark lordship, and blind agency,
Should force me on with it.

ILLO.

First hear him only,
And after weigh it.   [*Exeunt* TERZKY *and* ILLO.

SCENE IV.

WALLENSTEIN (*in soliloquy*).

Is it possible?
Is't so?   I can no longer what I *would?*
No longer draw back at my liking?   I
Must *do* the deed, because I *thought* of it?
And fed this heart here with a dream?   Because
I did not scowl temptation from my presence,
Dallied with thoughts of possible fulfilment,
Commenced no movement, left all time uncertain,
And only kept the road, the access open?
By the great God of Heaven! it was not
My serious meaning, it was ne'er resolved.
I but amused myself with thinking of it.
The free-will tempted me, the power to do
Or not to do it.—Was it criminal
To make the fancy minister to hope,
To fill the air with pretty toys of air,
And clutch fantastic sceptres moving t'ward me!
Was not the will kept free?   Beheld I not

The road of duty close beside me—but
One little step, and once more I was in it!
Where am I?   Whither have I been transported?
No road, no track behind me, but a wall,
Impenetrable, insurmountable,
Rises obedient to the spells I muttered
And meant not—my own doings tower behind me.
                    [*Pauses and remains in deep thought.*
A punishable man I seem: the guilt,
Try what I will, I cannot roll off from me;
The equivocal demeanour of my life
Bears witness on my prosecutor's party.
And even my purest acts from purest motives
Suspicion poisons with malicious gloss.
Were I that thing for which I pass, that traitor,
A goodly outside I had sure reserved,
Had drawn the coverings thick and double round me,
Been calm and chary of my utterance;
But being conscious of the innocence
Of my intent, my uncorrupted will,
I gave way to my humours, to my passion:
Bold were my words, because my deeds were *not*
Now every planless measure, chance event,
The threat of rage, the vaunt of joy and triumph,
And all the May-games of a heart o'erflowing.
Will they connect, and weave them all together
Into one web of treason; all will be plain,
My eye ne'er absent from the far-off mark,
Step tracing step, each step a politic progress;
And out of all they'll fabricate a charge
So specious, that I must myself stand dumb.
I am caught in my own net, and only force,
Nought but a sudden rent can liberate me.
                        [*Pauses again.*
How else! since that the heart's unbiass'd instinct
Impell'd me to the daring deed, which now
Necessity, self-preservation, orders.
Stern is the on-look of Necessity,
Not without shudder may a human hand
Grasp the mysterious urn of destiny.
My deed was mine, remaining in my bosom:

Once suffer'd to escape from its safe corner
Within the heart, its nursery and birth-place,
Sent forth into the Foreign, it belongs
For ever to those sly malicious powers
Whom never art of man conciliated.

> [*Paces in agitation through the chamber, then pauses, and,*
> *after the pause, breaks out again into audible soliloquy*

What is thy enterprise? thy aim? thy object?
Hast honestly confess'd it to thyself?
Power seated on a quiet throne thou'dst shake,
Power on an ancient consecrated throne,
Strong in possession. founded in all custom;
Power by a thousand tough and stringy roots
Fix'd to the people's pious nursery-faith.
This, this will be no strife of strength with strength.
That fear'd I not. I brave each combatant,
Whom I can look on, fixing eye to eye,
Who, full himself of courage, kindles courage
In me too. 'Tis a foe invisible
The which I fear—a fearful enemy,
Which in the human heart opposes me,
By its coward fear alone made fearful to me.
Not that, which full of life, instinct with power,
Makes known its present being; that is not
The true, the perilously formidable.
O no! it is the common, the quite common,
The thing of an eternal yesterday.
What ever was, and evermore returns,
Sterling to-morrow, for to-day 'twas sterling!
For of the wholly common is man made,
And custom is his nurse! Woe then to them,
Who lay irreverent hands upon his old
House furniture, the dear inheritance
From his forefathers! For time consecrates;
And what is grey with age becomes religion.
Be in possession, and thou hast the right,
And sacred will the many guard it for thee!

> [*To the* PAGE, *who here enters*

The Swedish officer?—Well, let him enter.

> [*The* PAGE *exit,* WALLENSTEIN *fixes his eye in deep*
> *thought on the door.*

Yet is it pure—as yet!—the crime has come
Not o'er this threshold yet—so slender is
The boundary that divideth life's two paths.

SCENE V.

WALLENSTEIN *and* WRANGEL.

WALLENSTEIN (*after having fixed a searching look on him*)
Your name is Wrangel?

WRANGEL.
                Gustave Wrangel, General
Of the Sudermanian Blues

WALLENSTEIN.
                It was a Wrangel
Who injured me materially at Stralsund,
And by his brave resistance was the cause
Of the opposition which that sea-port made

WRANGEL
It was the doing of the element
With which you fought, my Lord! and not my merit.
The Baltic Neptune did assert his freedom :
The sea and land, it seem'd, were not to serve
One and the same.

[WALLENSTEIN.
You pluck'd the Admiral's hat from off my head.

WRANGEL.
I come to place a diadem thereon.]

WALLENSTEIN (*makes the motion for him to take a seat, and
                seats himself*).
                And where are your credentials?
Come you provided with full powers, Sir General?

WRANGEL.
There are so many scruples yet to solve——

WALLENSTEIN (*having read the credentials*).
An able letter!—Ay—he is a prudent
Intelligent master whom you serve, Sir General!
The Chancellor writes me, that he but fulfils
His late departed Sovereign's own idea
In helping me to the Bohemian crown.

WRANGEL.

He says the truth.   Our great King, now in heaven,
Did ever deem most highly of your Grace's
Pre-eminent sense and military genius ;
And always the commanding Intellect,
He said, should have command, and be the King.

WALLENSTEIN.

Yes, he *might* say it safely.—General Wrangel,
            [*Taking his hand affectionately,*
Come, fair and open.   Trust me, I was always
A Swede at heart.   Eh ! that did you experience
Both in Silesia and at Nuremberg ;
I had you often in my power, and let you
Always slip out by some back door or other.
'Tis this for which the Court can ne'er forgive me,
Which drives me to this present step : and since
Our interests so run in one direction,
E'en let us have a thorough confidence
Each in the other.

WRANGEL.

Confidence will come
Has each but only first security.

WALLENSTEIN.

The Chancellor still, I see, does not quite trust me ;
And, I confess—the game does not lie wholly
To my advantage.   Without doubt he thinks,
If I can play false with the Emperor,
Who is my sovereign, I can do the like
With the enemy, and that *the one* too were
Sooner to be forgiven me than the *other.*
Is not this your opinion too, Sir General?

WRANGEL.

I have here a duty merely, no opinion.

WALLENSTEIN.

The Emperor hath urged me to the uttermost :
I can no longer honourably serve him
For my security, in self-defence.
I take this hard step, which my conscience blames

WRANGEL.

That I believe.   So far would no one go
Who was not forced to it.
                            [*After a pause,*

                              What may have impell'd
Your princely Highness in this wise to act
Toward your Sovereign Lord and Emperor,
Beseems not us to expound or criticise.
The Swede is fighting for his good old cause,
With his good sword and conscience.   This concurrence,
This opportunity, is in our favour,
And all advantages in war are lawful.
We take what offers without questioning ;
And if all have its due and just proportions——

WALLENSTEIN.

Of what then are ye doubting ? Of my will ?
Or of my power ?   I pledged me to the Chancellor,
Would he trust *me* with sixteen thousand men,
That I would instantly go over to them
With eighteen thousand of the Emperor's troops

WRANGEL.

Your Grace is known to be a mighty war-chief,
To be a second Attila and Pyrrhus.
'Tis talked of still with fresh astonishment,
How some years past, beyond all human faith,
You call'd an army forth, like a creation :
But yet——

WALLENSTEIN.

          But yet ?

WRANGEL.

                    But still the Chancellor thinks,
It might yet be an easier thing from nothing
To call forth sixty thousand men of battle,
Than to persuade one sixtieth part of them—

WALLENSTEIN.

What now ?   Out with it, friend ?

WRANGEL.

                         To break their oaths.

WALLENSTEIN.

And he thinks *so ?*   He judges like a Swede,
And like a Protestant.   You Lutherans
Fight for your Bible.   You are interested
About the cause ; and with your *hearts* you follow
Your banners.   Among *you*, whoe'er deserts

M 2

To the enemy, hath broken covenant
With two Lords at one time.   We've no such fancies.

WRANGEL.

Great God in Heaven!   Have then the people here
No house and home, no fireside, no altar?

WALLENSTEIN.

I will explain that to you, how it stands :—
The Austrian *has* a country, ay, and loves it,
And has good cause to love it—but this army,
That calls itself the Imperial, this that houses
Here in Bohemia, this has none—no country ;
This is an outcast of all foreign lands,
Unclaim'd by town or tribe, to whom belongs
Nothing, except the universal sun.
And this Bohemian land for which we fight
[Loves not the master whom the chance of war,
Not its own choice or will, hath given to it.
Men murmur at the oppression of their conscience,
And power hath only awed but not appeased them
A glowing and avenging mem'ry lives
Of cruel deeds committed on these plains ;
How can the son forget that here his father
Was hunted by the blood-hound to the mass?
A people thus oppress'd must still be feared,
Whether they suffer or avenge their wrongs.]

WRANGEL

But then the Nobles and the Officers?
Such a desertion, such a felony,
It is without example, my Lord Duke,
In the world's history.

WALLENSTEIN

                    They are all mine—
Mine unconditionally—mine on all terms.
Not me, your own eyes you must trust.
      [*He gives him the paper containing the written oath.
        WRANGEL reads it through, and, having read it, lays
        it on the table, remaining silent.*
                                    So then?

Now comprehend you?

WRANGEL.

Comprehend who can !
My Lord Duke, I will let the mask drop—yes !
I've full powers for a final settlement.
The Rhinegrave stands but four days' march from here
With fifteen thousand men, and only waits
For orders to proceed and join your army.
Those orders *I* give out, immediately
We're compromised.

WALLENSTEIN.

What asks the Chancellor ?

WRANGEL. (*considerately*).

Twelve regiments, every man a Swede—my head
The warranty —and all might prove at last
Only false play——

WALLENSTEIN (*starting*).

Sir Swede !

WRANGEL (*calmly proceeding*)

Am therefore forced
T' insist thereon, that he do formally,
Irrevocably break with the Emperor,
Else not a Swede is trusted to Duke Friedland.

WALLENSTEIN.

Come, brief, and open !   What is the demand ?

WRANGEL.

That he forthwith disarm the Spanish regiments
Attached to the Emp'ror, that he seize on Prague,
And to the Swedes give up that city, with
The strong pass Egra.

WALLENSTEIN.

That is much indeed !
Prague !—Egra's granted—but—but Prague !—'Twon't do.
I give you every security
Which you may ask of me in common reason —
But Prague—Bohemia—these, Sir General,
I can myself protect.

WRANGEL.

We doubt it not.
But 'tis not the protection that is now
Our sole concern.   We want security,

That we shall not expend our men and money
All to no purpose.

WALLENSTEIN.
'Tis but reasonable.

WRANGEL.
And till we are indemnified, so long
Stays Prague in pledge.

WALLENSTEIN.
                    Then trust you us so little?

WRANGEL (*rising*).
The Swede, if he would treat well with the German,
Must keep a sharp look-out.   We have been call'd
Over the Baltic, we have saved the empire
From ruin—with our best blood have we sealed
The liberty of faith, and gospel truth.
But now already is the benefaction
No longer felt, the load alone is felt.—
Ye look askance with evil eye upon us,
As foreigners, intruders in the empire,
And would fain send us, with some paltry sum
Of money, home again to our old forests.
No, no! my Lord Duke! no!—it never was
For Judas' pay, for chinking gold and silver,
That we did leave our King by the Great Stone *
No, not for gold and silver have there bled
So many of our Swedish Nobles—neither
Will we, with empty laurels for our payment,
Hoist sail for our own country.   *Citizens*
Will we remain upon the soil, the which
Our Monarch conquer'd for himself, and died

WALLENSTEIN.
Help to keep down the common enemy,
And the fair border land must needs be yours.

WRANGEL.
But when the common enemy lies vanquish'd,
Who knits together our new friendship then?
We know, Duke Friedland! though perhaps the Swede

---

* A great stone near Lützen, since called the Swede's Stone, the body of
their great king having been found at the foot of it, after the battle in which
he lost his life.

Ought not to have known it, that you carry on
Secret negociations with the Saxons.
Who is our warranty, that *we* are not
The sacrifices in those articles
Which 'tis thought needful to conceal from us?

WALLENSTEIN (*rises*).

Think you of something better, Gustave Wrangel!
Of Prague no more.

WRANGEL.

Here my commission ends.

WALLENSTEIN.

Surrender up to you my capital!
Far liever would I face about, and step
Back to my Emperor.

WRANGEL.

If time yet permits—

WALLENSTEIN.

That lies with me, even now, at any hour.

WRANGEL.

Some days ago, perhaps.   To-day, no longer;
No longer since Sesina's been a prisoner.

[WALLENSTEIN *is struck, and silenced*.

My Lord Duke, hear me—We believe that you
At present do mean honourably by us.
Since *yesterday* we're sure of that—and now
This paper warrants for the troops, there's nothing
Stands in the way of our full confidence.
Prague shall not part us.   Hear!   The Chancellor
Contents himself with Altstadt; to your Grace
He gives up Ratschin and the narrow side.
But Egra above all must open to us,
Ere we can think of any junction.

WALLENSTEIN.

You,
You therefore must I trust, and not you me?
I will consider of your proposition.

WRANGEL.

I must entreat, that your consideration
Occupy not too long a time.   Already
Has this negociation, my Lord Duke!

Crept on into the second year.   If nothing
Is settled this time, will the Chancellor
Consider it as broken off for ever.

WALLENSTEIN.

Ye press me hard.   A measure such as this,
Ought to be *thought* of.

WRANGEL

Ay! but think of this too,
That sudden action only can procure it
Success—think first of this, your Highness.

[*Exit* WRANGEL.

SCENE VI.

WALLENSTEIN, TERZKY, *and* ILLO (*re-enter*).

ILLO.

Is't all right?

TERZKY.

Are you compromised?

ILLO.

This Swede
Went smiling from you.   Yes! you're compromised

WALLENSTEIN.

As yet is nothing settled: and (well weighed)
I feel myself inclined to leave it so.

TERZKY.

How?   What is that?

WALLENSTEIN.

Come on me what will come,
The doing evil to avoid an evil
Cannot be good!

TERZKY.

Nay, but bethink you, Duke.

WALLENSTEIN.

To live upon the mercy of these Swedes!
Of these proud-hearted Swedes!—I could not bear it.

ILLO

Goest thou as fugitive, as mendicant?
Bringest thou not more to them than thou receivest?

[WALLENSTEIN.
How fared it with the brave and royal Bourbon
Who sold himself unto his country's foes,
And pierced the bosom of his father-land?
Curses were his reward, and men's abhorrence
Avenged th' unnatural and revolting deed.

ILLO.
Is that thy case?

WALLENSTEIN.
                    True faith, I tell thee,
Must ever be the dearest friend of man:
His nature prompts him to assert its rights.
The enmity of sects, the rage of parties,
Long cherish'd envy, jealousy,—unite:
And all the struggling elements of evil
Suspend their conflict, and together league
In one alliance 'gainst their common foe—
The savage beast that breaks into the fold,
Where men repose in confidence and peace.
For vain were man's own prudence to protect him.
'Tis only in the forehead nature plants
The watchful eye—the back, without defence,
Must find its shield in man's fidelity.

TERZKY.
Think not more meanly of thyself than do
Thy foes, who stretch their hands with joy to greet thee,
Less scrupulous far was the Imperial Charles,
The powerful head of this illustrious house;
With open arms he gave the Bourbon welcome;
For still by policy the world is ruled.]

SCENE VII
To these enter the COUNTESS TERZKY.

WALLENSTEIN.
Who sent for you? There is no business here
For women.

COUNTESS.
I am come to bid you joy.

WALLENSTEIN.
Use thy authority. Terzky; bid her go.

COUNTESS.

Come I perhaps too early?   I hope not.

WALLENSTEIN.

Set not this tongue upon me, I entreat you :
You know it is the weapon that destroys me.
I am routed, if a woman but attack me :
I cannot traffic in the trade of words
With that unreasoning sex.

COUNTESS.

I had already
Given the Bohemians a king.

WALLENSTEIN (*sarcastically*).

They have one,
In consequence, no doubt.

COUNTESS (*to the others*).

Ha ! what new scruple

TERZKY.

The Duke will not.

COUNTESS.

He *will not* what he *must !*

ILLO.

It lies with you now.   Try.   For I am silenced.
When folks begin to talk to me of conscience,
And of fidelity.

COUNTESS.

How ? then, when all
Lay in the far-off distance, when the road
Stretch'd out before thine eyes interminably,
Then hadst thou courage and resolve ; and now,
Now that the dream is being realized,
The purpose ripe, the issue ascertain'd,
Dost thou begin to play the dastard now?
Plann'd merely, 'tis a common felony ;
Accomplish'd, an immortal undertaking :
And with success comes pardon hand in hand
For all event is God's arbitrement.

SERVANT (*enters*).

The Colonel Piccolomini.

COUNTESS (*hastily*).

—Must wait

WALLENSTEIN.

I cannot see him now   Another time.

SERVANT.

But for two minutes he entreats an audience :
Of the most urgent nature is his business

WALLENSTEIN.

Who knows what he may bring us !   I will hear him

COUNTESS (*laughs*).

Urgent for him, no doubt ? but thou may'st wait.

WALLENSTEIN

What is it ?

COUNTESS

Thou shalt be inform'd hereafter
First let the Swede and thee be compromised.

[*Exit* SERVANT

WALLENSTEIN.

If there were yet a choice ! if yet some milder
Way of escape were possible—I still
Will choose it, and avoid the last extreme.

COUNTESS.

Desirest thou nothing further?   Such a way
Lies still before thee.   Send this Wrangel off.
Forget thou thy old hopes, cast far away
All thy past life ; determine to commence
A new one.   Virtue hath her heroes too,
As well as fame and fortune.—To Vienna
Hence—to the Emperor—kneel before the throne ;
Take a full coffer with thee—say aloud,
Thou didst but wish to prove thy fealty ;
Thy whole intention but to dupe the Swede

ILLO.

For that too 'tis too late.   They know too much ;
He would but bear his own head to the block.

COUNTESS.

I fear not that   They have not evidence
To attaint him legally, and they avoid
The avowal of an arbitrary power
They'll let the Duke resign without disturbance.
I see how all will end.   The King of Hungary

Makes his appearance, and 'twill of itself
Be understood, that then the Duke retires.
There will not want a formal declaration ·
The young King will administer the oath
To the whole army; and so all returns
To the old position.   On some morrow morning
The Duke departs; and now 'tis stir and bustle
Within his castles.   He will hunt, and build;
Superintend his horses' pedigrees,
Creates himself a court, gives golden keys,
And introduceth strictest ceremony
In fine proportions, and nice etiquette;
Keeps open table with high cheer: in brief,
Commenceth mighty King—in miniature.
And while he prudently demeans himself,
And gives himself no actual importance,
He will be let appear whate'er he likes:
And who dares doubt, that Friedland will appear
A mighty Prince to his last dying hour?
Well now, what then?   Duke Friedland is as others,
A fire-new Noble, whom the war hath raised
To price and currency, a Jonah's gourd,
An over-night creation of court-favour,
Which with an undistinguishable ease
Makes Baron or makes Prince.

WALLENSTEIN (in extreme agitation).

                                   Take her away.
Let in the young Count Piccolomini.

COUNTESS.

Art thou in earnest?   I entreat thee!   Canst thou
Consent to bear thyself to thy own grave,
So ignominiously to be dried up?
Thy life, that arrogated such an height
To end in such a nothing!   To be nothing,
When one was always nothing, is an evil
That asks no stretch of patience, a light evil;
But to become a nothing, having been——

WALLENSTEIN (starts up in violent agitation).

Show me a way out of this stifling crowd,
Ye powers of Aidance!   Show me such a way

As *I* am capable of going.   I
Am no tongue-hero, no fine virtue-prattler;
I cannot warm by thinking; cannot say
To the good luck that turns her back upon me,
Magnanimously; " Go; I need thee not."
Cease I to work, I am annihilated.
Dangers nor sacrifices will I shun,
If so I may avoid the last extreme;
But ere I sink down into nothingness,
Leave off so little, who began so great,
Ere that the world confuses me with those
Poor wretches, whom a day creates and crumbles,
This age and after ages * speak my name
With hate and dread; and Friedland be redemption
For each accursed deed.

COUNTESS.

         What is there here, then,
So against nature?   Help me to perceive it!
O let not Superstition's nightly goblins
Subdue thy clear bright spirit!   Art thou bid
To murder?—with abhorr'd, accursed poniard,
To violate the breasts that nourish'd thee?
That *were* against our nature, that might aptly
Make thy flesh shudder, and thy whole heart sicken †.
Yet not a few, and for a meaner object,
Have ventured even this, ay, and perform'd it.
What is there in thy case so black and monstrous?
Thou art accused of treason—whether with
Or without justice is not now the question—
Thou art lost if thou dost not avail thee quickly
Of the power which thou possessest—Friedland! *Duke!*
Tell me where lives that thing so meek and tame,
That doth not all his living faculties

---

   * Could I have hazarded such a Germanism, as the use of the word after-world, for posterity,—" Es spreche Welt und *Nachwelt* meinen Namen "—might have been rendered with more literal fidelity :—Let world and after-world speak out my name, etc.

   † I have not ventured to affront the fastidious delicacy of our age with a literal translation of this line,

werth
Die Eingeweide schaudernd aufzuregen.

Put forth in preservation of his life?
What deed so daring, which necessity
And desperation will not sanctify?

WALLENSTEIN.

Once was this Ferdinand so gracious to me;
He loved me; he esteem'd me; I was placed
The nearest to his heart.   Full many a time
We like familiar friends, both at one table,
Have banqueted together.   He and I—
And the young kings themselves held me the bason
Wherewith to wash me—and is't come to this?

COUNTESS.

So faithfully preservest thou each small favour,
And hast no memory for contumelies?
Must I remind thee, how at Regensburg
This man repaid thy faithful services?
All ranks and all conditions in the empire
Thou hadst wronged, to make him great,—hadst loaded on
     thee,
On *thee*, the hate, the curse of the whole world.
No friend existed for thee in all Germany,
And why? because thou hadst existed only
For the Emperor.   To the Emperor alone
Clung Friedland in that storm which gather'd round him
At Regensburg in the Diet—and he dropp'd thee!
He let thee fall! he let thee fall a victim
To the Bavarian, to that insolent!
Deposed, stript bare of all thy dignity
And power, amid the taunting of thy foes,
Thou wert let drop into obscurity.—
Say not, the restoration of thy honour
Has made atonement for that first injustice.
No honest good-will was it that replaced thee;
The law of hard necessity replaced thee,
Which they had fain opposed, but that they could not.

WALLENSTEIN.

Not to their good wishes, that is certain,
Nor yet to his affection I'm indebted
For this high office; and if I abuse it,
I shall therein abuse no confidence

COUNTESS.

Affection! confidence!—they *needed* thee.
Necessity, impetuous remonstrant!
Who not with empty names, or shows of proxy,
Is served, who'll have the thing and not the symbol,
Ever seeks out the greatest and the best,
And at the rudder places *him*, e'en though
She had been forced to take him from the rabble—
She, this Necessity, it was that placed thee
In this high office; it was she that gave thee
Thy letters patent of inauguration.
For, to the uttermost moment that they can,
This race still help themselves at cheapest rate
With slavish souls, with puppets!   At the approach
Of extreme peril, when a hollow image
Is found a hollow image and no more,
Then falls the power into the mighty hands
Of Nature, of the spirit giant-born,
Who listens only to himself, knows nothing
Of stipulations, duties. reverences,
And, like the emancipated force of fire,
Unmaster'd scorches. ere it reaches them,
Their fine-spun webs, their artificial policy.

WALLENSTEIN.

'Tis true! they saw me always as I am—
Always! I did not cheat them in the bargain.
I never held it worth my pains to hide
The bold all-grasping habit of my soul.

COUNTESS

Nay rather—thou hast ever shown thyself
A formidable man, without restraint:
Hast exercised the full prerogatives
Of thy impetuous nature, which had been
Once granted to thee.   Therefore, Duke, not *thou*
Who hast still remained consistent with thyself,
But *they* are in the wrong, who fearing thee,
Entrusted such a power in hand they fear'd.
For, by the laws of Spirit, in the right
Is every individual character
That acts in strict consistence with itself.

Self contradiction is the only wrong.
Wert thou another being, then, when thou
Eight years ago pursuedst thy march with fire,
And sword, and desolation, through the Circles
Of Germany, the universal scourge,
Didst mock all ordinances of the empire,
The fearful rights of strength alone exertedst,
Trampledst to earth each rank, each magistracy,
All to extend thy Sultan's domination ?
Then was the time to break thee in, to curb
Thy haughty will, to teach thee ordinance.
But no, the Emperor felt no touch of conscience ;
What served him pleased him, and without a murmur
He stamp'd his broad seal on these lawless deeds.
What at that time was right, because thou didst it
For him, to day is all at once become
Opprobrious, foul, because it is directed
Against him.—O most flimsy superstition !

WALLENSTEIN (*rising*).

I never saw it in this light before,
'Tis even so. The Emperor perpetrated
Deeds through my arm, deeds most unorderly.
And even this prince's mantle, which I wear,
I owe to what were services to him,
But most high misdemeanors 'gainst the empire.

COUNTESS.

Then betwixt thee and him (confess it Friedland !)
The point can be no more of right and duty,
Only of power and the opportunity.
That opportunity, lo ! it comes yonder
Approaching with swift steeds ; then with a swing
Throw thyself up into the chariot-seat,
Seize with firm hand the reins, ere thy opponent
Anticipate thee, and himself make conquest
Of the now empty seat. The moment comes ;
It is already here, when thou must write
The absolute total of thy life's vast sum.
The constellations stand victorious o'er thee,
The planets shoot good fortune in fair junctions,
And tell thee, " Now's the time !" The starry courses

Hast thou thy life-long measured to no purpose?
The quadrant and the circle, were they playthings?
                    [*Pointing to the different objects in the room*
The zodiacs, the rolling orbs of heaven,
Hast pictured on these walls, and all around thee
In dumb, foreboding symbols hast thou placed
These seven presiding Lords of Destiny —
For toys? Is all this preparation nothing?
Is there no marrow in this hollow art,
That even to thyself it doth avail
Nothing, and has no influence over thee
In the great moment of decision?——
    WALLENSTEIN (*during this last speech walks up and down
      with inward struggles, labouring with passion; stops sud-
      denly, stands still, then interrupting the Countess*).
Send Wrangel to me—I will instantly
Despatch three couriers——
           ILLO (*hurrying out*).
               God in heaven be praised!
           WALLENSTEIN.
It is *his* evil genius and *mine*.
Our evil genius! It chastises *him*
Through me, the instrument of his ambition;
And I expect no less, than that Revenge
E'en now is whetting for *my* breast the poniard.
Who sows the serpent's teeth, let him not hope
To reap a joyous harvest. Every crime
Has, in the moment of its perpetration,
Its own avenging angel—dark misgiving,
An ominous sinking at the inmost heart.
He can no longer trust me—Then no longer
Can I retreat—so come that which must come.—
Still destiny preserves its due relations,
The heart within us is its absolute
Vicegerent.   [*To* TERZKY.
    Go, conduct you Gustave Wrangel
To my state-cabinet.—Myself will speak to
The couriers.—And despatch immediately
A servant for Octavio Piccolomini.
    [*To the* COUNTESS, *who cannot conceal her triumph.*
No exultation! woman, triumph not!

                           N

For jealous are the Powers of Destiny
Joy premature, and shouts ere victory,
Encroach upon their rights and privileges.
We sow the seed, and they the growth determine.
[*While he is making his exit the curtain drops.*

ACT II.

SCENE I.

Scene, as in the preceding Act.

WALLENSTEIN, OCTAVIO PICCOLOMINI.

WALLENSTEIN (*coming forward in conversation*).
He sends me word from Linz, that he lies sick;
But I have sure intelligence, that he
Secretes himself at Frauenberg with Gallas.
Secure them both, and send them to me hither
Remember, thou takest on thee the command
Of those same Spanish regiments,—constantly
Make preparation, and be never ready;
And if they urge thee to draw out against me,
Still answer YES, and stand as thou wert fetter'd
I know, that it is doing thee a service
To keep thee out of action in this business.
Thou lovest to linger on in fair appearances;
Steps of extremity are not thy province,
Therefore have I sought out this part for thee.
Thou wilt this time be of most service to me
By thy inertness.   The mean time, if fortune
Declare itself on my side, thou wilt know
What is to do.

Enter MAX. PICCOLOMINI.
Now go, Octavio.
This night must thou be off, take my own horses:
Him here I keep with me—make short farewell—
Trust me, I think, we all shall meet again
In joy and thriving fortunes.

OCTAVIO (*to his son*).
I shall see you
Yet ere I go.

SCENE II.

WALLENSTEIN, MAX. PICCOLOMINI.

MAX. (*advances to him*).

My General!

WALLENSTEIN.

That I am no longer, if
Thou stylest thyself the Emperor's officer

MAX.

Then thou wilt leave the army, General?

WALLENSTEIN.

I have renounced the service of the Emperor

MAX

And thou wilt leave the army?

WALLENSTEIN.

Rather hope I
To bind it nearer still and faster to me.
[*He seats himself.*
Yes, Max., I have delay'd to open it to thee,
Even till the hour of acting 'gins to strike
Youth's fortunate feeling doth seize easily
The absolute right, yea, and a joy it is
To exercise the single apprehension
Where the sums square in proof;
But where it happens, that of two sure evils
One must be taken, where the heart not wholly
Brings itself back from out the strife of duties,
There 'tis a blessing to have no election,
And blank necessity is grace and favour.
—This is now present: do not look behind thee,—
It can no more avail thee. Look thou forwards!
Think not! judge not! prepare thyself to act!
The Court—it hath determined on my ruin,
Therefore I will be beforehand with them.
We'll join the Swedes—right gallant fellows are they,
And our good friends.
[*He stops himself, expecting* PICCOLOMINI's *answer.*

I have ta'en thee by surprise.   Answer me not.
I grant thee time to recollect thyself.
> [*He rises, retires at the back of the stage*   MAX. *re-
> mains for a long time motionless, in a trance of
> excessive anguish.   At his first motion* WALLEN-
> STEIN *returns, and places himself before him.*

MAX.

My General, this day thou makest me
Of age to speak in my own right and person,
For till this day I have been spared the trouble
To find out my own road.   Thee have I follow'd
With most implicit unconditional faith,
Sure of the right path if I follow'd thee.
To-day, for the first time, dost thou refer
Me to myself, and forcest me to make
Election between thee and my own heart.

WALLENSTEIN.

Soft cradled thee thy Fortune till to day;
Thy duties thou couldst exercise in sport,
Indulge all lovely instincts, act for ever
With undivided heart.   It can remain
No longer thus.   Like enemies, the roads
Start from each other.   Duties strive with duties.
Thou must needs choose thy party in the war
Which is now kindling 'twixt thy friend and him
Who is thy Emperor.

MAX.

          War! is that the name?
War is as frightful as heaven's pestilence
Yet it is good, is it heaven's will as that is
Is that a good war, which against the Emperor
Thou wagest with the Emperor's own army?
O God of heaven! what a change is this.
Beseems it me to offer such persuasion
To thee, who like the fix'd star of the pole
Wert all I gazed at on life's trackless ocean?
O! what a rent thou makest in my heart!
The ingrain'd instinct of old reverence,
The holy habit of obediency,
Must I pluck live asunder from thy name?

Nay, do not turn thy countenance upon me—
It always was as a god looking upon me!
Duke Wallenstein, its power has not departed ·
The senses still are in thy bonds, although,
Bleeding, the soul hath freed itself.

WALLENSTEIN.

Max. hear me.

MAX.

O! do it not, I pray thee, do it not!
There is a pure and noble soul within thee,
Knows not of this unblest unlucky doing.
Thy will is chaste, it is thy fancy only
Which hath polluted thee—and innocence,
It will not let itself be driven away
From that world-awing aspect.   Thou wilt **not**,
Thou canst not end in this.   It would **reduce**
All human creatures to disloyalty
Against the nobleness of their own nature.
'Twill justify the vulgar misbelief,
Which holdeth nothing noble in free will,
And trusts itself to impotence alone,
Made powerful only in an unknown power

WALLENSTEIN.

The world will judge me sternly, I expect it
Already have I said to my own self
All thou canst say to me.   Who but avoids
The extreme, can he by going round avoid it?
But here there is no choice.   Yes—I **must use**
Or suffer violence—so stands the case,
There remains nothing possible but that.

MAX.

O that is never possible for thee!
'Tis the last desperate resource of those
Cheap souls, to whom their honour, their good **name**
Is their poor *saving*, their last worthless *keep*,
Which having staked and lost, they stake **themselves**
In the mad rage of gaming   Thou art rich,
And glorious; with an unpolluted heart
Thou canst make conquest of whate'er seems **highest!**
But he, who once hath acted infamy,
Does nothing more in this world

WALLENSTEIN (*grasps his hand*).

Calmly, Max.!

Much that is great and excellent will we
Perform together yet.   And if we only
Stand on the height with dignity, 'tis soon
Forgotten, Max., by what road we ascended.
Believe me, many a crown shines spotless now,
That yet was deeply sullied in the winning.
To the evil spirit doth the earth belong,
Not to the good.   All, that the powers divine
Send from above, are universal blessings:
Their light rejoices us, their air refreshes,
But never yet was man enrich'd by them:
In their eternal realm no *property*
Is to be struggled for—all there is general
The jewel, the all-valued gold we win
From the deceiving Powers, depraved in nature,
That dwell beneath the day and blessed sun-light.
Not without sacrifices are they render'd
Propitious, and there lives no soul on earth
That e'er retired unsullied from their service

MAX.

Whate'er is human, to the human being
Do I allow—and to the vehement
And striving spirit readily I pardon
The excess of action; but to thee, my General!
Above *all* others make I large concession.
For thou must move a world, and be the master—
He kills thee, who condemns thee to inaction
So be it then! maintain thee in thy post
By violence.   Resist the Emperor,
And if it must be, force with force repel:
I will not praise it, yet I can forgive it.
But not—not to the *traitor*—yes!—the word
Is spoken out——
Not to the traitor can I yield a pardon.
That is no mere excess! that is no error
Of human nature—that is wholly different,
O that is black, black as the pit of hell!

[WALLENSTEIN *betrays a sudden agitation*.
Thou canst not hear it *named*, and wilt thou *do* it?

O turn back to thy duty.   That thou canst,
I hold it certain.   Send me to Vienna :
I'll make thy peace for thee with the Emperor.
He knows thee not.   But I do know thee.   He
Shall see thee, Duke ! with my unclouded eye,
And I bring back his confidence to thee.

WALLENSTEIN.

It is too late !   Thou knowest not what has happen'd.

MAX.

Were it too late, and were things gone so far,
That a crime only could prevent thy fall,
Then—fall ! fall honourably, even as thou stood'st,
Lose the command.   Go from the stage of war
Thou canst with splendour do it—do it too
With innocence.   Thou hast lived much for others,
At length live thou for thy own self.   I follow thee.
My destiny I never part from thine

WALLENSTEIN.

It is too late !   Even now, while thou art losing
Thy words, one after the other are the mile-stones
Left fast behind by my post couriers,
Who bear the order on to Prague and Egra.
  [MAX. *stands as convulsed, with a gesture and counte-*
    nance expressing the most intense anguish.
Yield thyself to it.   We act as we are forced.
I cannot give assent to my own shame
And ruin.   *Thou*—no—thou canst not forsake me !
So let us do, what must be done, with dignity,
With a firm step.   What am I doing worse
Than did famed Cæsar at the Rubicon,
When he the legions led against his country,
The which his country had delivered to him ?
Had he thrown down the sword, he had been lost,
As I were, if I but disarm'd myself.
I trace out something in me of this spirit ;
Give me his luck, *that other thing* I'll bear.
  [MAX. *quits him abruptly.* WALLENSTEIN *startled and*
    overpowered, continues looking after him, and is still in
    this posture when TERZKY *enters.*

SCENE III.

WALLENSTEIN, TERZKY

TERZKY.

Max. Piccolomini just left you?

WALLENSTEIN.

Where is Wrangel?

TERZKY.

He is already gone.

WALLENSTEIN.

In such a hurry?

TERZKY.

It is as if the earth had swallow'd him.
He had scarce left thee, when I went to seek him.
I wish'd some words with him—but he was gone.
How, when, and where, could no one tell me.   Nay,
I half believe it was the devil himself;
A human creature could not so at once
Have vanish'd.

ILLO (enters).

Is it true that thou wilt send
Octavio?

TERZKY.

How, Octavio!   Whither send him?

WALLENSTEIN.

He goes to Frauenburg, and will lead hither
The Spanish and Italian regiments.

ILLO.

No!

Nay, Heaven forbid!

WALLENSTEIN.

And why should Heaven forbid?

ILLO.

Him!—that deceiver!   Wouldst thou trust to him
The soldiery?   Him wilt thou let slip from thee,
Now in the very instant that decides us——

TERZKY.

Thou wilt not do this!—No! I pray thee, no!

WALLENSTEIN.

Ye are whimsical.

ILLO.

O but for this time, Duke,
Yield to our warning !   Let him not depart

WALLENSTEIN.

And why should 1 not trust him only this time,
Who have always trusted him ?   What, then, has happen'd
That I should lose my good opinion of him ?
In complaisance to your whims, not my own,
I must, forsooth, give up a rooted judgment.
Think not I am a woman Having trusted him
E'en till to-day, to-day too will I trust him.

TERZKY.

Must it be he—he only ?   Send another.

WALLENSTEIN.

t must be he, whom I myself have chosen ;
He is well fitted for the business.   Therefore
I gave it him.

ILLO

Because he's an Italian—
Therefore is he well fitted for the business !

WALLENSTEIN

I know you love them not—nor sire nor son—
Because that I esteem them, love them—visibly
Esteem them, love them more than you and others,
E'en as they merit.   Therefore are they eye-blights,
Thorns in your foot-path.   But your jealousies,
In what affect they me or my concerns ?
Are they the worse to *me* because you hate them ?
Love or hate one another as you will,
I leave to each man his own moods and likings ;
Yet know the worth of each of you *to* me.

ILLO.

Von Questenberg, while he was here, was always
Lurking about with this Octavio.

WALLENSTEIN.

It happen'd with my knowledge and permission.

ILLO.

I know that secret messengers came to him
From Gallas——

WALLENSTEIN.
That's not true.
ILLO.
O thou art blind,
With thy deep-seeing eyes!
WALLENSTEIN
Thou wilt not shake
My faith for me—my faith, which founds itself
On the profoundest science.   If 'tis false,
Then the whole science of the stars is false ;
For know, I have a pledge from Fate itself,
That he is the most faithful of my friends.
ILLO.
Hast thou a pledge, that this pledge is not false?
WALLENSTEIN.
There exist moments in the life of man,
When he is nearer the great Soul of the world
Than is man's custom, and possesses freely
The power of questioning his destiny :
And such a moment 'twas, when in the night
Before the action in the plains of Lützen,
Leaning against a tree, thoughts crowding thoughts
I look'd out far upon the ominous plain.
My whole life, past and future, in this moment
Before my mind's eye glided in procession,
And to the destiny of the next morning
The spirit, fill'd with anxious presentiment,
Did knit the most removed futurity.
Then said I also to myself, " So many
Dost thou command.   They follow all thy stars
And as on some great number set their All
Upon thy single head, and only man
The vessel of thy fortune.   Yet a day
Will come, when Destiny shall once more scatter
All these in many a several direction :
Few be they who will stand out faithful to thee."
I yearn'd to know which one was faithfullest
Of all, this camp included.   Great Destiny,
Give me a sign! And he shall be the man,
Who, on the approaching morning, comes the first
To meet me with a token of his love.

And thinking this, I fell into a slumber.
Then midmost in the battle was I led
In spirit.   Great the pressure and the tumult!
Then was my horse kill'd under me: I sank;
And over me away, all unconcernedly,
Drove horse and rider—and thus trod to pieces
I lay, and panted like a dying man;
Then seized me suddenly a saviour arm;
It was Octavio's—I awoke at once,
'Twas broad day, and *Octavio* stood before me.
" My brother," said he, " do not ride to-day
The dapple, as you're wont; but mount the horse
Which I have chosen for thee.   Do it, brother!
In love to me.   A strong dream warn'd me so."
It was the swiftness of this horse that snatch'd me
From the hot pursuit of Bannier's dragoons.
My cousin rode the dapple on that day,
And never more saw I or horse or rider.

ILLO

That was a chance.

WALLENSTEIN (significantly).

There's no such thing as chance ;
[And what to us seems merest accident
Springs from the deepest source of destiny.]
In brief, 'tis sign'd and seal'd that this Octavio
Is my good angel—and now no word more.

[He is retiring

TERZKY.

This is my comfort—Max. remains our hostage.

ILLO.

And he shall never stir from here alive.

WALLENSTEIN (stops and turns himself round).

Are ye not like the women, who for ever
Only recur to their first word, although
One had been talking reason by the hour !
Know, that the human being's thoughts and deeds
Are not like ocean billows, blindly moved.
The inner world, his microcosmus, is
The deep shaft, out of which they spring eternally.
They grow by certain laws, like the tree's fruit—
No juggling chance can metamorphose them.

Have I the human *kernel* first examined?
Then I know, too, the future will and action.   [*Exeunt.*

SCENE IV.
Chamber in the residence of Piccolomini.
OCTAVIO PICCOLOMINI (*attired for travelling*), AN ADJUTANT.

[OCTAVIO
Is the detachment here?

ADJUTANT
It waits below.

OCTAVIO.
And are the soldiers trusty, Adjutant?
Say, from what regiment hast thou chosen them?

ADJUTANT.
From Tiefenbach's

OCTAVIO.
That regiment is loyal,
Keep them in silence in the inner court,
Unseen by all, and when the signal peals
Then close the doors, keep watch upon the house,
And all ye meet be instantly arrested.   [*Exit Adjutant.*
I hope indeed I shall not need their service,
So certain feel I of my well laid plans ;
But when an empire's safety is at stake
Twere better too much caution than too little.]

SCENE V
A Chamber in PICCOLOMINI'S *Dwelling-House*
OCTAVIO PICCOLOMINI, ISOLANI, *entering*

ISOLANI.
Here am I — Well! who comes yet of the others?

OCTAVIO (*with an air of mystery*).
But, first, a word with you, Count Isolani

ISOLANI (*assuming the same air of mystery*).
Will it explode, ha?—Is the Duke about
To make the attempt?   In me, friend, you may place
Full confidence —Nay, put me to the proof.

OCTAVIO
That may happen.

ISOLANI
Noble brother, I am
Not one of those men who in words are valiant.

And when it comes to action skulk away.
The Duke has acted towards me as a friend
God knows it is so ; and I owe him all——
He may rely on my fidelity.

OCTAVIO.

That will be seen hereafter.

ISOLANI.

       Be on your guard,
All think not as I think ; and there are many
Who still hold with the Court—yes, and they say
That these stolen signatures bind them to nothing.

[OCTAVIO.

Indeed!   Pray name to me the chiefs that think so

ISOLANI.

Plague upon them! all the Germans think so;
Esterhazy, Kaunitz, Deodati, too,
Insist upon obedience to the Court.]

OCTAVIO.

I am rejoiced to hear it.

ISOLANI

     You rejoice!

OCTAVIO.

That the Emperor has yet such gallant servants,
And loving friends.

ISOLANI.

    Nay, jeer not, I entreat you.
They are no such worthless fellows, I assure you.

OCTAVIO.

I am assured already.   God forbid
That I should jest!—In very serious earnest,
I am rejoiced to see an honest cause
So strong.

ISOLANI.

   The Devil '—what !·—why, what means this?
Are you not, then——For what, then, am I here?

OCTAVIO.

That you may make full declaration, whether
You will be call'd the friend or enemy
Of the Emperor.

ISOLANI (with an air of defiance)

    That declaration, friend,

I'll make to him in whom a right is placed
To put that question to me.

OCTAVIO.

Whether, Count,
That right is mine, this paper may instruct you.

ISOLANI (*stammering*).

Why,—why—what! this is the Emperor's hand and seal!

[*Reads*

" Whereas, the officers collectively
Throughout our army will obey the orders
Of the Lieutenant-General Piccolomini.
As from ourselves."——*Hem!*—Yes! so!—Yes! yes!—
I—I give you joy, Lieutenant-General!

OCTAVIO.

And you submit you to the order?

ISOLANI.

I——

But you have taken me so by surprise—
Time for reflection one *must* have——

OCTAVIO.

Two minutes.

ISOLANI.

My God! But then the case is——

OCTAVIO.

Plain and simple
You must declare you, whether you determine
To act a treason 'gainst your Lord and Sovereign,
Or whether you will serve him faithfully.

ISOLANI.

Treason!—My God!—But who talks then of treason?

OCTAVIO.

That is the case. The Prince-duke is a traitor—
Means to lead over to the enemy
The Emperor's army.—Now, Count!—brief and full—
Say, will you break your oath to the Emperor?
Sell yourself to the enemy?—Say, will you?

ISOLANI.

What mean you? I—I break my oath, d'ye say,
To his Imperial Majesty?
Did I say so!—When, when have I said that?

OCTAVIO.

You have not said it yet—not yet. This instant
I wait to hear, Count, whether you *will* say it.

ISOLANI.

Ay! that delights me now, that you yourself
Bear witness for me that I never said so.

OCTAVIO.

And you renounce the Duke then?

ISOLANI.

If he's planning
Treason—why, treason breaks all bonds asunder.

OCTAVIO.

And are determined, too, to fight against him?

ISOLANI.

He has done me service—but if he's a villain,
Perdition seize him!—All scores are rubb'd off.

OCTAVIO.

I am rejoiced that you are so well disposed.
This night, break off in the utmost secrecy
With all the light-arm'd troops—it must appear
As came the order from the Duke himself.
At Frauenburg's the place of rendezvous;
There will Count Gallas give you further orders.

ISOLANI.

It shall be done.—But you'll remember me
With the Emperor—how well-disposed you found me.

OCTAVIO.

I will not fail to mention it honourably.
        [*Exit* ISOLANI.   *A Servant enters*
What, Colonel Butler!—Show him up.

ISOLANI (*returning*).

Forgive me too my bearish ways, old father!
Lord God! how should I know, then, what a great
Person I had before me.

OCTAVIO.

No excuses!

ISOLANI.

I am a merry lad, and if at time
A rash word might escape me 'gainst the Court
Amidst my wine—You know no harm was meant   [*Exit*

OCTAVIO.

You need not be uneasy on that score
That has succeeded.   Fortune favour us
With all the others only but as much!

SCENE VI.

OCTAVIO PICCOLOMINI, BUTLER

BUTLER.

At your command Lieutenant-general

OCTAVIO.

Welcome, as honour'd friend and visitor

BUTLER.

You do me too much honour.

OCTAVIO (*after both have seated themselves*
You have not
Return'd the advances which I made you yesterday—
Misunderstood them as mere empty forms.
That wish proceeded from my heart—I was
In earnest with you—for 'tis now a time
In which the honest should unite most closely.

BUTLER.

'Tis only the like-minded can unite.

OCTAVIO

True! and I name all honest men like-minded.
I never charge a man but with those acts
To which his character deliberately
Impels him; for alas! the violence
Of blind misunderstandings often thrusts
The very best of us from the right track.
You came through Frauenburg.   Did the Count Gallas
Say nothing to you?   Tell me.   He's my friend

BUTLER.

His words were lost on *me*.

OCTAVIO

It grieves me sorely,
To hear it: for his counsel was most wise.
I had myself the like to offer.

BUTLER

Spare
Yourself the trouble—me th' embarrassment,
To have deserved so ill your good opinion.

OCTAVIO.

The time is precious—let us talk openly.
You know how matters stand here.   Wallenstein
Meditates treason—I can tell you further,
He has committed treason; but few hours
Have past, since he a covenant concluded
With the enemy.   The messengers are now
Full on their way to Egra and to Prague.
To-morrow he intends to lead us over
To the enemy.   But he deceives himself:
For Prudence wakes—The Emperor has still
Many and faithful friends here, and they stand
In closest union, mighty though unseen.
This manifesto sentences the Duke—
Recalls the obedience of the army from him,
And summons all the loyal, all the honest,
To join and recognise in me their leader.
Choose—will you share with us an honest cause?
Or with the evil share an evil lot?

BUTLER (*rises*).

His lot is mine.

OCTAVIO.

Is that your last resolve?

BUTLER.

It is.

OCTAVIO.

Nay, but bethink you, Colonel Butler!
As yet you have time.   Within my faithful breast
That rashly utter'd word remains interr'd.
Recall it, Butler! choose a better party:
You have not chosen the right one.

BUTLER (*going*).

Any other
Commands for me, Lieutenant-General?

OCTAVIO.

See your white hairs: recall that word!

BUTLER.

Farewell!

OCTAVIO.

What! Would you draw this good and gallant sword
In such a cause?   Into a curse would you

o

Transform the gratitude which you have earn'd
By forty years' fidelity from Austria?

BUTLER (*laughing with bitterness*).

Gratitude from the House of Austria!   [*He is going.*

OCTAVIO (*permits him to go as far as the door, then calls after him*).

Butler!

BUTLER.

What wish you?

OCTAVIO.

How was't with the Count?

BUTLER

Count? what?

OCTAVIO (*coldly*).

The title that you wish'd, I mean.

BUTLER (*starts in sudden passion*).

Hell and damnation!

OCTAVIO (*coldly*).

You petition'd for it—
And your petition was repelled—Was it so?

BUTLER.

Your insolent scoff shall not go by unpunish'd.
Draw!

OCTAVIO.

Nay! your sword to 'ts sheath! and tell me calmly,
How all that happen'd.   I will not refuse you
Your satisfaction afterwards   Calmly, Butler!

BUTLER.

Be the whole world acquainted with the weakness
For which I never can forgive myself.
Lieutenant-General!   Yes; I have ambition.
Ne'er was I able to endure contempt.
It stung me to the quick, that birth and title
Should have more weight than merit has in the army
I would fain not be meaner than my equal,
So in an evil hour I let myself
Be tempted to that measure.   It was folly!
But yet so hard a penance it deserved not.
It might have been refused; but wherefore barb
And venom the refusal with contempt?

Why dash to earth and crush with heaviest scorn
The grey-hair'd man, the faithful veteran?
Why to the baseness of his parentage
Refer him with such cruel roughness, only
Because he had a weak hour and forgot himself?
But nature gives a sting e'en to the worm
Which wanton Power treads on in sport and insult.

OCTAVIO.

You must have been calumniated.   Guess you
The enemy who did you this ill service?

BUTLER.

Be't who it will—a most low-hearted scoundrel!
Some vile court-minion must it be, some Spaniard,
Some young squire of some ancient family,
In whose light I may stand; some envious knave,
Stung to his soul by my fair self-earn'd honours!

OCTAVIO.

But tell me, did the Duke approve that measure?

BUTLER.

Himself impell'd me to it, used his interest
In my behalf with all the warmth of friendship.

OCTAVIO.

Ay? are you sure of that?

BUTLER.
                         I read the letter.

OCTAVIO.

And so did I—but the contents were different.
                         [BUTLER *is suddenly struck.*
By chance I'm in possession of that letter—
Can leave it to your own eyes to convince you.
                         [*He gives him the letter*

BUTLER.

Ha! what is this?

OCTAVIO.
                    I fear me, Colonel Butler,
An infamous game have they been playing with you
The Duke, you say, impell'd you to this measure?
Now, in this letter, talks he in contempt
Concerning you; counsels the minister

o 2

To give sound chastisement to your conceit,
For so he calls it.

> [BUTLER *reads through the letter; his knees tremble,*
> *he seizes a chair, and sinks down in it.*

You have no enemy, no persecutor;
There's no one wishes ill to you.   Ascribe
The insult you received to the Duke only.
His aim is clear and palpable.   He wish'd
To tear you from your Emperor: he hoped
To gain from your revenge what he well knew
(What your long-tried fidelity convinced him)
He ne'er could dare expect from your calm reason
A blind tool would he make you, in contempt
Use you, as means of most abandoned ends.
He has gained his point.   Too well has he succeeded
In luring you away from that good path
On which you had been journeying forty years!

> BUTLER (*his voice trembling*).

Can e'er the Emperor's Majesty forgive me?

> OCTAVIO.

More than forgive you.   He would fain compensate
For that affront, and most unmerited grievance
Sustain'd by a deserving gallant veteran.
From his free impulse he confirms the present,
Which the Duke made you for a wicked purpose.
The regiment, which you now command, is yours.

> [BUTLER *attempts to rise, sinks down again.   He labours*
> *inwardly with violent emotions; tries to speak, and can-*
> *not.   At length he takes his sword from the belt, and*
> *offers it to* PICCOLOMINI.

> OCTAVIO.

What wish you?   Recollect yourself, friend.

> BUTLER.

> > Take it.

> OCTAVIO.

But to what purpose?   Calm yourself.

> BUTLER.

> > O take it!

I am no longer worthy of this sword.

> OCTAVIO.

Receive it then anew, from my hands—and

Wear it with honour for the right cause ever

BUTLER.

——Perjure myself to such a gracious Sovereign!

OCTAVIO.

You'll make amends.   Quick! break off from the Duke!

BUTLER.

Break off from him!

OCTAVIO.

What now? Bethink thyself.

BUTLER (*no longer governing his emotion*).

Only break off from him?   He dies! he dies!

OCTAVIO.

Come after me to Frauenburg, where now
All who are loyal, are assembling under
Counts Altringer and Gallas.   Many others
I've brought to a remembrance of their duty:
This night be sure that you escape from Pilsen.

BUTLER (*strides up and down in excessive agitation, then steps
up to* OCTAVIO *with resolved countenance*).

Count Piccolomini! dare that man speak
Of honour to you, who once broke his troth

OCTAVIO.

He, who repents so deeply of it, dares.

BUTLER.

Then leave me here upon my word of honour!

OCTAVIO.

What's your design?

BUTLER.

Leave me and my regiment.

OCTAVIO.

I have full confidence in you.   But tell me
What are you brooding?

BUTLER.

That the deed will tell you

Ask me no more at present.   Trust to me.
Ye may trust safely.   By the living God
Ye give him over, not to his good angel!
Farewell.   [*Exit* BUTLER

SERVANT (*enters with a billet*).

A stranger left it, and is gone.
The Prince-Duke's horses wait for you below.

[*Exit* Servant

OCTAVIO (*reads*).

" Be sure make haste! Your faithful Isolan."
—O that I had but left this town behind me.
To split upon a rock so near the haven!—
Away! This is no longer a safe place
For me! Where can my son be tarrying!

SCENE VII.

OCTAVIO *and* MAX. PICCOLOMINI.

MAX *enters almost in a state of derangement, from extreme
agitation; his eyes roll wildly, his walk is unsteady, and
he appears not to observe his father, who stands at a distance, and gazes at him with a countenance expressive of
compassion. He paces with long strides through the
chamber, then stands still again, and at last throws himself into a chair, staring vacantly at the object directly
before him*

OCTAVIO (*advances to him*).

I am going off, my son.

[*Receiving no answer, he takes his hand*
My son, farewell.

MAX.

Farewell.

OCTAVIO.

Thou wilt soon follow me?

MAX.

I follow thee?

Thy way is crooked—it is not my way.

[OCTAVIO *drops his hand, and starts back.*
O, hadst thou been but simple and sincere,
Ne'er had it come to this—all had stood otherwise.
He had not done that foul and horrible deed,
The virtuous had retain'd their influence o'er him:
He had not fallen into the snares of villains.
Wherefore so like a thief, and thief's accomplice
Didst creep behind him, lurking for thy prey!
O, unblest falsehood! Mother of all evil!
Thou misery-making demon, it is thou
That sink'st us in perdition. Simple truth,
Sustainer of the world, had saved us all!

Father, I will not. I can not excuse thee!
Wallenstein has deceived me—O, most foully!
But thou hast acted not much better.

OCTAVIO.

Son!

My son, ah! I forgive thy agony!

MAX. (*rises and contemplates his father with looks of suspicion*).
Was't possible? hadst thou the heart, my father,
Hadst thou the heart to drive it to such lengths,
With cold premeditated purpose? Thou—
Hadst thou the heart to wish to see him guilty
Rather than saved? Thou risest by his fall.
Octavio, 'twill not please me.

OCTAVIO.

God in heaven!

MAX.

O, woe is me! sure I have changed my nature
How comes suspicion here—in the free soul?
Hope, confidence, belief, are gone; for all
Lied to me, all that I e'er loved or honoured.
No, no! not all! She—she yet lives for me
And she is true, and open as the heavens!
Deceit is everywhere, hypocrisy,
Murder, and poisoning, treason, perjury:
The single holy spot is our love,
The only unprofaned in human nature.

OCTAVIO.

Max.!—we will go together. 'Twill be better.

MAX.

What? ere I've taken a last parting leave,
The very last—no, never!

OCTAVIO.

Spare thyself

The pang of necessary separation.
Come with me! Come, my son!

[*Attempts to take him with him.*

MAX.

No! as sure as God lives, no!

OCTAVIO (*more urgently*).

Come with me, I command thee! I, thy father

MAX.

Command me what is human.   I stay here

OCTAVIO

Max.! in the Emperor's name I bid thee come

MAX.

No Emperor has power to prescribe
Laws to the heart; and wouldst thou wish to rob me
Of the sole blessing which my fate has left me,
Her sympathy? Must then a cruel deed
Be done with cruelty?   The unalterable
Shall I perform ignobly—steal away,
With stealthy coward flight forsake her? No!
She shall behold my suffering, my sore anguish,
Hear the complaints of the disparted soul,
And weep tears o'er me.   Oh! the human race
Have steely souls—but she is as an angel.
From the black deadly madness of despair
Will she redeem my soul, and in soft words
Of comfort, plaining, loose this pang of death!

OCTAVIO.

Thou wilt not tear thyself away; thou canst not.
O, come, my son! I bid thee save thy virtue.

MAX.

Squander not thou thy words in vain.
The heart I follow, for I dare trust to it.

OCTAVIO (*trembling, and losing all self-command*).
Max.! Max.! if that most damned thing could be,
If thou—my son—my own blood—(dare I *think* it?
Do sell thyself to him, the infamous,
Do stamp this brand upon our noble house,
Then shall the world behold the horrible deed
And in unnatural combat shall the steel
Of the son trickle with the father's blood

MAX.

O hadst thou always better thought of men,
Thou hadst then acted better.   Curst suspicion
Unholy miserable doubt!   To him
Nothing on earth remains unwrench'd and firm,
Who has no faith

OCTAVIO.

And if I trust thy heart,
Will it be always in thy power to follow it?

MAX.

The heart's voice *thou* hast not o'erpowered— as little
Will Wallenstein be able to o'erpower it.

OCTAVIO.

O, Max.! I see thee never more again!

MAX.

Unworthy of thee wilt thou never see me.

OCTAVIO.

I go to Frauenberg—the Pappenheimers
I leave thee here, the Lothrings too ; Tsokana
And Tiefenbach remain here to protect thee.
They love thee, and are faithful to their oath,
And will far rather fall in gallant contest
Than leave their rightful leader, and their honour.

MAX.

Rely on this, I either leave my life
In the struggle, or conduct them out of Pilsen

OCTAVIO.

Farewell, my son!

MAX.

Farewell!

OCTAVIO.

How! not one look
Of filial love? No grasp of the hand at parting?
It is a bloody war to which we are going,
And the event uncertain and in darkness.
So used we not to part—it was not so!
Is it then true? I have a son no longer?

[MAX. *falls into his arms, they hold each other for a long
time in a speechless embrace, then go away at different
sides.*

(*The Curtain drops.*)

ACT III.

Scene I.

A Chamber in the House of the Duchess of Friedland.

COUNTESS TERZKY, THEKLA, LADY NEUBRUNN (*the two latter
sit at the same table at work*).

COUNTESS (*watching them from the opposite side*).

So you have nothing to ask me—nothing?
I have been waiting for a word from you.
And could you then endure in all this time
Not once to speak his name?

[THEKLA *remaining silent, the* COUNTESS *rises and advances to her.*

Why, how comes this!
Perhaps I am already grown superfluous,
And other ways exist, besides through me?
Confess it to me, Thekla: have you seen him?

THEKLA.

To-day and yesterday I have not seen him.

COUNTESS.

And not heard from him, either?   Come, be open.

THEKLA.

No syllable.

COUNTESS.

And still you are so calm?

THEKLA.

I am

COUNTESS.

May't please you, leave us, Lady Neubrunn.

[*Exit* LADY NEUBRUNN.

Scene II.

The COUNTESS, THEKLA.

COUNTESS.

It does not please me, Princess, that he holds
Himself so *still*, exactly at *this* time.

THEKLA.

Exactly at *this* time?

COUNTESS.

          He now knows **all**:
'Twere now the moment to declare himself.

THEKLA.

If I'm to understand you, speak less darkly.

COUNTESS.

'Twas for that purpose that I bade her leave us.
Thekla, you are no more a child. Your heart
Is now no more in nonage : for you love,
And boldness dwells with love—that *you* have proved
Your nature moulds itself upon your father's
More than your mother's spirit. Therefore may you
Hear, what were too much for her fortitude.

THEKLA.

Enough : no further preface, I entreat you.
At once, out with it ! Be it what it may,
It is not possible that it should torture me
More than this introduction. What have you
To say to me ? Tell me the whole, and briefly !

COUNTESS.

You'll not be frighten'd——

THEKLA.

          Name it, I entreat you.

COUNTESS.

It lies within your power to do your father
A weighty service——

THEKLA.

        Lies within *my* power ?

COUNTESS.

Max. Piccolomini loves you. You can link him
Indissolubly to your father.

THEKLA.

          I ?
What need of me for that ? And is he not
Already link'd to him ?

COUNTESS.

        He was.

THEKLA

          And wherefore
Should he not be so now—not be so always ?

COUNTESS
He cleaves to the Emperor too.

THEKLA.

Not more than duty
And honour may demand of him.

COUNTESS.

We ask
Proofs of his love, and not proofs of his honour.
Duty and honour!
Those are ambiguous words with many meanings
You should interpret them for him : his love
Should be the sole definer of his honour.

THEKLA.

How?

COUNTESS.

The Emperor or you must he renounce.

THEKLA.

He will accompany my father gladly
In his retirement.   From himself you heard,
How much he wish'd to lay aside the sword.

COUNTESS.

He must *not* lay the sword aside, we mean;
He must unsheath it in your father's cause.

THEKLA.

He'll spend with gladness and alacrity
His life, his heart's blood in my father's cause,
If shame or injury be intended him.

COUNTESS.

You will not understand me.   Well, hear then :—
Your father has fallen off from the Emperor,
And is about to join the enemy
With the whole soldiery· ——

THEKLA.

Alas, my mother !

COUNTESS.

There needs a great example to draw on
The army after him.   The Piccolomini
Possess the love and reverence of the troops ;
They govern all opinions, and wherever

They lead the way, none hesitate to follow.
The son secures the father to our interests—
You've much in your hands at this moment.

THEKLA.

My miserable mother! what a death-stroke
Awaits thee!—No! she never will survive it.

COUNTESS.

She will accommodate her soul to that
Which is and must be. I do know your mother:
The far-off future weighs upon her heart
With torture of anxiety; but is it
Unalterably, actually present,
She soon resigns herself, and bears it calmly.

THEKLA.

O my foreboding bosom! Even now,
E'en now 'tis here, that icy hand of horror!
And my young hope lies shuddering in its grasp;
I knew it well—no sooner had I enter'd,
An heavy ominous presentiment
Reveal'd to me that spirits of death were hovering
Over my happy fortune. But why think I
First of myself? My mother! O my mother!

COUNTESS

Calm yourself! Break not out in vain lamenting!
Preserve you for your father the firm friend,
And for yourself the lover, all will yet
Prove good and fortunate.

THEKLA.

Prove good! What good?
Must we not part?—part ne'er to meet again?

COUNTESS.

He parts not from you! He cannot part from you.

THEKLA.

Alas for his sore anguish! It will rend
His heart asunder.

COUNTESS.

If indeed he loves you,
His resolution will be speedily taken

THEKLA.

His resolution will be speedily taken—
O do not doubt of that!   A resolution!
Does there remain one to be taken?

COUNTESS.

Hush!
Collect yourself!   I hear your mother coming.

THEKLA.

How shall I bear to see her?

COUNTESS.

Collect yourself.

SCENE III.

To them enter the DUCHESS.

DUCHESS (*to the* COUNTESS).

Who was here, sister?   I heard some one talking,
And passionately too.

COUNTESS.

Nay! there was no one.

DUCHESS.

I am grown so timorous, every trifling noise
Scatters my spirits, and announces to me
The footstep of some messenger of evil.
And you can tell me, sister, what the event is?
Will he agree to do the Emperor's pleasure,
And send the horse-regiments to the Cardinal?
Tell me, has he dismiss'd Von Questenberg
With a favourable answer?

COUNTESS.

No, he has not.

DUCHESS.

Alas! then all is lost! I see it coming.
The worst that can come! Yes, they will depose him;
The accursed business of the Regensburg diet
Will all be acted o'er again!

COUNTESS.

No! never!
Make your heart easy, sister, as to that.

[THEKLA, *in extreme agitation, throws herself upon her
mother, and enfolds her in her arms, weeping*

DUCHESS.

Yes, my poor child !
Thou too hast lost a most affectionate godmother
In the Empress.   O that stern unbending man!
In this unhappy marriage what have I
Not suffer'd, not endured ?   For even as if
I had been link'd on to some wheel of fire
That restless, ceaseless, whirls impetuous onward,
I have pass'd a life of frights and horrors with him,
And ever to the brink of some abyss
With dizzy headlong violence he bears me.
Nay, do not weep, my child.   Let not my sufferings
Presignify unhappiness to thee,
Nor blacken with their shade the fate that waits thee.
There lives no second Friedland : thou, my child,
Hast not to fear thy mother's destiny.

THEKLA.

O let us supplicate him, dearest mother !
Quick! quick! here's no abiding place for us.
Here every coming hour broods into life
Some new affrightful monster

DUCHESS.

                  Thou wilt share
An easier, calmer lot, my child !   We too,
I and thy father, witnessed happy days.
Still think I with delight of those first years,
When he was making progress with glad effort,
When his ambition was a genial fire,
Not that consuming flame which now it is.
The Emperor loved him, trusted him : and all
He undertook could not but be successful.
But since that ill-starr'd day at Regensburg,
Which plunged him headlong from his dignity,
A gloomy uncompanionable spirit,
Unsteady and suspicious, has possess'd him.
His quiet mind forsook him, and no longer
Did he yield up himself in joy and faith
To his old luck, and individual power ;
But thenceforth turn'd his heart and best affections
All to those cloudy sciences, which never
Have yet made happy him who follow'd them

COUNTESS

You see it, sister! as your eyes permit you
But surely this is not the conversation
To pass the time in which we are waiting for him.
You know he will be soon here.   Would you have him
Find *her* in this condition?

DUCHESS

Come, my child!
Come wipe away thy tears, and show thy father
A cheerful countenance.   See, the tie-knot here
Is off—this hair must not hang so dishevell'd.
Come, dearest! dry thy tears up.   They deform
Thy gentle eye.—Well now—what was I saying?
Yes, in good truth, this Piccolomini -
Is a most noble and deserving gentleman.

COUNTESS.

That is he, sister!

THEKLA (*to the* COUNTESS, *with marks of great oppression of*
spirits).

Aunt, you will excuse me? (*Is going*).

COUNTESS.

But whither?   See, your father comes

THEKLA

I cannot see him now

COUNTESS.

Nay, but bethink you.

THEKLA.

Believe me, I cannot sustain his presence

COUNTESS.

But he will miss you, will ask after you.

DUCHESS.

What now?   Why is she going?

COUNTESS.

She's not well.

DUCHESS (*anxiously*).

What ails then my beloved child?

[*Both follow the* PRINCESS, *and endeavour to detain*
her.   During this WALLENSTEIN *appears, engaged*
in conversation with ILLO.

SCENE IV.

WALLENSTEIN, ILLO, COUNTESS, DUCHESS, THEKLA.

WALLENSTEIN.

All quiet in the camp?

ILLO.
It is all quiet.

WALLENSTEIN.

In a few hours may couriers come from Prague
With tidings, that this capital is ours.
Then we may drop the mask, and to the troops
Assembled in this town make known the measure
And its result together.   In such cases
Example does the whole.   Whoever is foremost
Still leads the herd.   An imitative creature
Is man.   The troops at Prague conceive no other,
Than that the Pilsen army has gone through
The forms of homage to us; and in Pilsen
They shall swear fealty to us, because
The example has been given them by Prague.
Butler, you tell me, has declared himself?

ILLO.
At his own bidding, unsolicited,
He came to offer you himself and regiment.

WALLENSTEIN.

I find we must not give implicit credence
To every warning voice that makes itself
Be listen'd to in the heart.   To hold us back,
Oft does the lying Spirit counterfeit
The voice of Truth and inward Revelation,
Scattering false oracles.   And thus have I
To intreat forgiveness, for that secretly
I've wrong'd this honourable gallant man,
This Butler: for a feeling, of the which
I am not master (*fear* I would not call it),
Creeps o'er me instantly, with sense of shuddering,
At his approach, and stops love's joyous motion.
And this same man, against whom I am warn'd,
This honest man is he, who reaches to me
The first pledge of my fortune.

P

ILLO.
                              And doubt not
That his example will win over to you
The best men in the army.

WALLENSTEIN.
                              Go and send
Isolani hither.   Send him immediately
He is under recent obligations to me:
With him will I commence the trial.   Go.   [*Exit* ILLO

WALLENSTEIN (*turns himself round to the females*).
Lo, there the mother with the darling daughter
For once we'll have an interval of rest—
Come! my heart yearns to live a cloudless hour
In the beloved circle of my family.

COUNTESS.
'Tis long since we've been thus together, brother.

WALLENSTEIN (*to the* COUNTESS *aside*).
Can she sustain the news?   Is she prepared?

COUNTESS.
Not yet.

WALLENSTEIN.
                  Come here, my sweet girl!   Seat thee by me
For there is a good spirit on thy lips.
Thy mother praised to me thy ready skill;
She says a voice of melody dwells in thee,
Which doth enchant the soul.   Now such a voice
Will drive away from me the evil demon
That beats his black wings close above my head.

DUCHESS.
Where is thy lute, my daughter?   Let thy father
Hear some small trial of thy skill.

THEKLA.
                              My mother!
1--

DUCHESS.
     Trembling?   Come, collect thyself.   Go, cheer
Thy father.

THEKLA.
          O my mother!   I—I cannot.

COUNTESS.
How, what is that, niece?

THEKLA (*to the* COUNTESS).
O spare me—sing—now—in this sore anxiety,
Of the o'erburthen'd soul—to sing to *him*,
Who is thrusting, even now, my mother headlong
Into her grave.

DUCHESS.
How, Thekla!   Humoursome!
What! shall thy father have express'd a wish
In vain?

COUNTESS.
Here is the lute.

THEKLA.
My God! how can I—
[*The orchestra plays.   During the ritornello* THEKLA *expresses
in her gestures and countenance the struggle of her feelings;
and at the moment that she should begin to sing, contracts
herself together, as one shuddering, throws the instrument
down, and retires abruptly.*

DUCHESS.
My child! O she is ill—

WALLENSTEIN.
What ails the maiden?
Say, is she often so?

COUNTESS
Since then herself
Has now betray'd it, I too must no longer
Conceal it.

WALLENSTEIN.
What?

COUNTESS.
She loves him!

WALLENSTEIN
Loves him!   **Whom?**

COUNTESS.
Max. does she love!   Max. Piccolomini.
Hast thou ne'er noticed it?   Nor yet my sister?

DUCHESS.

Was it this that lay so heavy on her heart?
God's blessing on thee, my sweet child!   Thou need'st
Never take shame upon thee for thy choice.

COUNTESS.

This journey, if 'twere not thy aim, ascribe it
To thine own self.   Thou shouldst have chosen another
To have attended her.

WALLENSTEIN

And does he know it?

COUNTESS.

Yes, and he hopes to win her!

WALLENSTEIN.

Hopes to win her!

Is the boy mad?

COUNTESS.

Well—hear it from themselves.

WALLENSTEIN.

He thinks to carry off Duke Friedland's daughter!
Ay?—The thought pleases me.
The young man has no grovelling spirit.

COUNTESS.

Since

Such and such constant favour you have shown him—

WALLENSTEIN.

He chooses finally to be my heir.
And true it is, I love the youth; yea, honour him.
But must he therefore be my daughter's husband?
Is it daughters only?   Is it only children
That we must show our favour by?

DUCHESS.

His noble disposition and his manners—

WALLENSTEIN.

Win him my heart, but not my daughter.

DUCHESS.

Then

His rank, his ancestors—

WALLENSTEIN.

Ancestors!   What?
He is a subject, and my son-in-law
I will seek out upon the thrones of Europe.

DUCHESS.

O dearest Albrecht!   Climb we not too high
Lest we should fall too low.

WALLENSTEIN.

               What! have I paid
A price so heavy to ascend this eminence,
And jut out high above the common herd,
Only to close the mighty part I play
In Life's great drama, with a common kinsman?
Have I for this—

            [*Stops suddenly, repressing himself*
          She is the only thing
That will remain behind of me on earth ;
And I will see a crown around her head,
Or die in the attempt to place it there.
I hazard all—all! and for this alone,
To lift her into greatness—
Yea, in this moment, in the which we are speaking—

              [*He recollects himself.*
And I must now, like a soft-hearted father,
Couple together in good peasant-fashion
The pair, that chance to suit each other's liking—
And I must do it now, even now, when I
Am stretching out the wreath that is to twine
My full accomplish'd work—no! she is the jewel,
Which I have treasured long, my last, my noblest,
And 'tis my purpose not to let her from me
For less than a king's sceptre.

DUCHESS.

             O my husband!
You're ever building, building to the clouds,
Still building higher, and still higher building,
And ne'er reflect, that the poor narrow basis
Cannot sustain the giddy tottering column.

WALLENSTEIN (*to the* COUNTESS).

Have you announced the place of residence
Which I have destined for her?

COUNTESS.

            No! not yet.
'Twere better you yourself disclosed it to her.

DUCHESS.

How?   Do we not return to Carinthia then?

WALLENSTEIN.

No

DUCHESS.

And to no other of your lands or seats?

WALLENSTEIN.

You would not be secure there.

DUCHESS.

Not secure
In the Emperor's realms, beneath the Emperor's
Protection?

WALLENSTEIN.

Friedland's wife may be permitted
No longer to hope *that.*

DUCHESS.

O God in heaven!
And have you brought it even to this!

WALLENSTEIN.

In Holland
You'll find protection.

DUCHESS.

In a Lutheran country?
What?   And you send us into Lutheran countries?

WALLENSTEIN.

Duke Franz of Lauenburg conducts you thither.

DUCHESS.

Duke Franz of Lauenburg?
The ally of Sweden, the Emperor's enemy.

WALLENSTEIN.

The Emperor's enemies are mine no longer.

DUCHESS (*casting a look of terror on the* DUKE *and the*
COUNTESS).

Is it then true?   It is.   You are degraded?
Deposed from the command?   O God in heaven!

COUNTESS (*aside to the* DUKE).

Leave her in this belief.   Thou seest she cannot
Support the real truth.

SCENE V.

To them enter COUNT TERZKY.

COUNTESS.

—Terzky!
What ails him?   What an image of affright!
He looks as he had seen a ghost

TERZKY (*leading* WALLENSTEIN *aside*).

Is it thy command that all the Croats —

WALLENSTEIN.

Mine!

TERZKY

We are betray'd.

WALLENSTEIN.

What?

TERZKY.

They are off!   This night
The Jägers likewise — all the villages
In the whole round are empty.

WALLENSTEIN.

Isolani!

TERZKY.

Him thou hast sent away.   Yes, surely.

WALLENSTEIN.

I?

TERZKY.

No!   Hast thou not sent him off?   Nor Deodati?
They are vanish'd both of them.

SCENE VI

To them enter ILLO.

ILLO.

Has Terzky told thee?

TERZKY.

He knows all.

ILLO

And likewise
That Esterhatzy, Goetz, Maradas, Kaunitz,
Kolalto, Palfi, have forsaken thee.

TERZKY

Damnation!

WALLENSTEIN (*winks at them*).

Hush!

COUNTESS (*who has been watching them anxiously from the
distance and now advances to them*).

Terzky! Heaven! What is it? What has happen'd?

WALLENSTEIN (*scarcely suppressing his emotions*).

Nothing! let us be gone!

TERZKY (*following him*).

Theresa, it is nothing.

COUNTESS (*holding him back*).

Nothing? Do I not see that all the life-blood
Has left your cheeks—look you not like a ghost?
That even my brother but affects a calmness?

PAGE (*enters*).

An Aide-de-Camp inquires for the Count Terzky.

[TERZKY *follows the* PAGE

WALLENSTEIN.

Go, hear his business.

[*To* ILLO.

This could not have happen'd
So unsuspected without mutiny.
Who was on guard at the gates?

ILLO.

'Twas Tiefenbach

WALLENSTEIN.

Let Tiefenbach leave guard without delay,
And Terzky's grenadiers relieve him.

ILLO (*is going*).

Stop!

Hast thou heard aught of Butler?

ILLO.

Him I met:
He will be here himself immediately.
Butler remains unshaken.

[ILLO *exit.* WALLENSTEIN *is following him.*

COUNTESS.

Let him not leave thee, sister! go, detain him!
There's some misfortune.

DUCHESS (*clinging to him*).

Gracious Heaven! What is it?

WALLENSTEIN.

Be tranquil ! leave me, sister ! dearest wife !
We are in camp, and this is nought unusual ;
Here storm and sunshine follow one another
With rapid interchanges.   These fierce spirits
Champ the curb angrily, and never yet
Did quiet bless the temples of the leader
If I am to stay, go you.   The plaints of women
Ill suit the scene where men must act.

[*He is going :* TERZKY *returns*

TERZKY.

Remain here.   From this window must we see it.

WALLENSTEIN (*to the* COUNTESS).

Sister, retire!

COUNTESS.

No—never

WALLENSTEIN.

'Tis my will.

TERZKY (*leads the* COUNTESS *aside, and drawing her attention
to the* DUCHESS).

Theresa !

DUCHESS.

Sister, come ! since he commands it.

SCENE VII.

WALLENSTEIN, TERZKY.

WALLENSTEIN (*stepping to the window*).

What now, then ?

TERZKY.

There are strange movements among all the troops,
And no one knows the cause.   Mysteriously,
With gloomy silentness, the several corps
Marshal themselves, each under its own banners
Tiefenbach's corps make threat'ning movements ; only
The Pappenheimers still remain aloof
In their own quarters, and let no one enter.

WALLENSTEIN.

Does Piccolomini appear among them ?

TERZKY.

We are seeking him : he is nowhere to be met with.

WALLENSTEIN.

What did the Aide-de-Camp deliver to you?

TERZKY.

My regiments had despatch'd him; yet once more
They swear fidelity to thee, and wait
The shout for onset, all prepared, and eager

WALLENSTEIN.

But whence arose this larum in the camp?
It should have been kept secret from the army,
Till fortune had decided for us at Prague.

TERZKY.

O that thou hadst believed me!   Yester evening
Did we conjure thee not to let that skulker,
That fox, Octavio, pass the gates of Pilsen.
Thou gavest him thy own horses to flee from thee

WALLENSTEIN.

The old tune still!   Now, once for all, no more
Of this suspicion—it is doting folly.

TERZKY.

Thou didst confide in Isolani too;
And lo! he was the first that did desert thee

WALLENSTEIN.

It was but yesterday I rescued him
From abject wretchedness.   Let that go by;
I never reckon'd yet on gratitude.
And wherein doth he wrong in going from me?
He follows still the god whom all his life
He has worshipp'd at the gaming-table.   With
My fortune, and my seeming destiny,
He made the bond, and broke it not with me.
I am but the ship in which his hopes were stow'd
And with the which, well-pleased and confident,
He traversed the open sea; now he beholds it
In eminent jeopardy among the coast-rocks,
And hurries to preserve his wares.   As light
As the free bird from the hospitable twig
Where it had nested, he flies off from me:
No human tie is snapp'd betwixt us two
Yea, he deserves to find himself deceived
Who seeks a heart in the unthinking man.

Like shadows on a stream, the forms of life
Impress their characters on the smooth forehead,
Nought sinks into the bosom's silent depth :
Quick sensibility of pain and pleasure
Moves the light fluids lightly; but no soul
Warmeth the inner frame.

TERZKY.

Yet, would I rather
Trust the smooth brow than that deep furrow'd one

SCENE VIII.

WALLENSTEIN, TERZKY, ILLO.

ILLO (*who enters agitated with rage*).
Treason and mutiny !

TERZKY.
And what further now ?

ILLO.
Tiefenbach's soldiers, when I gave the orders,
To go off guard—Mutinous villains !

TERZKY.
Well !

WALLENSTEIN
What followed ?

ILLO.
They refused obedience to them.

TERZKY.
Fire on them instantly !   Give out the order.

WALLENSTEIN.
Gently ! what cause did they assign ?

ILLO.
No other,
They said, had right to issue orders but
Lieutenant-General *Piccolomini*.

WALLENSTEIN (*in a convulsion of agony*).
What?   How is that?

ILLO.
He takes that office on him by commission,
Under sign-manual of the Emperor.

TERZKY.
From the Emperor—hear'st thou, Duke ?

ILLO
                      At his incitement
The Generals made that stealthy flight—

TERZKY
                      Duke! hear'st thou?

ILLO.
Caraffa too, and Montecuculi.
Are missing, with six other Generals,
All whom he had induced to follow him.
This plot he has long had in writing by him
From the Emperor; but 'twas finally concluded,
With all the detail of the operation,
Some days ago with the Envoy Questenberg.
      [WALLENSTEIN *sinks down into a chair, and covers his face.*

TERZKY.
O hadst thou but believed me!

SCENE IX.
To them enter the COUNTESS.

COUNTESS.
                      This suspense,
This horrid fear—I can no longer bear it.
For heaven's sake tell me what has taken place?

ILLO.
The regiments are all falling off from us.

TERZKY.
Octavio Piccolomini is a traitor.

COUNTESS.
O my foreboding!
                      [*Rushes out of the room.*

TERZKY
            Hadst thou but believed me!
Now seest thou how the stars have lied to thee.

WALLENSTEIN
The stars lie not; but we have here a work
Wrought counter to the stars and destiny.
The science is still honest: this false heart
Forces a lie on the truth-telling heaven.
On a divine law divination rests;
Where nature deviates from that law, and stumbles

Out of her limits, there all science errs.
True I did not suspect!   Were it superstition
Never by such suspicion t' have affronted
The human form, O may that time ne'er come
In which I shame me of the infirmity.
The wildest savage drinks not with the victim,
Into whose breast he means to plunge the sword.
This, this, Octavio, was no hero's deed:
'Twas not thy prudence that did conquer mine;
A bad heart triumph'd o'er an honest one.
No shield received the assassin stroke; thou plungest
Thy weapon on an unprotected breast—
Against such weapons I am but a child.

SCENE X.

To these enter BUTLER.

TERZKY (*meeting him*).

O look there! Butler! Here we've still a friend!

WALLENSTEIN (*meets him with outspread arms, and embraces
him with warmth*).

Come to my heart, old comrade!   Not the sun
Looks out upon us more revivingly
In the earliest month of spring,
Than a friend's countenance in such an hour

BUTLER.

My General: I come—

WALLENSTEIN (*leaning on* BUTLER's *shoulder*)
Know'st thou already?
That old man has betray'd me to the Emperor.
What say'st thou? Thirty years have we together
Lived out, and held out, sharing joy and hardship.
We have slept in one camp-bed, drunk from one glass,
One morsel shared!   I lean'd myself on *him*,
As now I lean me on *thy* faithful shoulder.
And now in the very moment, when, all love,
All confidence, my bosom beat to his,
He sees and takes the advantage, stabs the knife
Slowly into my heart.

[*He hides his face on* BUTLER's *breast.*

BUTLER.

Forget the false one.
What is your present purpose?

WALLENSTEIN.

Well remember d!
Courage, my soul!   I am still rich in friends,
Still loved by Destiny ; for in the moment
That it unmasks the plotting hypocrite,
It sends and proves to me one faithful heart.
Of the hypocrite no more!   Think not, his loss
Was that which struck the pang : O no! his treason
Is that which strikes this pang !   No more of him !
Dear to my heart, and honour'd were they both.
And the young man—yes—he did truly love me,
He—he—has not deceived me   But enough,
Enough of this—swift counsel now beseems us.
The Courier, whom Count Kinsky sent from Prague,
I expect him every moment : and whatever
He may bring with him, we must take good care
To keep it from the mutineers.   Quick then !
Despatch some messenger you can rely on
To meet him, and conduct him to me.

[ILLO *is going.*

BUTLER (*detaining him*).
My General, whom expect you then?

WALLENSTEIN.

The Courier
Who brings me word of the event at Prague.

BUTLER (*hesitating*).
Hem!

WALLENSTEIN.

And what now ?

BUTLER.

You do not know it ?

WALLENSTEIN.

Well ?

BUTLER.

From what that larum in the camp arose ?

WALLENSTEIN

From what?

BUTLER.

That Courier——

WALLENSTEIN (*with eager expectation*).

Well?

BUTLER.

Is already here. ·

TERZKY *and* ILLO (*at the same time*).

Already here?

WALLENSTEIN.

My Courier?

BUTLER.

For some hours.

WALLENSTEIN.

And I not know it?

BUTLER.

The sentinels detain him

In custody.

ILLO (*stamping with his foot*).

Damnation!

BUTLER.

And his letter

Was broken open, and is circulated
Through the whole camp.

WALLENSTEIN,

You know what it contains?

BUTLER.

Question me not!

TERZKY.

Illo! alas for us

WALLENSTEIN.

Hide nothing from me—I can hear the worst.
Prague then is lost.   It is.   Confess it freely.

BUTLER.

Yes! Prague is lost.   And all the several regiments
At Budweiss, Tabor, Braunau, Königingratz,
At Brunn and Znaym, have forsaken you,
And ta'en the oaths of fealty anew
To the Emperor.   Yourself, with Kinsky, Terzky,
And Illo have been sentenced.

[TERZKY *and* ILLO *express alarm and fury.* WAL-
LENSTEIN *remains firm and collected.*

WALLENSTEIN.
'Tis decided!
'Tis well!   I have received a sudden cure
From all the pangs of doubt : with steady stream
Once more my life-blood flows !   My soul's secure !
In the night only Friedland's stars can beam.
Lingering irresolute, with fitful fears
I drew the sword—'twas with an inward strife,
While yet the choice was mine.   The murderous knife
Is lifted for my heart !   Doubt disappears !
I fight now for my head and for my life.

        [*Exit* WALLENSTEIN ; *the others follow him.*

SCENE XI.
COUNTESS TERZKY (*enters from a side room*).
I can endure no longer   No !

                [*Looks around her.*
        Where are they !
No one is here.   They leave me all alone,
Alone in this sore anguish of suspense.
And I must wear the outward show of calmness
Before my sister, and shut in within me
The pangs and agonies of my crowded bosom.
It is not to be borne.   If all should fail ;
If—if he must go over to the Swedes,
An empty-handed fugitive, and not
As an ally, a covenanted equal,
A proud commander with his army following ,
If we must wander on from land to land,
Like the Count Palatine, of fallen greatness
An ignominious monument.   But no !
That day I will not see !   And could himself
Endure to sink so low, I would not bear
To see him so low sunken.

SCENE XII.
COUNTESS, DUCHESS, THEKLA.
THEKLA (*endeavouring to hold back the* DUCHESS)
Dear mother, do stay here !
             DUCHESS.
        No !   Here is yet
Some frightful mystery that is hidden from me.

Why does my sister shun me?   Don't I see her
Full of suspense and anguish roam about
From room to room?   Art thou not full of terror?
And what import these silent nods and gestures
Which stealthwise thou exchangest with her?

THEKLA.

Nothing:

Nothing, dear mother!

DUCHESS (*to the* COUNTESS).

Sister, I will know.

COUNTESS.

What boots it now to hide it from her?   Sooner
Or later she *must* learn to hear and bear it.
'Tis not the time now to indulge infirmity;
Courage beseems us now, a heart collect,
And exercise and previous discipline
Of fortitude.   One word, and over with it!
Sister, you are deluded.   You believe
The Duke has been deposed—the Duke is not
Deposed—he is——

THEKLA (*going to the* COUNTESS).

What? do you wish to kill her?

COUNTESS.

The Duke is——

THEKLA (*throwing her arms round her mother*).

O stand firm! stand firm, my mother!

COUNTESS.

Revolted is the Duke; he is preparing
To join the enemy; the army leave him,
And all has fail'd.

SCENE XIII.

A spacious Room in the Duke of Friedland's Palace.

WALLENSTEIN (*in armour*).

Thou hast gain'd thy point, Octavio!   Once more am I
Almost as friendless as at Regensburg.
There I had nothing left me, but myself;
But what one man can do, you have now experience.
The twigs have you hew'd off, and here I stand
A leafless trunk.   But in the sap within

Q

Lives the creating power, and a new world
May sprout forth from it.   Once already have I
Proved myself worth an army to you—I alone!
Before the Swedish strength your troops had melted;
Beside the Lech sank Tilly your last hope;
Into Bavaria, like a winter torrent,
Did that Gustavus pour, and at Vienna
In his own palace did the Emperor tremble
Soldiers were scarce, for still the multitude
Follow the luck : all eyes were turn'd on me,
Their helper in distress : the Emperor's pride
Bow'd itself down before the man he had injured.
'Twas I must rise, and with creative word
Assemble forces in the desolate camps.
I did it.   Like a god of war, my name
Went through the world.   The drum was beat ; and, lo ;
The plough, the workshop is forsaken, all
Swarm to the old familiar long-loved banners ;
And as the wood-choir rich in melody
Assemble quick around the bird of wonder,
When first his throat swells with his magic song,
So did the warlike youth of Germany
Crowd in around the image of my eagle
I feel myself the being that I was.
It is the soul that builds itself a body,
And Friedland's camp will not remain unfill'd
Lead then your thousands out to meet me—true !
They are accustom'd under me to conquer,
But not against me.   If the head and limbs
Separate from each other, 'twill be soon
Made manifest, in which the soul abode
                    (ILLO *and* TERZKY *enter.*)
Courage, friends ! courage ! we are still unvanquish'd
I feel my footing firm ; five regiments, Terzky,
Are still our own, and Butler's gallant troops ;
And an host of sixteen thousand Swedes to-morrow.
I was not stronger when, nine years ago,
I marched forth, with glad heart and high of hope,
To conquer Germany for the Emperor.

SCENE XIV.

WALLENSTEIN, ILLO, TERZKY
(To them enter NEUMANN, *who leads* TERZKY *aside, and talks
with him.)*

TERZKY.

What do they want?

WALLENSTEIN.
What now?

TERZKY.

Ten Cuirassiers
From Pappenheim request leave to address you
In the name of the regiment.

WALLENSTEIN *(hastily to* NEUMANN).
Let them enter.
[*Exit* NEUMANN
This
May end in something.   Mark you.   They are still
Doubtful, and may be won

SCENE XV

WALLENSTEIN, TERZKY, ILLO, *ten* Cuirassiers *(led by an* AN-
SPESSADE **, march up and arrange themselves, after the
word of command, in one front before the Duke, and make
their obeisance.   He takes his hat off, and immediately
covers himsif again).*

ANSPESSADE.

Halt! Front! Present!

WALLENSTEIN *(after he has run through them with his eye, to
the* ANSPESSADE).
I know thee well.   Thou art out of Brüggen in Flanders:
Thy name is Mercy

ANSPESSADE.
Henry Mercy

WALLENSTEIN.

Thou wert cut off on the march, surrounded by the Hes-
sians, and didst fight thy way with an hundred and eighty
men through their thousand.

* Anspessade, in German Gefreiter, a soldier inferior to a corporal, but
above the sentinels.   The German name implies that he is exempt from
mounting guard.

ANSPESSADE
'Twas even so, General!

WALLENSTEIN.
What reward hadst thou for this gallant exploit?

ANSPESSADE.
That which I asked for: the honour to serve in this corps

WALLENSTEIN (*turning to a second*).
Thou wert among the volunteers that seized and made booty of the Swedish battery at Altenburg.

SECOND CUIRASSIER.
Yes, General!

WALLENSTEIN.
I forget no one with whom I have exchanged words. (*A pause.*) Who sends you?

ANSPESSADE.
Your noble regiment, the Cuirassiers of Piccolomini.

WALLENSTEIN.
Why does not your colonel deliver in your request, according to the custom of service?

ANSPESSADE.
Because we would first know *whom* we serve.

WALLENSTEIN.
Begin your address.

ANSPESSADE (*giving the word of command*)
Shoulder your arms!

WALLENSTEIN (*turning to a third*).
Thy name is Risbeck; Cologne is thy birth-place.

THIRD CUIRASSIER.
Risbeck of Cologne.

WALLENSTEIN.
It was thou that broughtest in the Swedish colonel, Dübald, prisoner, in the camp at Nüremberg.

THIRD CUIRASSIER.
It was not I, General.

WALLENSTEIN
Perfectly right! It was thy elder brother: thou hadst a younger brother too: Where did he stay?

THIRD CUIRASSIER.
He is stationed at Olmütz, with the Imperial army.

WALLENSTEIN (*to the* ANSPESSADE).
Now then—begin.

ANSPESSADE.
There came to hand a letter from the Emperor
Commanding us—

WALLENSTEIN (*interrupting him*).
Who chose you?

ANSPESSADE.
Every company
Drew its own man by lot.

WALLENSTEIN.
Now! to the business.

ANSPESSADE
There came to hand a letter from the Emperor
Commanding us collectively, from thee
All duties of obedience to withdraw,
Because thou wert an enemy and traitor

WALLENSTEIN.
And what did you determine?

ANSPESSADE.
All our comrades
At Braunau, Budweiss, Prague and Olmütz, have
Obey'd already; and the regiments here,
Tiefenbach and Toscano, instantly
Did follow their example.   But—but we
Do not believe that thou art an enemy
And traitor to thy country, hold it merely
For lie and trick, and a trumped up Spanish story!
[*With warmth.*

Thyself shalt tell us what thy purpose is,
For we have found thee still sincere and true :
No mouth shall interpose itself betwixt
The gallant General and the gallant troops.

WALLENSTEIN.
Therein I recognise my Pappenheimers.

ANSPESSADE.
And this proposal makes thy regiment to thee ·
Is it thy purpose merely to preserve
In thine own hands this military sceptre,
Which so becomes thee, which the Emperor
Made over to thee by a covenant!

Is it thy purpose merely to remain
Supreme commander of the Austrian armies?—
We will stand by thee, General! and guarantee
Thy honest rights against all opposition.
And should it chance, that all the other regiments
Turn from thee, by ourselves will we stand forth
Thy faithful soldiers, and, as is our duty,
Far rather let ourselves be cut to pieces,
Than suffer thee to fall.   But if it be
As the Emperor's letter says, if it be true,
That thou in traitorous wise wilt lead us over
To the enemy, which God in heaven forbid!
Then we too will forsake thee, and obey
That letter—

WALLENSTEIN.

Hear me, children!

ANSPESSADE.

Yes, or no!

There needs no other answer

WALLENSTEIN

Yield attention.

You're men of sense, examine for yourselves;
Ye think, and do not follow with the herd:
And therefore have I always shown you honour
Above all others, suffer'd you to reason;
Have treated you as free men, and my orders
Were but the echoes of your prior suffrage.—

ANSPESSADE.

Most fair and noble has thy conduct been
To us, my General! With thy confidence
Thou hast honour'd us, and shown us grace and favo
Beyond all other regiments; and thou seest
We follow not the common herd.   We will
Stand by thee faithfully.   Speak but one word—
Thy word shall satisfy us, that it is not
A treason which thou meditatest—that
Thou meanest not to lead the army over
To the enemy; nor e'er betray thy country.

WALLENSTEIN.

Me, me are they betraying.   The Emperor
Hath sacrificed me to my enemies,

And I must fall, unless my gallant troops
Will rescue me.   See! I confide in you.
And be your hearts my stronghold! At this **breast**
The aim is taken, at this hoary head.
This is your Spanish gratitude, this is our
Requital for that murderous fight at Lutzen!
For this we threw the naked breast against
The halbert, made for this the frozen earth
Our bed, and the hard stone our pillow! never stream
Too rapid for us, nor wood too impervious;
With cheerful spirit we pursued that Mansfeldt
Through all the turns and windings of his flight:
Yea, our whole life was but one restless march:
And homeless, as the stirring wind, we travell'd
O'er the war-wasted earth.   And now, even now,
That we have well nigh finish'd the hard toil,
The unthankful, the curse-laden toil of weapons,
With faithful indefatigable arm
Have roll'd the heavy war-load up the hill,
Behold! this boy of the Emperor's bears away
The honours of the peace, an easy prize!
He'll weave, forsooth, into his flaxen locks
The olive branch, the hard-earn'd ornament
Of this grey head, grown grey beneath the helmet.
                    ANSPESSADE.
That shall he not, while we can hinder it!
No one, but thou, who hast conducted it
With fame, shall end this war, this frightful war
Thou leddest us out to the bloody field
Of death; thou and no other shalt conduct us home,
Rejoicing, to the lovely plains of peace—
Shalt share with us the fruits of the long toil—
                    WALLENSTEIN.
What! Think you then at length in late old age
To enjoy the fruits of toil? Believe it not.
Never, no never, will you see the end
Of the contest! you and me, and all of us,
This war will swallow up! War, war, not peace.
Is Austria's wish; and therefore, because I
Endeavour'd after peace, therefore I fall
For what cares Austria, how long the war

Wears out the armies and lays waste the world!
She will but wax and grow amid the ruin
And still win new domains
    [*The* Cuirassiers *express agitation by their gestures*
                Ye're moved—I see
A noble rage flash from your eyes, ye warriors!
Oh that my spirit might possess you now
Daring as once it led you to the battle!
Ye would stand by me with your veteran arms,
Protect me in my rights; and this is noble!
But think not that *you* can accomplish it,
Your scanty number! to no purpose will you
Have sacrificed you for your General.   [*Confidentially.*
No! let us tread securely, seek for friends;
The Swedes have proffer'd us assistance, let us
Wear for a while the appearance of good will,
And use them for your profit, till we both
Carry the fate of Europe in our hands,
And from our camp to the glad jubilant world
Lead Peace forth with the garland on her head!

ANSPESSADE.

'Tis then but mere appearances which thou
Dost put on with the Swede! Thou'lt not betray
The Emperor? Wilt not turn us into Swedes?
This is the only thing which we desire
To learn from thee.

WALLENSTEIN.

               What care I for the Swedes?
I hate them as I hate the pit of hell,
And under Providence I trust right soon
To chase them to their homes across their Baltic.
My cares are only for the whole: I have
A heart—it bleeds within me for the miseries
And piteous groaning of my fellow Germans.
Ye are but common men, but yet ye think
With minds not common; ye appear to me
Worthy before all others, that I whisper ye
A little word or two in confidence!
See now! already for full fifteen years,
The war-torch has continued burning, yet
No rest, no pause of conflict. Swede and German,

Papist and Lutheran! neither will give way
To the other, every hand's against the other.
Each one is party and no one a judge.
Where shall this end?   Where's he that will unravel
This tangle, ever tangling more and more
It must be cut asunder.
I feel that I am the man of destiny,
And trust, with your assistance, to accomplish it.

SCENE XVI.

To these enter BUTLER.

BUTLER (passionately)
General!   This is not right!

WALLENSTEIN.
What is not right?

BUTLER.
It must needs injure us with all honest men

WALLENSTEIN.
But what?

BUTLER.
It is an open proclamation
Of insurrection.

WALLENSTEIN.
Well, well—but what is it?

BUTLER.
Count Terzky's regiments tear the Imperial Eagle
From off the banners, and instead of it
Have rear'd aloft their arms.

ANSPESSADE (abruptly to the Cuirassiers).
Right about! March!

WALLENSTEIN.
Cursed be this counsel, and accursed who gave it!
[To the Cuirassiers, who are retiring
Halt, children, halt! There's some mistake in this;
Hark!—I will punish it severely.   Stop!
They do not hear. (To ILLO). Go after them, assure them,
And bring them back to me, cost what it may.
[ILLO hurries out
This hurls us headlong.   Butler! Butler!
You are my evil genius, wherefore must you
Announce it in their presence?   It was all

In a fair way. They were half won! those madmen
With their improvident over-readiness—
A cruel game is Fortune playing with me.
The zeal of friends it is that razes me,
And not the hate of enemies.

SCENE XVII.

To these enter the DUCHESS, *who rushes into the Chamber*
THEKLA and the COUNTESS *follow her*

DUCHESS.
                    O Albrecht!
What hast thou done ?

WALLENSTEIN.
                    And now comes this beside,

COUNTESS.
Forgive me, brother!   It was not in my power—
They know all.

DUCHESS.
What hast thou done ?

COUNTESS (*to* TERZKY)
Is there no hope ?   Is all lost utterly ?

TERZKY.
All lost. No hope. Prague in the Emperor's hands,
The soldiery have ta'en their oaths anew

COUNTESS.
That lurking hypocrite, Octavio !
Count Max. is off too.

TERZKY.
                    Where can he be ?   He's
Gone over to the Emperor with his father.
    [THEKLA *rushes out into the arms of her mother, hiding*
    her face in her bosom.

DUCHESS (*enfolding her in her arms*)
Unhappy child! and more unhappy mother !

WALLENSTEIN (*aside to* TERZKY).
Quick ! Let a carriage stand in readiness
In the court behind the palace.   Scherfenberg
Be their attendant ; he is faithful to us ·

To Egra he'll conduct them, and we follow.

[To ILLO, who returns.

Thou hast not brought them back ?

ILLO.

Hear'st thou the uproar ?
The whole corps of the Pappenheimers is
Drawn out : the younger Piccolomini,
Their colonel, they require : for they affirm,
That he is in the palace here, a prisoner ;
And if thou dost not instantly deliver him,
They will find means to free him with the sword.

[All stand amazed

TERZKY.

What shall we make of this ?

WALLENSTEIN.

Said I not so ?
O my prophetic heart ! he is still here.
He has not betray'd me—he could not betray me.
I never doubted of it.

COUNTESS.

If he be
Still here, then all goes well ; for I know what

[Embracing THEKLA.

Will keep him here for ever.

TERZKY

It can't be.
His father has betray'd us, is gone over
To the Emperor—the son could not have ventured
To stay behind.

THEKLA (*her eye fixed on the door*).
There he is !

SCENE XVIII.

To these enter MAX PICCOLOMINI

MAX.

Yes ! here he is !   I can endure no longer
To creep on tiptoe round this house, and lurk
In ambush for a favourable moment :
This loitering, this suspense exceeds my powers

[Advancing to THEKLA, *who has thrown herself into her
mother's arms*

Turn not thine eyes away.   O look upon me !
Confess it freely before all.   Fear no one.
Let who will hear that we both love each other
Wherefore continue to conceal it?   Secrecy
Is for the happy—misery, hopeless misery,
Needeth no veil!   Beneath a thousand suns
It dares act openly.

> [*He observes the* COUNTESS *looking on* THEKLA *with
> expressions of triumph*

                         No, Lady !   No !
Expect not, hope it not.   I am not come
To stay : to bid farewell, farewell for ever.
For this I come !   'Tis over !   I must leave thee !
Thekla, I must—*must* leave thee !   Yet thy hatred
Let me not take with me.   I pray thee, grant me
One look of sympathy, only one look.
Say that thou dost not hate me.   Say it to me Thekla !
> [*Grasps her hand*
O God !   I cannot leave this spot—I cannot !
Cannot let go this hand.   O tell me, Thekla !
That thou dost suffer with me, art convinced
That I can not act otherwise.

> [THEKLA, *avoiding his look, points with her hand to
> her father.* MAX. *turns round to the Duke, whom he
> had not till then perceived.*

Thou here?   It was not thou, whom here I sought.
I trusted never more to have beheld thee
My business is with her alone.   Here will I
Receive a full acquittal from this heart—
For any other I am no more concern'd.

                    WALLENSTEIN
Think'st thou that, fool-like, I shall let thee go,
And act the mock-magnanimous with thee ?
Thy father is become a villain to me ;
I held thee for his son, and nothing more :
Nor to no purpose shalt thou have been given
Into my power.   Think not, that I will honour
That ancient love, which so remorselessly
He mangled.   They are now past by, those hours
Of friendship and forgiveness   Hate and vengeance

Succeed—'tis now their turn—I too can throw
All feelings of the man aside—can prove
Myself as much a monster as thy father!

MAX. (calmly).

Thou wilt proceed with me, as thou hast power.
Thou know'st, I neither brave nor fear thy rage.
What has detain'd me here, that too thou know'st.

[Taking THEKLA by the hand

See, Duke! All—all would I have owed to thee,
Would have received from thy paternal hand
The lot of blessed spirits. This hast thou
Laid waste for ever—that concerns not thee.
Indifferent thou tramplest in the dust
Their happiness, who most are thine. The god
Whom thou dost serve, is no benignant deity.
Like as the blind irreconcileable
Fierce element, incapable of compact,
Thy heart's wild impulse only dost thou follow *.

---

* I have here ventured to omit a considerable number of lines. I fear
that I should not have done amiss, had I taken this liberty more frequently
It is, however, incumbent on me to give the original, with a literal translation.

Weh denen, die auf Dich vertraun, an Dich
Die sichre Hütte ihres Glückes lehnen,
Gelockt von deiner geistlichen Gestalt.
Schnell unverhofft, bei nächtlich stiller Weile
Gährts in dem tückschen Feuerschlunde, ladet
Sich aus mit tobender Gewalt, und weg
Treibt über alle Pflanzungen der Menschen
Der wilde Strom in grausender Zerstörung.

WALLENSTEIN.

Du schilderst deines Vaters Herz. Wie Du's
Beschreibst, so ist's in seinem Eingeweide,
In dieser schwarzen Heuchlers Brust gestaltet.
O, mich hat Höllenkunst getäuscht! Mir sandte
Der Abgrund den verflecktesten der Geister,
Den Lügenkundigsten herauf, und stellt' ihn
Als Freund an meiner Seite. Wer vermag
Der Hölle Macht zu widerstehn! Ich zog
Den Basilisken auf an meinem Busen,
Mit meinem Herzblut nährt ich ihn, er sog
Sich schwelgend voll an meiner Liebe Brüsten,
Ich hatte nimmer Arges gegen ihn,
Weit offen liess ich des Gedankens Thore,

WALLENSTEIN.

Thou art describing thy own father's heart.
The adder!   O, the charms of hell o'erpowered me
He dwelt within me, to my inmost soul
Still to and fro he pass'd, suspected never
On the wide ocean, in the starry heaven
Did mine eyes seek the enemy, whom I
In my heart's heart had folded!   Had I been
To *Ferdinand* what Octavio was to *me*,
War had I ne'er denounced against him   No,
I never could have done it.   The Emperor was
My austere master only, not my friend
There was already war 'twixt him and me
When he deliver'd the Commander's Staff
Into my hands; for there's a natural
Unceasing war 'twixt cunning and suspicion;
Peace exists only betwixt confidence
And faith.   Who poisons confidence, he murders
The future generations

MAX.
I will not
Defend my father.   Woe is me, I cannot!
Hard deeds and luckless have ta'en place; one crime
Drags after it the other in close link.
But we are innocent: how have we fallen

Und warf die Schlüssel weiser Vorsicht weg,
Am Sternenhimmel, etc.

LITERAL TRANSLATION.

Alas! for those who place their confidence on thee, against thee lean the secure hut of their fortune, allured by thy hospitable form.   Suddenly, unexpectedly, in a moment still as night, there is a fermentation in the treacherous gulf of fire; it discharges itself with raging force, and away over all the plantations of men drives the wild stream in frightful devastation.—WALLENSTEIN.   Thou art portraying thy father's heart; as thou describest, even so is it shaped in his entrails, in this black hypocrite's breast. O, the art of hell has deceived me!   The Abyss sent up to me the most spotted of the spirits, the most skilful in lies, and placed him as a friend by my side.   Who may withstand the power of hell?   I took the basilisk to my bosom, with my heart's blood I nourished him; he sucked himself glutfull at the breasts of my love.   I never harboured evil towards him; wide open did I leave the door of my thoughts; I threw away the key of wise foresight.   In the starry heaven, &c.—We find a difficulty in believing this to have been written by SCHILLER.

Into this circle of mishap and guilt?
To whom have we been faithless?　Wherefore must
The evil deeds and guilt reciprocal
Of our two fathers twine like serpents round us?
　　　　　　　Why must our fathers'
Unconquerable hate rend us asunder,
Who love each other?

WALLENSTEIN.

　　　　　Max., remain with me.
Go you not from me, Max.!　Hark!　I will tell thee—
How when at Prague, our winter quarters, thou
Wert brought into my tent a tender boy,
Not yet accustom'd to the German winters;
Thy hand was frozen to the heavy colours
Thou wouldst not let them go.—
At that time did I take thee in my arms,
And with my mantle did I cover thee;
I was thy nurse, no woman could have been
A kinder to thee; I was not ashamed
To do for thee all little offices,
However strange to me; I tended thee
Till life return'd; and when thine eyes first open'd,
I had thee in my arms　Since then, when have
Alter'd my feelings towards thee?　Many thousands
Have I made rich, presented them with lands;
Rewarded them with dignities and honours;
Thee have I *loved* : my heart, my self, I gave
To thee!　They all were aliens : THOU wert
Our child and inmate*.　Max.!　Thou canst not leave me;
It cannot be; I may not, will not think
That Max. can leave me.

MAX.

　　　O my God!

WALLENSTEIN.

　　　　　　　　I have

---

* This is a poor and inadequate translation of the affectionate simplicity
of the original—
　　　　　Sie alle waren Fremdlinge, *Du* warst
　　　　　Das Kind des Hauses.

Indeed the whole speech is in the best style of Massinger.　O si sic
omnia!

Held and sustain'd thee from thy tottering childhood
What holy bond is there of natural love,
What human tie, that does not knit thee to me?
I love thee, Max.! What did thy father for thee,
Which I too have not done, to the height of duty?
Go hence, forsake me, serve thy Emperor;
He will reward thee with a pretty chain
Of gold; with his ram's fleece will he reward thee;
For that the friend, the father of thy youth,
For that the holiest feeling of humanity,
Was nothing worth to thee.

MAX.

      O God! how can I
Do otherwise? Am I not forced to do it,
My oath—my duty—my honour—

WALLENSTEIN

      How? Thy duty?
Duty to whom? Who art thou? Max.! bethink thee
What duties mayst *thou* have? If *I* am acting
A criminal part toward the Emperor,
It is my crime, not thine. Dost thou belong
To thine own self? Art thou thine own commander?
Stand'st thou, like me, a freeman in the world,
That in thy actions thou shouldst plead free agency?
On me thou'rt planted, I am thy Emperor;
To obey *me*, to *belong* to me, this is
Thy honour, this a law of nature to thee!
And if the planet, on the which thou livest
And hast thy dwelling, from its orbit starts
It is not in thy choice, whether or no
Thou'lt follow it. Unfelt it whirls thee onward
Together with his ring, and all his moons.
With little guilt stepp'st thou into this contest;
Thee will the world not censure, it will praise thee,
For that thou held'st thy friend more worth to thee
Than names and influences more removed
For justice is the virtue of the ruler,
Affection and fidelity the subject's.
Not every one doth it beseem to question
The far-off high Arcturus. Most securely

Wilt thou pursue the nearest duty : let
The pilot fix his eye upon the pole-star.

SCENE XIX

To these enter NEUMANN

WALLENSTEIN

What now?

NEUMANN.

The Pappenheimers are dismounted,
And are advancing now on foot, determined
With sword in hand to storm the house, and free
The Count, their colonel.

WALLENSTEIN (*to* TERZKY).

Have the cannon planted.
I will receive them with chain-shot.

[*Exit* TERZKY.

Prescribe to me with sword in hand!   Go, Neumann ,
'Tis my command that they retreat this moment,
And in their ranks in silence wait my pleasure.

[NEUMANN *exit*.   ILLO *steps to the window*

COUNTESS

Let him go, I entreat thee, let him go

ILLO (*at the window*)

Hell and perdition !

WALLENSTEIN.

What is it?

ILLO.

They scale the council-house, the roof's uncovered,
They level at this house the cannon—

MAX.

Madmen !

ILLO.

They are making preparations now to fire on us.

DUCHESS *and* COUNTESS.

Merciful heaven !

MAX. (*to* WALLENSTEIN)

Let me go to them !

WALLENSTEIN.

Not a step !

R

MAX. (*pointing to* THEKLA *and the* DUCHESS).
But their life! Thine!

WALLENSTEIN.
What tidings bring'st thou, Terzky?

SCENE XX.

To these TERZKY *returning*

TERZKY.
Message and greeting from our faithful regiments.
Their ardour may no longer be curb'd in.
They entreat permission to commence the attack;
And if thou wouldst but give the word of onset,
They could now charge the enemy in rear,
Into the city wedge them, and with ease
O'erpower them in the narrow streets.

ILLO.
                              O come!
Let not their ardour cool.   The soldiery
Of Butler's corps stand by us faithfully;
We are the greater number.   Let us charge them,
And finish here in Pilsen the revolt.

WALLENSTEIN
What? shall this town become a field of slaughter,
And brother-killing Discord, fire-eyed,
Be let loose through its streets to roam and rage?
Shall the decision be deliver'd over
To deaf remorseless Rage, that hears no leader?
Here is not room for battle, only for butchery.
Well, let it be!   I have long thought of it,
So let it burst then!

                              [*Turns to* MAX
            Well, how is it with thee?
Wilt thou attempt a heat with me.   Away!
Thou art free to go   Oppose thyself to me,
Front against front, and lead them to the battle;
Thou'rt skill'd in war, thou hast learn'd somewhat under me,
I need not be ashamed of my opponent,
And never hadst thou fairer opportunity
To pay me for thy schooling.

COUNTESS
Is it then,
Can it have come to this?—What! Cousin, cousin!
Have you the heart?

MAX.
The regiments that are trusted to my care
I have pledged my troth to bring away from Pilsen
True to the Emperor; and this promise will I
Make good, or perish. More than this no duty
Requires of me. I will not fight against thee,
Unless compell'd; for though an enemy,
Thy head is holy to me still.

   [*Two reports of cannon.* ILLO *and* TERZKY *hurry to the window*

WALLENSTEIN.
What's that?

TERZKY
He falls.

WALLENSTEIN.
Falls! Who?

ILLO.
Tiefenbach's corps
Discharged the ordnance.

WALLENSTEIN.
Upon whom?

ILLO.
On Neumann
Your messenger.

WALLENSTEIN (*starting up*).
Ha! Death and hell! I will—

TERZKY
Expose thyself to their blind frenzy?

DUCHESS *and* COUNTESS.
No!
For God's sake, no!

ILLO.
Not yet, my General!
O hold him! hold him!

WALLENSTEIN.
Leave me —

R 2

MAX.
                              Do it not;
Not yet! This rash and bloody deed has thrown them
Into a frenzy-fit—allow them time——

WALLENSTEIN.
Away! too long already have I loiter'd.
They are emboldened to these outrages,
Beholding not my face.   They shall behold
My countenance, shall hear my voice——
Are they not *my* troops?   Am I not their General,
And their long-fear'd commander!   Let me see,
Whether indeed they do no longer know
That countenance, which was their sun in battle!
From the balcony (mark!) I show myself
To these rebellious forces, and at once
Revolt is mounded, and the high-swoln current
Shrinks back into the old bed of obedience.
                [*Exit* WALLENSTEIN; ILLO, TERZKY, *and* BUTLER
                follow.

SCENE XXI.

COUNTESS, DUCHESS, MAX. and THEKLA.,

                COUNTESS (*to the* DUCHESS).
Let them but see him—there is hope still, sister.
                              DUCHESS.
Hope! I have none!

MAX (*who during the last scene has been standing at a dis-
        tance, in a visible struggle of feelings, advances*).
                              This can I not endure.
With most determined soul did I come hither;
My purposed action seem'd unblamable
To my own conscience—and I must stand here
Like one abhorr'd, a hard inhuman being:
Yea, loaded with the curse of all I love!
Must see all whom I love in this sore anguish,
Whom I with one word can make happy—O!
My heart revolts within me, and two voices
Make themselves audible within my bosom.
My soul's benighted; I no longer can
Distinguish the right track.   O, well and truly

Didst thou say, father, I relied too much
On my own heart.　My mind moves to and fro—
I know not what to do.

COUNTESS.

　　　　　　　What! you know not?
Does not your own heart tell you?　O! then I
Will tell it you.　Your father is a traitor,
A frightful traitor to us—he has plotted
Against our General's life, has plunged us all
In misery—and you're his son!　'Tis yours
To make the *amends*—Make you the son's fidelity
Outweigh the father's treason, that the name
Of Piccolomini be not a proverb
Of infamy, a common form of cursing
To the posterity of Wallenstein.

MAX.

Where is that voice of truth which I dare follow!
It speaks no longer in *my* heart.　We all
But utter what our passionate wishes dictate:
O that an angel would descend from heaven,
And scoop for me the right, the uncorrupted,
With a pure hand from the pure Fount of Light.

　　　　　　　　[*His eyes glance on* THEKLA.

What other angel seek I?　To this heart,
To this unerring heart, will I submit it;
Will ask thy love, which has the power to bless
The happy man alone, averted ever
From the disquieted and guilty—*canst* thou
Still love me, if I stay?　Say that thou canst,
And I am the Duke's——

COUNTESS.

　　　　　Think, niece——

MAX.

　　　　　　　　Think, nothing, Thekla!
Speak what thou *feelest*.

COUNTESS.

　　　　　Think upon your father

MAX

I did not question thee, as Friedland's daughter.
Thee, the beloved and the unerring god
Within thy heart, I question.　What's at stake?

Not whether diadem of royalty
Be to be won or not—that mightst thou *think* on.
Thy friend, and his soul's quiet, are at stake :
The fortune of a thousand gallant men,
Who will all follow me ; shall I forswear
My oath and duty to the Emperor ?
Say, shall I send into Octavio s camp
The parricidal ball?   For when the ball
Has left its cannon, and is on its flight,
It is no longer a dead instrument!
It lives, a spirit passes into it.
The avenging furies seize possession of it,
And with sure malice guide it the worst way.

THEKLA.

O! Max.——

MAX. (*interrupting her*).
        Nay, not precipitately either, Thekla.
I understand thee.   To thy noble heart
The hardest duty might appear the highest.
The human, not the great part, would I act
Even from my childhood to this present hour.
Think what the Duke has done for me, how loved me
And think, too, how my father has repaid him.
O likewise the free lovely impulses
Of hospitality, the pious friend's
Faithful attachment, these, too, are a holy
Religion to the heart ; and heavily
The shudderings of nature do avenge
Themselves on the barbarian that insults them
Lay all upon the balance, all—then speak.
And let thy heart decide it.

THEKLA
        O, thy own
Hath long ago decided.   Follow thou
Thy heart's first feeling——

COUNTESS.
        Oh ! ill-fated woman !

THEKLA.
Is it possible, that that can be the right,
The which thy tender heart did not at first
Detect and seize with instant impulse?   Go,

Fulfil thy duty !   I should ever love thee
Whate'er thou hadst chosen, thou wouldst still have acted
Nobly and worthy of thee—but repentance
Shall ne'er disturb thy soul's fair peace.

MAX.

Then I
Must leave thee, must part from thee !

THEKLA.

Being faithful
To thine own self, thou art faithful, too, to me ·
If our fates part, our hearts remain united.
A bloody hatred will divide for ever
The houses Piccolomini and Friedland ;
But we belong not to our houses.   Go !
Quick ! quick ! and separate thy righteous cause
From our unholy and unblessed one !
The curse of Heaven lies upon our head :
'Tis dedicate to ruin.   Even me
My father's guilt drags with it to perdition.
Mourn not for me :
My destiny will quickly be decided.

> [MAX. *clasps her in his arms in extreme emotion.   There
> is heard from behind the Scene a loud, wild, long con
> tinued cry,* Vivat Ferdinandus ! *accompanied by war-
> like instruments.*   MAX. *and* THEKLA *remain without
> motion in each other's embraces.*

SCENE XXII.

To the above enter TERZKY.

COUNTESS (*meeting him*).

What meant that cry ?   What was it ?

TERZKY.

All is lost !

COUNTESS.

What! they regarded not his countenance ?

TERZKY.

'Twas all in vain.

DUCHESS.
They shouted Vivat !

TERZKY.
                                        To the Emperor.
                    COUNTESS.
The traitors!

                    TERZKY.
            Nay! he was not permitted
Even to address them.   Soon as he began,
With deafening noise of warlike instruments
They drown'd his words.   But here he comes.

                SCENE XXIII.

To these enter WALLENSTEIN, *accompanied by* ILLO *and*
                    BUTLER.
            WALLENSTEIN (*as he enters*).
                                        Terzky!
                    TERZKY.
My General!

                    WALLENSTEIN.
            Let our regiments hold themselves
In readiness to march; for we shall lave
Pilsen ere evening.   [*Exit* TERZKY
            Butler!
                    BUTLER
                        Yes, my General

                    WALLENSTEIN.
The Governor of Egra is your friend
And countryman.   Write to him instantly
By a post courier.   He must be advised,
That we are with him early on the morrow.
You follow us yourself, your regiment with you.
                    BUTLER.
It shall be done, my General!
WALLENSTEIN (*steps between* MAX. *and* THEKLA, *who have re-
        mained during this time in each other's arms*).
                                        Part!
                    MAX.
                                        O God!
[Cuirassiers *enter with drawn swords, and assemble in the
    back-ground.   At the same time there are heard from below
    some spirited passages out of the Pappenheim March, which
    seem to address* MAX.

WALLENSTEIN (*to the* Cuirassiers).
Here he is, he is at liberty : I keep him
No longer.
> [*He turns away, and stands so that* MAX. *cannot pass by him nor approach the* PRINCESS.

MAX.
Thou know'st that I have not yet learnt to live
Without thee ! I go forth into a desert,
Leaving my all behind me.   O do not turn
Thine eyes away from me !   O once more show me
Thy ever dear and honour'd countenance.
> [MAX *attempts to take his hand, but is repelled: he turns to the* COUNTESS.

Is there no eye that has a look of pity for me ?
> [*The* COUNTESS *turns away from him ; he turns to the* DUCHESS.

My mother !

DUCHESS.
Go where duty calls you   Haply
The time may come, when you may prove to us
A true friend, a good angel at the throne
Of the Emperor

MAX.
You give me hope ; you would not
Suffer me wholly to despair.   No ! no !
Mine is a certain misery.   Thanks to Heaven !
That offers me a means of ending it.
> [*The military music begins again.   The stage fills more and more with armed men.* MAX. *sees* BUTLER *and addresses him.*

And you here, Colonel Butler—and will you
Not follow me ?   Well, then ! remain more faithful
To your new lord, than you have proved yourself
To the Emperor.   Come, Butler ! promise me.
Give me your hand upon it, that you'll be
The guardian of his life, its shield, its watchman.
He is attainted, and his princely head
Fair booty for each slave that trades in murder.
Now he doth need the faithful eye of friendship,
And those whom here I see—
> [*Casting suspicious looks on* ILLO *and* BUTLER.

ILLO.

Go—seek for traitors
In Gallas', in your father's quarters.   Here
Is only one.   Away! away! and free us
From his detested sight!   Away!

[MAX. *attempts once more to approach* THEKLA. WALLEN-
STEIN *prevents him.* MAX. *stands irresolute, and in
apparent anguish.   In the mean time the stage fills more
and more; and the horns sound from below louder
and louder, and each time after a shorter interval.*

MAX.

Blow, blow!   O were it but the Swedish Trumpets,
And all the naked swords, which I see here,
Were plunged into my breast!   What purpose you?
You come to tear me from this place!   Beware,
Ye drive me not to desperation.   Do it not!
Ye may repent it!

[*The stage is entirely filled with armed men*

Yet more! weight upon weight to drag me down!
Think what ye're doing.   It is not well done
To choose a man despairing for your leader;
You tear me from my happiness.   Well, then,
I dedicate your souls to vengeance.   Mark!
For your own ruin you have chosen me:
Who goes with me, must be prepared to perish.

[*He turns to the background, there ensues a sudden and
violent movement among the Cuirassiers; they sur
round him, and carry him off in wild tumult.* WAL-
LENSTEIN *remains immoveable.* THEKLA *sinks into her
mother's arms.   The curtain falls.   The music becomes
loud and overpowering, and passes into a complete war
march—the orchestra joins it—and continues during
the interval between the second and third Act.*

ACT IV.

SCENE I.

The BURGOMASTER's *House at Egra.*

BUTLER (*just arrived*).

Here then he is, by his destiny conducted.
Here, Friedland! and no farther!   From Bohemia

Thy meteor rose, traversed the sky awhile,
And here upon the borders of Bohemia
Must sink.
          Thou hast foresworn the ancient colours,
Blind man! yet trustest to thy ancient fortunes.
Profaner of the altar and the hearth,
Against thy Emperor and fellow citizens
Thou mean'st to wage the war. Friedland, beware—
The evil spirit of revenge impels thee—
Beware thou, that revenge destroy thee not!

SCENE II.

BUTLER *and* GORDON.

GORDON.

                       Is it you?
How my heart sinks! The Duke a fugitive traitor!
His princely head attainted! O my God!
[Tell me, General, I implore thee, tell me
In full, of all these sad events at Pilsen.]

BUTLER

You have received the letter which I sent you
By a post-courier?

GORDON.

               Yes: and in obedience to it
Open'd the stronghold to him without scruple,
For an imperial letter orders me
To follow your commands implicitly.
But yet forgive me! when even now I saw
The Duke himself, my scruples recommenced.
For truly, not like an attainted man,
Into this town did Friedland make his entrance;
His wonted majesty beam'd from his brow,
And calm, as in the days when all was right,
Did he receive from me the accounts of office.
'Tis said, that fallen pride learns condescension ·
But sparing and with dignity the Duke
Weigh'd every syllable of approbation,
As masters praise a servant who has done
His duty and no more.

BUTLER.

'Tis all precisely
As I related in my letter.   Friedland
Has sold the army to the enemy,
And pledged himself to give up Prague and Egra
On this report the regiments all forsook him,
The five excepted that belong to Terzky,
And which have follow'd him, as thou hast seen
The sentence of attainder is pass'd on him,
And every loyal subject is required
To give him in to justice, dead or living.

GORDON.

A traitor to the Emperor.   Such a noble !
Of such high talents !   What is human greatness !
I often said, this can't end happily.
His might, his greatness, and this obscure power
Are but a cover'd pit-fall.   The human being
May not be trusted to self-government.
The clear and written law, the deep trod foot-marks
Of ancient custom, are all necessary
To keep him in the road of faith and duty.
The authority entrusted to this man
Was unexampled and unnatural,
It placed him on a level with his Emperor,
Till the proud soul unlearn'd submission.   Wo is me;
I mourn for him ! for where he fell, I deem
Might none stand firm.   Alas ! dear General,
We in our lucky mediocrity
Have ne'er experienced, cannot calculate,
What dangerous wishes such a height may breed
In the heart of such a man.

BUTLER.

Spare your laments
Till he need sympathy ; for at this present
Ho is still mighty, and still formidable.
The Swedes advance to Egra by forced marches,
And quickly will the junction be accomplish'd.
This must not be !   The Duke must never leave
This stronghold on free footing ; for I have
Pledged life and honour here to hold him prisoner,
And your assistance 'tis on which I calculate.

GORDON.

O that I had not lived to see this day!
From his hand I received this dignity,
He did himself entrust this stronghold to me,
Which I am now required to make his dungeon.
We subalterns have no will of our own:
The free, the mighty man alone may listen
To the fair impulse of his human nature.
Ah! we are but the poor tools of the law,
Obedience the sole virtue we dare aim at!

BUTLER.

Nay! let it not afflict you, that your power
Is circumscribed. Much liberty, much error!
The narrow path of duty is securest.

GORDON.

And all then have deserted him you say?
He has built up the luck of many thousands;
For kingly was his spirit: his full hand
Was ever open! Many a one from dust
                    [*With a sly glance on* BUTLER.
Hath he selected, from the very dust
Hath raised him into dignity and honour
And yet no friend, not one friend hath he purchased,
Whose heart beats true to him in the evil hour.

BUTLER.

Here's one, I see.

GORDON.

           I have enjoy'd from him
No grace or favour. I could almost doubt,
If ever in his greatness he once thought on
An old friend of his youth. For still my office
Kept me at distance from him; and when first
He to this citadel appointed me,
He was sincere and serious in his duty
I do not then abuse his confidence,
If I preserve my fealty in that
Which to my fealty was first delivered.

BUTLER.

Say, then, will you fulfil th' attainder on him,
[And lend your aid to take him in arrest?]

GORDON (*pauses, reflecting—then as in deep dejection*).
If it be so—if all be as you say—

If he've betray'd the Emperor, his master,
Have sold the troops, have purposed to deliver
The strongholds of the country to the enemy—
Yea, truly!—there is no redemption for him!
Yet it is hard, that me the lot should destine
To be the instrument of his perdition;
For we were pages at the court of Bergau
At the same period; but I was the senior

BUTLER.

I have heard so——

GORDON.

    'Tis full thirty years since then,
A youth who scarce had seen his twentieth year
Was Wallenstein, when he and I were friends:
Yet even then he had a daring soul:
His frame of mind was serious and severe
Beyond his years: his dreams were of great objects.
He walk'd amidst us of a silent spirit,
Communing with himself; yet I have known him
Transported on a sudden into utterance
Of strange conceptions; kindling into splendour,
His soul reveal'd itself, and he spake so
That we look'd round perplex'd upon each other,
Not knowing whether it were craziness,
Or whether it were a god that spoke in him.

BUTLER.

But was it where he fell two story high
From a window-ledge, on which he had fallen asleep
And rose up free from injury? From this day
(It is reported) he betrayed clear marks
Of a distemper'd fancy.

GORDON.

    He became
Doubtless more self-enwrapt and melancholy;
He made himself a Catholic*. Marvellously
His marvellous preservation had transform'd him.
Thenceforth he held himself for an exempted
And privileged being, and, as if he were
Incapable of dizziness or fall,

---

* It appears that the account of his conversion being caused by such a
fall, and other stories of his juvenile character, are not well authenticated.

He ran along the unsteady rope of life
But now our destinies drove us asunder,
He paced with rapid step the way of greatness,
Was Count, and Prince, Duke-regent, and Dictator
And now is all, all this too little for him;
He stretches forth his hands for a king's crown,
And plunges in unfathomable ruin.

BUTLER.

No more, he comes.

Scene III

To these enter WALLENSTEIN, *in conversation with the* BURGO-
MASTER *of Egra.*

WALLENSTEIN

You were at one time a free town.   I see,
Ye bear the half eagle in your city arms.
Why the *half* eagle only?

BURGOMASTER.

We were free,
But for these last two hundred years has Egra
Remain'd in pledge to the Bohemian crown;
Therefore we bear the half eagle, the other half
Being cancell'd till the empire ransom us,
If ever that should be.

WALLENSTEIN.

Ye merit freedom.
Only be firm and dauntless.   Lend your ears
To no designing whispering court-minions.
What may your imposts be?

BURGOMASTER.

So heavy that
We totter under them.   The garrison
Lives at our costs.

WALLENSTEIN.

I will relieve you   Tell me,
There are some Protestants among you still?

[*The* BURGOMASTER *hesitates*

Yes, yes; I know it.   Many lie conceal'd
Within these walls—Confess now—you yourself—

[*Fixes his eye on him.   The* BURGOMASTER *alarmed*

Be not alarm'd.   I hate the Jesuits.
Could my will have determined it, they had
Been long ago expell'd the empire.   Trust me—
Mass-book or bible, 'tis all one to me.
Of that the world has had sufficient proof.
I built a church for the Reform'd in Glogau
At my own instance.   Harkye, Burgomaster!
What is your name?

> BURGOMASTER.
>
> Pachhalbel, may it please you.
>
> WALLENSTEIN

Harkye!——
But let it go no further, what I now
Disclose to you in confidence.

> [Laying his hand on the BURGOMASTER's shoulder
> with a certain solemnity.

The times
Draw near to their fulfilment, Burgomaster!
The high will fall, the low will be exalted.
Harkye! But keep it to yourself! The end
Approaches of the Spanish double monarchy—
A new arrangement is at hand.   You saw
The three moons that appear'd at once in the Heaven

> BURGOMASTER.

With wonder and affright!

> WALLENSTEIN.
>
> Whereof did two
Strangely transform themselves to bloody daggers,
And only one, the middle moon, remained
Steady and clear

> BURGOMASTER.
>
> We applied it to the Turks.
>
> WALLENSTEIN.

The Turks! That all?—I tell you, that two empires
Will set in blood, in the East and in the West,
And Luth'ranism alone remain.

> [Observing GORDON and BUTLER
> I' faith,
'Twas a smart cannonading that we heard
This evening, as we journey'd hitherward;
'Twas on our left hand   Did you hear it here?

GORDON.

Distinctly. The wind brought it from the south.

BUTLER.

It seem'd to come from Weiden or from Neustadt.

WALLENSTEIN.

'Tis likely. That's the route the Swedes are taking.
How strong is the garrison?

GORDON.

Not quite two hundred
Competent men, the rest are invalids

WALLENSTEIN.

Good! And how many in the vale of Jochim?

GORDON.

Two hundred arquebusiers have I sent thither
To fortify the posts against the Swedes.

WALLENSTEIN.

Good! I commend your foresight. At the works too
You have done somewhat?

GORDON.

Two additional batteries
I caused to be run up. They were needless
The Rhinegrave presses hard upon us, General!

WALLENSTEIN.

You have been watchful in your Emperor's service.
I am content with you, Lieutenant-Colonel.

[*To* BUTLER

Release the outposts in the vale of Jochim
With all the stations in the enemy's route.

[*To* GORDON.

Governor, in your faithful hands I leave
My wife, my daughter, and my sister. I
Shall make no stay here, and wait but the arrival
Of letters to take leave of you, together
With all the regiments.

SCENE IV

To these enter COUNT TERZKY.

TERZKY

Joy, General; joy! I bring you welcome tidings

J

WALLENSTEIN.

And what may they be?

TERZKY.

There has been an engagement
At Neustadt; the Swedes gain'd the victory.

WALLENSTEIN.

From whence did you receive the intelligence?

TERZKY.

A countryman from Tirschenreut convey'd it.
Soon after sunrise did the fight begin!
A troop of the Imperialists from Tachau
Had forced their way into the Swedish camp;
The cannonade continued full two hours;
There were left dead upon the field a thousand
Imperialists, together with their Colonel;
Further than this he did not know.

WALLENSTEIN.

How came
Imperial troops at Neustadt?   Altringer,
But yesterday, stood sixty miles from there.
Count Gallas' force collects at Frauenberg,
And have not the full complement.   Is it possible
That Suys perchance had ventured so far onward?
It cannot be

TERZKY.

We shall soon know the whole,
For here comes Illo, full of haste, and joyous

SCENE V.

To these enter ILLO.

ILLO (*to* WALLENSTEIN).

A courier, Duke! he wishes to speak with thee.

TERZKY (*eagerly*).

Does he bring confirmation of the victory?

WALLENSTEIN (*at the same time*).

What does he bring?   Whence comes he?

ILLO.

From the Rhinegrave
And what he brings I can announce to you

Beforehand.   Seven leagues distant are the Swedes;
At Neustadt did Max. Piccolomini
Throw himself on them with the cavalry :
A murderous fight took place! o'erpower'd by numbers
The Pappenheimers all, with Max. their leader,

              [WALLENSTEIN *shudders and turns pale*

Were left dead on the field.

      WALLENSTEIN (*after a pause in a low voice*).

Where is the messenger?   Conduct me to him.

    [WALLENSTEIN *is going, when* LADY NEUBRUNN *rushes*
      into the room.   Some servants follow her and run
      across the stage.

              NEUBRUNN

Help! Help!

    ILLO *and* TERZKY (*at the same time*).

          What now?

             NEUBRUNN.

              The Princess!

      WALLENSTEIN *and* TERZKY.

                       Does she know it?

     NEUBRUNN (*at the same time with them*).

She is dying!

   [*Hurries off the stage, when* WALLENSTEIN *and* TERZEY
    follow her.

          SCENE VI.

        BUTLER *and* GORDON.

            GORDON.

What's this?

            BUTLER.

      She has lost the man she loved—

Young Piccolomini who fell in the battle.

            GORDON

Unfortunate Lady!

            BUTLER.

      You have heard what Illo

Reporteth, that the Swedes are conquerors,
And marching hitherward

            GORDON.

        Too well I heard it.

                         s 2

BUTLER.

They are twelve regiments strong, and there are five
Close by us to protect the Duke. We have
Only my single regiment; and the garrison
Is not two hundred strong.

GORDON.

        'Tis even so.

BUTLER.

It is not possible with such small force
To hold in custody a man like him.

GORDON

I grant it.

BUTLER.

    Soon the numbers would disarm us,
And liberate him.

GORDON.

    It were to be fear'd

BUTLER (*after a pause*)

Know, I am warranty for the event;
With my head have I pledged myself for his.
Must make my word good, cost it what it will,
And if alive we cannot hold him prisoner,
Why—death makes all things certain!

GORDON.

        Butler! What?
Do I understand you? Gracious God! You could—

BUTLER.

He must not live.

GORDON.

    And *you* can do the deed!

BUTLER.

Either you or I.   This morning was his last

GORDON.

You would assassinate him.

BUTLER.

    'Tis my purpose.

GORDON.

Who leans with his whole confidence upon you!

BUTLER.

Such is his evil destiny '

GORDON.
                              Your General!
The sacred person of your General!

BUTLER.
My General he *has been*.

GORDON.
                         That 'tis only
An "*has been*" washes out no villany.
And without judgment pass'd?

BUTLER.
                    The execution
Is here instead of judgment.

GORDON.
                    This were murder,
Not justice.   The most guilty should be heard

BUTLER.
His guilt is clear, the Emperor has pass'd judgment,
And we but execute his will.

GORDON.
                         We should not
Hurry to realize a bloody sentence.
A word may be recall'd, a life can never be.

BUTLER.
Despatch in service pleases sovereigns.

GORDON.
No honest man's ambitious to press forward
To the hangman's service.

BUTLER.
                    And no brave man loses
His colour at a daring enterprise.

GORDON.
A brave man hazards life, but not his conscience.

BUTLER.
What then?   Shall he go forth anew to kindle
The unextinguishable flame of war?

GORDON
Seize him, and hold him prisoner—do not kill him

BUTLER.
Had not the Emperor's army been defeated,
I might have done so.—But 'tis now past by.

GORDON.
O, wherefore open'd I the stronghold to him?

BUTLER

His destiny and not the place destroys him.

GORDON.

Upon these ramparts, as bescem'd a soldier,
I had fallen. defending the Emperor's citadel!

BUTLER.

Yes! and a thousand gallant men have perish'd

GORDON.

Doing their duty—that adorns the man!
But murder's a black deed, and nature curses it.

BUTLER (*brings out a paper*).

Here is the manifesto which commands us
To gain possession of his person.   See—
It is addressed to you as well as me.
Are you content to take the consequences,
If through our fault he escape to the enemy?

GORDON.

I?—Gracious God!

BUTLER.

Take it on yourself.
Come of it what may, on you I lay it.

GORDON.

O God in heaven!

BUTLER.

Can you advise aught else
Wherewith to execute the Emperor's purpose?
Say if you can.   For I desire his fall,
Not his destruction

GORDON.

Merciful heaven! what must be
I see as clear as you.   Yet still the heart
Within my bosom beats with other feelings!

BUTLER.

Mine is of harder stuff!   Necessity
In her rough school hath steel'd me.   And this Illo,
And Terzky likewise, they must not survive him

GORDON.

I feel no pang for these.   Their own bad hearts
Impell'd them, not the influence of the stars.
'Twas they who strew'd the seeds of evil passions
In his calm breast. and with officious villany

Water d and nursed the pois'nous plants. May they
Receive their earnests to the uttermost mite !

BUTLER.

And their death shall precede his!
We meant to have taken them alive this evening
Amid the merry-making of a feast.
And keep them prisoners in the citadel.
But this makes shorter work. I go this instant
To give the necessary orders.

SCENE VII.

To these enter ILLO *and* TERZKY.

TERZKY

Our luck is on the turn. To-morrow come
The Swedes—twelve thousand gallant warriors, Illo !
Then straightwise for Vienna. Cheerily, friend !
What ! meet such news with such a moody face ?

ILLO

It lies with us at present to prescribe
Laws, and take vengeance on those worthless traitors,
Those skulking cowards that deserted us ;
One has already done his bitter penance,
The Piccolomini : be his the fate
Of all who wish us evil ! This flies sure
To the old man s heart; he has his whole life long
Fretted and toil'd to raise his ancient house
From a Count's title to the name of prince;
And now must seek a grave for his only son.

BUTLER.

'Twas pity, though ! A youth of such heroic
And gentle temperament ! The Duke himself,
'Twas easily seen, how near it went to his heart

ILLO.

Hark ye, old friend ! That is the very point
That never pleased me in our General—
He ever gave the preference to the Italians.
Yea, at this very moment, by my soul !
He'd gladly see us all dead ten times over,
Could he thereby recall his friend to life.

TERZKY.

Hush, hush ! Let the dead rest ! This evening's business
Is, who can fairly drink the other down—

Your regiment, Illo! gives the entertainment
Come! we will keep a merry carnival—
The night for once be day, and 'mid full glasses
Will we expect the Swedish avant-garde.

ILLO.

Yes, let us be of good cheer for to-day,
For there's hot work before us, friends! This sword
Shall have no rest, till it be bathed to the hilt
In Austrian blood

GORDON.

Shame, shame! what talk is this
My Lord Field-Marshal? Wherefore foam you so
Against your Emperor?

BUTLER.

Hope not too much
From this first victory   Bethink you, sirs!
How rapidly the wheel of Fortune turns;
The Emperor still is formidably strong.

ILLO

The Emperor has soldiers, no commander,
For this King Ferdinand of Hungary
Is but a tyro.   Gallas? He's no luck,
And was of old the ruiner of armies.
And then this viper, this Octavio,
Is excellent at stabbing in the back,
But ne'er meets Friedland in the open field.

TERZKY.

Trust me, my friends, it cannot but succeed;
Fortune, we know, can ne'er forsake the Duke!
And only under Wallenstein can Austria
Be conqueror.

ILLO

The Duke will soon assemble
A mighty army: all comes crowding, streaming
To banners, dedicate by destiny,
To fame, and prosperous fortune. I behold
Old times come back again! he will become
Once more the mighty Lord which he has been
How will the fools, who've now deserted him,
Look then? I can't but laugh to think of them,
For lands will he present to all his friends,

And like a King and Emperor reward
True services; but we've the nearest claims

[*To* GORDON.

You will not be forgotten, Governor!
He'll take you from this nest, and bid you shine
In higher station : your fidelity
Well merits it.

GORDON

I am content already,
And wish to climb no higher; where great height is,
The fall must needs be great. " Great height, great depth."

ILLO.

Here you have no more business, for to-morrow
The Swedes will take possession of the citadel.
Come, Terzky, it is supper-time. What think you?
Nay, shall we have the town illuminated
In honour of the Swede? And who refuses
To do it is a Spaniard and a traitor

TERZKY

Nay! nay! not that, it will not please the Duke—

ILLO.

What! we are masters here; no soul shall dare
Avow himself Imperial where we've the rule.
Gordon! good night, and for the last time, take
A fair leave of the place. Send out patroles
To make secure, the watch-word may be alter'd
At the stroke of ten ; deliver in the keys
To the Duke himself, and then you've quit for ever
Your wardship of the gates, for on to-morrow
The Swedes will take possession of the citadel.

TERZKY (*as he is going, to* BUTLER).

You come, though, to the castle?

BUTLER.

At the right time.

[*Exeunt* TERZKY *and* ILLO.

SCENE VIII.

GORDON *and* BUTLER.

GORDON (*looking after them*).

Unhappy men! How free from all foreboding!
They rush into the outspread net of murder.

In the blind drunkenness of victory;
I have no pity for their fate.   This Illo,
This overflowing and foolhardy villain,
That would fain bathe himself in his Emperor's blood.——

BUTLER.

Do as he order'd you.   Send round patroles,
Take measures for the citadel's security;
When they are within I close the castle-gate
That nothing may transpire.

GORDON (*with earnest anxiety*).

Oh! haste not so!

Nay, stop; first tell me——

BUTLER.

You have heard already,
To-morrow to the Swedes belongs.   This night
Alone is ours.   They make good expedition.
But we will make still greater.   Fare you well

GORDON.

Ah! your looks tell me nothing good   Nay, Butler,
I pray you, promise me!

BUTLER

The sun has set;
A fateful evening doth descend upon us,
And brings on their long night!   Their evil stars
Deliver them unarm'd into our hands,
And from their drunken dream of golden fortunes
The dagger at their heart shall rouse them.   Well,
The Duke was ever a great calculator;
His fellow-men were figures on his chess-board,
To move and station, as his game required.
Other men's honour, dignity, good name,
Did he shift like pawns, and made no conscience of
Still calculating, calculating still;
And yet at last his calculation proves
Erroneous; the whole game is lost; and lo!
His own life will be found among the forfeits.

GORDON.

O think not of his errors now! remember
His greatness, his munificence; think on all

The lovely features of his character,
On all the noble exploits of his life,
And let them, like an angel's arm, unseen,
Arrest the lifted sword.

BUTLER.

It is too late.

I suffer not myelf to feel compassion,
Dark thoughts and bloody are my *duty* now:

[*Grasping* GORDON's *hand.*

Gordon! 'tis not my hatred, (I pretend not
To love the Duke, and have no cause to love him,)
Yet 'tis not now my hatred that impels me
To be his murderer.   'Tis his evil fate.
Hostile concurrences of many events
Control and subjugate me to the office.
In vain the human being meditates
Free action.   He is but the wire-work'd * puppet
Of the blind Power, which out of its own choice
Creates for him a dread necessity.
What too would it avail him, if there were
A something pleading for him in my heart—
Still I must kill him.

GORDON.

If your heart speak to you.

Follow its impulse.   'Tis the voice of God.
Think you your fortunes will grow prosperous
Bedew'd with blood—his blood?   Believe it not!

BUTLER.

You know not.   Ask not!   Wherefore should it happen,
That the Swedes gain'd the victory, and hasten
With such forced marches hitherwards?   Fain would I
Have given him to the Emperor's mercy.   Gordon!
I do not wish his blood—But I must ransom
The honour of my word,—it lies in pledge—
And he must die, or——

[*Passionately grasping* GORDON's *hand.*

Listen then, and know,

I am *dishonour'd* if the Duke escape us.

---

* We doubt the propriety of putting so blasphemous a statement in the
mouth of any character.—T.

GORDON.

O! to save such a man——

BUTLER.

What!

GORDON.

It is worth
A sacrifice. Come, friend! Be noble-minded!
Our own heart, and not other men's opinions,
Forms our true honour.

BUTLER (*with a cold and haughty air*).

He is a great Lord,
This Duke—and I am but of mean importance.
This is what you would say! Wherein concerns it
The world at large, you mean to hint to me,
Whether the man of low extraction keeps
Or blemishes his honour—
So that the man of princely rank be saved?
We all do stamp our value on ourselves :
The price we challenge for ourselves is given us.
There does not live on earth the man so station'd,
That I despise myself compared with him.
Man is made great or little by his own will ;
Because I am true to mine, therefore he dies.

GORDON.

I am endeavouring to move a rock.
Thou hadst a mother, yet no human feelings.
I cannot hinder you, but may some God
Rescue him from you!   [*Exit* GORDON.

BUTLER * (*alone*).

I treasured my good name all my life long ;
The Duke has cheated me of life's best jewel,
So that I blush before this poor weak Gordon!
He prizes above all his fealty ;
His conscious soul accuses him of nothing :
In opposition to his own soft heart
He subjugates himself to an iron duty.

---

* [This soliloquy, which, according to the former arrangement, constituted
the whole of Scene IX., and concluded the Fourth Act, is omitted in all the
printed German editions. It seems probable that it existed in the original
manuscript from which Mr. Coleridge translated.—*Ed.*]

Me in a weaker moment passion warp'd;
I stand beside him, and must feel myself
The worse man of the two.   What, though the world
Is ignorant of my purposed treason, yet
One man does know it, and can prove it too—
High-minded Piccolomini!
There lives the man who can dishonour me!
This ignominy blood alone can cleanse!
Duke Friedland, thou or I—Into my own hands
Fortune delivers me—The dearest thing a man has is him-
    self.

SCENE IX.

A Gothic and gloomy Apartment at the DUCHESS FRIEDLAND'S
THEKLA on a seat, pale, her eyes closed.   The DUCHESS *and*
LADY NEUBRUNN *busied about her.*   WALLENSTEIN *and the*
COUNTESS *in conversation*

WALLENSTEIN

How knew she it so soon?

COUNTESS.
                          She seems to have
Foreboded some misfortune.   The report
Of an engagement, in the which had fallen
A colonel of the Imperial army, frighten'd her.
I saw it instantly   She flew to meet
The Swedish courier, and with sudden questioning,
Soon wrested from him the disastrous secret.
Too late we missed her, hasten'd after her,
We found her lying in his arms, all pale
And in a swoon.

WALLENSTEIN.
            A heavy, heavy blow!
And she so unprepared!   Poor child! how is it?
                          [*Turning to the* DUCHESS.
Is she coming to herself?

DUCHESS
            Her eyes are opening
COUNTESS
She lives!

THEKLA (*looking around her*),
Where am I?

WALLENSTEIN (*steps to her, raising her up in his arms*)
Come, cheerly, Thekla! be my own brave girl!
See, there's thy loving mother.   Thou art in
Thy father's arms.

THEKLA (*standing up*).
Where is he?   Is he gone?

DUCHESS.
Who gone, my daughter?

THEKLA.
He—the man who utter'd
That word of misery

DUCHESS.
O! think not of it,
My Thekla!

WALLENSTEIN.
Give her sorrow leave to talk!
Let her complain—mingle your tears with hers,
For she hath suffer'd a deep anguish; but
She'll rise superior to it, for my Thekla
Hath all her father's unsubdued heart.

THEKLA.
I am not ill.   See, I have power to stand.
Why does my mother weep?   Have I alarm'd her?
It is gone by—I recollect myself—
[*She casts her eyes round the room, as seeking some one*
Where is he?   Please you, do not hide him from me.
You see I have strength enough: now I will hear him

DUCHESS.
No; never shall this messenger of evil
Enter again into thy presence, Thekla!

THEKLA
My father—

WALLENSTEIN
Dearest daughter!

THEKLA.
I'm not weak—
Shortly I shall be quite myself again.
You'll grant me one request?

WALLENSTEIN.

Name it, my daughter.

THEKLA.

Permit the stranger to be called to me,
And grant me leave, that by myself I may
Hear his report and question him.

DUCHESS.

No, never!

COUNTESS.

'Tis not advisable—assent not to it.

WALLENSTEIN

Hush! Wherefore wouldst thou speak with him, my
   daughter?

THEKLA.

Knowing the whole, I shall be more collected;
I will not be deceived. My mother wishes
Only to spare me. I will not be spared—
The worst is said already: I can hear
Nothing of deeper anguish!

COUNTESS *and* DUCHESS.

Do it not.

THEKLA.

The horror overpower'd me by surprise.
My heart betray'd me in the stranger's presence:
He was a witness of my weakness, yea,
I sank into his arms: and that has shamed me.
I must replace myself in his esteem,
And I must speak with him, perforce, that he,
The stranger, may not think ungently of me.

WALLENSTEIN.

I see she is in the right, and am inclined
To grant her this request of hers. Go, call him.

              [LADY NEUBRUNN *goes to call him*

DUCHESS.

But I, thy mother, will be present—

THEKLA.

'Twere

More pleasing to me, if alone I saw him:
Trust me, I shall behave myself the more
Collectedly.

WALLENSTEIN.

Permit her her own will.
Leave her alone with him: for there are sorrows,
Where of necessity the soul must be
Its own support.   A strong heart will rely
On its own strength alone.   In her own bosom,
Not in her mother's arms, must she collect
The strength to rise superior to this blow.
It is mine own brave girl.   I'll have her treated
Not as the woman, but the heroine.   [*Going.*

COUNTESS (*detaining him*).

Where art thou going?   I heard Terzky say
That 'tis *thy* purpose to depart from hence
To-morrow early, but to leave us here.

WALLENSTEIN.

Yes, ye stay here, placed under the protection
Of gallant men.

COUNTESS.

O take us with you, brother.
Leave us not in this gloomy solitude
To brood o'er anxious thoughts.   The mists of doubt
Magnify evils to a shape of horror.

WALLENSTEIN.

Who speaks of evil ?   I entreat you, sister,
Use words of better omen.

COUNTESS

Then take us with you.
O leave us not behind you in a place
That forces us to such sad omens.   Heavy
And sick within me is my heart——
These walls breathe on me, like a church yard vault.
I cannot tell you, brother, how this place
Doth go against my nature.   Take us with you.
Come, sister, join you your entreaty !   Niece,
Yours too.   We all entreat you, take us with you!

WALLENSTEIN.

The place's evil omens will I change,
Making it that which shields and shelters for me
My best beloved.

LADY NEUBRUNN (*returning*).
The Swedish officer.

WALLENSTEIN.
Leave her alone with me.

DUCHESS (*to* THEKLA, *who starts and shivers*)
There—pale as death! Child, 'tis impossible
That thou shouldst speak with him. Follow thy mother.

THEKLA.
The Lady Neubrunn then may stay with me.
[*Exeunt* DUCHESS *and* COUNTESS

SCENE X.

THEKLA, THE SWEDISH CAPTAIN, LADY NEUBRUNN

CAPTAIN (*respectfully approaching her*).
Princess—I must entreat your gentle pardon—
My inconsiderate rash speech. How could I—

THEKLA (*with dignity*).
You have beheld me in my agony.
A most distressful accident occasion'd
You from a stranger to become at once
My confidant.

CAPTAIN.
I fear you hate my presence,
For my tongue spake a melancholy word.

THEKLA.
The fault is mine. Myself did wrest it from you.
The horror which came o'er me interrupted
Your tale at its commencement. May it please you,
Continue it to the end.

CAPTAIN.
Princess, 'twill
Renew your anguish.

THEKLA.
I am firm,——
I *will* be firm. Well—how began the engagement?

CAPTAIN.
We lay, expecting no attack, at Neustadt,
Entrench'd but insecurely in our camp,

T

When towards evening rose a cloud of dust
From the wood thitherward: our vanguard fled
Into the camp, and sounded the alarm.
Scarce had we mounted, ere the Pappenheimers,
Their horses at full speed, broke through the lines,
And leapt the trenches; but their heedless courage
Had borne them onward far before the others—
The infantry were still at distance, only
The Pappenheimers follow'd daringly
Their daring leader——

[THEKLA *betrays agitation in her gestures.* The officer
pauses till she makes a sign to him to proceed.

CAPTAIN.

                    Both in van and flanks
With our whole cavalry we now received them;
Back to the trenches drove them, where the foot
Stretch'd out a solid ridge of pikes to meet them
They neither could advance, nor yet retreat;
And as they stood on every side wedged in,
The Rhinegrave to their leader call'd aloud,
Inviting a surrender; but their leader,
Young Piccolomini——

[THEKLA, *as giddy, grasps a chair*
Known by his plume,
And his long hair, gave signal for the trenches;
Himself leapt first: the regiment all plunged after.
His charger, by a halbert gored, rear'd up,
Flung him with violence off, and over him
The horses, now no longer to be curbed.——

[THEKLA, *who has accompanied the last speech with all
the marks of increasing agony, trembles through her
whole frame, and is falling.* The LADY NEUBRUNN
runs to her, and receives her in her arms.

NEUBRUNN

My dearest lady——

CAPTAIN.

I retire

THEKLA

                    'Tis over.
Proceed to the conclusion.

CAPTAIN.
> Wild despair
Inspired the troops with frenzy when they saw
Their leader perish ; every thought of rescue
Was spurned ; they fought like wounded tigers ; their
Frantic resistance roused our soldiery ;
A murderous fight took place, nor was the contest
Finish'd before their last man fell.

THEKLA (*faltering*).
> And where——
Where is—You have not told me all

CAPTAIN (*after a pause*).
> This morning
We buried him.   Twelve youths of noblest birth
Did bear him to interment ; the whole army
Follow'd the bier.   A laurel deck'd his coffin ;
The sword of the deceased was placed upon it,
In mark of honour, by the Rhinegrave's self.
Nor tears were wanting ; for there are among us
Many, who had themselves experienced
The greatness of his mind, and gentle manners ;
All were affected at his fate.   The Rhinegrave
Would willingly have saved him ; but himself
Made vain the attempt—'tis said he wish'd to die.

NEUBRUNN (*to* THEKLA, *who has hidden her countenance*)
Look up, my dearest lady——

THEKLA.
> Where is his grave ?

CAPTAIN
At Neustadt, lady ; in a cloister church
Are his remains deposited, until
We can receive directions from his father.

THEKLA.
What is the cloister's name ?

CAPTAIN.
> Saint Catherine's

THEKLA.
And how far is it thither ?

CAPTAIN.
> Near twelve leagues.
> > T 2

THEKLA.

And which the way?

CAPTAIN.
You go by Tirschenreut
And Falkenberg, through our advanced posts.

THEKLA.
Who
Is their commander?

CAPTAIN.
Colonel Seckendorf.

[THEKLA *steps to the table, and takes a ring from a casket.*

THEKLA.
You have beheld me in my agony,
And shown a feeling heart.   Please you, accept
[*Giving him the ring.*
A small memorial of this hour.   Now go!

CAPTAIN (*confusedly*).
Princess——

[THEKLA *silently makes signs to him to go, and turns from him.   The* CAPTAIN *lingers, and is about to speak.* LADY NEUBRUNN *repeats the signal, and he retires.*

SCENE XI.

THEKLA, LADY NEUBRUNN.

THEKLA (*falls on* LADY NEUBRUNN'S *neck*).
Now, gentle Neubrunn, show me the affection
Which thou hast ever promised—prove thyself
My own true friend and faithful fellow-pilgrim.
This night we must away!

NEUBRUNN.
Away! and whither?

THEKLA.
Whither! There is but one place in the world
Thither, where he lies buried! To his coffin!

NEUBRUNN.
What would you do there?

THEKLA.
What do there?
That wouldst thou not have ask'd, hadst thou e'er loved.
There, there is all that still remains of him!
That single spot is the whole earth to me.

NEUBRUNN.
That place of death——

THEKLA.
Is now the only place
Where life yet dwells for me: detain me not!
Come and make preparations; let us think
Of means to fly from hence.

NEUBRUNN.
Your father's **rage** ——

THEKLA.
That time is past——
And now I fear no human being's rage.

NEUBRUNN.
The sentence of the world! The tongue of calumny!

THEKLA.
Whom am I seeking? Him who is no more.
Am I then hastening to the arms——O God!
I haste but to the grave of the beloved.

NEUBRUNN.
And we alone, two helpless feeble women?

THEKLA.
We will take weapons: my arm shall protect thee.

NEUBRUNN.
In the dark night-time?

THEKLA.
Darkness will conceal us

NEUBRUNN.
This rough tempestuous night——

THEKLA.
Had he a soft bed
Under the hoofs of his war-horses?

NEUBRUNN.
Heaven!
And then the many posts of the enemy

THEKLA.

They are human beings. Misery travels free
Through the whole earth.

NEUBRUNN.

The journey's weary length——

THEKLA.

The pilgrim, travelling to a distant shrine
Of hope and healing, doth not count the leagues.

NEUBRUNN.

How can we pass the gates?

THEKLA.

Gold opens them

Go, do but go

NEUBRUNN.

Should we be recognised——

THEKLA.

In a despairing woman, a poor fugitive,
Will no one seek the daughter of Duke Friedland.

NEUBRUNN.

And where procure we horses for our flight?

THEKLA.

My equerry procures them. Go and fetch him.

NEUBRUNN.

Dares he, without the knowledge of his lord?

THEKLA.

He will. Go, only go. Delay no longer

NEUBRUNN.

Dear lady! and your mother?

THEKLA.

Oh! my mother!

NEUBRUNN.

So much as she has suffer'd too already;
Your tender mother—Ah! how ill prepared
For this last anguish!

THEKLA.

Woe is me! my mother!
[Pause.

Go instantly.

NEUBRUNN.
But think what you are doing!

THEKLA.
What *can* be thought, already has been thought.

NEUBRUNN.
And being there, what purpose you to do?

THEKLA.
There a Divinity will prompt my soul.

NEUBRUNN.
Your heart, dear lady, is disquieted!
And this is not the way that leads to quiet,

THEKLA.
To a deep quiet, such as he has found.
It draws me on, I know not what to name it,
Resistless does it draw me to his grave.
There will my heart be eased, my tears will flow
O hasten, make no further questioning!
There is no rest for me till I have left
These walls—they fall in on me—a dim power
Drives me from hence—Oh mercy! What a feeling!
What pale and hollow forms are those! They fill,
They crowd the place! I have no longer room here!
Mercy! Still more! More still! The hideous swarm,
They press on me; they chase me from these walls—
Those hollow, bodiless forms of living men!

NEUBRUNN.
You frighten me so, lady, that no longer
I dare stay here myself. I go and call
Rosenberg instantly.   [*Exit* LADY NEUBRUNN

SCENE XII.

THEKLA.
His spirit 'tis that calls me: 'tis the troop
Of his true followers, who offer'd up
Themselves to avenge his death: and they accuse me
Of an ignoble loitering—*they* would not
Forsake their leader even in his death—*they* died for him
And shall *I* live?—
For me too was that laurel-garland twined
That decks his bier. Life is an empty casket!

I throw it from me. O ! my only hope ;—
To die beneath the hoofs of trampling steeds—
That is the lot of heroes upon earth !

[Exit Thekla*.

(*The Curtain drops.*)

Scene XIII.

Thekla, Lady Neubrunn, *and* Rosenberg.

[Neubrunn

Ho is here lady, and he will procure them.

THEKLA.

Wilt thou provide us horses, Rosenberg?

ROSENBERG.

I will, my lady.

THEKLA.

And go with us as well?

ROSENBERG.

To the world's end, my lady.

THEKLA

But consider,

Thou never canst return unto the Duke.

ROSENBERG.

I will remain with thee.

THEKLA.

1 will reward thee,

And will commend thee to another master,
Canst thou unseen conduct us from the castle?

ROSENBERG.

I can.

THEKLA

When can I go ?

ROSENBERG.

This very hour

But whither would you, Lady?

THEKLA

To—— Tell him, Neubrunn.

---

* The soliloquy of Thekla consists in the original of six-and-twenty lines, twenty of which are in rhymes of irregular recurrence. I thought it prudent to abridge it. Indeed the whole scene between Thekla and Lady Neubrunn might, perhaps, have been omitted without injury to the play.—C.

NEUBRUNN.

To Neustadt

ROSENBERG.

So;—I leave you to get ready.   [*Exit.*

NEUBRUNN.

O see, your mother comes.

THEKLA.

Indeed!   O Heav'n!

SCENE XIV.

THEKLA, LADY NEUBRUNN, *the* DUCHESS

DUCHESS.

He's gone!   I find thee more composed, my child

THEKLA.

I am so, mother; let me only now
Retire to rest, and Neubrunn here be with me.
I want repose.

DUCHESS.

My Thekla, thou shalt have it.
I leave thee now consoled, since I can calm
Thy father's heart.

THEKLA.

Good night, beloved mother!
(*Falling on her neck and embracing her with deep emotion.*)

DUCHESS.

Thou scarcely art composed e'en now, my daughter.
Thou tremblest strongly, and I feel thy heart
Beat audibly on mine.

THEKLA.

Sleep will appease
Its beating: now good night, good night, dear mother.]
(*As she withdraws from her mother's arms the curtain falls.*)

ACT V

SCENE I.

Butler's Chamber.

BUTLER, *and* MAJOR GERALDIN.

BUTLER.

Find me twelve strong dragoons, arm them with pikes,
For there must be no firing——

Conceal them somewhere near the banquet-room,
And soon as the dessert is served up, rush all in
And cry—" Who is loyal to the Emperor!"
I will overturn the table—while you attack
Illo and Terzky, and despatch them both.
The castle-palace is well barr'd and guarded,
That no intelligence of this proceeding
May make its way to the Duke.   Go instantly;
Have you yet sent for Captain Devereux
And the Macdonald?——

GERALDIN
          They'll be here anon.
                    [*Exit* GERALDIN.

BUTLER
Here's no room for delay.   The citizens
Declare for him, a dizzy drunken spirit
Possesses the whole town.   They see in the Duke
A Prince of peace, a founder of new ages
And golden times.   Arms too have been given out
By the town-council, and a hundred citizens
Have volunteered themselves to stand on guard.
Despatch! then, be the word; for enemies
Threaten us from without and from within.

SCENE II.

BUTLER, CAPTAIN DEVEREUX, *and* MACDONALD

MACDONALD.
Here we are, Genera.

DEVEREUX.
          What's to be the watchword?

BUTLER.
Long live the Emperor!

BOTH (*recoiling*).
          How?

BUTLER.
                    Live the House of Austria

DEVEREUX.
Have we not sworn fidelity to Friedland?

MACDONALD.
Have we not march'd to this place to protect him?

BUTLER.

Protect a traitor, and his country's enemy?

DEVEREUX.

Why, yes! in his name you administer'd
Our oath

MACDONALD

And follow'd him yourself to Egra.

BUTLER

I did it the more surely to destroy him

DEVEREUX

So then!

MACDONALD

An alter'd case!

BUTLER (*to* DEVEREUX).

Thou wretched man
So easily leavest thou thy oath and colours?

DEVEREUX.

The devil!—I but follow'd your example,
If you could prove a villain, why not we?

MACDONALD.

We've nought to do with *thinking*—that s your business.
You are our General, and give out the orders :
We follow you, though the track lead to hell.

BUTLER (*appeased*)

Good then! we know each other.

MACDONALD.

I should hope so.

DEVEREUX.

Soldiers of fortune are we—who bids most,
He has us.

MACDONALD.

'Tis e'en so!

BUTLER.

Well, for the present
Ye must remain honest and faithful soldiers.

DEVEREUX

We wish no other.

BUTLER

Ay, and make your fortunes,

MACDONALD.

That is still better.

Listen!

BOTH.

We attend.

BUTLER.

It is the Emperor's will and ordinance
To seize the person of the Prince-Duke Friedland,
Alive or dead.

DEVEREUX.

It runs so in the letter

MACDONALD.

Alive or dead—these were the very words

BUTLER.

And he shall be rewarded from the State
In land and gold, who proffers aid thereto

DEVEREUX.

Ay! that sounds well   The *words* sound always well
That travel hither from the Court.   Yes! yes!
We know already what Court-words import.
A golden chain perhaps in sign of favour,
Or an old charger, or a parchment patent,
And such like.—The Prince-Duke pays better

MACDONALD.

Yes

The Duke's a splendid paymaster.

BUTLER.

All over

With that, my friends! His lucky stars are set.

MACDONALD.

And is that certain!

BUTLER.

You have my word for it

DEVEREUX.

His lucky fortunes all past by?

BUTLER.

For ever

He is as poor as we.

MACDONALD.

As poor as we?

DEVEREUX

Macdonald, we'll desert him.

BUTLER.

We'll desert him?

Full twenty thousand have done that already;
We must do more, my countrymen!   In short—
We—we must kill him.

BOTH (*starting back*).

Kill him!

BUTLER.

Yes, must kill him;

And for that purpose have I chosen you.

BOTH.

Us!

BUTLER.

You, Captain Devereux, and thee, Macdonald

DEVEREUX (*after a pause*).

Choose you some other.

BUTLER.

What! art dastardly?

Thou, with full thirty lives to answer for—
Thou conscientious of a sudden?

DEVEREUX.

Nay

To assassinate our Lord and General——

MACDONALD.

To whom we've sworn a soldier's oath——

BUTLER.

The oath

Is null, for Friedland is a traitor.

DEVEREUX.

No, no! it is too bad!

MACDONALD.

Yes, by my soul!!

It is too bad.   One has a conscience too—·

DEVEREUX.

If it were not our Chieftain, who so long
Has issued the commands, and claim'd our duty--

BUTLER.

Is that the objection?

DEVEREUX

Were it my own father,
And the Emperor's service should demand it of me,
It might be done perhaps—But we are soldiers,
And to assassinate our Chief Commander,
That is a sin, a foul abomination,
From which no monk or confessor absolves us

BUTLER.

I am your Pope, and give you absolution.
Determine quickly!

DEVEREUX.

'Twill not do

MACDONALD.

'Twon't do!

BUTLER.

Well, off then! and—send Pestalutz to me

DEVEREUX (*hesitates*).

The Pestalutz——

MACDONALD.

What may you want with him?

BUTLER.

If you reject it, we can find enough—

DEVEREUX.

Nay, if he must fall, we may earn the bounty
As well as any other.   What think you,
Brother Macdonald?

MACDONALD.

Why, if he *must* fall,
And *will* fall, and it can't be otherwise,
One would not give place to this Pestalutz.

DEVEREUX (*after some reflection*).

When do you purpose he should fall?

BUTLER.

This night.

To-morrow will the Swedes be at our gates.

DEVEREUX.

You take upon you all the consequences?

BUTLER

I take the whole upon me.

DEVEREUX.

                                        And it is
The Emperor's will, his express absolute will?
For we have instances, that folks may like
The murder, and yet hang the murderer.

BUTLER

The manifesto says—" alive or dead."
Alive—'tis not possible—you see it is not.

DEVEREUX.

Well, dead then! dead! But how can we come at him
The town is filled with Terzky's soldiery.

MACDONALD.

Ay! and then Terzky still remains, and Illo——

BUTLER.

With these you shall begin—you understand me?

DEVEREUX.

How! And must they too perish?

BUTLER.

                                        They the first

MACDONALD

Hear, Devereux! A bloody evening this.

DEVEREUX.

Have you a man for that? Commission me—

BUTLER

'Tis given in trust to Major Geraldin;
This is a carnival night, and there's a feast
Given at the castle—there we shall surprise them,
And hew them down. The Pestalutz and Lesley
Have that commission. Soon as that is finish'd—

DEVEREUX.

Hear, General! It will be all one to you—
Hark ye, let me exchange with Geraldin

BUTLER.

'Twill be the lesser danger with the Duke.

DEVEREUX.

Danger! The devil! What do you think me, General
'Tis the Duke's eye, and not his sword, I fear

BUTLER

What can his eye do to thee?

DEVEREUX.

Death and hell!
Thou know'st that I'm no milksop, General!
But 'tis not eight days since the Duke did send me
Twenty gold pieces for this good warm coat
Which I have on! and then for him to see me
Standing before him with the pike, his murderer.
That eye of his looking upon this coat—
Why—why—the devil fetch me! I'm no milksop!

BUTLER.

The Duke presented thee this good warm coat,
And thou, a needy wight, hast pangs of conscience
To run him through the body in return.
A coat that is far better and far warmer
Did the Emperor give to him, the Prince's mantle.
How doth he thank the Emperor?   With revolt,
And treason.

DEVEREUX.

That is true. The devil take
Such thankers! I'll despatch him.

BUTLER.

And would'st quiet
Thy conscience, thou hast nought to do but simply
Pull off the coat; so canst thou do the deed
With light heart and good spirits.

DEVEREUX.

You are right
That did not strike me.   I'll pull off the coat—
So there's an end of it.

MACDONALD.

Yes, but there's another
Point to be thought of.

BUTLER.

And what's that, Macdonald?

MACDONALD.

What avails sword or dagger against *him*?
He is not to be wounded—he is—

BUTLER (*starting up*).

What?

MACDONALD.

Safe against shot, and stab, and flash! Hard frozen,

Secured and warranted by the black art!
His body is impenetrable, I tell you.

DEVEREUX

In Ingolstadt there was just such another:
His whole skin was the same as steel; at last
We were obliged to beat him down with gunstocks.

MACDONALD.

Hear what I'll do.

DEVEREUX.
        Well.

MACDONALD.
                In the cloister here
There's a Dominican, my countryman.
I'll make him dip my sword and pike for me
In holy water, and say over them
One of his strongest blessings   That's probatum!
Nothing can stand 'gainst that.

BUTLER
                So do, Macdonald!
But now go and select from out the regiment
Twenty or thirty able-bodied fellows,
And let them take the oaths to the Emperor.
Then when it strikes eleven, when the first rounds
Are pass'd, conduct them silently as may be
To the house—I will myself be not far off.

DEVEREUX.

But how do we get through Hartschier and Gordon
That stand on guard there in the inner chamber?

BUTLER
I have made myself acquainted with the place,
I lead you through a back door that's defended
By one man only.   Me my rank and office
Give access to the Duke at every hour.
I'll go before you—with one poniard-stroke
Cut Hartschier's windpipe, and make way for you.

DEVEREUX.
And when we are there, by what means shall we gain
The Duke's bed-chamber, without his alarming
The servants of the Court: for he has here
A numerous company of followers?

                                U

BUTLER.

The attendants fill the right wing : he hates bustle,
And lodges in the left wing quite alone.

DEVEREUX.

Were it well over — hey, Macdonald? I
Feel queerly on the occasion, devil knows !

MACDONALD.

And I too   'Tis too great a personage.
People will hold us for a brace of villains.

BUTLER.

In plenty, honour, splendour—you may safely
Laugh at the people's babble.

DEVEREUX.

                              If the business
Squares with one's honour—if that be quite certain —

BUTLER.

Set your hearts quite at ease.   Ye save for Ferdinand
His crown and empire.   The reward can be
No small one

DEVEREUX

And 'tis his purpose to dethrone the Emperor?

BUTLER.

Yes !—Yes !—to rob him of his crown and life.

DEVEREUX

And he must fall by the executioner's hands,
Should we deliver him up to the Emperor
Alive ?

BUTLER.

It were his certain destiny

DEVEREUX.

Well ! Well ! Come then, Macdonald, he shall not
Lie long in pain.

    [*Exeunt* BUTLER *through one door,* MACDONALD
    DEVEREUX *through the other.*

SCENE III.

*A Saloon, terminated by a Gallery which extends far into the
background.*

WALLENSTEIN *sitting at a table.   The* SWEDISH CAPTAIN
standing before him

WALLENSTEIN

Commend me to your lord.   I sympathize

In his good fortune; and if you have seen me
Deficient in the expressions of that joy,
Which such a victory might well demand,
Attribute it to no lack of good will,
For henceforth are our fortunes one.   Farewell.
And for your trouble take my thanks.   To-morrow
The citadel shall be surrender'd to you
On your arrival.

> [*The* SWEDISH CAPTAIN *retires.* WALLENSTEIN *sits
> lost in thought, his eyes fixed vacantly, and his
> head sustained by his hand.   The* COUNTESS
> TERZKY *enters, stands before him for awhile, un-
> observed by him; at length he starts, sees her and
> recollects himself*

WALLENSTEIN.

Comest thou from her?   Is she restored?   How is she?

COUNTESS.

My sister tells me, she was more collected
After her conversation with the Swede.
She has now retired to rest.

WALLENSTEIN.

　　　　　　　The pang will soften,
She will shed tears.

COUNTESS.

　　　　　　I find thee alter'd too,
My brother!   After such a victory
I had expected to have found in thee
A cheerful spirit.   O remain *thou* firm!
Sustain, uphold us!   For our light thou art,
Our sun.

WALLENSTEIN.

　　　　Be quiet.   I ail nothing.   Where's
Thy husband?

COUNTESS

　　　　At a banquet—he and Illo.

WALLENSTEIN (*rises and strides across the saloon*).
The night's far spent.   Betake thee to thy chamber.

COUNTESS.

Bid me not go, O let me stay with thee!

WALLENSTEIN (*moves to the window*).

There is a busy motion in the Heaven,
The wind doth chase the flag upon the tower,
Fast sweep the clouds, the sickle * of the moon,
Struggling, darts snatches of uncertain light
No form of star is visible! That one
White stain of light, that single glimmering yonder,
Is from Cassiopeia, and therein
Is Jupiter. (*A pause*). But now
The blackness of the troubled element hides him!
    [*He sinks into profound melancholy, and looks
        vacantly into the distance.*

COUNTESS (*looks on him mournfully, then grasps his hand*).
What art thou brooding on?

WALLENSTEIN.

                              Methinks,
If I but saw him, 'twould be well with me.
He is the star of my nativity,
And often marvellously hath his aspect
Shot strength into my heart.

COUNTESS.

                        Thou'lt see him again.

WALLENSTEIN (*remains for a while with absent mind, then assumes a livelier manner, and turning suddenly to the Countess*).
See him again? O never, never again!

* These four lines are expressed in the original with exquisite felicity

    Am Himmel ist geschäftige Bewegung.
    Des Thurmes Fahne jagt der Wind, schnell geht
    Der Wolken Zug, die *Mondessichel wankt*,
    Und durch die Nacht zuckt ungewisse Helle.

The word " moon-sickle," reminds me of a passage in Harris, as quoted by Johnson, under the word " falcated." " The enlightened part of the moon appears in the form of a sickle or reaping-hook, which is while she is moving from the conjunction to the opposition, or from the new moon to the full: but from full to a new again, the enlightened part appears gibbous, and the dark *falcated*."
    The words " wanken " and " schweben " are not easily translated. The English words, by which we attempt to render them, are either vulgar or pedantic, or not of sufficiently general application. So " der Wolken Zug "—The Draft, the Procession of clouds.—The Masses of the Clouds sweep onward in swift *stream*.

COUNTESS

How?

WALLENSTEIN.
> He is gone—is dust.

COUNTESS.
> Whom meanest thou, then?

WALLENSTEIN.
He, the more fortunate! yea, he hath finish'd!
For him there is no longer any future,
His life is bright—bright without spot it *was*,
And cannot cease to be. No ominous hour
Knocks at his door with tidings of mishap,
Far off is he, above desire and fear;
No more submitted to the change and chance
Of the unsteady planets. O 'tis well
With *him!* but who knows what the coming hour
Veil'd in thick darkness brings for us?

COUNTESS.
> Thou speakest
Of Piccolomini. What was his death?
The courier had just left thee as I came.

> [WALLENSTEIN *by a motion of his hand makes signs to
> her to be silent.*

Turn not thine eyes upon the backward view,
Let us look forward into sunny days,
Welcome with joyous heart the victory,
Forget what it has cost thee. Not to-day,
For the first time, thy friend was to thee dead;
To thee he died, when first he parted from thee

WALLENSTEIN.
This anguish will be wearied down*, I know;
What pang is permanent with man? From the highest,
As from the vilest thing of every day,
He learns to wean himself: for the strong hours

---

* A very inadequate translation of the original:—
> Verschmerzen werd' ich diesen Schlag, das weiss ich,
> Denn was verschmerzte nicht der Mensch!

LITERALLY.
I shall *grieve down* this blow, of that I'm conscious:
What does not man grieve down?

Conquer him.   Yet I feel what I have lost
In him.   The bloom is vanish'd from my life
For O ! he stood beside me, like my youth,
Transform'd for me the real to a dream,
Clothing the palpable and the familiar
With golden exhalations of the dawn.
Whatever fortunes wait my future toils,
The *beautiful* is vanish'd—and returns not.

COUNTESS.

O be not treacherous to thy own power.
Thy heart is rich enough to vivify
Itself.   Thou lovest and prizest virtues in him,
The which thyself didst plant, thyself unfold.

WALLENSTEIN (*stepping to the door*).

Who interrupts us now at this late hour ?
It is the Governor.   He brings the keys
Of the Citadel.   'Tis midnight.   Leave me, sister !

COUNTESS.

O 'tis so hard to me this night to leave thee—
A boding fear possesses me !

WALLENSTEIN.

                              Fear ! Wherefore ?

COUNTESS.

Shouldst thou depart this night, and we at waking
Never more find thee !

WALLENSTEIN.

                    Fancies !

COUNTESS.

                              O my soul
Has long been weigh'd down by these dark forebodings
And if I combat and repel them waking,
They still crush down upon my heart in dreams
I saw thee yesternight with thy first wife
Sit at a banquet, gorgeously attired.

WALLENSTEIN.

This was a dream of favourable omen,
That marriage being the founder of my fortunes.

COUNTESS.

To-day I dreamt that I was seeking thee
In thy own chamber   As I enter'd, lo !

It was no more a chamber : the Chartreuse
At Gitschin 'twas, which thou thyself hast founded,
And where it is thy will that thou should'st bo
Interr'd.

WALLENSTEIN.

Thy sou¹ is busy with these thoughts

COUNTESS.

What! dost thou not believe that oft in dreams
A voice of warning speaks prophetic to us?

WALLENSTEIN

There is no doubt that there exist such voices
Yet I would not call *them*
Voices of warning that announce to us
Only the inevitable.   As the sun,
Ere it is risen, sometimes paints its image
In the atmosphere, so often do the spirits
Of great events stride on before the events,
And in to-day already walks to-morrow.
That which we read of the fourth Henry's death
Did ever vex and haunt me like a tale
Of my own future destiny.   The king
Felt in his breast the phantom of the knife,
Long ere Ravaillac arm'd himself therewith.
His quiet mind forsook him : the phantasma
Started him in his Louvre, chased him forth
Into the open air : like funeral knells
Sounded that coronation festival :
And still with boding sense he heard the tread
Of those feet that even then were seeking him
Throughout the streets of Paris.

COUNTESS.

And to *thee*

The voice within thy soul bodes nothing?

WALLENSTEIN

Nothing

Be wholly tranquil.

COUNTESS.

And another time

I hasten'd after thee, and thou rann'st from me
Through a long suite, through many a spacious hall.
There seem'd no end of it : doors creak'd and clapp'd ;

I follow'd panting, but could not o'ertake thee;
When on a sudden did I feel myself
Grasp'd from behind—the hand was cold that grasped me—
'Twas thou, and thou didst kiss me, and there seem'd
A crimson covering to envelop us.

WALLENSTEIN.

That is the crimson tapestry of my chamber

COUNTESS (*gazing on him*).

If it should come to that—if I should see thee,
Who standest now before me in the fulness
Of life—   [*She falls on his breast and weeps*

WALLENSTEIN.

The Emperor's proclamation weighs upon thee—
Alphabets wound not—and he finds no hands.

COUNTESS.

If he *should* find them, my resolve is taken—
I bear about me my support and refuge.

                    [*Exit* COUNTESS.

SCENE IV.

WALLENSTEIN, GORDON

WALLENSTEIN.

All quiet in the town?

GORDON.

            The town is quiet.

WALLENSTEIN.

I hear a boisterous music! and the Castle
Is lighted up.   Who are the revellers?

GORDON.

There is a banquet given at the Castle
To the Count Terzky, and Field Marshal Illo.

WALLENSTEIN

In honour of the victory—This tribe
Can show their joy in nothing else but feasting.

        [*Rings. The* GROOM OF THE CHAMBER *enters*
Unrobe me.   I will lay me down to sleep.

        [WALLENSTEIN *takes the keys from* GORDON
So we are guarded from all enemies,
And shut in with sure friends

For all must cheat me, or a face like this
                    [*Fixing his eye on* GORDON
Was ne'er a hypocrite's mask.
          [*The* GROOM OF THE CHAMBER *takes off his mantle,*
          collar, and scarf

                         WALLENSTEIN.
                              Take care—what is that?
                  GROOM OF THE CHAMBER.
The golden chain is snapped in two.
                       WALLENSTEIN.
Well, it has lasted long enough.   Here—give it.
                         [*He takes and looks at the chain*
'Twas the first present of the Emperor.
He hung it round me in the war of Friule,
He being then Archduke ; and I have worn it
Till now from habit——
From superstition, if you will.   Belike,
It was to be a talisman to me ;
And while I wore it on my neck in faith,
It was to chain to me all my life long
The volatile fortune, whose first pledge it was.
Well, be it so ! Henceforward a new fortune
Must spring up for me; for the potency
Of this charm is dissolved.
          [GROOM OF THE CHAMBER *retires with the vestments*
          WALLENSTEIN *rises, takes a stride across the room,*
          and stands at last before GORDON *in a posture of*
          meditation.
How the old time returns upon me ! I
Behold myself once more at Burgau, where
We two were Pages of the Court together
We oftentimes disputed : thy intention
Was ever good ; but thou wert wont to play
The Moralist and Preacher, and wouldst rail at me
That I strove after things too high for me,
Giving my faith to bold unlawful dreams,
And still extol to me the golden mean
——Thy wisdom hath been proved a thriftless friend
To thy own self.   See, it has made thee early
A superannuated man, and (but

That my munificent stars will intervene)
Would let thee in some miserable corner
Go out like an untended lamp.

GORDON

My Prince!
With light heart the poor fisher moors his boat,
And watches from the shore the lofty ship
Stranded amid the storm.

WALLENSTEIN.

Art thou already
In harbour then, old man?   Well! I am not
The unconquer'd spirit drives me o'er life's billows;
My planks still firm, my canvas swelling proudly.
Hope is my goddess still, and Youth my inmate;
And while we stand thus front to front almost
I might presume to say, that the swift years
Have passed by powerless o'er my unblanched hair.

[*He moves with long strides across the Saloon, and
remains on the opposite side over against* GORDON.

Who now persists in calling Fortune false?
To me she has proved faithful; with fond love
Took me from out the common ranks of men,
And like a mother goddess, with strong arm
Carried me swiftly up the steps of life.
Nothing is common in my destiny,
Nor in the furrows of my hand.   Who dares
Interpret then my life for me as 'twere
One of the undistinguishable many?
True, in this present moment I appear
Fallen low indeed; but I shall rise again.
The high flood will soon follow on this ebb;
The fountain of my fortune, which now stops
Repress'd and bound by some malicious star.
Will soon in joy play forth from all its pipes.

GORDON.

And yet remember I the good old proverb.
" Let the night come before we praise the day."
I would be slow from long-continued fortune
To gather hope: for Hope is the companion
Given to the unfortunate by pitying Heaven.

Fear hovers round the head of prosperous men
For still unsteady are the scales of fate.

WALLENSTEIN (*smiling*).
I hear the very Gordon that of old
Was wont to preach, now once more preaching;
I know well, that all sublunary things
Are still the vassals of vicissitude.
The unpropitious gods demand their tribute
This long ago the ancient Pagans knew:
And therefore of their own accord they offer'd
To themselves injuries, so to atone
The jealousy of their divinities:
And human sacrifices bled to Typhon.

[*After a pause, serious, and in a more subdued manner.*
I too have sacrificed to him—For me
There fell the dearest friend, and through my fault
He fell! No joy from favourable fortune
Can overweigh the anguish of this stroke
The envy of my destiny is glutted:
Life pays for life.   On his pure head the lightning
Was drawn off which would else have shatter'd *me*

SCENE V

To these enter SENI.

WALLENSTEIN.
Is not that Seni! and beside himself,
If one may trust his looks?   What brings thee hither
At this late hour, Baptista?

SENI.
Terror, Duke!
On thy account.

WALLENSTEIN.
What now?

SENI
Flee ere the day break!
Trust not thy person to the Swedes!

WALLENSTEIN.
What now
Is in thy thoughts

SENI (*with louder voice*).
Trust not thy person to the Swedes.

WALLENSTEIN.
What is it, then?

SENI (*still more urgently*).
O wait not the arrival of these Swedes!
An evil near at hand is threatening thee
From false friends.   All the signs stand full of horror!
Near, near at hand the net-work of perdition—
Yea, even now 'tis being cast around thee!

WALLENSTEIN.
Baptista, thou art dreaming!—Fear befools thee.

SENI.
Believe not that an empty fear deludes me.
Come, read it in the planetary aspects;
Read it thyself, that ruin threatens thee
From false friends.

WALLENSTEIN.
From the falseness of my friends
Has risen the whole of my unprosperous fortunes.
The warning should have come before!   At present
I need no revelation from the stars
To know that

SENI.
Come and see! trust thine own eyes
A fearful sign stands in the house of life—
An enemy; a fiend lurks close behind
The radiance of thy planet.—O be warn'd!
Deliver not up thyself to these heathens,
To wage a war against our holy church.

WALLENSTEIN (*laughing gently*).
The oracle rails that way!   Yes, yes!   Now
I recollect.   This junction with the Swedes
Did never please thee—lay thyself to sleep,
Baptista!   Signs like these I do not fear.

GORDON (*who during the whole of this dialogue has shown marks
of extreme agitation. and now turns to* WALLENSTEIN).
My Duke and General!   May I dare presume?

WALLENSTEIN
Speak freely

GORDON.

What if 'twere no mere creation
Of fear, if God's high providence vouchsafed
To interpose its aid for your deliverance,
And made that mouth its organ?

WALLENSTEIN.

Ye're both feverish!
How can mishap come to me from the Swedes!
They sought this junction with me—'tis their interest.

GORDON (with difficulty suppressing his emotion).

But what if the arrival of these Swedes—
What if this were the very thing that wing'd
The ruin that is flying to your temples?

[Flings himself at his feet

There is yet time, my Prince

SENI.

O hear him! hear him!

GORDON (rises).

The Rhinegrave's still far off.　Give but the orders.
This citadel shall close its gates upon him.
If then he will besiege us, let him try it.
But this I say; he'll find his own destruction
With his whole force before these ramparts, sooner
Than weary down the valour of our spirit.
He shall experience what a band of heroes,
Inspirited by an heroic leader,
Is able to perform.　And if indeed
It be thy serious wish to make amend
For that which thou hast done amiss,—this, this
Will touch and reconcile the Emperor,
Who gladly turns his heart to thoughts of mercy:
And Friedland, who returns repentant to him,
Will stand yet higher in his Emperor's favour,
Than e'er he stood when he had never fallen

WALLENSTEIN (contemplates him with surprise, remains
awhile, betraying strong emotion).

Gordon—your zeal and fervour lead you far
Well, well—an old friend has a privilege.
Blood, Gordon, has been flowing. Never, never
Can the Emperor pardon me: and if he could,

Yet I—I ne'er could let myself be pardon'd.
Had I foreknown what now has taken place,
That he, my dearest friend, would fall for me
My first death-offering; and had the heart
Spoken to me, as now it has done—Gordon,
It may be, I might have bethought myself
It may be too, I might not.   Might or might not
Is now an idle question.   All too seriously
Has it begun to end in nothing, Gordon!
Let it then have its course.   [*Stepping to the window.*
All dark and silent—at the castle too
All is now hush'd—Light me, Chamberlain!

> [*The* GROOM OF THE CHAMBER, *who had entered dur-
> ing the last dialogue, and had been standing at a
> distance and listening to it with visible expressions
> of the deepest interest, advances in extreme agita-
> tion, and throws himself at the* DUKE's *feet.*

And thou too!   But I know why thou dost wish
My reconcilement with the Emperor.
Poor man! he hath a small estate in Carinthia,
And fears it will be forfeited because
He's in my service.   Am I then so poor
That I no longer can indemnify
My servants?   Well! to no one I employ
Means of compulsion.   If 'tis thy belief
That fortune has fled from me, go! forsake me.
This night for the last time mayst thou unrobe me,
And then go over to thy Emperor.
Gordon, good night! I think to make a long
Sleep of it: for the struggle and the turmoil
Of this last day or two was great.   May't please you!
Take care that they awake me not too early.

> [*Exit* WALLENSTEIN, *the* GROOM OF THE CHAMBER
> lighting him.   SENI *follows,* GORDON *remains on
> the darkened stage, following the* DUKE *with his
> eye, till he disappears at the farther end of the
> gallery: then by his gestures the old man expresses
> the depth of his anguish and stands leaning
> against a pillar*

SCENE VI

GORDON, BUTLER (*at first behind the scenes*).

BUTLER (*not yet come into view of the stage*).
Here stand in silence till I give the signal.

GORDON (*starts up*).
'Tis he! he has already brought the murderers.

BUTLER.
The lights are out   All lies in profound sleep.

GORDON.
What shall I do, shall I attempt to save him?
Shall I call up the house? alarm the guards?

BUTLER (*appears, but scarcely on the stage*).
A light gleams hither from the corridor.
It leads directly to the Duke's bed-chamber.

GORDON.
But then I break my oath to the Emperor;
If he escape and strengthen the enemy,
Do I not hereby call down on my head
All the dread consequences?

BUTLER (*stepping forward*).
            Hark!   Who speaks there?

GORDON.
'Tis better, I resign it to the hands
Of Providence. For what am I, that I
Should take upon myself so great a deed?
I have not murdered him, if he be murder'd;
But all his rescue were *my* act and deed:
Mine—and whatever be the consequences,
I must sustain them.

BUTLER (*advances*).
            I should know that voice

GORDON.
Butler!

BUTLER
    'Tis Gordon.   What do *you* want here?
Was it so late then, when the Duke dismiss'd you?

GORDON.
Your hand bound up and in a scarf?

BUTLER.

'Tis wounded.
That Illo fought as he were frantic, till
At last we threw him on the ground.

GORDON (*shuddering*).

Both dead?

BUTLER.

Is he in bed?

GORDON.

Ah, Butler!

BUTLER.

Is he? speak.

GORDON.

He shall *not* perish! Not through you! The Heaven
Refuses *your* arm. See—'tis wounded!—

BUTLER.

There is no need of *my* arm

GORDON.

The most guilty
Have perish'd, and enough is given to justice.

[*The* GROOM OF THE CHAMBER *advances from the
Gallery with his finger on his mouth commanding
silence.*

GORDON.

He sleeps! O murder not the holy sleep!

BUTLER.

No! he shall die awake.   [*Is going.*

GORDON

His heart still cleaves
To earthly things: he's not prepared to step
Into the presence of his God!

BUTLER (*going*).

God's merciful!

GORDON (*holds him*).
Grant him but this night's respite.

BUTLER (*hurrying off*).

The next moment
May ruin all.

GORDON (*holds him still*)
One hour!——

BUTLER.

Unhold me!   What
Can that short respite profit him?

GORDON.

O—Time
Works miracles.   In one hour many thousands
Of grains of sand run out; and quick as they,
Thought follows thought within the human soul.
Only one hour!   *Your* heart may change its purpose,
His heart may change its purpose—some new tidings
May come; some fortunate event, decisive,
May fall from Heaven and rescue him.   O what
May not one hour achieve!

BUTLER.

You but remind me,
How precious every minute is!

[*He stamps on the floor*

SCENE VII.

To these enter MACDONALD *and* DEVEREUX, *with the* HAL-
BERDIERS.

GORDON (*throwing himself between him and them*).

No, monster!
First over my dead body thou shalt tread.
I will not live to see the accursed deed!

BUTLER (*forcing him out of the way*).
Weak-hearted dotard!

[*Trumpets are heard in the distance*
DEVEREUX *and* MACDONALD.

Hark!   The Swedish trumpets!
The Swedes before the ramparts!   Let us hasten!

GORDON (*rushes out*).
O, God of mercy!

BUTLER (*calling after him*).
Governor, to your post!

GROOM OF THE CHAMBER (*hurries in*).
Who dares make larum here?   Hush!   The Duke sleeps

X

DEVEREUX (*with loud harsh voice*).
Friend, it is time now to make larum.

GROOM OF THE CHAMBER.
Help!

Murder!

BUTLER.
Down with him!

GROOM OF THE CHAMBER (*run through the body by DEVEREUX, falls at the entrance of the Gallery*).
Jesus Maria

BUTLER.
Burst the doors open.
[*They rush over the body into the Gallery—two doors are heard to crash one after the other.—Voices, deadened by the distance—clash of arms—then all at once a profound silence*

SCENE VIII

COUNTESS TERZKY (*with a light*).
Her bed-chamber is empty; she herself
Is nowhere to be found! The Neubrunn too,
Who watch'd by her, is missing. If she should
Be flown —— but whither flown? We must call up
Every soul in the house. How will the Duke
Bear up against these worst bad tidings? O
If that my husband now were but return'd
Home from the banquet!—Hark! I wonder whether
The Duke is still awake! I thought I heard
Voices and tread of feet here! I will go
And listen at the door. Hark! what is that?
'Tis hastening up the steps!

SCENE IX.

COUNTESS, GORDON.

GORDON (*rushes in out of breath*).
'Tis a mistake!
'Tis not the Swedes—Ye must proceed no further—
Butler!—O God! where is he?

GORDON (*observing the* COUNTESS).
                  Countess! Say——

COUNTESS.
You are come then from the castle? Where's my husband?

GORDON (*in an agony of affright*).
Your husband!—Ask not!—To the Duke——

COUNTESS.
                                        Not he!
You have discover'd to me——

GORDON
                  On this moment
Does the world hang.   For God's sake! to the Duke.
While we are speaking ——   [*Calling loudly*
                  Butler! Butler! God!

COUNTESS.
Why, he is at the castle with my husband.
                  [BUTLER *comes from the Gallery*

GORDON.
'Twas a mistake—'Tis not the Swedes—it is
The Imperialists' Lieutenant-General
Has sent me hither—will be here himself
Instantly.—You must not proceed.

BUTLER.
                  He comes
Too late.   [GORDON *dashes himself against the wall*

GORDON.
    O God of mercy!

COUNTESS
                  What too late?
Who will be here himself? Octavio
In Egra? Treason! Treason!—Where's the Duke?
                  [*She rushes to the Gallery*

SCENE X.

*Servants run acoss the Stage full of terror.   The whole Scene
must be spoken entirely without pauses*).

SENI (*from the Gallery*)
O bloody frightful deed!
                                        x 2

COUNTESS.
What is it, Seni?
PAGE (*from the Gallery*).

O piteous sight!

[*Other Servants hasten in with torches*
COUNTESS

What is it? For God's sake!

SENI.

And do *you* ask?

Within, the Duke lies murder'd—and your husband
Assassinated at the Castle.

[*The* COUNTESS *stands motionless.*
FEMALE SERVANT (*rushing across the Stage*).

Help! help! the Duchess!

BURGOMASTER (*enters*).

What mean these confused
Loud cries, that wake the sleepers of this house?

GORDON.

Your house is cursed to all eternity.
In your house doth the Duke lie murder'd!

BURGOMASTER (*rushing out*).

Heaven forbid!

FIRST SERVANT.

Fly! fly! they murder us all!

SECOND SERVANT (*carrying silver plate*).

That way! the lower
Passages are block'd up.

VOICE (*from behind the Scene*).

Make room for the Lieutenant-General!

[*At these words the* COUNTESS *starts from her stupor, collects herself, and retires suddenly.*

VOICE (*from behind the Scene*)

Keep back the people! Guard the door!

SCENE XI.

To these enter OCTAVIO PICCOLOMINI *with all his train   At
the same time* DEVEREUX *and* MACDONALD *enter from out
the Corridor with the Halberdiers.*—WALLENSTEIN'S *dead
body is carried over the back part of the Stage, wrapped in a
piece of crimson tapestry.*

OCTAVIO (*entering abruptly*)

It must not be! It is not possible!

Butler! Gordon!
I'll not believe it.   Say no!
> [GORDON, *without answering, points with his hand to the
> body of* WALLENSTEIN *as it is carried over the back of
> the stage.*   OCTAVIO *looks that way, and stands over-
> powered with horror.*

DEVEREUX (*to* BUTLER).
Here is the golden fleece—the Duke's sword—

MACDONALD.
Is it your order—

BUTLER (*pointing to* OCTAVIO).
Here stands he who now
Hath the sole power to issue orders.
> [DEVEREUX *and* MACDONALD *retire with marks of obeis-
> ance.   One drops away after the other, till only* BUT-
> LER, OCTAVIO, *and* GORDON, *remain on the Stage*

OCTAVIO (*turning to* BUTLER).
Was that my purpose, Butler, when we parted?
O God of Justice!
To thee I lift my hand! I am not guilty
Of this foul deed

BUTLER.
Your *hand* is pure   You have
Avail'd yourself of mine.

OCTAVIO
Merciless man!
Thus to abuse the orders of thy Lord—
And stain thy Emperor's holy name with murder,
With bloody, most accursed assassination!

BUTLER (*calmly*).
I've but fulfilled the Emperor's own sentence

OCTAVIO.
O curse of Kings,
Infusing a dread life into their words,
And linking to the sudden transient thought
The unchanging irrevocable deed.
Was there necessity for such an eager
Despatch?   Couldst thou not grant the merciful
A time for mercy?   Time is man's good Angel.

To leave no interval between the sentence,
And the fulfilment of it, doth beseem
God only, the immutable!

> BUTLER.
> For what
Rail you against me?   What is my offence?
The Empire from a fearful enemy
Have I deliver'd, and expect reward.
The single difference betwixt you and me
Is this: you placed the arrow in the bow:
I pull'd the string.   You sow'd blood, and yet stand
Astonish'd that blood is come up.   I always
Knew what I did, and therefore no result
Hath power to frighten or surprise my spirit
Have you aught eise to order; for this instant
I make my best speed to Vienna; place
My bleeding sword before my Emperor's throne,
And hope to gain the applause which undelaying
And punctual obedience may demand
From a just judge.   [*Exit* BUTLER.

Scene XII.

To these enter the COUNTESS TERZKY, *pale and disordered.
Her utterance is slow and feeble, and unimpassioned.*

> OCTAVIO (*meeting her*).
O, Countess Terzky! These are the results
Of luckless unblest deeds.

> COUNTESS.
> They are the fruits
Of your contrivances.   The Duke is dead,
My husband too is dead, the Duchess struggles
In the pangs of death, my niece has disappear'd
This house of splendour, and of princely glory,
Doth now stand desolated: the affrighted servants
Rush forth through all its doors.   I am the last
Therein; I shut it up, and here deliver
The keys.

> OCTAVIO (*with a deep anguish*).
O Countess! my house, too, is desolate.

COUNTESS

Who next is to be murder'd? Who is next
To be maltreated? Lo! the Duke is dead,
The Emperor's vengeance may be pacified!
Spare the old servants; let not their fidelity
Be imputed to the faithful as a crime—
The evil destiny surprised my brother
Too suddenly: he could not think on them.

OCTAVIO.

Speak not of vengeance! Speak not of maltreatment!
The Emperor is appeased; the heavy fault
Hath heavily been expiated—nothing
Descended from the father to the daughter,
Except his glory and his services.
The Empress honours your adversity,
Takes part in your afflictions, opens to you
Her motherly arms! Therefore no farther fears;
Yield yourself up in hope and confidence
To the Imperial Grace!

COUNTESS (*with her eye raised to heaven*).

To the grace and mercy of a greater Master
Do I yield up myself. Where shall the body
Of the Duke have its place of final rest?
In the Chartreuse, which he himself did found
At Gitschin, rests the Countess Wallenstein;
And by her side, to whom he was indebted
For his first fortunes, gratefully he wish'd
He might sometime repose in death! O let him
Be buried there. And likewise, for my husband's
Remains, I ask the like grace. The Emperor
Is now the proprietor of all our castles.
This sure may well be granted us—one sepulchre
Beside the sepulchres of our forefathers!

OCTAVIO

Countess, you tremble, you turn pale!

COUNTESS (*reassembles all her powers, and speaks with energy
and dignity*)

You think
More worthily of me, than to believe
I would survive the downfall of my house.

We did not hold ourselves too mean to grasp
After a monarch's crown—the crown did fate
Deny, but not the feeling and the spirit
That to the crown belong!. We deem a
Courageous death more worthy of our free station
Than a dishonour'd life.—I have taken poison.

OCTAVIO.

Help! Help! Support her!

COUNTESS.

Nay, it is too late.
In a few moments is my fate accomplish'd

[*Exit* COUNTESS.

GORDON.

O house of death and horrors!

[*An* OFFICER *enters, and brings a letter with the great seal.*
GORDON *steps forward and meets him.*

What is this?

It is the Imperial Seal.

[*He reads the address, and delivers the letter to* OCTAVIO
*with a look of reproach, and with an emphasis on the
word.*

To the *Prince* Piccolomini.

[OCTAVIO, *with his whole frame expressive of sudden
anguish, raises his eyes to heaven*

The Curtain drops.

END OF THE DEATH OF WALLENSTEIN.

WILHELM TELL.

TRANSLATED BY

SIR THEODORE MARTIN, K.C.B., LL.D.

WILHELM TELL.

DRAMATIS PERSONÆ.

HERMANN GESSLER, *Governor of Switz and Uri.*

WERNER, *Baron of Attinghausen, free noble of Switzerland.*

ULRICH VON RUDENZ, *his Nephew.*

WERNER STAUFFACHER,
CONRAD HUNN,
HANS AUF DER MAUER,
JORG IM HOFE,
ULRICH DER SCHMIDT,
JOST VON WEILER,
ITEL REDING, } *People of Schwytz.*

WALTER FURST,
WILHELM TELL,
RÖSSELMANN, *the Priest,*
PETERMANN, *Sacristan,*
KUONI, *Herdsman,*
WERNI, *Huntsman,*
RUODI, *Fisherman,* } *of Uri.*

ARNOLD OF MELCHTHAL,
CONRAD BAUMGARTEN,
MEYER VON SARNEN,
STRUTH VON WINKELRIED,
KLAUS VON DER FLUE,
BURKHART AM BUHEL,
ARNOLD VON SEWA, } *of Unter- wald.*

PFEIFFER OF LUCERNE.

KUNZ OF GERSAU.

JENNI, *Fisherman's son.*

SEPPI, *Herdsman's son.*

GERTRUDE, *Stauffacher's wife.*

HEDWIG, *wife of Tell, daughter of Fürst.*

BERTHA OF BRUNECK, *a rich heiress.*

ARMGART,
MECHTHILD,
ELSBETH,
HILDEGARD, } *Peasant women.*

WALTER,
WILHELM, } *Tell's sons.*

FRIESSHARDT,
LEUTHOLD, } *Soldiers.*

RUDOLPH DER HARRAS, *Gessler's master of the horse.*

JOHANNES PARRICIDA, *Duke of Suabia.*

STUSSI, *Overseer.*

THE MAYOR OF URI.

A COURIER.

MASTER STONEMASON, COMPANIONS, AND WORKMEN.

TASKMASTER.

A CRIER.

MONKS OF THE ORDER OF CHARITY.

HORSEMEN OF GESSLER AND LANDEN-BERG.

MANY PEASANTS; MEN AND WOMEN FROM THE WALDSTETTEN.

ACT I.

SCENE I.

A high rocky shore of the lake of Lucerne opposite Schwytz The lake makes a bend into the land ; a hut stands at a short distance from the shore ; the fisher boy is rowing about in his boat. Beyond the lake are seen the green meadows, the hamlets and farms of Schwytz, lying in the clear sunshine On the left are observed the peaks of the Hacken, surrounded with clouds; to the right, and in the remote distance, appear the Glaciers. The Ranz des Vaches, and the tinkling of cattle bells, continue for some time after the rising of the curtain.

FISHER BOY (*sings in his boat*).
Melody of the Ranz des Vaches.
The clear smiling lake woo'd to bathe in its deep,
A boy on its green shore had laid him to sleep ;
  Then heard he a melody
   Flowing and soft,
  And sweet, as when angels
   Are singing aloft.
And as thrilling with pleasure he wakes from his rest,
The waters are murmuring over his breast :
  And a voice from the deep cries,
   "With me thou must go,
  I charm the young shepherd,
   I lure him below."

HERDSMAN (*on the mountains*).
Air.—Variation of the Ranz des Vaches.
  Farewell, ye green meadows,
   Farewell, sunny shore,
  The herdsman must leave you,
   The summer is o'er.
We go to the hills, but you'll see us again,
 When the cuckoo is calling, and woodnotes are gay,
When flow'rets are blooming in dingle and plain,
 And the brooks sparkle up in the sunshine of May.
  Farewell, ye green meadows,
   Farewell, sunny shore,
  The herdsman must leave you,
   The summer is o'er

CHAMOIS HUNTER (*appearing on the top of a cliff*)

Second Variation of the Ranz des Vaches.

On the heights peals the thunder, and trembles the bridge,
The huntsman bounds on by the dizzying ridge.
   Undaunted he hies him
   O'er ice-covered wild,
  Where leaf never budded,
  Nor Spring ever smiled :
And beneath him an ocean of mist, where his eye
No longer the dwellings of man can espy ;
  Through the parting clouds only
   The earth can be seen,
  Far down 'neath the vapour
   The meadows of green.

[*A change comes over the landscape. A rumbling,
cracking noise is heard among the mountains. Shadows of clouds sweep across the scene.*

[RUODI, *the fisherman, comes out of his cottage.* WERNI,
the huntsman, descends from the rocks. KUONI, *the
shepherd, enters, with a milkpail on his shoulders,
followed by* SEPPI, *his assistant.*

RUODI. Bestir thee, Jenni, haul the boat on shore.
 The grizzly Vale-King* comes, the Glaciers moan,
 The lofty Mytenstein† draws on his hood,
 And from the Stormcleft chilly blows the wind;
 The storm will burst, before we are prepared.

KUONI. 'Twill rain ere long ; my sheep browse eagerly,
 And Watcher there is scraping up the earth.

WERNI. The fish are leaping, and the water-hen
 Dives up and down. A storm is coming on

KUONI (*to his boy*).
 Look, Seppi, if the cattle are not straying.

SEPPI. There goes brown Liesel, I can hear her bells.

KUONI. Then all are safe : she ever ranges farthest.

RUODI. You've a fine yoke of bells there, master herdsman.

WERNI. And likely cattle, too. Are they your own?

---

* The German is, *Thalvogt*, Ruler of the Valley—the name given figura-
tively to a dense grey mist which the south wind sweeps into the valleys from
the mountain tops.   It is well known as the precursor of stormy weather.

† A steep reck, standing on the north of Rütli, and nearly opposite to
Brunnen.

KUONI. I'm not so rich.   They are the noble lord's
  Of Attinghaus, and trusted to my care.
RUODI. How gracefully yon heifer bears her ribbon!
KUONI. Ay, well she knows she's leader of the herd,
  And, take it from her, she'd refuse to feed.
RUODI. You're joking now.   A beast devoid of reason—
WERNI That's easy said.   But beasts have reason, too,—
  And that we know, we men that hunt the chamois
  They never turn to feed—sagacious creatures!
  Till they have placed a sentinel ahead,
  Who pricks his ears whenever we approach,
  And gives alarm with clear and piercing pipe.
RUODI (*to the shepherd*
  Are you for home?
KUONI.   The Alp is grazed quite bare
WERNI. A safe return, my friend!
KUONI.   The same to you!
  Men come not always back from tracks like yours.
RUODI. But who comes here, running at topmost speed?
WERNI. I know the man; 'tis Baumgart of Alzellen.
KONRAD BAUMGARTEN (*rushing in breathless*).
  For God's sake, ferryman, your boat!
RUODI.   How now?
  Why all this haste?
BAUM.   Cast off! My life's at stake!
  Set me across!
KUONI   Why, what's the matter, friend?
WERNI Who are pursuing you?   First tell us that.
BAUM. (*to the fisherman*).
  Quick, quick, e'en now they're close upon my heels!
  The Viceroy's horsemen are in hot pursuit!
  I'm a lost man, should they lay hands upon me.
RUODI. Why are the troopers in pursuit of you?
BAUM. First save my life, and then I'll tell you all.
WERNI. There's blood upon your garments—how is this?
BAUM. The imperial Seneschal, who dwelt at Rossberg—
KUONI. How! What! The Wolfshot*? Is it he pursues you?

---

 * In German, *Wolfenschiessen*—a young man of noble family, and a native
of Unterwalden, who attached himself to the House of Austria, and was appointed *Burgvogt*, or Seneschal, of the Castle of Rossberg.   He was killed by
Baumgarten in the manner, and for the cause, mentioned in the text.

BAUM.　He'll ne'er hurt man again ; I've settled him.

ALL (*starting back*).

> Now, God forgive you, what is this you've done !

BAUM　What every free man in my place had done.
> I have but used mine own good household right
> 'Gainst him that would have wrong'd my wife—my
> honour.

KUONI.　And has he wrong'd you in your honour, then?

BAUM.　That he did not fulfil his foul desire,
> Is due to God and to my trusty axe.

WERNI. You've cleft his skull then, have you, with your axe ?

KUONI.　O, tell us all !　You've time enough, before
> The boat can be unfastened from its moorings.

BAUM.　When I was in the forest felling timber,
> My wife came running out in mortal fear.
> " The Seneschal," she said, " was in my house,
> Had order'd her to get a bath prepared,
> And thereupon had ta'en unseemly freedoms,
> From which she rid herself, and flew to me."
> Arm'd as I was, I sought him, and my axe
> Has given his bath a bloody benediction.

WERNI. And you did well; no man can blame the deed.

KUONI.　The tyrant! Now he has his just reward!
> We men of Unterwald have owed it long.

BAUM.　The deed got wind, and now they're in pursuit.
> Heavens! whilst we speak, the time is flying fast.
>> [*It begins to thunder.*

KUONI.　Quick, ferryman, and set the good man over.

RUODI.　Impossible! a storm is close at hand,
> Wait till it pass ! You must.

BAUM.　　　　　　　　　　　　Almighty heavens !
> I cannot wait ; the least delay is death.

KUONI (*to the fisherman*).

> Push out—God with you! We should help our neigh-
> bours ;
> The like misfortune may betide us all.
>> [*Thunder and the roaring of the wind*

RUODI　The South-wind's up * ! See how the lake is rising!
> I cannot steer against both storm and wave.

---

* Literally, The *Föhn* is loose ! " When," says Müller, in his History of
Switzerland, "the wind called the Föhn is high, the navigation of the lake

BAUM. (*clasping him by the knees*).

    God so help you, as now you pity me!

WERNI. His life's at stake. Have pity on him, man!

KUONI. He is a father: has a wife and children.

                   [*Repeated peals of thunder.*

RUODI What! and have I not, then, a life to lose,

    A wife and child at home as well as he?

    See, how the breakers foam, and toss, and whirl,

    And the lake eddies up from all its depths!

    Right gladly would I save the worthy man,

    But 'tis impossible, as you must see.

BAUM. (*still kneeling*).

    Then must I fall into the tyrant's hands,

    And with the port of safety close in sight!

    Yonder it lies! My eyes can measure it,

    My very voice can echo to its shores.

    There is the boat to carry me across,

    Yet must I lie here helpless and forlorn.

KUONI. Look! who comes here?

RUODI.   'Tis Tell, brave Tell, of Bürglen♦

                [*Enter* TELL *with a crossbow.*

TELL. Who is the man that here implores for aid?

KUONI. He is from Alzellen, and to guard his honour

    From touch of foulest shame, has slain the Wolfshot,

    The Imperial Seneschal, who dwelt at Rossberg.

    The Viceroy's troopers are upon his heels;

    He begs the boatman here to take him over,

    But he, in terror of the storm, refuses.

RUODI. Well, there is Tell can steer as well as I,

    He'll be my judge, if it be possible.

[*Violent peals of thunder—the lake becomes more tempestuous.*

    Am I to plunge into the jaws of hell?

    I should be mad to dare the desperate act.

TELL. The brave man thinks upon himself the last.

    Put trust in God, and help him in his need!

---

becomes extremely dangerous. Such is its vehemence, that the laws of the
country require that the fires shall be extinguished in the houses while it
lasts, and the night watches are doubled. The inhabitants lay heavy stones
upon the roofs of their houses, to prevent their being blown away."

   * Bürglen, the birthplace and residence of Tell. A chapel, erected in
1522, remains on the spot formerly occupied by his house.

RUODI Safe in the port, 'tis easy to advise.
   There is the boat, and there the lake! Try you!
TELL. The lake may pity, but the Viceroy will not.
   Come, venture, man!
SHEPHERD *and* HUNTSMAN.
       O save him! save him! save him!
RUODI Though 'twere my brother, or my darling child,
   I would not go. It is St. Simon's day,
   The lake is up, and calling for its victim.
TELL Nought's to be done with idle talking here.
   Time presses on—the man must be assisted
   Say, boatman, will you venture?
RUODI.   No; not I
TELL In God's name, then, give me the boat! I will,
   With my poor strength, see what is to be done!
KUONI. Ha, noble Tell!
WERNI   That's like a gallant huntsman!
BAUM. You are my angel, my preserver, Tell.
TELL. I may preserve you from the Viceroy's power,
   But from the tempest's rage another must.
   Yet you had better fall into God's hands,
   Than into those of men   [*To the herdsman*
        Herdsman, do thou
   Console my wife, should aught of ill befall me.
   I do but what I may not leave undone.
        [*He leaps into the boat*
KUONI (*to the fisherman*).
   A pretty man to be a boatman, truly!
   What Tell could risk, you dared not venture on.
RUODI. Far better men than I would not ape Tell.
   There does not live his fellow 'mong the mountains
WERNI (*who has ascended a rock*).
   He pushes off. God help thee now, brave sailor!
   Look how his bark is reeling on the waves!
KUONI (*on the shore*).
   The surge has swept clean over it. And now
   'Tis out of sight. Yet stay, there 'tis again!
   Stoutly he stems the breakers, noble fellow!
SEPPI. Here come the troopers hard as they can ride!
KUONI Heavens! so they do! Why, that was help, indeed.
       [*Enter a troop of horsemen*
          Y

1st H   Give up the murderer! You have him here!
2nd H   This way he came! 'Tis useless to conceal him!
RUODI *and* KUONI.
    Whom do you mean?
FIRST HORSEMAN (*discovering the boat*).
                The devil! What do I see?
WERNI (*from above*).
    Is't he in yonder boat ye seek? Ride on,
    If you lay to, you may o'ertake him yet.
2nd H.   Curse on you, he's escaped!
FIRST HORSEMAN (*to the shepherd and fisherman*).
             You help'd him off,
    And you shall pay for it. Fall on their herds!
    Down with the cottage! burn it! beat it down!
                    [*They rush off.*
SEPPI (*hurrying after them*). Oh my poor lambs!
KUONI (*following him*). Unhappy me, my herds!
WERNI. The tyrants!
RUODI (*wringing his hands*).
    Righteous Heaven! Oh, when will come
    Deliverance to this devoted land? [*Exeunt severally.*

SCENE II.

A lime tree in front of STAUFFACHER'S *house at Steinen, in
Schwytz, upon the public road, near a bridge.*

WERNER STAUFFACHER *and* PFEIFFER, *of Lucerne, enter
into conversation.*

PFEIFF. Ay, ay, friend Stauffacher, as I have said,
    Swear not to Austria, if you can help it.
    Hold by the Empire stoutly as of yore,
    And God preserve you in your ancient freedom!
            [*Presses his hand warmly and is going.*
STAUFF Wait till my mistress comes. Now do! You are
    My guest in Schwytz—I in Lucerne am yours.
PFEIFF. Thanks! thanks! But I must reach Gersau to day.
    Whatever grievances your rulers' pride
    And grasping avarice may yet inflict,
    Bear them in patience—soon a change may come.

Another emperor may mount the throne.
But Austria's once, and you are hers for ever. [*Exit,*
    [STAUFFACHER *sits down sorrowfully upon a bench*
    under the lime tree. Gertrude, his wife, enters,
    and finds him in this posture. She places herself
    near him, and looks at him for some time in
    silence

GERT   So sad, my love! I scarcely know thee now
For many a day in silence I have mark'd
A moody sorrow furrowing thy brow.
Some silent grief is weighing on thy heart.
Trust it to me   I am thy faithful wife,
And I demand my half of all thy cares
    [STAUFFACHER *gives her his hand and is silent,*
Tell me what can oppress thy spirits thus?
Thy toil is blest—the world goes well with thee—
Our barns are full—our cattle, many a score;
Our handsome team of sleek and well-fed steeds
Brought from the mountain pastures safely home,
To winter in their comfortable stalls.
There stands thy house—no nobleman's more fair!
'Tis newly built with timber of the best,
All grooved and fitted with the nicest skill;
Its many glistening windows tell of comfort!
'Tis quarter'd o'er with scutcheons of all hues,
And proverbs sage. which passing travellers
Linger to read, and ponder o'er their meaning.

STAUFF The house is strongly built, and handsomely,
But, ah! the ground on which we built it totters.

GERT   Tell me, dear Werner, what you mean by that?

STAUFF No later since than yesterday, I sat
Beneath this linden, thinking with delight,
How fairly all was finished, when from Kussnacht,
The Viceroy and his men came riding by.
Before this house he halted in surprise:
At once I rose, and, as beseemed his rank,
Advanced respectfully to greet the lord,
To whom the Emperor delegates his power,
As judge supreme within our Canton here.
" Who is the owner of this house?" he asked,
With mischief in his thoughts, for well he knew.

With prompt decision, thus I answered him :
" The Emperor, your grace—my lord and yours,
And held by me in fief." On this he answered,
" I am the Emperor's viceregent here,
And will not that each peasant churl should build
At his own pleasure, bearing him as freely
As though he were the master in the land
I shall make bold to put a stop to this!"
So saying, he, with menaces, rode off,
And left me musing with a heavy heart,
On the fell purpose that his words betray'd.

GERT.   Mine own dear lord and husband! Wilt thou take
A word of honest counsel from thy wife?
I boast to be the noble Iberg's child,
A man of wide experience. Many a time,
As we sat spinning in the winter nights,
My sisters and myself, the people's chiefs
Were wont to gather round our father's hearth,
To read the old imperial charters, and
To hold sage converse on the country's weal.
Then heedfully I listened, marking well
What or the wise man thought, or good man wished
And garner'd up their wisdom in my heart.
Hear then, and mark me well ; for thou wilt see,
I long have known the grief that weighs thee down.
The Viceroy hates thee, fain would injure thee,
For thou hast cross'd his wish to bend the Swiss
In homage to this upstart house of princes,
And kept them staunch, like their good sires of old,
In true allegiance to the Empire. Say,
Is't not so, Werner? Tell me, am I wrong?

STAUFF. 'Tis even so. For this doth Gessler hate me.

GERT.   He burns with envy, too, to see thee living
Happy and free on thine inheritance,
For he has none. From the Emperor himself
Thou hold'st in fief the lands thy fathers left thee
There's not a prince i'the Empire that can show
A better title to his heritage ;
For thou hast over thee no lord but one,
And he the mightiest of all Christian kings
Gessler, we know, is but a younger son,

His only wealth the knightly cloak he wears:
He therefore views an honest man's good fortune
With a malignant and a jealous eye
Long has he sworn to compass thy destruction.
As yet thou art uninjured.　Wilt thou wait,
Till he may safely give his malice scope?
A wise man would anticipate the blow.

STAUFF　What's to be done?

GERT.　　　　　　　　Now hear what I advise
Thou knowest well, how here with us in Schwytz
All worthy men are groaning underneath
This Gessler's grasping, grinding tyranny.
Doubt not the men of Unterwald as well,
And Uri, too, are chafing like ourselves,
At this oppressive and heart-wearying yoke.
For there, across the lake, the Landenberg
Wields the same iron rule as Gessler here—
No fishing-boat comes over to our side,
But brings the tidings of some new encroachment,
Some outrage fresh, more grievous than the last.
Then it were well, that some of you—true men—
Men sound at heart, should secretly devise,
How best to shake this hateful thraldom off.
Well do I know, that God would not desert you,
But lend his favour to the righteous cause.
Hast thou no friend in Uri, say, to whom
Thou frankly may'st unbosom all thy thoughts?

STAUFF.　I know full many a gallant fellow there,
And nobles, too,—great men, of high repute,
In whom I can repose unbounded trust.　　[Rising
Wife! What a storm of wild and perilous thoughts
Hast thou stirr'd up within my tranquil breast?
The darkest musings of my bosom thou
Hast dragg'd to light, and placed them full before me;
And what I scarce dared harbour e'en in thought,
Thou speakest plainly out, with fearless tongue.
But hast thou weigh'd well what thou argest thus?
Discord will come, and the fierce clang of arms,
To scare this valley's long unbroken peace,
If we, a feeble shepherd race, shall dare
Him to the fight, that lords it o'er the world.

Ev'n now they only wait some fair pretext
For setting loose their savage warrior hordes,
To scourge and ravage this devoted land,
To lord it o'er us with the victor's rights,
And, 'neath the show of lawful chastisement,
Despoil us of our chartered liberties.

GERT   You, too, are men; can wield a battle axe
As well as they.   God ne'er deserts the brave

STAUFF   Oh wife! a horrid, ruthless fiend is war,
That strikes at once the shepherd and his flock.

GERT   Whate'er great Heaven inflicts, we must endure;
No heart of noble temper brooks injustice.

STAUFF.   This house—thy pride—war, unrelenting war.
Will burn it down.

GERT   And did I think this heart
Enslaved and fettered to the things of earth,
With *my* own hand I'd hurl the kindling torch.

STAUFF.   Thou hast faith in human kindness, wife; but war
Spares not the tender infant in its cradle

GERT.   There is a friend to innocence in heaven!
Look forward, Werner—not behind you, now!

STAUFF.   We men may perish bravely, sword in hand;
But oh, what fate, my Gertrude, may be thine?

GERT   None are so weak, but one last choice is left.
A spring from yonder bridge, and I am free!

STAUFF. (*embracing her*).
Well may he fight for hearth and home, that clasps
A heart so rare as thine against his own!
What are the hosts of Emperors to him?
Gertrude, farewell!   I will to Uri straight
There lives my worthy comrade, Walter Fürst;
His thoughts and mine upon these times are one
There, too, resides the noble Banneret
Of Attinghaus.   High though of blood he be,
He loves the people, honours their old customs.
With both of these I will take counsel, how
To rid us bravely of our country's foe.
Farewell! and while I am away, bear thou
A watchful eye in management at home.
The pilgrim, journeying to the house of God,
And pious monk, collecting for his cloister,

To these give liberally from purse and garner.
Stauffacher's house would not be hid.   Right out
Upon the public way it stands, and offers
To all that pass an hospitable roof.

[*While they are retiring,* TELL *enters with* BAUMGARTEN

TELL   Now, then, you have no further need of me.
Enter yon house.   'Tis Werner Stauffacher's,
A man that is a father to distress.
See, there he is, himself!   Come, follow me.

[*They retire up.   Scene changes*

SCENE III.

*A common near Altdorf.   On an eminence in the back-ground
a Castle in progress of erection, and so far advanced that the
outline of the whole may be distinguished.   The back part
is finished; men are working at the front.   Scaffolding, on
which the workmen are going up and down.   A slater is seen
upon the highest part of the roof.   All is bustle and activity.*

TASKMASTER, MASON, WORKMEN *and* LABOURERS.

TASK   (*with a stick, urging on the workmen*).
Up, up! You've rested long enough. To work!
The stones here! Now the mortar, and the lime!
And let his lordship see the work advanced,
When next he comes.   These fellows crawl like
snails!

[*To two labourers, with loads*
What! call ye that a load?   Go, double it.
Is this the way ye earn your wages, laggards?
1ST W   'Tis very hard that we must bear the stones,
To make a keep and dungeon for ourselves!
TASK   What's that you mutter?   'Tis a worthless race,
And fit for nothing but to milk their cows,
And saunter idly up and down the mountains
OLD MAN (*sinks down exhausted*).
I can no more
TASK (*shaking him*).
Up, up, old man, to work!
1ST W   Have you no bowels of compassion, thus
To press so hard upon a poor old man,
That scarce can drag his feeble limbs along?

MASTER MASON *and* WORKMEN.

        Shame, shame upon you—shame! It cries to heaven!

TASK.   Mind your own business. I but do my duty.

1ST W.   Pray, master, what's to be the name of this
        Same castle, when 'tis built?

TASK.   The Keep of Uri;
        For by it we shall keep you in subjection.

WORK.   The Keep of Uri?

TASK.   Well, why laugh at that?

2ND W.   So you'll keep Uri with this paltry place!

1ST W.   How many molehills such as that must first
        Be piled above each other, ere you make
        A mountain equal to the least in Uri?

                        [TASKMASTER *retires up the stage.*

MAS. M.   I'll drown the mallet in the deepest lake,
        That served my hand on this accursed pile.

                    [*Enter* TELL *and* STAUFFACHER

STAUFF.   O, that I had not lived to see this sight!

TELL.   Here 'tis not good to be. Let us proceed.

STAUFF. Am I in Uri, in the land of freedom?

MAS. M.   O, sir, if you could only see the vaults
        Beneath these towers. The man that tenants them
        Will never hear the cock crow more.

STAUFF.   O God!

MASON.   Look at these ramparts and these buttresses,
        That seem as they were built to last for ever.

TELL.   Hands can destroy whatever hands have rear'd.

                  [*Pointing to the mountains.*
  That house of freedom God hath built for us.

        [*A drum is heard. People enter bearing a cap
          upon a pole, followed by a crier. Women and
          children thronging tumultuously after them*

1ST W.   What means the drum? Give heed!

MASON.   Why, here's a mumming!
        And look, the cap—what can they mean by that?

CRIER.   In the Emperor's name, give ear!

WORK.   Hush! silence! hush

CRIER.   Ye men of Uri, ye do see this cap!
        It will be set upon a lofty pole
        In Altdorf, in the market place: and this
        Is the Lord Governor's good will and pleasure,

The cap shall have like honour as himself,
And all shall reverence it with bended knee,
And head uncovered : thus the king will know
Who are his true and loyal subjects here;
His life and goods are forfeit to the crown,
That shall refuse obedience to the order.

    [The people burst out into laughter. The drum
    beats, and the procession passes on

1ST W A strange device to fall upon, indeed !
Do reverence to a cap! A pretty farce!
Heard ever mortal anything like this ?

MAS.M Down to a cap on bended knee, forsooth !
Rare jesting this with men of sober sense!

1ST W. Nay, were it but the imperial crown, indeed !
But 'tis the cap of Austria! I've seen it
Hanging above the throne in Gessler's hall.

MASON The cap of Austria? Mark that! A snare
To get us into Austria's power, by Heaven !

WORK. No freeborn man will stoop to such disgrace.

MAS. M. Come—to our comrades, and advise with them !

    [They retire up.

TELL (*to* STAUFFACHER).
    You see how matters stand.   Farewell, my friend !

STAUFF. Whither away ? Oh, leave us not so soon.

TELL. They look for me at home.   So fare ye well.

STAUFF. My heart's so full, and has so much to tell you

TELL. Words will not make a heart that's heavy light.

STAUFF. Yet words may possibly conduct to deeds.

TELL. All we can do is to endure in silence.

STAUFF. But shall we bear what is not to be borne ?

TELL. Impetuous rulers have the shortest reigns.
When the fierce Southwind rises from his chasms,
Men cover up their fires, the ships in haste
Make for the harbour, and the mighty spirit
Sweeps o'er the earth, and leaves no trace behind.
Let every man live quietly at home ;
Peace to the peaceful rarely is denied.

STAUFF. And is it thus you view our grievances ?

TELL. The serpent stings not, till it is provoked.
Let them alone ; they'll weary of themselves,
Whene'er they see we are not to be roused.

STAUFF. Much might be done—did we stand fast together.
TELL.   When the ship founders, he will best escape,
        Who seeks no other's safety but his own.
STAUFF. And you desert the common cause so coldly?
TELL.   A man can safely count but on himself!
STAUFF. Nay, even the weak grow strong by union.
TELL.   But the strong man is strongest when alone.
STAUFF Your country, then, cannot rely on you,
        If in despair she rise against her foes
TELL.   Tell rescues the lost sheep from yawning gulphs:
        Is he a man, then, to desert his friends?
        Yet, whatsoe'er you do, spare me from council!
        I was not born to ponder and select;
        But when your course of action is resolved,
        Then call on Tell; you shall not find him fail.
              [*Exeunt severally. A sudden tumult is heard
                 around the scaffolding.*
MASON (*running in*). What's wrong?
FIRST WORKMAN (*running forward*).
                        The slater's fallen from the roof.
BERTHA (*rushing in*).
        Is he dashed to pieces? Run—save him, help!
        If help be possible, save him! Here is gold.
                    [*Throws her trinkets among the people*
MASON. Hence with your gold,—your universal charm,
        And remedy for ill! When you have torn
        Fathers from children, husbands from their wives,
        And scattered woe and wail throughout the land,
        You think with gold to compensate for all.
        Hence! Till we saw you, we were happy men;
        With you came misery and dark despair.
BERTHA (*to the* TASKMASTER, *who has returned*).
        Lives he?
                        [TASKMASTER *shakes his head.*
        Ill-fated towers, with curses built,
        And doomed with curses to be tenanted!   [*Exit*

SCENE IV

The House of WALTER FÜRST. WALTER FURST *and* ARNOLD
VON MELCHTHAL *enter simultaneously at different sides*

MELCH. Good Walter Fürst

FURST   If we should be surprised!
    Stay where you are. We are beset with spies.

MELCH. Have you no news for me from Unterwald?
    What of my father? 'Tis not to be borne,
    Thus to be pent up like a felon here!
    What have I done of such a heinous stamp,
    To skulk and hide me like a murderer?
    I only laid my staff across the fingers
    Of the pert varlet, when before my eyes,
    By order of the governor, he tried
    To drive away my handsome team of oxen.

FURST You are too rash by far. He did no more
    Than what the governor had ordered him.
    You had transgress'd, and therefore should have paid
    The penalty, however hard, in silence.

MELCH. Was I to brook the fellow's saucy words?
    " That if the peasant must have bread to eat,
    " Why, let him go and draw the plough himself!"
    It cut me to the very soul to see
    My oxen, noble creatures, when the knave
    Unyoked them from the plough. As though they felt
    The wrong, they lowed and butted with their horns.
    On this I could contain myself no longer,
    And, overcome by passion, struck him down.

FURST. O, we old men can scarce command ourselves!
    And can we wonder youth should break its bounds?

MELCH. I'm only sorry for my father's sake!
    To be away from him, that needs so much
    My fostering care! The governor detests him,
    Because he hath, whene'er occasion served,
    Stood stoutly up for right and liberty.
    Therefore they'll bear him hard--the poor old man!
    And there is none to shield him from their gripe.
    Come what come may, I must go home again.

FURST Compose yourself, and wait in patience till
    We get some tidings o'er from Unterwald.

Away! away! I hear a knock! Perhaps
A message from the Viceroy! Get thee in!
You are not safe from Landenberger's* arm
In Uri, for these tyrants pull together.

MELCH. They teach us Switzers what *we* ought to do.

FURST. Away! I'll call you when the coast is clear.

[MELCHTHAL *retires.*

Unhappy youth! I dare not tell him all
The evil that my boding heart predicts!
Who's there? The door ne'er opens, but I look
For tidings of mishap. Suspicion lurks
With darkling treachery in every nook.
Even to our inmost rooms they force their way,
These myrmidons of power; and soon we'll need
To fasten bolts and bars upon our doors.

[*He opens the door, and steps back in surprise as*
WERNER STAUFFACHER *enters.*

What do I see? You, Werner? Now, by Heaven!
A valued guest, indeed. No man e'er set
His foot across this threshold, more esteem'd
Welcome! thrice welcome, Werner, to my roof!
What brings you here? What seek you here in Uri?

STAUFF. (*shakes* FURST *by the hand*).
The olden times and olden Switzerland.

FURST   You bring them with you. See how I'm rejoiced,
My heart leaps at the very sight of you.
Sit down—sit down, and tell me how you left
Your charming wife, fair Gertrude? Iberg's child,
And clever as her father. Not a man,
That wends from Germany, by Meinrad's Cell,†
To Italy, but praises far and wide
Your house's hospitality. But say,
Have you come here direct from Flüelen,
And have you noticed nothing on your way,
Before you halted at my door?

---

* Berenger von Landenberg, a man of noble family in Thurgau, and
Governor of Unterwald, infamous for his cruelties to the Swiss, and particu
larly to the venerable Henry of the Halden. He was slain at the battle of
Morgarten, in 1315.

† A cell built in the 9th century, by Meinrad, Count of Hohenzollern, the
founder of the Convent of Einsiedeln, subsequently alluded to in the text.

STAUFF. (*sits down*).   I saw
        A work in progress, as I came along,
        I little thought to see—that likes me ill
FURST. O friend ! you've lighted on my thought at once.
STAUFF Such things in Uri ne'er were known before.
        Never was prison here in man's remembrance,
        Nor ever any stronghold but the grave.
FURST   You name it well.   It is the grave of freedom.
STAUFF Friend, Walter Fürst, I will be plain with you.
        No idle curiosity it is,
        That brings me here, but heavy cares.   I left
        Thraldom at home, and thraldom meets me here.
        Our wrongs, e'en now, are more than we can bear,
        And who shall tell us where they are to end ?
        From eldest time the Switzer has been free,
        Accustom'd only to the mildest rule.
        Such things as now we suffer, ne'er were known,
        Since herdsman first drove cattle to the hills.
FURST   Yes, our oppressions are unparallel'd !
        Why, even our own good lord of Attinghaus,
        Who lived in olden times, himself declares,
        They are no longer to be tamely borne.
STAUFF. In Unterwalden yonder 'tis the same ;
        And bloody has the retribution been.
        The imperial Seneschal, the Wolfshot, who
        At Rossberg dwelt, long'd for forbidden fruit—
        Baumgarten's wife, that lives at Alzellen,
        He wished to overcome in shameful sort,
        On which the husband slew him with his axe.
FURST. O, Heaven is just in all its judgments still !
        Baumgarten, say you?   A most worthy man.
        Has he escaped, and is he safely hid ?
STAUFF Your son-in-law conveyed him o'er the lake,
        And he lies hidden in my house at Steinen.
        He brought the tidings with him of a thing
        That has been done at Sarnen, worse than all,
        A thing to make the very heart run blood !
FURST (*attentively*).
        Say on   What is it ?
STAUFF.   There dwells in Melchthal, then,
        Just as you enter by the road from Kerns,

An upright man, named Henry of the Halden,
A man of weight and influence in the Diet.

FURST. Who knows him not? But what of him? Proceed.

STAUFF. The Landenberg, to punish some offence.
Committed by the old man's son, it seems,
Had given command to take the youth's best pair
Of oxen from his plough ; on which the lad
Struck down the messenger and took to flight

FURST. But the old father—tell me, what of him?

STAUFF. The Landenberg sent for him, and required
He should produce his son upon the spot :
And when th' old man protested, and with truth,
That he knew nothing of the fugitive,
The tyrant call'd his torturers.

FURST (*springs up and tries to lead him to the other side*).
                   Hush, no more !

STAUFFACHER (*with increasing warmth*).
"And though thy son," he cried, "has 'scaped me
    now,
I have thee fast, and thou shalt feel my vengeance."
With that they flung the old man to the earth,
And plunged the pointed steel into his eyes.

FURST. Merciful Heaven !

MELCH. (*rushing out*).
                 Into his eyes, his eyes?

STAUFF (*addresses himself in astonishment to* WALTER FURST).
Who is this youth?

MELCH. (*grasping him convulsively*).
             Into his eyes? Speak, speak\

FURST. Oh, miserable hour !

STAUFF   Who is it, tell me?
             [STAUFFACHER *makes a sign to him*
It is his son! All righteous heaven !

MELCH.   And I
Must be from thence ! What! into both his eyes ?

FURST. Be calm, be calm ; and bear it like a man !

MELCH. And all for me—for my mad wilful folly !
Blind, did you say? Quite blind—and both his eyes?

STAUFF. Ev'n so. The fountain of his sight's dried up
He ne'er will see the blessed sunshine more.

FURST. Oh, spare his anguish !

MELCH.   Never, never more!
[*Presses his hands upon his eyes and is silent for
   some moments: then turning from one to the
   other, speaks in a subdued tone, broken by sobs*
O the eye's light, of all the gifts of Heaven,
The dearest, best! From light all beings live—
Each fair created thing—the very plants
Turn with a joyful transport to the light,
And he—he must drag on through all his days
In endless darkness! Never more for him
The sunny meads shall glow, the flow'rets bloom ;
Nor shall he more behold the roseate tints
Of the iced mountain top! To die is nothing,
But to have life, and not have sight,—oh, that
Is misery indeed! Why do you look
So piteously at me? I have two eyes,
Yet to my poor blind father can give neither!
No, not one gleam of that great sea of light,
That with its dazzling splendour floods my gaze

STAUFF. Ah, I must swell the measure of your grief,
Instead of soothing it. The worst, alas!
Remains to tell. They've stripp'd him of his all ;
Nought have they left him, save his staff, on which.
Blind, and in rags, he moves from door to door.

MELCH. Nought but his staff to the old eyeless man!
Stripp'd of his all—even of the light of day,
The common blessing of the meanest wretch
Tell me no more of patience, of concealment!
Oh, what a base and coward thing am I,
That on mine own security I thought,
And took no care of thine! Thy precious head
Left as a pledge within the tyrant's grasp!
Hence, craven-hearted prudence, hence! And all
My thoughts be vengeance, and the despot's blood!
I'll seek him straight—no power shall stay me now—
And at his hands demand my father's eyes.
I'll beard him 'mid a thousand myrmidons!
What's life to me, if in his heart's best blood
I cool the fever of this mighty anguish. [*He is going*

FURST. Stay, this is madness, Melchthal! What avails
Your single arm against his power? He sits

At Sarnen high within his lordly keep,
And, safe within its battlemented walls,
May laugh to scorn your unavailing rage.

MELCH. And though he sat within the icy domes
Of yon far Schreckhorn—ay, or higher, where
Veil'd since eternity, the Jungfrau soars,
Still to the tyrant would I make my way;
With twenty comrades minded like myself,
I'd lay his fastness level with the earth!
And if none follow me, and if you all,
In terror for your homesteads and your herds,
Bow in submission to the tyrant's yoke,
I'll call the herdsmen on the hills around me,
And there beneath heaven's free and boundless roof,
Where men still feel as men, and hearts are true,
Proclaim aloud this foul enormity!

STAUFF. (to FURST).
'Tis at its height—and are we then to wait
Till some extremity——

MELCHTHAL.　　　　　　What extremity
Remains for apprehension, when men's eyes
Have ceased to be secure within their sockets?
Are we defenceless? Wherefore did we learn
To bend the cross-bow,—wield the battle-axe?
What living creature, but in its despair,
Finds for itself a weapon of defence?
The baited stag will turn, and with the show
Of his dread antlers hold the hounds at bay;
The chamois drags the huntsman down th' abyss;
The very ox, the partner of man's toil,
The sharer of his roof, that meekly bends
The strength of his huge neck beneath the yoke,
Springs up, if he's provoked, whets his strong horn,
And tosses his tormentor to the clouds.

FURST. If the three Cantons thought as we three do,
Something might, then, be done, with good effect.

STAUFF When Uri calls, when Unterwald replies,
Schwytz will be mindful of her ancient league *.

---

* The League, or Bond, of the Three Cantons was of very ancient origin.
They met and renewed it from time to time, especially when their liberties

MELCH. I've many friends in Unterwald, and none
That would not gladly venture life and limb,
If fairly back'd and aided by the rest.
Oh, sage and reverend fathers of this land,
Here do I stand before your riper years,
An unskill'd youth, whose voice must in the Diet
Still be subdued into respectful silence.
Do not, because that I am young, and want
Experience, slight my counsel and my words.
'Tis not the wantonness of youthful blood

were threatened with danger. A remarkable instance of this occurred in
the end of the 13th century, when Albert, of Austria, became Emperor, and
when, possibly, for the first time, the Bond was reduced to writing. As it
is important to the understanding of many passages of the play, a translation is subjoined of the oldest known document relating to it. The original,
which is in Latin and German, is dated in August, 1291, and is under the
seals of the whole of the men of Schwytz, the commonalty of the vale of
Uri and the whole of the men of the upper and lower vales of Stanz.

THE BOND.

Be it known to every one, that the men of the Dale of Uri, the Com-
munity of Schwytz, as also the men of the mountains of Unterwald, in
consideration of the evil times, have full confidently bound themselves, and
sworn to help each other with all their power and might, property and
people, against all who shall do violence to them, or any of them. That is
our Ancient Bond.

Whoever hath a Seignior, let him obey according to the conditions of his
service.

We are agreed to receive into these dales no Judge, who is not a countryman and indweller, or who hath bought his place.

Every controversy amongst the sworn confederates shall be determined by
some of the sagest of their number, and if any one shall challenge their
judgment, then shall he be constrained to obey it by the rest.

Whoever intentionally or deceitfully kills another, shall be executed
and whoever shelters him shall be banished.

Whoever burns the property of another shall no longer be regarded as a
countryman, and whoever shelters him shall make good the damage done.

Whoever injures another, or robs him, and hath property in our country
shall make satisfaction out of the same.

No one shall distrain a debtor without a judge, nor any one who is not
his debtor, or the surety for such debtor.

Every one in these dales shall submit to the judge, or we, the sworn
confederates, all will take satisfaction for all the injury occasioned by his
contumacy. And if in any internal division the one party will not accept
justice, all the rest shall help the other party. These decrees shall, God
willing, endure eternally for our general advantage.

Z

That fires my spirit ; but a pang so deep
That e'en the flinty rocks must pity me.
You, too, are fathers, heads of families,
And you must wish to have a virtuous son,
To reverence your grey hairs, and shield your eyes
With pious and affectionate regard.
Do not, I pray, because in limb and fortune
You still are unassail'd, and still your eyes
Revolve undimm'd and sparkling in their spheres ;
Oh, do not, therefore, disregard our wrongs !
Above you, too, doth hang the tyrant's sword.
You, too, have striven to alienate the land
From Austria.　This was all my father's crime :
You share his guilt, and may his punishment.

STAUFFACHER (to FURST).

Do thou resolve ! I am prepared to follow.

FURST.　First let us learn, what steps the noble lords
Von Sillinen and Attinghaus propose.
Their names would rally thousands in the cause.

MELCH.　Is there a name within the Forest Mountains
That carries more respect than thine—and thine ?
To names like these the people cling for help
With confidence—such names are household words.
Rich was your heritage of manly virtue,
And richly have you added to its stores.
What need of nobles ?　Let us do the work
Ourselves.　Although we stood alone, methinks,
We should be able to maintain our rights.

STAUFF.　The nobles' wrongs are not so great as ours.
The torrent, that lays waste the lower grounds,
Hath not ascended to the uplands yet.
But let them see the country once in arms,
They'll not refuse to lend a helping hand.

FURST.　Were there an umpire 'twixt ourselves and Austria,
Justice and law might then decide our quarrel.
But our oppressor is our emperor too,
And judge supreme.　'Tis God must help us, then,
And our own arm !　Be yours the task to rouse
The men of Schwytz ; I'll rally friends in Uri
But whom are we to send to Unterwald ?

MELCH.　Thither send me.　Whom should it more concern ?

FURST. No, Melchthal, no; thou art my guest, and I
    Must answer for thy safety.
MELCHTHAL.   Let me go.
    I know each forest track and mountain pass;
    Friends too I'll find, be sure, on every hand,
    To give me willing shelter from the foe.
STAUFF. Nay, let him go : no traitors harbour there :
    For tyranny is so abhorred in Unterwald,
    No minions can be found to work her will.
    In the low valleys, too, the Alzeller
    Will gain confederates, and rouse the country.
MELCH. But how shall we communicate, and not
    Awaken the suspicion of the tyrants?
STAUFF. Might we not meet at Brunnen or at Treib,
    Hard by the spot where merchant vessels land?
FURST. We must not go so openly to work.
    Hear my opinion. On the lake's left bank,
    As we sail hence to Brunnen, right against
    The Mytenstein, deep-hidden in the wood
    A meadow lies, by shepherds called the Rootli,
    Because the wood has been uprooted there.
    'Tis where our Canton bound'ries verge on yours ;—
                         [*To* MELCHTHAL
    Your boat will carry you across from Schwytz.
                        [*To* STAUFFACHER
    Thither by lonely bypaths let us wend
    At midnight, and deliberate o'er our plans.
    Let each bring with him there ten trusty men,
    All one at heart with us ; and then we may
    Consult together for the general weal,
    And, with God's guidance, fix our onward course.
STAUFF. So let it be. And now your true right hand!
    Yours, too, young man ! and as we now three men
    Among ourselves thus knit our hands together
    In all sincerity and truth, e'en so
    Shall we three Cantons, too, together stand
    In victory and defeat, in life and death
FURST *and* MELCHTHAL.
    In life and death.
       [*They hold their hands clasped together for some*
      moments in silence.

MELCHTHAL.   Alas, my old blind father!
Thou canst no more behold the day of freedom;
But thou shalt hear it. When from Alp to Alp
The beacon fires throw up their flaming signs,
And the proud castles of the tyrants fall,
Into thy cottage shall the Switzer burst,
Bear the glad tidings to thine ear, and o'er
Thy darken'd way shall Freedom's radiance pour.

ACT II.

Scene I.

The Mansion of the Baron of Attinghausen *A Gothic
Hall, decorated with escutcheons and helmets. The* Baron,
*a grey-headed man, eighty-five years old, tall and of a com-
manding mien, clad in a furred pelisse, and leaning on a
staff tipped with chamois horn.* Kuoni *and six hinds standing round him with rakes and scythes* Ulrich of Rudenz
enters in the costume of a Knight.

Rud. . . Uncle, I'm here! Your will?
Attinghausen.   First let me share,
After the ancient custom of our house,
The morning cup, with these my faithful servants!
     [*He drinks from a cup, which is then passed round.*
Time was, I stood myself in field and wood,
With mine own eyes directing all their toil,
Even as my banner led them in the fight,
Now I am only fit to play the steward;
And, if the genial sun come not to me,
I can no longer seek it on the mountains.
Thus slowly, in an ever narrowing sphere,
I move on to the narrowest and the last,
Where all life's pulses cease. I now am **but**
The shadow of my former self, and that
Is fading fast—'twill soon be but a **name**
Kuoni (*offering* Rudenz *the cup*).
A pledge, young master!
         [Rudenz *hesitates to take the cup.*
       Nay, Sir, drink it off!
One cup, one heart! You know our proverb, **Sir?**

ATTING. Go, children, and at eve, when work is done,
　　　　We'll meet and talk the country's business over.
　　　　　　　　　　　　　　　　　　[Exeunt Servants
　　　　Belted and plumed, and all thy bravery on!
　　　　Thou art for Altdorf—for the castle, boy?
RUD. . . Yes, uncle.　Longer may I not delay—
ATTINGHAUSEN (*sitting down*).
　　　　Why in such haste? Say, are thy youthful hours
　　　　Doled in such niggard measure, that thou must
　　　　Be chary of them to thy aged uncle?
RUD. . . I see, my presence is not needed here,
　　　　I am but as a stranger in this house.
ATTINGHAUSEN (*gazes fixedly at him for a considerable time*).
　　　　Alas, thou art indeed! Alas, that home
　　　　To thee has grown so strange! Oh, Uly! Uly!
　　　　I scarce do know thee now, thus deck'd in silks,
　　　　The peacock's feather * flaunting in thy cap,
　　　　And purple mantle round thy shoulders flung;
　　　　Thou look'st upon the peasant with disdain,
　　　　And takest with a blush his honest greeting.
RUD.　. All honour due to him I gladly pay,
　　　　But must deny the right he would usurp.
ATTING. The sore displeasure of the king is resting
　　　　Upon the land, and every true man's heart
　　　　Is full of sadness for the grievous wrongs
　　　　We suffer from our tyrants.　Thou alone
　　　　Art all unmoved amid the general grief
　　　　Abandoning thy friends, thou tak'st thy stand
　　　　Beside thy country's foes, and, as in scorn
　　　　Of our distress, pursuest giddy joys,
　　　　Courting the smiles of princes, all the while
　　　　Thy country bleeds beneath their cruel scourge
RUD 　The land is sore oppress'd, I know it, uncle.
　　　　But why? Who plunged it into this distress?
　　　　A word, one little easy word, might buy
　　　　Instant deliverance from such dire oppression,
　　　　And win the good will of the Emperor.

---

* The Austrian knights were in the habit of wearing a plume of peacocks feathers in their helmets. After the overthrow of the Austrian dominion in Switzerland, it was made highly penal to wear the peacock's feather at any public assembly there.

Woe unto those, who seal the people's eyes,
And make them adverse to their country's good—
The men, who, for their own vile selfish ends,
Are seeking to prevent the Forest States
From swearing fealty to Austria's House,
As all the countries round about have done.
It fits their humour well, to take their seats
Amid the nobles on the Herrenbank*;
They'll have the Cæsar for their lord, forsooth,—
That is to say, they'll have no lord at all.

ATTING. Must I hear this, and from thy lips, rash boy!

RUD... You urged me to this answer.   Hear me out.
What, uncle, is the character you've stoop'd
To fill contentedly through life?   Have you
No higher pride, than in these lonely wilds
To be the Landamman or Banneret†,
The petty chieftain of a shepherd race?
How! Were it not a far more glorious choice,
To bend in homage to our royal lord,
And swell the princely splendours of his court,
Than sit at home, the peer of your own vassals,
And share the judgment-seat with vulgar clowns?

ATTING. Ah, Uly, Uly; all too well I see,
The tempter's voice has caught thy willing ear,
And pour'd its subtle poison in thy heart.

RUD .. Yes, I conceal it not.   It doth offend
My inmost soul, to hear the stranger's gibes,
That taunt us with the name of " Peasant Nobles!"
Think you the heart that's stirring here can brook,
While all the young nobility around
Are reaping honour under Habsburg's banner,
That I should loiter, in inglorious ease,
Here on the heritage my fathers left,
And, in the dull routine of vulgar toil,
Lose all life's glorious spring?   In other lands
Deeds are achieved.   A world of fair renown
Beyond these mountains stirs in martial pomp.

* The bench reserved for the nobility.
† The Landamman was an officer chosen by the Swiss Gemeinde, or Diet,
to preside over them.   The Banneret was an officer entrusted with the
keeping of the State Banner, and such others as were taken in battle.

My helm and shield are rusting in the hall;
The martial trumpet's spirit-stirring blast,
The herald's call, inviting to the lists,
Rouse not the echoes of these vales, where nought,
Save cowherd's horn and cattle bell, is heard,
In one unvarying dull monotony.

ATTING Deluded boy, seduced by empty show!
Despise the land that gave thee birth! Ashamed
Of the good ancient customs of thy sires!
The day will come, when thou, with burning tears,
Wilt long for home, and for thy native hills,
And that dear melody of tuneful herds,
Which now, in proud disgust, thou dost despise!
A day when thou wilt drink its tones in sadness,
Hearing their music in a foreign land.
Oh! potent is the spell that binds to home!
No, no, the cold, false world is not for thee.
At the proud court, with thy true heart, thou wilt
For ever feel a stranger among strangers.
The world asks virtues of far other stamp
Than thou hast learned within these simple vales.
But go—go thither,—barter thy free soul,
Take land in fief, become a prince's vassal,
Where thou might'st be lord paramount, and prince
Of all thine own unburden'd heritage!
O, Uly, Uly, stay among thy people!
Go not to Altdorf.   Oh, abandon not
The sacred cause of thy wrong'd native land!
I am the last of all my race.   My name
Ends with me.   Yonder hang my helm and shield;
They will be buried with me in the grave*.
And must I think, when yielding up my breath,
That thou but wait'st the closing of mine eyes,
To stoop thy knee to this new feudal court,
And take in vassalage from Austria's hands
The noble lands, which I from God received,
Free and unfetter'd as the mountain air!

RUD. . . 'Tis vain for us to strive against the king.
The world pertains to him :—shall we alone,

---

* According to the custom, by which, when the last male descendant of a
noble family died, his sword, helmet, and shield, were buried with him.

In mad presumptuous obstinacy. strive
To break that mighty chain of lands, which he
Hath drawn around us with his giant grasp.
His are the markets, his the courts,—his too
The highways ; nay, the very carrier's horse,
That traffics on the Gotthardt, pays him toll.
By his dominions, as within a net,
We are enclosed. and girded round about.
—And will the Empire shield us ? Say, can it
Protect itself 'gainst Austria's growing power?
To God, and not to emperors must we look!
What store can on their promises be placed,
When they, to meet their own necessities,
Can pawn, and even alienate the towns
That flee for shelter 'neath the Eagle's wings * ?
No, uncle! It is wise and wholesome prudence,
In times like these, when faction's all abroad,
To own attachment to some mighty chief.
The imperial crown's transferred from line to line †.
It has no memory for faithful service :
But to secure the favour of these great
Hereditary masters, were to sow
Seed for a future harvest.

ATTINGHAUSEN.   Art so wise?
Wilt thou see clearer than thy noble sires,
Who battled for fair freedom's costly gem,
With life, and fortune, and heroic arm ?
Sail down the lake to Lucern, there inquire,
How Austria's rule doth weigh the Cantons down.
Soon she will come to count our sheep, our cattle,
To portion out the Alps, e'en to their summits,
And in our own free woods to hinder us
From striking down the eagle or the stag ;
To set her tolls on every bridge and gate,
Impoverish us, to swell her lust of sway,
And drain our dearest blood to feed her wars

---

* This frequently occurred. But in the event of an imperial city being
mortgaged for the purpose of raising money, it lost its freedom, and was considered as put out of the realm.

† An allusion to the circumstance of the Imperial Crown not being
hereditary, but conferred by election on one of the Counts of the Empire.

No, if our blood must flow, let it be shed
In our own cause! We purchase liberty
More cheaply far than bondage.

RUDENZ.   What can we,
A shepherd race, against great Albert's hosts?

ATTING Learn, foolish boy, to know this shepherd race!
I know them, I have led them on in fight,—
I saw them in the battle at Favenz.
Austria will try, forsooth, to force on us
A yoke we are determined not to bear!
Oh, learn to feel from what a race thou'rt sprung!
Cast not, for tinsel trash and idle show,
The precious jewel of thy worth away.
To be the chieftain of a free born race,
Bound to thee only by their unbought love,
Ready to stand—to fight—to die with thee,
Be that thy pride, be that thy noblest boast!
Knit to thy heart the ties of kindred—home—
Cling to the land, the dear land of thy sires,
Grapple to that with thy whole heart and soul!
Thy power is rooted deep and strongly here,
But in yon stranger world thou'lt stand alone,
A trembling reed beat down by every blast.
Oh come! 'tis long since we have seen thee, Uly!
Tarry but this one day. Only to-day
Go not to Altdorf. Wilt thou? Not to-day!
For this one day, bestow thee on thy friends.

                                      [*Takes his hand*

RUD.   . I gave my word. Unhand me! I am bound.

ATTING. (*drops his hand and says sternly*)
Bound, didst thou say? Oh yes, unhappy boy,
Thou art indeed. But not by word or oath.
'Tis by the silken mesh of love thou'rt bound.

                                      [RUDENZ *turns away*

Ay, hide thee, as thou wilt. 'Tis she, I know,
Bertha of Bruneck, draws thee to the court;
'Tis she that chains thee to the Emperor's service,
Thou think'st to win the noble knightly maid
By thy apostacy. Be not deceived.
She is held out before thee as a lure;
But never meant for innocence like thine

RUD...No more, I've heard enough.   So fare you well.

[*Exit*

ATTING. Stay, Uly! Stay! Rash boy, he's gone!   I can
Nor hold him back, nor save him from destruction
And so the Wolfshot has deserted us ;—
Others will follow his example soon.
This foreign witchery, sweeping o'er our hills,
Tears with its potent spell our youth away :
O luckless hour, when men and manners strange
Into these calm and happy valleys came,
To warp our primitive and guileless ways.
The new is pressing on with might.   The old,
The good, the simple, fleeteth fast away.
New times come on.   A race is springing up,
That think not as their fathers thought before!
What do I here?   All, all are in the grave
With whom erewhile I moved, and held converse ;
My age has long been laid beneath the sod :
Happy the man, who may not live to see
What shall be done by those that follow me !

SCENE II.

*A meadow surrounded by high rocks and wooded ground.
On the rocks are tracks, with rails and ladders, by which the
peasants are afterwards seen descending.   In the back-ground
the lake is observed, and over it a moon rainbow in the early
part of the scene.   The prospect is closed by lofty mountains,
with glaciers rising behind them.   The stage is dark · but
the lake and glaciers glisten in the moonlight.*

MELCHTHAL, BAUMGARTEN, WINKELRIED, MEYER VON SAR
NEN, BURKHART AM BUHEL, ARNOLD VON SEWA.
KLAUS VON DER FLUE, *and four other peasants, all armed*

MELCHTHAL (*behind the scenes*).
The mountain pass is open.   Follow me!
I see the rock, and little cross upon it :
This is the spot; here is the Rootli.

[*They enter with torches*

WINKELRIED   Hark!
SEWA. The coast is clear

MEYER.   None of our comrades come?
We are the first, we Unterwaldeners.
MELCH. How far is't i' the night?
BAUM.   The beacon watch
Upon the Selisberg has just called two.
                              [*A bell is heard at a distance*
MEYER. Hush! Hark!
BUHEL.   The forest chapel's matin bell
Chimes clearly o'er the lake from Switzerland.
VON F. The air is clear, and bears the sound so far.
MELCH. Go, you and you, and light some broken boughs,
Let's bid them welcome with a cheerful blaze.
                              [*Two peasants exeunt*
SEWA.   The moon shines fair to-night.   Beneath its beams
The lake reposes, bright as burnish'd steel.
BUHEL. They'll have an easy passage.
WINK. (*pointing to the lake*).   Ha! look there!
See you nothing?
MEYER.   What is it? Ay, indeed!
A rainbow in the middle of the night.
MELCH. Formed by the bright reflection of the moon!
VON F. A sign most strange and wonderful, indeed!
Many there be, who ne'er have seen the like
SEWA. 'Tis doubled, see, a paler one above!
BAUM. A boat is gliding yonder right beneath it.
MELCH. That must be Werner Stauffacher!   I knew
The worthy patriot would not tarry long.
                              [*Goes with* BAUMGARTEN *towards the shore*
MEYER. The Uri men are like to be the last.
BUHEL. They're forced to take a winding circuit through
The mountains; for the Viceroy's spies are out.
                    [*In the meanwhile the two peasants have kindled
                    a fire in the centre of the stage.*
MELCH. (*on the shore*).
Who's there? The word?
STAUFF. (*from below*).   Friends of the country.
                    [*All retire up the stage, towards the party landing
                    from the boat. Enter* STAUFFACHER, ITEL RED-
                    ING, HANS AUF DER MAUER, JORG IM HOFE,
                    CONRAD HUNN, ULRICH DER SCHMIDT, JOST VON
                    WEILER, *and three other peasants, armed.*

ALL   Welcome!

[While the rest remain behind exchanging greet-
ings, MELCHTHAL. *comes forward with* STAUF-
FACHER.

MELCH. Oh worthy Stauffacher, I've look'd but now
        On him, who could not look on me again.
        I've laid my hands upon his rayless eyes,
        And on their vacant orbits sworn a vow
        Of vengeance, only to be cool'd in blood.

STAUFF Speak not of vengeance. We are here, to meet
        The threatened evil, not to avenge the past.
        Now tell me what you've done, and what secured,
        To aid the common cause in Unterwald,
        How stand the peasantry disposed, and how
        Yourself escaped the wiles of treachery?

MELCH. Through the Surenen's fearful mountain chain,
        Where dreary ice-fields stretch on every side,
        And sound is none, save the hoarse vulture's cry,
        I reach'd the Alpine pasture, where the herds
        From Uri and from Engelberg resort,
        And turn their cattle forth to graze in common.
        Still as I went along, I slaked my thirst
        With the coarse oozings of the lofty glacier,
        That thro' the crevices come foaming down,
        And turned to rest me in the herdsmen's cots*,
        Where I was host and guest, until I gain'd
        The cheerful homes and social haunts of men.
        Already through these distant vales had spread
        The rumour of this last atrocity;
        And wheresoe'er I went, at every door,
        Kind words and gentle looks were there to greet me
        I found these simple spirits all in arms
        Against our rulers' tyrannous encroachments.
        For as their Alps through each succeeding year
        Yield the same roots,—their streams flow ever on
        In the same channels,—nay, the clouds and winds
        The selfsame course unalterably pursue,

---

* These are the cots, or shealings, erected by the herdsmen for shelter,
while pasturing their herds on the mountains during the summer. These
are left deserted in winter, during which period Melchthal's journey was
taken

So have old customs there, from sire to son,
Been handed down, unchanging and unchanged;
Nor will they brook to swerve or turn aside
From the fixed even tenor of their life.
With grasp of their hard hands they welcomed me,—
Took from the walls their rusty falchions down,—
And from their eyes the soul of valour flash'd
With joyful lustre, as I spoke those names,
Sacred to every peasant in the mountains,
Your own and Walter Fürst's.   Whate'er your voice
Should dictate as the right, they swore to do;
And you they swore to follow e'en to death.
—So sped I on from house to house, secure
In the guest's sacred privilege;—and when
I reached at last the valley of my home,
Where dwell my kinsmen, scatter'd far and near—
And when I found my father, stript and blind.
Upon the stranger's straw, fed by the alms
Of charity——

STAUFFACHER.   Great Heaven!
MELCHTHAL.   Yet wept I not!
No—not in weak and unavailing tears
Spent I the force of my fierce burning anguish;
Deep in my bosom, like some precious treasure,
I lock'd it fast, and thought on deeds alone.
Through every winding of the hills I crept,—
No valley so remote but I explored it;
Nay, even at the glacier's ice-clad base,
I sought and found the homes of living men;
And still, where'er my wandering footsteps turn'd,
The selfsame hatred of these tyrants met me.
For even there, at vegetation's verge,
Where the numb'd earth is barren of all fruits,
Their grasping hands had been stretch'd forth for
   plunder.
Into the hearts of all this honest race,
The story of my wrongs struck deep, and now
They, to a man, are ours; both heart and hand.

STAUFF. Great things, indeed, you've wrought in little time.
MELCH. I did still more than this.   The fortresses,

Rossberg and Sarnen, are the country's dread;
For from behind their rocky walls the foe
Swoops, as the eagle from his eyrie, down,
And, safe himself, spreads havoc o'er the land
With my own eyes I wish'd to weigh its strength,
So went to Sarnen, and explored the castle.

STAUFF. How! Risk thyself e'en in the tiger's den?

MELCH. Disguised in pilgrim's weeds I entered it;
I saw the Viceroy feasting at his board—
Judge if I'm master of myself or no!
I saw the tyrant, and I slew him not!

STAUFF. Fortune, indeed, has smiled upon your boldness.
          [*Meanwhile the others have arrived and join*
               MELCHTHAL *and* STAUFFACHER.
Yet tell me now, I pray, who are the friends,
The worthy men, who came along with you?
Make me acquainted with them, that we may
Speak frankly, man to man, and heart to heart.

MEYER. In the three Cantons, who, sir, knows not you?
Meyer of Sarnen is my name; and this
Is Struth of Winkelried, my sister's son.

STAUFF. No unknown name.   A Winkelried it was,
Who slew the dragon in the fen at Weiler,
And lost his life in the encounter, too.

WINK. That, Master Stauffacher, was my grandfather.

MELCH. (*pointing to two peasants*).
These two are men belonging to the convent
Of Engelberg, and live behind the forest.
You'll not think ill of them, because they're serfs,
And sit not free upon the soil, like us.
They love the land, and bear a good repute.

STAUFFACHER (*to them*).
Give me your hands.   He has good cause for thanks,
That unto no man owes his body's service.
But worth is worth, no matter where 'tis found

HUNN. That is Herr Reding, sir, our old Landamman.

MEYER. I know him well.   There is a suit between us,
About a piece of ancient heritage.
Herr Reding, we are enemies in court,
Here we are one   [*Shakes his hand*

STAUFFACHER. That's well and bravely said.

WINK. Listen ! They come. Hark to the horn of Uri !
    [*On the right and left armed men are seen descend-*
    ing the rocks with torches.

MAUER. Look, is not that God's pious servant there ?
    A worthy priest ! The terrors of the night,
    And the way's pains and perils scare not him
    A faithful shepherd caring for his flock.

BAUM. The Sacrist follows him, and Walter Fürst.
    But where is Tell ? I do not see him there.
    [WALTER FURST, ROSSELMANN *the Pastor,* PETER-
    MANN *the Sacrist,* KUONI *the Shepherd,* WERNI
    the Huntsman, RUODI *the Fisherman, and five*
    other countrymen, thirty-three in all, advance
    and take their places round the fire.

FURST. Thus must we, on the soil our fathers left us,
    Creep forth by stealth to meet like murderers,
    And in the night, that should her mantle lend
    Only to crime and black conspiracy,
    Assert our own good rights, which yet are clear
    As is the radiance of the noonday sun.

MELCH. So be it. What is woven in gloom of night
    Shall free and boldly meet the morning light

ROSSEL. Confederates ! listen to the words which God
    Inspires my heart withal. Here we are met,
    To represent the general weal. In us
    Are all the people of the land convened.
    Then let us hold the Diet, as of old,
    And as we're wont in peaceful times to do.
    The time's necessity be our excuse,
    If there be aught informal in this meeting.
    Still, wheresoe'er men strike for justice, there
    Is God, and now beneath his heav'n we stand

STAUFF. 'Tis well advised.—Let us, then, hold the Diet,
    According to our ancient usages.—
    Though it be night, there's sunshine in our cause.

MELCH. Few though our numbers be, the hearts are here
    Of the whole people ; here the BEST are met.

HUNN. The ancient books may not be near at hand,
    Yet are they graven in our inmost hearts.

Rossel. 'Tis well.   And now, then, let a ring be formed,
         And plant the swords of power within the ground *
Mauer   Let the Landamman step into his place,
         And by his side his secretaries stand.
Sacrist There are three Cantons here. Which hath the right
         To give the head to the united Council ?
         Schwytz may contest that dignity with Uri,
         We Unterwald'ners enter not the field.
Melch. We stand aside.   We are but suppliants here,
         Invoking aid from our more potent friends.
Stauff. Let Uri have the sword.   Her banner takes,
         In battle, the precedence of our own.
Furst   Schwytz, then, must share the honour of the sword;
         For she's the honoured ancestor of all
Rossel. Let me arrange this generous controversy.
         Uri shall lead in battle—Schwytz in Council.
Furst (gives Stauffacher his hand).
         Then take your place.
Stauffacher.   Not I. Some older man.
Hofe   Ulrich, the Smith, is the most aged here.
Mauer. A worthy man, but he is not a freeman ;
         —No bondman can be judge in Switzerland.
Stauff. Is not Herr Reding here, our old Landamman ?
         Where can we find a worthier man than he?
Furst. Let him be Amman and the Diet's chief!
         You that agree with me, hold up your hands !
                         [All hold up their right hands
Reding (stepping into the centre).
         I cannot lay my hands upon the books ;
         But by you everlasting stars I swear,
         Never to swerve from justice and the right.
             [The two swords are placed before him, and a circle
              formed ; Schwytz in the centre, Uri on his right
              Unterwald on his left.
Reding (resting on his battle sword).
         Why, at the hour when spirits walk the earth,
         Meet the three Cantons of the mountains here,

---

* It was the custom at the Meetings of the Landes Gemeinde, or Diet, to
set swords upright in the ground as emblems of authority.

Upon the lake's inhospitable shore?
And what the purport of the new alliance
We here contract beneath the starry Heaven?

STAUFFACHER (*entering the circle*).

No new alliance do we now contract,
But one our fathers framed, in ancient times,
We purpose to renew!   For know, confederates,
Though mountain ridge and lake divide our bounds
And every Canton's ruled by its own laws,
Yet are we but one race, born of one blood,
And all are children of one common home

WINK.   Then is the burden of our legends true,
That we came hither from a distant land?
Oh, tell us what you know, that our new league
May reap fresh vigour from the leagues of old.

STAUFF   Hear, then, what aged herdsmen tell.   There dwelt
A mighty people in the land that lies
Back to the north.   The scourge of famine came;
And in this strait twas publicly resolved,
That each tenth man, on whom the lot might fall,
Should leave the country   They obey'd—and forth,
With loud lamentings, men and women went,
A mighty host; and to the south moved on,
Cutting their way through Germany by the sword,
Until they gained these pine-clad hills of ours;
Nor stopp'd they ever on their forward course,
Till at the shaggy dell they halted, where
The Müta flows through its luxuriant meads
No trace of human creature met their eye,
Save one poor hut upon the desert shore,
Where dwelt a lonely man, and kept the ferry.
A tempest raged—the lake rose mountains high
And barr'd their further progress.   Thereupon
They view'd the country—found it rich in wood,
Discover'd goodly springs, and felt as they
Were in their own dear native land once more.
Then they resolved to settle on the spot;
Erected there the ancient town of Schwytz;
And many a day of toil had they to clear
The tangled brake and forest's spreading roots
Meanwhile their numbers grew, the soil became

2 A

Unequal to sustain them, and they cross'd
To the black mountain, far as Weissland, where,
Conceal'd behind eternal walls of ice,
Another people speak another tongue.
They built the village Stanz, beside the Kernwald;
The village Altdorf, in the vale of Reuss;
Yet, ever mindful of their parent stem,
The men of Schwytz, from all the stranger race,
That since that time have settled in the land,
Each other recognize. Their hearts still know,
And beat fraternally to kindred blood.

[Extends his hand right and left

MAUER. Ay, we are all one heart, one blood, one race!
ALL (*joining hands*).
      We are one people, and will act as one.
STAUFF. The nations round us bear a foreign yoke;
      For they have yielded to the conqueror.
      Nay, e'en within our frontiers may be found
      Some, that owe villein service to a lord,
      A race of bonded serfs from sire to son.
      But we, the genuine race of ancient Swiss,
      Have kept our freedom from the first till now.
      Never to princes have we bow'd the knee;
      Freely we sought protection of the Empire.
ROSSEL. Freely we sought it—freely it was given.
      'Tis so set down in Emperor Frederick's charter.
STAUFF. For the most free have still some feudal lord.
      There must be still a chief, a judge supreme,
      To whom appeal may lie, in case of strife.
      And therefore was it, that our sires allow'd,
      For what they had recover'd from the waste,
      This honour to the Emperor, the lord
      Of all the German and Italian soil;
      And, like the other free men of his realm,
      Engaged to aid him with their swords in war;
      And this alone should be the free man's duty,
      To guard the Empire that keeps guard for him.
MELCH. He's but a slave that would acknowledge more.
STAUFF. They followed, when the Heribann* went forth,

* The Heribann was a muster of warriors similar to the *arrière ban* of
France.

The imperial standard, and they fought its battles!
To Italy they march'd in arms, to place
The Cæsars' crown upon the Emperor's head.
But still at home they ruled themselves in peace,
By their own laws and ancient usages.
The Emperor's only right was to adjudge
The penalty of death ; he therefore named
Some mighty noble as his delegate,
That had no stake or interest in the land
He was call'd in, when doom was to be pass'd,
And, in the face of day, pronounced decree,
Clear and distinctly. fearing no man's hate.
What traces here, that we are bondsmen?   Speak,
If there be any can gainsay my words!

HOFE. No! You have spoken but the simple truth :
We never stoop'd beneath a tyrant's yoke.

STAUFF Even to the Emperor we refused obedience.
When he gave judgment in the church's favour;
For when the Abbey of Einsiedlen claimed
The Alp our fathers and ourselves had grazed,
And showed an ancient charter, which bestowed
The land on them as being ownerless—
For our existence there had been concealed—
What was our answer? This. " The grant is void,
No Emperor can bestow what is our own :
And if the Empire shall deny us justice,
We can, within our mountains, right ourselves !"
Thus spake our fathers!   And shall we endure
The shame and infamy of this new yoke.
And from the vassal brook what never king
Dared, in the fulness of his power, attempt?
This soil we have created for ourselves,
By the hard labour of our hands ; we've changed
The giant forest, that was erst the haunt
Of savage bears, into a home for man :
Extirpated the dragon's brood, that wont
To rise, distent with venom, from the swamps ;
Rent the thick misty canopy that hung
Its blighting vapours on the dreary waste ;
Blasted the solid rock : o'er the abyss
Thrown the firm bridge for the wayfaring man

2 A 2

By the possession of a thousand years
The soil is ours.   And shall an alien lord,
Himself a vassal, dare to venture here.
On our own hearths insult us,—and attempt
To forge the chains of bondage for our hands,
And do us shame on our own proper soil?
Is there no help against such wrong as this?

　　　　　　　[*Great sensation among the people*

Yes! there's a limit to the despot's power!
When the oppress'd looks round in vain for justice,
When his sore burden may no more be borne,
With fearless heart he makes appeal to Heaven,
And thence brings down his everlasting rights,
Which there abide, inalienably his,
And indestructible as are the stars.
Nature's primæval state returns again,
Where man stands hostile to his fellow man;
And if all other means shall fail his need,
One last resource remains—his own good sword.
Our dearest treasures call to us for aid,
Against the oppressor's violence; we stand
For country, home, for wives, for children here!

ALL (*clashing their swords*).

　　Here stand we for our homes, our wives, and
　　children.

ROSSELMANN (*stepping into the circle*).

　　Bethink ye well, before ye draw the sword.
　　Some peaceful compromise may yet be made:
　　Speak but one word, and at your feet you'll see
　　The men who now oppress you   Take the terms
　　That have been often tendered you; renounce
　　The Empire, and to Austria swear allegiance!

MAUER. What says the priest? To Austria allegiance?

BUHEL. Hearken not to him!

WINKELRIED. 　　　　　　　　'Tis a traitor's counsel,

　　His country's foe!

REDING 　　　　　　　Peace, peace, confederates!

SERVA. Homage to Austria, after wrongs like these!

FLUE. Shall Austria extort from us by force,

　　What we denied to kindness and entreaty?

MEYER Then should we all be slaves, deservedly.

MAUER. Yes! Let him forfeit all a Switzer's rights,
    Who talks of yielding to the yoke of Austria!
    I stand on this, Landamman.   Let this be
    The foremost of our laws!
MELCHTHAL   Even so! Whoe'er
    Shall talk of tamely bearing Austria's yoke,
    Let him be stripp'd of all his rights and honours;
    And no man hence receive him at his hearth!
ALL (raising their right hands).
    Agreed! Be this the law!
REDING (after a pause).   The law it is.
ROSSEL. Now you are free—by this law you are free.
    Never shall Austria obtain by force
    What she has fail'd to gain by friendly suit.
WEIL.   On with the order of the day! Proceed!
REDING. Confederates! Have all gentler means been tried?
    Perchance the Emp'ror knows not of our wrongs;
    It may not be his will that thus we suffer:
    Were it not well to make one last attempt,
    And lay our grievances before the throne,
    Ere we unsheath the sword?   Force is at best
    A fearful thing e'en in a righteous cause;
    God only helps, when man can help no more.
STAUFF. (to KONRAD HUNN).
    Here you can give us information.   Speak!
HUNN   I was at Rheinfeld, at the Emperor's palace,
    Deputed by the Cantons to complain
    Of the oppressions of these governors,
    And claim the charter of our ancient freedom,
    Which each new king till now has ratified.
    I found the envoys there of many a town,
    From Suabia and the valley of the Rhine,
    Who all received their parchments as they wish'd,
    And straight went home again with merry heart.
    They sent for me, your envoy, to the council,
    Where I was soon dismiss'd with empty comfort;
    " The Emperor at present was engaged;
    Some other time he would attend to us!"
    I turn'd away, and passing through the hall,
    With heavy heart, in a recess I saw

The Grand Duke John * in tears, and by his side
The noble lords of Wart and Tegerfeld,
Who beckon'd me, and said, " Redress yourselves.
Expect not justice from the Emperor.
Does he not plunder his own brother's child,
And keep from him his just inheritance ?
The Duke claims his maternal property,
Urging he's now of age, and 'tis full time
That he should rule his people and dominions ;
What is the answer made to him ? The king
Places a chaplet on his head ; " Behold
The fitting ornament," he cries, " of youth !"

MAUER   You hear. Expect not from the Emperor
       Or right or justice ! Then redress yourselves !

REDING.   No other course is left us. Now, advise
       What plan most likely to ensure success.

FURST   To shake a thraldom off that we abhor,
       To keep our ancient rights inviolate,
       As we received them from our fathers,—this,
       Not lawless innovation, is our aim.
       Let Cæsar still retain what is his due ;
       And he that is a vassal, let him pay
       The service he is sworn to faithfully.

MEYER   I hold my land of Austria in fief.

FURST.   Continue, then, to pay your feudal service

WEIL.   I'm tenant of the lords of Rappersweil.

FURST.   Continue, then, to pay them rent and tithe.

ROSSEL.   Of Zurich's Lady I'm the humble vassal.

FURST.   Give to the cloister, what the cloister claims.

STAUFF.   The Empire only is my feudal lord

FURST.   What needs must be, we'll do, but nothing further
       We'll drive these tyrants and their minions hence,
       And raze their towering strongholds to the ground,
       Yet shed. if possible, no drop of blood.
       Let the Emperor see, that we were driven to cast
       The sacred duties of respect away ;
       And when he finds we keep within our bounds,
       His wrath, belike, may yield to policy ;

* The Duke of Suabia, who soon afterwards assassinated his uncle, for withholding his patrimony from him.

For truly is that nation to be fear'd,
That, when in arms, is temp'rate in its wrath.
REDING. But prithee tell us how may this be done?
The enemy is arm'd as well as we,
And, rest assured, he will not yield in peace.
STAUFF. He will, whene'er he sees us up in arms;
We shall surprise him, ere he is prepared.
MEYER. 'Tis easily said, but not so easily done.
Two fortresses of strength command the country—
They shield the foe, and should the King invade us,
The task would then be dangerous indeed.
Rossberg and Sarnen both must be secured,
Before a sword is drawn in either Canton.
STAUFF. Should we delay the foe will soon be warned;
We are too numerous for secrecy.
MEYER. There is no traitor in the Forest States.
ROSSEL. But even zeal may heedlessly betray.
FURST. Delay it longer, and the keep at Altdorf
Will be complete,—the governor secure
MEYER. You think but of yourselves.
SACRISTAN.   You are unjust!
MEYER. Unjust! said you?   Dares Uri taunt us so?
REDING. Peace, on your oath!
MEYER.   If Schwytz be leagued with Uri,
Why, then, indeed, we must perforce be silent.
REDING. And let me tell you, in the Diet's name,
Your hasty spirit much disturbs the peace.
Stand we not all for the same common cause?
WINK. What, if we delay till Christmas?   'Tis then
The custom for the serfs to throng the castle,
Bringing the governor their annual gifts.
Thus may some ten or twelve selected men
Assemble unobserved, within its walls,
Bearing about their persons pikes of steel,
Which may be quickly mounted upon staves,
For arms are not admitted to the fort.
The rest can fill the neighb'ring wood, prepared
To sally forth upon a trumpet's blast,
Whene'er their comrades have secured the gate;
And thus the castle will be ours with ease
MELCH The Rossberg I will undertake to scale,

I have a sweetheart in the garrison,
Whom with some tender words I could persuade
To lower me at night a hempen ladder.
Once up, my friends will not be long behind.

REDING Are all resolved in favour of delay?

[*The majority raise their hands*

STAUFF (*counting them*).
Twenty to twelve is the majority.

FURST. If on the appointed day the castles fall,
From mountain on to mountain we shall pass
The fiery signal: in the capital
Of every Canton quickly rouse the Landsturm*
Then, when these tyrants see our martial front,
Believe me, they will never make so bold
As risk the conflict, but will gladly take
Safe conduct forth beyond our boundaries.

STAUFF Not so with Gessler. He will make a stand.
Surrounded with his dread array of horse,
Blood will be shed before he quits the field,
And even expell'd he'd still be terrible.
'Tis hard, indeed 'tis dangerous, to spare him

BAUM. Place me where'er a life is to be lost;
I owe my life to Tell, and cheerfully
Will pledge it for my country. I have clear'd
My honour, and my heart is now at rest.

REDING. Counsel will come with circumstance. Be patient!
Something must still be trusted to the moment.
Yet, while by night we hold our Diet here,
The morning, see, has on the mountain tops
Kindled her glowing beacon   Let us part,
Ere the broad sun surprise us.

FURST.   Do not fear.
The night wanes slowly from these vales of ours.

[*All have involuntarily taken off their caps, and
contemplate the breaking of day, absorbed in
silence.*

ROSSEL. By this fair light which greeteth us, before
Those other nations, that, beneath us far,
In noisome cities pent, draw painful breath,

* A sort of national militia.

Swear we the oath of our confederacy !
We swear to be a nation of true brothers,
Never to part in danger or in death !
   [They repeat his words with three fingers raised.
We swear we will be free, as were our sires,
And sooner die than live in slavery !
                 [All repeat as before.
We swear to put our trust in God Most High,
And not to quail before the might of man !
   [All repeat as before, and embrace each other.

STAUFF Now every man pursue his several way
Back to his friends, his kindred, and his home.
Let the herd winter up his flock, and gain,
In silence, friends for our confederacy !
What for a time must be endured, endure,
And let the reckoning of the tyrants grow,
Till the great day arrive, when they shall pay
The general and particular debt at once.
Let every man control his own just rage,
And nurse his vengeance for the public wrongs:
For he whom selfish interests now engage,
Defrauds the general weal of what to it belongs.
   [As they are going off in profound silence, in
      three different directions, the orchestra plays a
      solemn air   The empty scene remains open for
      some time, showing the rays of the sun rising
      over the Glaciers.

ACT III.

SCENE I.

Court before TELL'S *house.* TELL *with an axe.* HEDWIG
engaged in her domestic duties. WALTER *and* WILHELM *in
the back-ground, playing with a little cross-bow*

(WALTER *sings*).
With his cross-bow, and his quiver,
   The huntsman speeds his way,
Over mountain, dale, and river,
   At the dawning of the day.

As the eagle, on wild pinion,
  Is the king in realms of air,
So the hunter claims dominion
  Over crag and forest lair.

Far as ever bow can carry,
  Thro' the trackless airy space,
All he sees he makes his quarry,
  Soaring bird and beast of chase

WILHELM (*runs forward*).
  My string has snapt! Wilt mend it for me, father?
TELL.   Not I; a true-born archer helps himself. [*Boys retire.*
HEDW.   The boys begin to use the bow betimes.
TELL.   'Tis early practice only makes the master.
HEDW.   Ah! Would to Heaven they never learnt the art!
TELL.   But they shall learn it, wife, in all its points.
  Whoe'er would carve an independent way
  Through life, must learn to ward or plant a blow
HEDW   Alas, alas! and they will never rest
  Contentedly at home.
TELL.   No more can I!
  I was not framed by nature for a shepherd.
  Restless I must pursue a changing course;
  I only feel the flush and joy of life,
  In starting some fresh quarry every day
HEDW   Heedless the while of all your wife's alarms,
  As she sits watching through long hours at home.
  For my soul sinks with terror at the tales
  The servants tell about your wild adventures.
  Whene'er we part, my trembling heart forebodes,
  That you will ne'er come back to me again.
  I see you on the frozen mountain steeps,
  Missing, perchance, your leap from cliff to cliff.
  I see the chamois, with a wild rebound,
  Drag you down with him o'er the precipice.
  I see the avalanche close o'er your head,—
  The treacherous ice give way, and you sink down
  Intombed alive within its hideous gulf.
  Ah! in a hundred varying forms does death
  Pursue the Alpine huntsman on his course
  That way of life can surely ne'er be blessed,
  Where life and limb are perill'd every hour.

TELL.   The man that bears a quick and steady eye,
          And trusts to God, and his own lusty sinews,
          Passes, with scarce a scar, through every danger.
          The mountain cannot awe the mountain child.
              [*Having finished his work, he lays aside his tools*
          And now, methinks, the door will hold awhile.—
          The axe at home oft saves the carpenter
                                            [*Takes his cap*
HEDW.   Whither away?
TELL.   To Altdorf, to your father.
HEDW.   You have some dangerous enterprise in view?
          Confess!
TELL.   Why think you so?
HEDWIG.   Some scheme's on foot,
          Against the governors.   There was a Diet
          Held on the Rootli—that I know—and you
          Are one of the confederacy, I'm sure.
TELL.   I was not there.   Yet will I not hold back,
          Whene'er my country calls me to her aid
HEDW.   Wherever danger is, will you be placed.
          On you, as ever, will the burden fall.
TELL.   Each man shall have the post that fits his powers
HEDW.   You took—ay, 'mid the thickest of the storm—
          The man of Unterwald across the lake.
          'Tis a marvel you escaped.   Had you no thought
          Of wife and children, then?
TELL.   Dear wife, I had;
          And therefore saved the father for his children.
HEDW.   To brave the lake in all its wrath!   'Twas not
          To put your trust in God!   'Twas tempting him.
TELL.   The man that's over cautious will do little.
HEDW.   Yes, you've a kind and helping hand for all :
          But be in straits, and who will lend you aid?
TELL.   God grant I ne'er may stand in need of it!
                              [*Takes up his crossbow and arrows*
HEDW   Why take your crossbow with you? Leave it here
TELL.   I want my right hand, when I want my bow.
                                        [*The boys return*
WALT.   Where, father, are you going?
TELL.   To grand-dad, boy—
          To Altdorf.   Will you go?

364   WILHELM TELL.   [ACT III.

WALTER.   Ay, that I will!
HEDW. The Viceroy's there just now. Go not to Altdorf!
TELL. He leaves to-day.
HEDWIG.   Then let him first be gone
  Cross not his path.—You know he bears us grudge
TELL. His ill-will cannot greatly injure me.
  I do what's right, and care for no man's hate.
HEDW. 'Tis those who do what's right, whom most he hates.
TELL. Because he cannot reach them. Me, I ween,
  His knightship will be glad to leave in peace.
HEDW. Ay!—Are you sure of that?
TELL.   Not long ago,
  As I was hunting through the wild ravines
  Of Shechenthal, untrod by mortal foot,—
  There, as I took my solitary way
  Along a shelving ledge of rocks, where 'twas
  Impossible to step on either side;
  For high above rose, like a giant wall,
  The precipice's side, and far below
  The Shechen thunder'd o'er its rifted bed;—
    [*The boys press towards him, looking upon him
    with excited curiosity.*
  There, face to face, I met the Viceroy. He
  Alone with me—and I myself alone—
  Mere man to man, and near us the abyss.
  And when his lordship had perused my face,
  And knew the man he had severely fined
  On some most trivial ground, not long before;
  And saw me, with my sturdy bow in hand,
  Come striding t'wards him, then his cheek grew pale.
  His knees refused their office, and I thought
  He would have sunk against the mountain side.
  Then, touch'd with pity for him, I advanced,
  Respectfully, and said, " 'Tis I, my lord."
  But ne'er a sound could he compel his lips
  To frame in answer. Only with his hand
  He beckoned me in silence to proceed.
  So I pass'd on, and sent his train to seek him.
HEDW. He trembled then before you? Woe the while
  You saw his weakness; that he'll ne'er forgive
TELL. I shun him, therefore, and he'll not seek me.

HEDW. But stay away to-day.   Go hunting rather!
TELL.   What do you fear?
HEDWIG.   I am uneasy.   Stay
TELL.   Why thus distress yourself without a cause?
HEDW. Because there is no cause.   Tell, Tell! stay here!
TELL.   Dear wife, I gave my promise I would go.
HEDW. Must you,—then go.   But leave the boys with me.
WALT.   No, mother dear. I'm going with my father.
HEDW. How, Walter! will you leave your mother then?
WALT.   I'll bring you pretty things from grandpapa.
                          [*Exit with his father.*
WILH.   Mother, I'll stay with you!
HEDWIG (*embracing him*).   Yes, yes! thou art
          My own dear child.   Thou'rt all that's left to me
              [*She goes to the gate of the court, and looks
              anxiously after* TELL *and her son for a con-
              siderable time.*

SCENE II

*A retired part of the Forest.—Brooks dashing in spray over
the rocks.*

Enter BERTHA *in a hunting dress.   Immediately afterwards*
                          RUDENZ

BERTH. He follows me.   Now to explain myself!
RUDENZ (*entering hastily*).
          At length, dear lady, we have met alone.
          In this wild dell, with rocks on every side,
          No jealous eye can watch our interview.
          Now let my heart throw off this weary silence.
BERTH. But are you sure they will not follow us?
RUD. . . See, yonder goes the chase.   Now, then, or never!
          I must avail me of the precious moment,—
          Must hear my doom decided by thy lips,
          Though it should part me from thy side for ever
          Oh, do not arm that gentle face of thine
          With looks so stern and harsh!   Who—who am I,
          That dare aspire so high, as unto thee?
          Fame hath not stamp'd me yet; nor may I take

My place amid the courtly throng of knights,
That, crown'd with glory's lustre, woo thy smiles.
Nothing have I to offer, but a heart
That overflows with truth and love for thee

BERTHA (*sternly and with severity*).
And dare you speak to me of love—cf truth?
You, that are faithless to your nearest ties!
You, that are Austria's slave—bartered and sold
To her—an alien, and your country's tyrant!

UD. . . How! This reproach from thee! Whom do I seek,
On Austria's side, my own beloved, but thee?

BERTH. Think you to find me in the traitor's ranks?
Now, as I live, I'd rather give my hand
To Gessler's self, all despot though he be,
Than to the Switzer who forgets his birth,
And stoops to be the minion of a tyrant.

RUD. . . Oh heaven, what must I hear!

BERTHA.   Say! what can lie
Nearer the good man's heart, than friends and
      kindred?
What dearer duty to a noble soul,
Than to protect weak, suffering innocence,
And vindicate the rights of the oppress'd?
My very soul bleeds for your countrymen.
I suffer with them, for I needs must love them;
They are so gentle, yet so full of power;
They draw my whole heart to them. Every day
I look upon them with increased esteem.
But you, whom nature and your knightly vow,
Have given them as their natural protector,
Yet who desert them and abet their foes,
In forging shackles for your native land,
You—you it is, that deeply grieve and wound me
I must constrain my heart, or I shall hate you.

RUD. . . Is not my country's welfare all my wish?
What seek I for her, but to purchase peace
'Neath Austria's potent sceptre?

BERTHA.   Bondage, rather!
You would drive freedom from the last stronghold
That yet remains for her upon the earth.

The people know their own true int'rests better:
Their simple natures are not warp'd by show.
But round your head a tangling net is wound.

RUD. . . Bertha, you hate me—you despise me!

BERTHA. 　　　　　　　　　　　　Nay!
And if I did, 'twere better for my peace.
But to see him despised and despicable,—
The man whom one might love—

RUDENZ. 　　　　　　　　　Oh, Bertha! You
Show me the pinnacle of heavenly bliss,
Then, in a moment, hurl me to despair!

BERTH No, no! the noble is not all extinct
Within you. It but slumbers,—I will rouse it
It must have cost you many a fiery struggle,
To crush the virtues of your race within you.
But, Heaven be praised, 'tis mightier than yourself,
And you are noble in your own despite!

RUD. . . You trust me, then? Oh, Bertha, with thy love
What might I not become!

BERTHA. 　　　　　　　　　　Be only that
For which your own high nature destin'd you
Fill the position you were born to fill;—
Stand by your people and your native land—
And battle for your sacred rights!

RUDENZ 　　　　　　　　　　　　Alas!
How can I hope to win you— to possess you,
If I take arms against the Emperor?
Will not your potent kinsmen interpose,
To dictate the disposal of your hand?

BERTH All my estates lie in the Forest Cantons;
And I am free, when Switzerland is free.

RUD. . Oh! what a prospect, Bertha, hast thou shown me!

BERTH Hope not to win my hand by Austria's favour;
Fain would they lay their grasp on my estates,
To swell the vast domains which now they hold.
The selfsame lust of conquest, that would rob
You of your liberty, endangers mine
Oh, friend, I'm mark'd for sacrifice;—to be
The guerdon of some parasite, perchance!
They'll drag me hence to the Imperial court,
That hateful haunt of falsehood and intrigue;

There do detested marriage bonds await me.
Love, love alone,—your love can rescue me.

RUD.   . And thou couldst be content, love, to live here;
In my own native land to be my own?
Oh, Bertha, all the yearnings of my soul
For this great world and its tumultuous strife,
What were they, but a yearning after thee?
In glory's path I sought for thee alone,
And all my thirst of fame was only love.
But if in this calm vale thou canst abide
With me, and bid earth's pomps and pride adieu,
Then is the goal of my ambition won;
And the rough tide of the tempestuous world
May dash and rave around these firm-set hills!
No wandering wishes more have I to send
Forth to the busy scene that stirs beyond.
Then may these rocks, that girdle us, extend
Their giant walls impenetrably round,
And this sequestered happy vale alone
Look up to heaven, and be my paradise!

BERTH. Now art thou all my fancy dream'd of thee.
My trust has not been given to thee in vain

RUD .   Away, ye idle phantoms of my folly!
In mine own home I'll find my happiness.
Here, where the gladsome boy to manhood grew,
Where ev'ry brook, and tree, and mountain peak,
Teems with remembrances of happy hours,
In mine own native land thou wilt be mine.
Ah, I have ever loved it well, I feel
How poor without it were all earthly joys.

BERTH. Where should we look for happiness on earth,
If not in this dear land of innocence?
Here, where old truth hath its familiar home,
Where fraud and guile are strangers, envy ne'er
Shall dim the sparkling fountain of our bliss,
And ever bright the hours shall o'er us glide.
There do I see thee, in true manly worth,
The foremost of the free and of thy peers,
Revered with homage pure and unconstrain'd,
Wielding a power that kings might envy thee.

RUD .. And thee I see, thy sex's crowning gem,

With thy sweet woman grace and wakeful love,
Building a heaven for me within my home,
And, as the spring-time scatters forth her flowers,
Adorning with thy charms my path of life,
And spreading joy and sunshine all around.

BERTH. And this it was, dear friend, that caused my grief,
To see thee blast this life's supremest bliss,
With thine own hand.   Ah ! what had been my fate,
Had I been forced to follow some proud lord,
Some ruthless despot, to his gloomy castle !
Here are no castles, here no bastion'd walls
Divide me from a people I can bless.

RUD .. Yet, how to free myself; to loose the coils
Which I have madly twined around my head ?

BERTH. Tear them asunder with a man's resolve.
Whatever the event, stand by thy people.
. It is thy post by birth.

        [*Hunting horns are heard in the distance.*
                      But hark ! The chase !
Farewell,—'tis needful we should part—away !
Fight for thy land ; thou fightest for thy love.
One foe fills all our souls with dread ; the blow
That makes one free, emancipates us all.

                    [*Exeunt severally.*

SCENE III.

A meadow near Altdorf.   Trees in the fore-ground.   At the back of the stage a cap upon a pole.   The prospect is bounded by the Bannberg, which is surmounted by a snow-capped mountain.

     FRIESSHARDT *and* LEUTHOLD *on guard*

FRIESS. We keep our watch in vain.   There's not a soul
Will pass, and do obeisance to the cap.
But yesterday the place swarm'd like a fair ;
Now the whole green looks like a very desert,
Since yonder scarecrow hung upon the pole.

LEUTH. Only the vilest rabble show themselves,
And wave their tattered caps in mockery at us.
All honest citizens would sooner make
A tedious circuit over half the town,

                           2 B

Than bend their backs before our master's **cap**

FRIESS. They were obliged to pass this way at noon,
As they were coming from the Council House.
I counted then upon a famous catch,
For no one thought of bowing to the cap.
But Rosselmann, the priest, was even with **me** :
Coming just then from some sick penitent,
He stands before the pole,—raises the Host—
The Sacrist, too, must tinkle with his bell,—
When down they dropp'd on knee—myself and **all**
In reverence to the Host, but not the cap.

LEUTH. Hark ye, companion, I've a shrewd suspicion,.
Our post's no better than the pillory.
It is a burning shame. a trooper should
Stand sentinel before an empty cap,
And every honest fellow must despise **us**
To do obeisance to a cap, too! Faith,
I never heard an order so absurd !

FRIESS. Why not, an't please thee, to an empty cap ?
Thou'st duck'd, I'm sure, to many an empty sconce.

[HILDEGARD, MECHTHILD, *and* ELSBETH *enter
with their children, and station themselves
around the pole.*

LEUTH. And thou art an officious sneaking knave,
That's fond of bringing honest folks to trouble.
For my part, he that likes, may pass the cap :—
I'll shut my eyes and take no note of him.

MECH. There hangs the Viceroy ! Your obeisance, children !

ELS. . . I would to God he'd go, and leave his cap !
The country would be none the worse for it.

FRIESSHARDT (*driving them away*).
Out of the way ! Confounded pack of gossips !
Who sent for you ? Go, send your husbands here,
If they have courage to defy the order.

[TELL *enters with his crossbow, leading his son*
WALTER *by the hand. They pass the hat without noticing it, and advance to the front of the
stage.*

WALTER (*pointing to the Bannberg*).
Father, is't true, that on the mountain there,
The trees, if wounded with a hatchet, bleed ?

TELL.   Who says so, boy?

WALTER.   The master herdsman, father!
He tells us, there's a charm upon the trees,
And if a man shall injure them, the hand
That struck the blow will grow from out the grave

TELL   There is a charm about them—that's the truth.
Dost see those glaciers yonder—those white horns—
That seem to melt away into the sky?

WALT   They are the peaks that thunder so at night,
And send the avalanches down upon us

TELL.   They are; and Altdorf long ago had been
Submerged beneath these avalanches' weight,
Did not the forest there above the town
Stand like a bulwark to arrest their fall.

WALTER (after musing a little).
And are there countries with no mountains, father?

TELL.   Yes, if we travel downwards from our heights,
And keep descending in the rivers' courses,
We reach a wide and level country, where
Our mountain torrents brawl and foam no more,
And fair large rivers glide serenely on.
All quarters of the heaven may there be scann'd
Without impediment.   The corn grows there
In broad and lovely fields, and all the land
Is fair as any garden to the view.

WALT   But, father, tell me, wherefore haste we not
Away to this delightful land, instead
Of toiling here, and struggling as we do?

TELL.   The land is fair and bountiful as Heaven;
But they who till it, never may enjoy
The fruits of what they sow.

WALTER.   Live they not free,
As you do, on the land their fathers left them?

TELL.   The fields are all the bishop's or the king's.

WALT.   But they may freely hunt among the woods?

TELL.   The game is all the monarch's—bird and beast.

WALT.   But they, at least, may surely fish the streams?

TELL.   Stream, lake, and sea, all to the king belong.

WALT.   Who is this king, of whom they're so afraid?

TELL.   He is the man who fosters and protects them.

          Have they not courage to protect themselves?

TELL.   The neighbour there dare not his neighbour trust.

WALT.   I should want breathing room in such a land.
          I'd rather dwell beneath the avalanches.

TELL   'Tis better, child, to have these glacier peaks
          Behind one's back, than evil minded men!
                    [They are about to pass on

WALT.   See, father, see the cap on yonder pole!

TELL.   What is the cap to us?   Come, let's begone
            [As he is going, FRIESSHARDT, *presenting his pike,*
              stops him.

FRIESS.   Stand, I command you, in the Emperor's name!

TELL (*seizing the pike*).
          What would ye?   Wherefore do ye stop my path?

FRIESS.   You've broke the mandate, and must go with us.

LEUTH.   You have not done obeisance to the cap.

TELL.   Friend, let me go.

FRIESS.   Away, away to prison!

WALT.   Father to prison Help!
              [Calling to the side scene.
            This way, you men!
         Good people, help! They're dragging him to prison!
            *[*ROSSELMANN *the Priest, and the* SACRISTAN, *with*
              three other men, enter.

SACRIS.   What's here amiss?

ROSS.   Why do you seize this man?

FRIESS.   He is an enemy of the King—a traitor.

TELL (*seizing him with violence*).
          A traitor, I!

ROSSELMANN.   Friend, thou art wrong.   'Tis Tell,
          An honest man, and worthy citizen.

WALTER (*descries* FURST *and runs up to him*).
          Grandfather, help, they want to seize my father!

FRIESS.   Away to prison!

FURST (*running in*).   Stay, I offer bail.
          For God's sake, Tell, what is the matter here?
            *[*MELCHTHAL, *and* STAUFFACHER *enter*

LEUTH.   He has contemn'd the Viceroy's sovereign power
          Refusing flatly to acknowledge it

STAUFF.   Has Tell done this?

MELCHTHAL.   Villain, thou knowest 'tis false!
LEUTH. He has not made obeisance to the cap.
FURST. And shall for this to prison? Come, my friend,
    Take my security, and let him go.
FRIESS. Keep your security for yourself—you'll need it.
    We only do our duty. Hence with him.
MELCHTHAL (*to the country people*).
    This is too bad—shall we stand by, and see them
    Drag him away before our very eyes?
SACRIS. We are the strongest. Don't endure it, friends.
    Our countrymen will back us to a man.
FRIESS Who dares resist the governor's commands?
OTHER THREE PEASANTS (*running in*).
    We'll help you. What's the matter? Down with
    them !
        [HILDEGARD. MECHTHILD *and* ELSBETH *return*.
TELL. Go, go, good people, I can help myself.
    Think you, had I a mind to use my strength,
    These pikes of theirs should daunt me?
MELCHTHAL (*to* FRIESSHARDT).   Only try—
    Try. if you dare, to force him from amongst us.
FURST *and* STAUFFACHER.
    Peace, peace, friends !
FRIESSHARDT (*loudly*).   Riot! Insurrection, ho !
        [*Hunting horns without*
WOMEN The Governor!
FRIESSHARDT (*raising his voice*). Rebellion! Mutiny!
STAUFF. Roar, till you burst, knave !
ROSSELMANN *and* MELCHTHAL.   Will you hold your tongue?
FRIESSHARDT (*calling still louder*).
    Help, 'elp. I say, the servants of the law!
FURST. The `   eroy here! Then we shall smart for this!
     [*ter* GESSLER *on horseback, with a falcon on*
     ': rist ; RUDOLPH DER HARRAS, BERTHA, *and*
     R _ENZ, and a numerous train of armed at-
     tendants, who form a circle of lances round the
     whole stage.
HAR. . Room for the Viceroy !
GESSLER.   Drive the clowns apart.
    Why throng the people thus? Who calls for help?
        [*General silence*

Who was it?   I will know

[FRIESSHARDT *steps forward.*

And who art thou?

And why hast thou this man in custody?

[*Gives his falcon to an attendant.*

FRIESS. Dread sir, I am a soldier of your guard,
And station'd sentinel beside the cap;
This man I apprehended in the act
Of passing it without obeisance due,
So I arrested him, as you gave order
Whereon the people tried to rescue him.

GESSLER (*after a pause*).
And do you, Tell, so lightly hold your king,
And me, who act as his vicegerent here,
That you refuse the greeting to the cap
I hung aloft to test your loyalty?
I read in this a disaffected spirit.

TELL. Pardon me, good my lord! The action sprung
From inadvertence,—not from disrespect.
Were I discreet, I were not William Tell ·
Forgive me now—I'll not offend again.

GESSLER (*after a pause*).
I hear, Tell, you're a master with the bow,—
And bear the palm away from every rival.

WALT. That must be true, sir! At a hundred yards
He'll shoot an apple for you off the tree.

GESSL. Is that boy thine, Tell?

TELL.   Yes, my gracious lord

GESSL. Hast any more of them?

TELL.   Two boys, my lord.

GESSL And, of the two, which dost thou love the most?

TELL. Sir, both the boys are dear to me alike.

GESSL Then, Tell, since at a hundred yards thou canst
Bring down the apple from the tree, thou shalt
Approve thy skill before me.   Take thy bow—
Thou hast it there at hand—and make thee ready
To shoot an apple from the stripling's head!
But take this counsel,—look well to thine aim,
See, that thou hitt'st the apple at the first,
For, shouldst thou miss, thy head shall pay the forfeit

[*All give signs of horror*

TELL. What monstrous thing, my lord, is this you ask?
That I, from the head of mine own child!—No, no!
It cannot be, kind sir, you meant not that—
God, in His grace, forbid! You could not ask
A father seriously to do that thing!

GESSL. Thou art to shoot an apple from his head!
I do desire—command it so.

TELL. What I!
Level my crossbow at the darling head
Of mine own child? No—rather let me die!

GESSL Or thou must shoot, or with thee dies the boy.

TELL. Shall I become the murd'rer of my child!
You have no children, sir—you do not know
The tender throbbings of a father's heart.

GESSL. How now, Tell, so discreet upon a sudden
I had been told thou wert a visionary,—
A wanderer from the paths of common men.
Thou lov'st the marvellous. So have I now
Cull'd out for thee a task of special daring.
Another man might pause and hesitate;—
Thou dashest at it, heart and soul, at once.

BERTH. Oh, do not jest, my lord, with these poor souls!
See, how they tremble, and how pale they look,
So little used are they to hear thee jest.

GESSL. Who tells thee, that I jest?
[Grasping a branch above his head.
Here is the apple.
Room there, I say! And let him take his distance—
Just eighty paces,—as the custom is,—
Not an inch more or less! It was his boast,
That at a hundred he could hit his man.
Now, archer, to your task, and look you miss not!

HAR. . Heavens! this grows serious—down, boy, on your
knees,
And beg the governor to spare your life.

FURST (aside to MELCHTHAL, who can scarcely restrain his
impatience).
Command yourself,—bo calm, I beg of you!

BERTHA (to the governor).
Let this suffice you, sir! It is inhuman

         To trifle with a father's anguish thus.
         Although this wretched man had forfeited
         Both life and limb for such a slight offence,
         Already has he suffer'd tenfold death.
         Send him away uninjured to his home;
         He'll know thee well in future; and this hour
         He and his children's children will remember.

GESSL   Open a way there—quick! Why this delay?
         Thy life is forfeited; I might despatch thee,
         And see I graciously repose thy fate
         Upon the skill of thine own practis'd hand.
         No cause has he to say his doom is harsh,
         Who's made the master of his destiny.
         Thou boastest of thy steady eye. 'Tis well!
         Now is a fitting time to show thy skill.
         The mark is worthy, and the prize is great.
         To hit the bull's eye in the target;—that
         Can many another do as well as thou;
         But he, methinks, is master of his craft,
         Who can at all times on his skill rely,
         Nor lets his heart disturb or eye or hand

FÜRST   My lord, we bow to your authority;
         But oh, let justice yield to mercy here.
         Take half my property, nay, take it all,
         But spare a father this unnatural doom!

WALT   Grandfather, do not kneel to that bad man!
         Say, where am I to stand? I do not fear;
         My father strikes the bird upon the wing,
         And will not miss now when 'twould harm his boy!

STAUFF. Does the child's innocence not touch your heart?

ROSSEL. Bethink you, sir, there is a God in heaven,
         To whom you must account for all your deeds.

GESSLER (pointing to the boy).
         Bind him to yonder lime tree straight!

WALTER.   Bind me?
         No, I will not be bound! I will be still,
         Still as a lamb—nor even draw my breath!
         But if you bind me, I can not be still.
         Then I shall writhe and struggle with my bonds

HAR. . . But let your eyes at least be bandaged, boy!

WALT. And why my eyes? No! Do you think I fear
An arrow from my father's hand? Not I!
I'll wait it firmly, nor so much as wink!
Quick, father, show them that thou art an archer!
He doubts thy skill—he thinks to ruin us.
Shoot then, and hit, though but to spite the tyrant!
    [*He goes to the lime tree, and an apple is placed
      on his head.*

MELCHTHAL (*to the country people*).
What! Is this outrage to be perpetrated
Before our very eyes? Where is our oath?

STAUFF. 'Tis all in vain. We have no weapons here;
And see the wood of lances that surrounds us!

MELCH. Oh! would to Heaven that we had struck at once!
God pardon those, who counsell'd the delay!

GESSLER (*to* TELL).
Now, to thy task! Men bear not arms for nought.
'Tis dangerous to carry deadly weapons,
And on the archer oft his shaft recoils.
This right, these haughty peasant churls assume,
Trenches upon their master's privileges.
None should be armed, but those who bear command.
It pleases you to wear the bow and bolt;—
Well,—be it so. I will provide the mark.

TELL (*bends the bow, and fixes the arrow*).
A lane there! Room!

STAUFFACHER. What, Tell? You would—no, no!
You shake—your hand's unsteady—your knees tremble.

TELL (*letting the bow sink down*).
There's something swims before mine eyes!

WOMEN. Great Heaven!

TELL. Release me from this shot! Here is my heart!
    [*Tears open his breast*
Summon your troopers—let them strike me down!

GESSL. I do not want thy life, Tell, but the shot.
Thy talent's universal! Nothing daunts thee!
Thou canst direct the rudder like the bow!
Storms fright not thee, when there's a life at stake.
Now, saviour, help thyself.—thou savest all!
    [TELL *stands fearfully agitated by contending*

emotions, his hands moving convulsively, and
his eyes turning alternately to the governor and
Heaven.   Suddenly he takes a second arrow
from his quiver, and sticks it in his belt   The
governor watches all these motions

WALTER (*beneath the lime tree*).
    Come, father, shoot! I'm not afraid!
TELL   It must be '
    [*Collects himself and levels the bow*
RUDENZ (*who all the while has been standing in a state of*
    violent excitement, and has with difficulty restrained
    himself, advances).
    My lord, you will not urge this matter further
    You will not.   It was surely but a test.
    You've gained your object.   Rigour push'd too far
    Is sure to miss its aim, however good,
    As snaps the bow that's all too straitly bent.
GESSL.   Peace, till your counsel's ask'd for!
RUDENZ   I will speak!
    Ay, and I dare!   I reverence my king;
    But acts like these must make his name abhorr'd.
    He sanctions not this cruelty.   I dare
    Avouch the fact.   And you outstep your powers
    In handling thus an unoffending people.
GESSL.   Ha! thou grow'st bold, methinks!
RUDENZ.   I have been dumb
    To all the oppressions I was doom'd to see.
    I've closed mine eyes, that they might not behold
        them,
    Bade my rebellious, swelling heart be still,
    And pent its struggles down within my breast.
    But to be silent longer, were to be
    A traitor to my king and country both.
BERTHA (*casting herself between him and the governor*).
    Oh Heavens! you but exasperate his rage:
RUD. .   My people I forsook—renounced my kindred—
    Broke all the ties of nature, that I might
    Attach myself to you.   I madly thought,
    That I should best advance the general weal.

By adding sinews to the Emperor's power.
The scales have fallen from mine eyes—I see
The fearful precipice on which I stand.
You've led my youthful judgment far astray,—
Deceived my honest heart.　With best intent,
I had well nigh achiev'd my country's ruin.

GESSL　Audacious boy, this language to thy lord?

RUD. .　The Emperor is my lord, not you!　I'm free
As you by birth, and I can cope with you
In every virtue that beseems a knight.
And if you stood not here in that King's name,
Which I respect e'en where 'tis most abused,
I'd throw my gauntlet down, and you should give
An answer to my gage in knightly fashion.
Ay, beckon to your troopers!　Here I stand;
But not like these　　　　　[*Pointing to the people.*
　　　　　—unarmed.　I have a sword,
And he that stirs one step——

STAUFFACHER (*exclaims*).　　　　The apple's down!

　　　　[*While the attention of the crowd has been directed
　　　　to the spot where* BERTHA *had cast herself be-
　　　　tween* RUDENZ *and* GESSLER, TELL *has shot.*

ROSSEL. The boy's alive!

MANY VOICES.　　　　　The apple has been struck!

　　　　[WALTER FURST *staggers, and is about to fall*
　　　　BERTHA *supports him*

GESSLER (*astonished*).
　　　　How? Has he shot? The madman!

BERTHA.　　　　　　　　　　　Worthy father!
Pray you, compose yourself.　The boy's alive.

WALTER (*runs in with the apple*).
Here is the apple, father!　Well I knew,
You would not harm your boy

　　　　[TELL *stands with his body bent forwards, as
　　　　though he would follow the arrow.　His bow
　　　　drops from his hand.　When he sees the boy
　　　　advancing, he hastens to meet him with open
　　　　arms, and embracing him passionately sinks
　　　　down with him quite exhausted　All crowd
　　　　round them deeply affected.*

BERTHA.　　　　　　　　　Oh, ye kind Heavens!

Furst (*to father and son*).   My children, my dear children!

Stauffacher   God be praised!

Leuth   Almighty powers!   That was a shot indeed!
It will be talked of to the end of time.

Har. .   This feat of Tell, the archer, will be told
While yonder mountains stand upon their base.

                          [*Hands the apple to* Gessler

Gessl.   By Heaven! the apple's cleft right through the core
It was a master shot, I must allow.

Rossel. The shot was good.   But woe to him, who drove
The man to tempt his God by such a feat!

Stauff Cheer up, Tell, rise!   You've nobly freed yourself,
And now may go in quiet to your home.

Rossel. Come, to the mother let us bear her son!

                          [*They are about to lead him off*

Gessl   A word, Tell

Tell.   Sir, your pleasure?

Gessler.   Thou didst place
A second arrow in thy belt—nay, nay!
I saw it well—what was thy purpose with it?

Tell (*confused*).   It is a custom with all archers, Sir

Gessl.   No, Tell, I cannot let that answer pass.
There was some other motive, well I know.
Frankly and cheerfully confess the truth;—
Whate'er it be, I promise thee thy life,
Wherefore the second arrow?

Tell.   Well, my lord,
Since you have promised not to take my life,
I will, without reserve, declare the truth.

                          [*He draws the arrow from his belt, and fixes his
                          eyes sternly upon the governor*

If that my hand had struck my darling child,
This second arrow I had aimed at you,
And, be assured, I should not then have miss'd.

Gessl.   Well, Tell, I promised thou shouldst have thy life;
I gave my knightly word, and I will keep it.
Yet, as I know the malice of thy thoughts,
I will remove thee hence to sure confinement,
Where neither sun nor moon shall reach thine eyes
Thus from thy arrows I shall be secure.
Seize on him, guards, and bind him! [*They bind him.*

STAUFFACHER.   How, my lord—
    How can you treat in such a way a man.
    On whom God's hand has plainly been reveal'd ?
GESSL. Well, let us see if it will save him twice!
    Remove him to my ship; I'll follow straight
    In person I will see him lodged at Küssnacht.
ROSSEL. You dare not do't. Nor durst the Emperor's self
    So violate our dearest chartered rights.
GESSL. Where are they? Has the Emp'ror confirm'd them?
    He never has. And only by obedience
    Need you expect to win that favour from him.
    You are all rebels 'gainst the Emp'ror's power,—
    And bear a desperate and rebellious spirit.
    I know you all—I see you through and through.
    Him do I single from amongst you now,
    But in his guilt you all participate.
    The wise will study silence and obedience.
        [*Exit, followed by* BERTHA, RUDENZ, HARRAS,
        and attendants. FRIESSHARDT *and* LEUTHOLD
        remain.
FURST (*in violent anguish*).
    All's over now! He is resolved, to bring
    Destruction on myself and all my house.
STAUFF. (*to* TELL). Oh, why did you provoke the tyrant's rage?
TELL.   Let him be calm who feels the pangs I felt.
STAUFF. Alas! alas! Our every hope is gone.
    With you we all are fettered and enchain'd
COUNTRY PEOPLE (*surrounding* TELL).
    Our last remaining comfort goes with you!
LEUTH. (*approaching him*).
    I'm sorry for you, Tell, but must obey
TELL.   Farewell!
WALTER TELL (*clinging to him in great agony*).
    Oh, father, father, my dear father!
TELL (*pointing to Heaven*).
    Thy father is on high—appeal to him!
STAUFF. Hast thou no message, Tell, to send thy wife?
TELL. (*clasping the boy passionately to his breast*).
    The boy's uninjured; God will succour me!
        [*Tears himself suddenly away, and follows the sol-
        diers of the guard*

ACT IV.
Scene I.

*Eastern shore of the Lake of Lucerne; rugged and singularly
shaped rocks close the prospect to the west. The lake is agitated, violent roaring and rushing of wind, with thunder and
lightning at intervals.*

Kunz of Gersau, Fisherman *and* Boy.

Kunz   I saw it with these eyes!   Believe me, friend,
      It happen'd all precisely as I've said.

Fisher. Tell made a prisoner and borne off to Küssnacht?
      The best man in the land, the bravest arm,
      Had we resolved to strike for liberty!

Kunz.   The Viceroy takes him up the lake in person:
      They were about to go on board, as I
      Left Flüelen; but still the gathering storm,
      That drove me here to land so suddenly,
      Perchance has hindered their abrupt departure.

Fisher. Our Tell in chains, and in the Viceroy's power!
      O, trust me, Gessler will entomb him, where
      He never more shall see the light of day;
      For, Tell once free, the tyrant well might dread
      The just revenge of one so deep incensed.

Kunz.   The old Landamman, too—von Attinghaus—
      They say, is lying at the point of death.

Fisher Then the last anchor of our hopes gives way!
      He was the only man that dared to raise
      His voice in favour of the people's rights.

Kunz.   The storm grows worse and worse. So, fare ye well!
      I'll go and seek out quarters in the village.
      There's not a chance of getting off to-day.   [*Exit.*

Fisher. Tell dragg'd to prison, and the Baron dead!
      Now, tyranny, exalt thy insolent front,—
      Throw shame aside! The voice of truth is silenced,
      The eye that watch'd for us, in darkness closed,
      The arm that should have struck thee down, in chains!

Boy. . 'Tis hailing hard—come, let us to the cottage!
      This is no weather to be out in, father!

Fisher. Rage on, ye winds! Ye lightnings, flash your fires!
      Burst, ye swollen clouds! Ye cataracts of Heaven,
      Descend, and drown the country! In the germ,

Destroy the generations yet unborn!
Ye savage elements, be lords of all!
Return, ye bears; ye ancient wolves, return
To this wide howling waste! The land is yours
Who would live here, when liberty is gone!

Boy... Hark! How the wind whistles, and the whirlpool roars,
I never saw a storm so fierce as this!

Fisher. To level at the head of his own child!
Never had father such command before.
And shall not nature, rising in wild wrath,
Revolt against the deed? I should not marvel,
Though to the lake these rocks should bow their heads,
Though yonder pinnacles, yon towers of ice,
That, since creation's dawn, have known no thaw,
Should, from their lofty summits, melt away.—
Though yonder mountains, yon primeval cliffs,
Should topple down, and a new deluge whelm
Beneath its waves all living men's abodes!

　　　　　　　　　　　　　　　[Bells heard

Boy　Hark, they are ringing on the mountain, yonder!
They surely see some vessel in distress.
And toll the bell that we may pray for it.

　　　　　　　　　　　　　　　[Ascends a rock

Fisher. Woe to the bark that now pursues its course,
Rock'd in the cradle of these storm-tost waves!
Nor helm nor steersman here can aught avail;
The storm is master. Man is like a ball,
Toss'd 'twixt the winds and billows. Far or near,
No haven offers him its friendly shelter!
Without one ledge to grasp, the sheer smooth rocks
Look down inhospitably on his despair,
And only tender him their flinty breasts.

Boy (*calling from above*).
Father, a ship; and bearing down from Flüelen

Fisher. Heaven pity the poor wretches! When the storm
Is once entangled in this strait of ours,
It rages like some savage beast of prey,
Struggling against its cage's iron bars!
Howling, it seeks an outlet—all in vain;
For the rocks hedge it round on every side,
Walling the narrow pass as high as Heaven.

　　　　　　　　　　　　　　　[He ascends a cliff

BOY. . . It is the Governor of Uri's ship ;
            By its red poop I know it, and the flag.

FISHER. Judgments of Heaven!   Yes, it is he himself
            It is the governor!   Yonder he sails,
            And with him bears the burden of his crimes
            Soon has the arm of the avenger found him ;
            Now over him he knows a mightier lord.
            These waves yield no obedience to his voice,
            These rocks bow not their heads before his cap.
            Boy, do not pray ; stay not the Judge's arm!

BOY. . . I pray not for the governor—I pray
            For Tell, who is on board the ship with him

FISHER. Alas, ye blind, unreasoning elements!
            Must ye, in punishing one guilty head,
            Destroy the vessel and the pilot too?

BOY.   . See, see, they've clear'd the Buggisgrat* ; but now
            The blast, rebounding from the Devil's Minster*,
            Has driven them back on the Great Axenberg *
            I cannot see them now.

FISHERMAN.   The Hakmesser*
            Is there, that's founder'd many a gallant ship.
            If they should fail to double that with skill,
            Their bark will go to pieces on the rocks,
            That hide their jagged peaks below the lake.
            They have on board the very best of pilots.
            If any man can save them, Tell is he ;
            But he is manacled both hand and foot

                [*Enter* WILLIAM TELL., *with his crossbow. He
                enters precipitately, looks wildly round, and tes-
                tifies the most violent agitation.   When he reaches
                the centre of the stage, he throws himself upon his
                knees, and stretches out his hands, first towards
                the earth, then towards Heaven.*

BOY (*observing him*).
            See, father ! Who is that man, kneeling yonder?
FISHER. He clutches at the earth with both his hands,
            And looks as though he were beside himself.
BOY (*advancing*).
            What do I see ?   Father, come here, and look !

                * Rocks on the shore of the Lake of Lucerne.

FISHERMAN (*approaches*).
    Who is it?   God in Heaven! What! William Tell
    How came you hither? Speak. Tell!
BOY.   Were you not
    In yonder ship, a prisoner, and in chains?
FISHER. Were they not bearing you away to Küssnacht?
TELL (*rising*).   I am released
FISHERMAN *and* BOY.   Released, oh miracle!
BOY. . Whence came you here?
TELL.   From yonder vessel!
FISHERMAN   What?
BOY.   Where is the Viceroy?
TELL   Drifting on the waves.
FISHER. Is't possible? But you! How are you here?
    How 'scaped you from your fetters and the storm?
TELL. By God's most gracious providence.   Attend.
FISHER *and* BOY. Say on, say on!
TELL.   You know what passed at Altdorf?
FISHER. I do—say on!
TELL.   How I was seized and bound,
    And order'd by the governor to Küssnacht.
FISHER. And how with you at Flüelen he embarked.
    All this we know.   Say, how have you escaped?
TELL. I lay on deck, fast bound with cords, disarm'd,
    In utter hopelessness.   I did not think
    Again to see the gladsome light of day,
    Nor the dear faces of my wife and children,
    And eyed disconsolate the waste of waters.—
FISHER. Oh, wretched man!
TELL.   Then we put forth; the Viceroy.
    Rudolph der Harras, and their suite.   My bow
    And quiver lay astern beside the helm;
    And just as we had reached the corner, near
    The Little Axen*, Heaven ordain'd it so,
    That from the Gotthardt's gorge, a hurricane
    Swept down upon us with such headlong force,
    That every rower's heart within him sank,
    And all on board look'd for a watery grave.
    Then heard I one of the attendant train,

* A rock on the shore of the Lake of Lucerne.

Turning to Gessler, in this strain accost him:
"You see our danger, and your own, my lord,
And that we hover on the verge of death.
The boatmen there are powerless from fear,
Nor are they confident what course to take:—
Now, here is Tell, a stout and fearless man,
And knows to steer with more than common skill
How if we should avail ourselves of him
In this emergency?" The Viceroy then
Address'd me thus: "If thou wilt undertake
To bring us through this tempest safely, Tell,
I might consent to free thee from thy bonds."
I answer'd, "Yes, my lord, with God's assistance,
I'll see what can be done, and help us Heaven!"
On this they loosed me from my bonds, and I
Stood by the helm and fairly steer'd along;
Yet ever eyed my shooting gear askance,
And kept a watchful eye upon the shore,
To find some point where I might leap to land:
And when I had descried a shelving crag,
That jutted, smooth atop, into the lake

FISHER. I know it. 'Tis at foot of the Great Axen:
But looks so steep, I never could have dreamt
'Twere possible to leap it from the boat.

TELL. I bade the men put forth their utmost might,
Until we came before the shelving crag.
For there, I said, the danger will be past!
Stoutly they pull'd, and soon we near'd the point:
One prayer to God for his assisting grace,
And straining every muscle, I brought round
The vessel's stern close to the rocky wall;
Then snatching up my weapons, with a bound
I swung myself upon the flattened shelf,
And with my feet thrust off, with all my might,
The puny bark into the hell of waters.
There let it drift about, as Heaven ordains!
Thus am I here, deliver'd from the might
Of the dread storm, and man, more dreadful still.

FISHER. Tell, Tell, the Lord has manifestly wrought
A miracle in thy behalf! I scarce
Can credit my own eyes. But tell me, now,

Whither you purpose to betake yourself?
For you will be in peril, should the Viceroy
Chance to escape this tempest with his life.

TELL. I heard him say, as I lay bound on board,
His purpose was to disembark at Brunnen;
And, crossing Schwytz, convey me to his castle.

FISHER. Means he to go by land?

TELL.   So he intends

FISHER. Oh, then, conceal yourself without delay!
Not twice will Heaven release you from his grasp

TELL. Which is the nearest way to Arth and Küssnacht?

FISHER. The public road leads by the way of Steinen,
But there's a nearer road, and more retired,
That goes by Lowerz, which my boy can show you

TELL (gives him his hand).
May Heaven reward your kindness! Fare ye well.
    [As he is going, he comes back
Did not you also take the oath at Rootli?
I heard your name, methinks.

FISHERMAN.   Yes, I was there,
And took the oath of the confederacy.

TELL. Then do me this one favour: speed to Bürglen—
My wife is anxious at my absence—tell her
That I am free, and in secure concealment.

FISHER. But whither shall I tell her you have fled?

TELL. You'll find her father with her, and some more,
Who took the oath with you upon the Rootli;
Bid them be resolute, and strong of heart,—
For Tell is free and master of his arm:
They shall hear further news of me ere long.

FISHER. What have you, then, in view? Come, tell me
    frankly!

TELL. When once 'tis done, 'twill be in every mouth. [Exit.

FISHER. Show him the way, boy. Heaven be his support!
Whate'er he has resolved, he'll execute.   [Exit.

SCENE II.

Baronial mansion of Attinghausen. The BARON upon a
couch dying. WALTER FURST, STAUFFACHER, MELCHTHAL,
and BAUMGARTEN attending round him. WALTER TELL
kneeling before the dying man..   .   ..

FURST, All now is over with him. He is gone

STAUFF. He lies not like one dead.   The feather, see,
Moves on his lips! His sleep is very calm,
And on his features plays a placid smile.
[BAUMGARTEN *goes to the door and speaks with
some one.*
FURST. Who's there?
BAUMGARTEN (*returning*).
Tell's wife, your daughter, she insists
That she must speak with you, and see her boy.
[WALTER TELL *rises.*
FURST. I who need comfort—can I comfort her?
Does every sorrow centre on my head?
HEDWIG (*forcing her way in*).
Where is my child? Unhand me! I must see him.
STAUFF. Be calm! Reflect you're in the house of death!
HEDWIG (*falling upon her boy's neck*).
My Walter! Oh, he yet is mine!
WALTER.   Dear mother!
HEDW And is it surely so? Art thou unhurt?
[*Gazing at him with anxious tenderness*
And is it possible he aim'd at thee?
How could he do it?   Oh, he has no heart—
And he could wing an arrow at his child!
FURST His soul was rack'd with anguish when he did it.
No choice was left him, but to shoot or die!
HEDW. Oh, if he had a father's heart, he would
Have sooner perish'd by a thousand deaths!
STAUFF. You should be grateful for God's gracious care,
That ordered things so well.
HEDWIG.   Can I forget
What might have been the issue.   God of Heaven.
Were I to live for centuries, I still
Should see my boy tied up,—his father's mark,—
And still the shaft would quiver in my heart!
MELCH. You know not how the Viceroy taunted him!
HEDW. Oh, ruthless heart of man!   Offend his pride,
And reason in his breast forsakes her seat;
In his blind wrath he'll stake upon a cast
A child's existence, and a mother's heart!
BAUM. Is then your husband's fate not hard enough,
That you embitter it by such reproaches?
Have you no feeling for his sufferings?

HEDWIG (*turning to him and gazing full upon him*).

> Hast thou tears only for thy friend's distress?
> Say, where were you when he—my noble Tell,
> Was bound in chains? Where was your friendship
> then?
> The shameful wrong was done before your eyes;
> Patient you stood, and let your friend be dragg'd,
> Ay, from your very hands. Did ever Tell
> Act thus to you? Did he stand whining by
> When on your heels the Viceroy's horsemen press'd,
> And full before you roared the storm-toss'd lake?
> Oh not with idle tears he show'd his pity;
> Into the boat he sprung, forgot his home,
> His wife, his children, and delivered thee!

FURST. It had been madness to attempt his rescue,
> Unarm'd, and few in numbers as we were?

HEDWIG (*casting herself upon his bosom*).

> Oh, father, and thou, too, hast lost my Tell!
> The country—all have lost him! All lament
> His loss; and, oh, how he must pine for us!
> Heaven keep his soul from sinking to despair!
> No friend's consoling voice can penetrate
> His dreary dungeon walls. Should he fall sick!
> Ah! In the vapours of the murky vault
> He must fall sick. Even as the Alpine rose
> Grows pale and withers in the swampy air,
> There is no life for him, but in the sun,
> And in the balm of Heaven's refreshing breeze.
> Imprison'd! Liberty to him is breath:
> He cannot live in the rank dungeon air!

STAUFF. Pray you be calm! And hand in hand, we'll all
> Combine to burst his prison doors.

HEDWIG.   Without him,

> What have you power to do? While Tell was free.
> There still, indeed, was hope—weak innocence
> Had still a friend, and the oppress'd a stay.
> Tell saved you all! You cannot all combined
> Release him from his cruel prison bonds.

> [*The* BARON *wakes*

BAUM. Hush, hush! He starts!

ATTINGHAUSEN (*sitting up*).   Where is he?

STAUFFACHER.   Who?

ATTINGHAUSEN.   He leaves me,—
In my last moments he abandons me.

STAUFF. He means his nephew. Have they sent for him?

FURST. He has been summoned. Cheerly sir! Take comfort!
He has found his heart at last, and is our own.

ATTING. Say, has he spoken for his native land?

STAUFF. Ay, like a hero!

ATTINGHAUSEN.   Wherefore comes he not,
That he may take my blessing ere I die?
I feel my life fast ebbing to a close.

STAUFF. Nay, talk not thus, dear sir! This last short sleep
Has much refresh'd you, and your eye is bright.

ATTING. Life is but pain, and even that has left me;
My sufferings, like my hopes, have pass'd away.
                    [*Observing the boy*
What boy is that?

FURST.   Bless him. Oh, good my lord!
He is my grandson, and is fatherless.
                    [HEDWIG *kneels with the boy before the dying man*

ATTING. And fatherless—I leave you all, ay all!
Oh, wretched fate, that these old eyes should see
My country's ruin, as they close in death!
Must I attain the utmost verge of life,
To feel my hopes go with me to the grave?

STAUFFACHER (*to* FURST).
Shall he depart 'mid grief and gloom like this?
Shall not his parting moments be illumed
By hope's delightful beams? My noble lord,
Raise up your drooping spirit! We are not
Forsaken quite—past all deliverance.

ATTING. Who shall deliver you?

FURST.   Ourselves. For know
The Cantons three are to each other pledged,
To hunt the tyrants from the land. The league
Has been concluded, and a sacred oath
Confirms our union. Ere another year
Begins its circling course—the blow shall **fall**
In a free land your ashes shall repose.

ATTING. The league concluded! Is it really so?

MELCH. On one day shall the Cantons rise together

All is prepared to strike—and to this hour
The secret closely kept, though hundreds share it;
The ground is hollow 'neath the tyrants' feet;
Their days of rule are number'd, and ere long
No trace of their dominion shall remain.

ATTING. Ay, but their castles, how to master them?

MELCH. On the same day they, too, are doom'd to fall.

ATTING. And are the nobles parties to this league?

STAUFF. We trust to their assistance should we need it;
As yet the peasantry alone have sworn.

ATTING. (*raising himself up, in great astonishment.*)
And have the peasantry dared such a deed
On their own charge, without the nobles' aid—
Relied so much on their own proper strength?
Nay then, indeed, they want our help no more;
We may go down to death cheer'd by the thought,
That after us the majesty of man
Will live, and be maintain'd by other hands.

[*He lays his hand upon the head of the child, who
is kneeling before him.*

From this boy's head, whereon the apple lay,
Your new and better liberty shall spring;
The old is crumbling down—the times are changing—
And from the ruins blooms a fairer life.

STAUFFACHER (*to* FURST).
See, see, what splendour streams around his eye!
This is not Nature's last expiring flame,
It is the beam of renovated life.

ATTING From their old towers the nobles are descending,
And swearing in the towns the civic oath.
In Uechtland and Thurgau the work's begun:
The noble Bern lifts her commanding head,
And Freyburg is a stronghold of the free:
The stirring Zurich calls her guilds to arms;—
And now, behold!—the ancient might of kings
Is shiver'd 'gainst her everlasting walls.

[*He speaks what follows with a prophetic tone;
his utterance rising into enthusiasm.*

I see the princes and their haughty peers,
Clad all in steel, come striding on to crush
A harmless shepherd race with mailèd hand.

Desp'rate the conflict: 'tis for life or death;
And many a pass will tell to after years
Of glorious victories sealed in foemen's blood *
The peasant throws himself with naked breast,
A willing victim on their serried lances
They yield—the flower of chivalry's cut down,
And freedom waves her conquering banner high!
          [*Grasps the hands of* WALTER FURST *and* STAUF-
          FACHER.
Hold fast together, then,—for ever fast!
Let freedom's haunts be one in heart and mind!
Set watches on your mountain tops, that league
May answer league, when comes the hour to strike.
Be one—be one—be one——
          [*He falls back upon the cushion. His lifeless
          hands continue to grasp those of* FURST *and*
          STAUFFACHER, *who regard him for some mo-
          ments in silence, and then retire, overcome with
          sorrow. Meanwhile the servants have quietly
          pressed into the chamber, testifying different de-
          grees of grief. Some kneel down beside him
          and weep on his body: while this scene is pass-
          ing, the castle bell tolls.*

RUDENZ (*entering hurriedly*).
          Lives he? Oh say, can he still hear my voice?
FURST (*averting his face*).
          You are our seignior and protector now;
          Henceforth this castle bears another name.
RUDENZ (*gazing at the body with deep emotion*).
          Oh, God! Is my repentance, then, too late?
          Could he not live some few brief moments more,
          To see the change that has come o'er my heart?
          Oh, I was deaf to his true counselling voice
          While yet he walked on earth. Now he is gone,—

          * An allusion to the gallant self-devotion of Arnold Struthan of Winkel
ried, at the battle of Sempach, [9th July, 1386,] who broke the Austrian
phalanx by rushing on their lances, grasping as many of them as he could
reach, and concentrating them upon his breast. The confederates rushed
forward through the gap thus opened by the sacrifice of their comrade, broke
and cut down their enemy's ranks, and soon became the masters of the field.
"Dear and faithful confederates, I will open you a passage. Protect my
wife and children," were the words of Winkelried, as he rushed to death.

Gone, and for ever,—leaving me the debt—
The heavy debt I owe him—undischarged!
Oh, tell me! did he part in anger with me?

STAUFF. When dying, he was told what you had done,
And bless'd the valour that inspired your words!

RUDENZ *(kneeling down beside the dead body)*.
Yes, sacred relics of a man beloved!
Thou lifeless corpse! Here, on thy death-cold hand,
Do I abjure all foreign ties for ever!
And to my country's cause devote myself.
I am a Switzer, and will act as one,
With my whole heart and soul.   [*Rises.*
                       Mourn for our friend.
Our common parent, yet be not dismay'd!
'Tis not alone his lands that I inherit,—
His heart—his spirit, have devolved on me;
And my young arm shall execute the task,
For which his hoary age remain'd your debtor.
Give me your hands, ye venerable fathers!
Thine, Melchthal, too! Nay, do not hesitate,
Nor from me turn distrustfully away.
Accept my plighted vow—my knightly oath!

FURST. Give him your hands, my friends! A heart like his,
That sees and owns its error, claims our trust

MELCH. You ever held the peasantry in scorn,
What surety have we, that you mean us fair?

RUD. . . Oh, think not of the error of my youth!

STAUFFACHER (*to* MELCHTHAL).
Be one! They were our father's latest words.
See they be not forgotten!

MELCH.   Take my hand,—
A peasant's hand,—and with it, noble sir,
The gage and the assurance of a man!
Without us, sir, what would the nobles be?
Our order is more ancient, too, than yours!

RUD. . . I honour it, and with my sword will shield it!

MELCH. The arm, my lord, that tames the stubborn earth,
And makes its bosom blossom with increase,
Can also shield a man's defenceless breast.

RUD. . . Then you shall shield my breast, and I will yours
Thus each be strengthen'd by the others aid!

Yet wherefore talk we, while our native land
Is still to alien tyranny a prey?
First let us sweep the foeman from the soil,
Then reconcile our difference in peace!
                    [*After a moment's pause.*
How! You are silent! Not a word for me?
And have I yet no title to your trust?—
Then must I force my way, despite your will,
Into the League you secretly have form'd.
You've held a Diet on the Rootli,—I
Know this,—know all that was transacted there!
And though I was not trusted with your secret,
I still have kept it like a sacred pledge.
Trust me, I never was my country's foe,
Nor would I e'er have ranged myself against you!
Yet you did wrong—to put your rising off.
Time presses! We must strike, and swiftly too!
Already Tell has fallen a sacrifice
To your delay.

STAUFF.   We swore to wait till Christmas.

RUD.   I was not there,—I did not take the oath.
        If you delay, I will not!

MELCHTHAL.   What! You would——

RUD.   . I count me now among the country's fathers,
        And to protect you is my foremost duty.

FURST. Within the earth to lay these dear remains,
        That is your nearest and most sacred duty.

RUD... When we have set the country free, we'll place
        Our fresh victorious wreaths upon his bier.
        Oh, my dear friends, 'tis not your cause alone!—
        I have a cause to battle with the tyrants,
        That more concerns myself. Know, that my Bertha
        Has disappear'd,—been carried off by stealth,—
        Stolen from amongst us by their ruffian hands!

STAUFF. And has the tyrant dared so fell an outrage
        Against a lady free and nobly born?

RUD.   . Alas! my friends, I promised help to you,
        And I must first implore it for myself!
        She that I love, is stolen—is forced away,
        And who knows where the tyrant has conceal'd her.
        Or with what outrages his ruffian crew

May force her into nuptials she detests ?
Forsake me not !—Oh help me to her rescue.
She loves you !   Well, oh well, has she deserved,
That all should rush to arms in her behalf !
STAUFF. What course do you propose ?
RUDENZ.   Alas ! I know not.
In the dark mystery that shrouds her fate,—
In the dread agony of this suspense,—
Where I can grasp at nought of certainty,—
One single ray of comfort beams upon me.
From out the ruins of the tyrant's power
Alone can she be rescued from the grave.
Their strongholds must be levell'd ! every one,
Ere we can pierce into her gloomy prison.
MELCH. Come, lead us on ! We follow ! Why defer
Until to-morrow, what to-day may do ?
Tell's arm was free when we at Rootli swore,
This foul enormity was yet undone.
And change of circumstance brings change of law ;
Who such a coward as to waver still ?
RUDENZ (*to* WALTER FURST).
Meanwhile to arms, and wait in readiness
The fiery signal on the mountain tops.
For swifter than a boat can scour the lake
Shall you have tidings of our victory ;
And when you see the welcome flames ascend,
Then, like the lightning, swoop upon the foe,
And lay the despots and their creatures low !

SCENE III.

The pass near Küssnacht, sloping down from behind, with rocks
on either side.   The travellers are visible upon the heights,
before they appear on the stage.   Rocks all round the stage
Upon one of the foremost a projecting cliff overgrown with
brushwood.
TELL. (*enters with his crossbow*).
Here thro' this deep defile he needs must pass ;
There leads no other road to Küssnacht :—here
I'll do it:—the opportunity is good.
Yon alder tree stands well for my concealment,
Thence my avenging shaft will surely reach him

The straitness of the path forbids pursuit.
Now, Gessler, balance thine account with **Heaven**!
Thou must away from earth,—thy sand is run.

I led a peaceful inoffensive life ;—
My bow was bent on forest game alone,
And my pure soul was free from thoughts of murder—
But thou hast scared me from my dream of peace;
The milk of human kindness thou hast turn'd
To rankling poison in my breast ; and made
Appalling deeds familiar to my soul.
He who could make his own child's head his mark,
Can speed his arrow to his foeman's heart.

My children dear, my lov'd and faithful wife,
Must be protected, tyrant, from thy fury !—
When last I drew my bow—with trembling hand—
And thou, with murderous joy, a father forced
To level at his child—when, all in vain.
Writhing before thee, I implored thy mercy—
Then in the agony of my soul, I vow'd
A fearful oath, which met God's ear alone,
That when my bow next wing'd an arrow's flight,
Its aim should be thy heart.—The vow I made,
Amid the hellish torments of that moment,
I hold a sacred debt, and I will pay it.

Thou art my lord, my Emperor's delegate;
Yet would the Emperor not have stretch'd his power
So far as thou.—He sent thee to these Cantons
To deal forth law—stern law—for he is anger'd ;
But not to wanton with unbridled will
In every cruelty, with fiend-like joy :—
There is a God to punish and avenge.

Come forth, thou bringer once of bitter pangs,
My precious jewel now,—my chiefest treasure—
A mark I'll set thee, which the cry of grief
Could never penetrate,—but thou shalt pierce it.—
And thou, my trusty bowstring, that so oft
'Has served me faithfully in sportive scenes,

Desert me not in this most serious hour —
Only be true this once, my own good cord,
That hast so often wing'd the biting shaft:—
For shouldst thou fly successless from my hand,
I have no second to send after thee.

      [Travellers pass over the stage.

 I'll sit me down upon this bench of stone,
Hewn for the way-worn traveller's brief repose—
For here there is no home.—Each hurries by
The other, with quick step and careless look,
Nor stays to question of his grief.—Here goes
The merchant, full of care,—the pilgrim, next,
With slender scrip,—and then the pious monk,
The scowling robber, and the jovial player,
The carrier with his heavy-laden horse,
That comes to us from the far haunts of men ;
For every road conducts to the world's end.
They all push onwards — every man intent
On his own several business—mine is murder.

         [Sits down.
 Time was, my dearest children, when with joy
You hail'd your father's safe return to home
From his long mountain toils; for, when he came,
He ever brought some little present with him
A lovely Alpine flower—a curious bird—
Or elf-boat, found by wanderer on the hills.—
But now he goes in quest of other game :
In the wild pass he sits, and broods on murder;
And watches for the life-blood of his foe.—
But still his thoughts are fixed on you alone,
Dear children.—'Tis to guard your innocence,
To shield you from the tyrant's fell revenge,
He bends his bow to do a deed of blood! *[Rises.*

 Well—I am watching for a noble prey—
Does not the huntsman, with severest toil,
Roam for whole days, amid the winter's cold,
Leap with a daring bound from rock to rock,—
And climb the jagged, slippery steeps, to which
His limbs are glued by his own streaming blood—

WILHELM TELL.

398   WILHELM TELL.   [ACT IV

And all this but to gain a wretched chamois
A far more precious prize is now my aim—
The heart of that dire foe, who would destroy me.

[*Sprightly music heard in the distance, which comes
gradually nearer.*

From my first years of boyhood I have used
The bow—been practised in the archer's feats;
The bull's eye many a time my shafts have hit,
And many a goodly prize have I brought home,
Won in the games of skill.—This day I'll make
My master-shot, and win the highest prize
Within the whole circumference of the mountains.

[*A marriage train passes over the stage, and goes
up the pass. TELL gazes at it, leaning on his
bow. He is joined by STUSSI the Ranger.*

STUSSI. There goes the bridal party of the steward
Of Mörlischachen's cloister. He is rich!
And has some ten good pastures on the Alps.
He goes to fetch his bride from Imisee,
There will be revelry to-night at Küssnacht.
Come with us—ev'ry honest man's invited.
TELL. A gloomy guest fits not a wedding feast.
STUSSI. If grief oppress you, dash it from your heart!
Bear with your lot. The times are heavy now,
And we must snatch at pleasure while we can.
Here 'tis a bridal, there a burial.
TELL. And oft the one treads close upon the other.
STUSSI So runs the world at present. Everywhere
We meet with woe and misery enough.
There's been a slide of earth in Glarus, and
A whole side of the Glärnisch has fallen in.
TELL. Strange! And do even the hills begin to totter?
There is stability for nought on earth
STUSSI. Strange tidings, too, we hear from other parts.
I spoke with one but now, that came from Baden,
Who said a knight was on his way to court,
And, as he rode along, a swarm of wasps
Surrounded him, and settling on his horse,
So fiercely stung the beast, that it fell dead,
And he proceeded to the court on foot.

TELL.   Even the weak are furnish'd with a sting.

ARMGART (*enters with several children, and places herself at the
          entrance of the pass*).

STUSSI.   'Tis thought to bode disaster to the country,—
          Some horrid deed against the course of nature.

TELL.   Why, every day brings forth such fearful deeds;
          There needs no miracle to tell their coming.

STUSSI.   Too true! He's bless'd, who tills his field in peace,
          And sits untroubled by his own fireside.

TELL.   The very meekest cannot rest in quiet,
          Unless it suits with his ill neighbour's humour
              [TELL *looks frequently with restless expectation to-
              wards the top of the pass*

STUSSI.   So fare you well! You're waiting some one here?

TELL.   I am.

STUSSI.   A pleasant meeting with your friends!
          You are from Uri, are you not? His grace
          The governor's expected thence to-day.

TRAVELLER (*entering*).
          Look not to see the governor to-day.
          The streams are flooded by the heavy rains,
          And all the bridges have been swept away.
                                      [TELL *rises*

ARMGART (*coming forward*).
          The Viceroy not arriv'd?

STUSSI.   And do you seek him?

ARM...   Alas, I do!

STUSSI.   But why thus place yourself
          Where you obstruct his passage down the pass?

ARM...   Here he cannot escape me.   He *must* hear me.

FRIESS. (*coming hastily down the pass, and calls upon the stage*)
          Make way, make way! My lord, the governor,
          Is coming down on horseback close behind me.
                                      [*Exit* TELL.

ARMGART (*with animation*).
          The Viceroy comes!
              [*She goes towards the pass with her children*
              GESSLER *and* RUDOLPH DER HARRAS *appear
              upon the heights on horseback.*

STUSSI (*to* FRIESSHARDT).   How got ye through the stream,
          When all the bridges have been carried down?

FRIESS. We've battled with the billows; and, my friend,
   An Alpine torrent's nothing after that.
STUSSI. How! Were you out, then, in that dreadful storm?
FRIESS. Ay, that we were! I shall not soon forget it.
STUSSI. Stay, speak—
FRIESS.   I cannot.   I must to the castle,
   And tell them, that the governor's at hand.   [Exit.
STUSSI. If honest men, now, had been in the ship,
   It had gone down with every soul on board:—
   Some folks are proof 'gainst fire and water both.
                              [Looking round
   Where has the huntsman gone, with whom I spoke?
                              [Exit

Enter GESSLER and RUDOLPH DER HARRAS on horseback

GESSL. Say what you please; I am the Emperor's servant,
   And my first care must be to do his pleasure.
   He did not send me here to fawn and cringe
   And coax these boors into good humour.   No!
   Obedience he must have.   We soon shall see,
   If king or peasant is to lord it here?
ARM... Now is the moment! Now for my petition!
GESSL. 'Twas not in sport that I set up the cap
   In Altdorf—or to try the people's hearts—
   All this I knew before.   I set it up
   That they might learn to bend those stubborn necks
   They carry far too proudly—and I placed
   What well I knew their eyes could never brook
   Full in the road, which they perforce must pass,
   That, when their eye fell on it, they might call
   That lord to mind whom they too much forget.
HAR... But surely, sir, the people have some rights—
GESSL. This is no time to settle what they are.
   Great projects are at work, and hatching now
   The Imperial house seeks to extend its power.
   Those vast designs of conquest, which the sire
   Has gloriously begun, the son will end.
   This petty nation is a stumbling-block—
   One way or other, it must be subjected.
       [They are about to pass on. ARMGART throws
       herself down before GESSLER.

ARM. . Mercy, lord governor! Oh, pardon, pardon!

GESSL. Why do you cross me on the public road?
       Stand back, I say.

ARMGART.   My husband lies in prison;
       My wretched orphans cry for bread.   Have pity,
       Pity, my lord, upon our sore distress!

HAR. . . Who are you, woman; and who is your husband?

ARM. . . A poor wild-hay-man of the Rigiberg,
       Kind sir, who on the brow of the abyss,
       Mows down the grass from steep and craggy shelves,
       To which the very cattle dare not climb.

HARRAS (*to* GESSLER).
       By Heaven! a sad and miserable life!
       I prithee, give the wretched man his freedom.
       How great soever his offence may be,
       His horrid trade is punishment enough.
                              [*To* ARMGART
       You shall have justice.   To the castle bring
       Your suit.   This is no place to deal with it.

ARM. . . No, no, I will not stir from where I stand,
       Until your grace restore my husband to me.
       Six months already has he been in prison,
       And waits the sentence of a judge in vain.

GESSL. How! would you force me, woman? Hence! Begone!

ARM. . . Justice, my lord! Ay, justice! Thou art judge:
       The deputy of the Emperor—of Heaven.
       Then do thy duty,—as thou hopest for justice
       From Him who rules above, show it to us!

GESSL. Hence, drive this daring rabble from my sight!

ARMGART (*seizing his horse's reins*).
       No, no, by Heaven, I've nothing more to lose.—
       Thou stirr'st not, Viceroy, from this spot, until
       Thou dost me fullest justice.   Knit thy brows,
       And roll thy eyes—I fear not.   Our distress
       Is so extreme, so boundless, that we care
       No longer for thine anger.

GESSLER.   Woman, hence!
       Give way, I say, or I will ride thee down.

ARM. . . Well, do so—there—
              [*Throws her children and herself upon the ground
              before him.*

                                             2 D

                              Here on the ground I lie,
        I and my children.   Let the wretched orphans
        Be trodden by thy horse into the dust!
        It will not be the worst, that thou hast done
HAR. . . Are you mad, woman?
ARMGART (*continuing with vehemence*).
                              Many a day thou hast
        Trampled the Emperor's lands beneath thy feet
        Oh, I am but a woman! Were I man,
        I'd find some better thing to do, than here
        Lie grovelling in the dust.
                [*The music of the wedding party is again heard
                   from the top of the pass, but more softly*
GESSLER.   Where are my knaves?
        Drag her away, lest I forget myself,
        And do some deed I may repent hereafter.
HAR . . My lord, the servants cannot force a passage;
        The pass is block'd up by a marriage party.
GESSL. Too mild a ruler am I to this people,
        Their tongues are all too bold—nor have they yet
        Been tamed to due submission, as they shall be.
        I must take order for the remedy;
        I will subdue this stubborn mood of theirs,
        And crush the Soul of Liberty within them.
        I'll publish a new law throughout the land;
        I will—
                [*An arrow pierces him,—he puts his hand on his
                   heart, and is about to sink—with a feeble voice,*
                Oh God, have mercy on my soul!
HAR. . . My lord! my lord! Oh God! What's this? Whence
        came it?
ARMGART (*starts up*).
        Dead, dead! He reels, he falls! 'Tis in his heart!
HARRAS (*springs from his horse*).
        This is most horrible! Oh Heavens! sir knight,
        Address yourself to God and pray for mercy,—
        You are a dying man.
GESSLER.   That shot was Tell's
                [*He slides from his horse into the arms of Ru-
                   DOLPH DER HARRAS, who lays him down upon
                   the bench. TELL appears above upon the rocks.*

TELL.   Thou know'st the archer, seek no other hand
Our cottages are free, and innocence
Secure from thee : thou'lt be our curse no more.
                    [TELL *disappears. People rush in*
STUSSI   What is the matter?   Tell me what has happen'd?
ARM... The governor is shot,—kill'd by an arrow!
PEOPLE (*running in*).
Who has been shot?
                    [*While the foremost of the marriage party are
                    coming on the stage, the hindmost are still upon
                    the heights.   The music continues.*
HARRAS   He's bleeding fast to death.
Away, for help—pursue the murderer!
Unhappy man, is't thus that thou must die?
Thou wouldst not heed the warnings that I gave
     thee!
STUSSI. By Heaven, his cheek is pale! His life ebbs fast.
MANY VOICES
Who did the deed?
HARRAS   What! Are the people mad,
That they make music to a murder? Silence!
                    [*Music breaks off suddenly. People continue to
                    flock in.*
Speak, if thou canst, my lord.   Hast thou no charge
To intrust me with?
                    [GESSLER *makes signs with his hand, which he
                    repeats with vehemence, when he finds they are
                    not understood.*
                              What would you have me do?
Shall I to Küssnacht?   I can't guess your meaning.
Do not give way to this impatience.   Leave
All thoughts of earth, and make your peace with
     Heaven.
                    [*The whole marriage party gather round the
                    dying man.*
STUSSI. See there! how pale he grows! Death's gathering
     now
About his heart :—his eyes grow dim and glazed.
ARMGART (*holds up a child*).
Look, children, how a tyrant dies!

                              2 D 2

HARRAS   Mad hag!
Have you no touch of feeling, that you look
On horrors such as these, without a shudder?
Help me—take hold.   What, will not one assist
To pull the torturing arrow from his breast?
WOMEN. We touch the man whom God's own hand has struck!
HAR.   All curses light on you !   [*Draws his sword.*
STUSSI *(seizes his arm).*   Gently, sir knight!
Your power is at an end.   'Twere best forbear.
Our country's foe is fallen.   We will brook
No further violence.   We are free men.
ALL.   The country's free !
HARRAS.   And is it come to this?
Fear and obedience at an end so soon?
         [*To the soldiers of the guard, who are thronging in.*
You see, my friends, the bloody piece of work
They've acted here.   'Tis now too late for help,
And to pursue the murderer were vain.
New duties claim our care.   Set on to Küssnacht,
And let us save that fortress for the king!
For in an hour like this, all ties of order,
Fealty and faith, are scatter'd to the winds.
No man's fidelity is to be trusted.
         [*As he is going out with the soldiers, six* FRATRES
              MISERICORDIÆ *appear.*
ARM.   . Here come the brotherhood of mercy.   Room!
STUSSI. The victim's slain, and now the ravens stoop.
BROTHERS OF MERCY (*form a semicircle round the body, and
              sing in solemn tones).*
With hasty step death presses on,
    Nor grants to man a moment's stay,
He falls ere half his race be run,
    In manhood's pride is swept away :
Prepar'd, or unprepar'd, to die,
He stands before his Judge on high.
         [*While they are repeating the two last lines, the
           curtain falls.*

ACT V.

SCENE I.

A common near Altdorf. In the background to the right the
Keep of Uri, with the scaffold still standing, as in the Third
Scene of the first Act To the left, the view opens upon nu
merous mountains, on all of which signal fires are burning.
Day is breaking, and bells are heard ringing from various
distances

RUODI, KUONI, WERNI, MASTER MASON, *and many other*
country people, also women and children

RUODI. Look at the fiery signals on the mountains!

MASON. Hark to the bells above the forest there!

RUODI. The enemy's expelled.

MASON.   The forts are taken.

RUODI. And we of Uri, do we still endure
Upon our native soil, the tyrant's Keep?
Are we the last to strike for liberty?

MASON. Shall the yoke stand, that was to bow our necks?
Up! Tear it to the ground!

ALL.   Down, down with it!

RUODI. Where is the Stier of Uri?

URI. . .   Here. What would ye?

RUODI. Up to your tower, and wind us such a blast,
As shall resound afar, from hill to hill ;
Rousing the echoes of each peak and glen,
And call the mountain men in haste together!
                [*Exit* STIER OF URI—*enter* WALTER FURST

FURST. Stay, stay, my friends! As yet we have not learn'd
What has been done in Unterwald and Schwytz.
Let's wait till we receive intelligence!

RUODI. Wait, wait for what?   The accursed tyrant's dead,
And the bright day of liberty has dawn'd!

MASON. How! Do these flaming signals not suffice,
That blaze on every mountain top around?

RUODI. Come all, fall to—come, men and women, all!
Destroy the scaffold! Tear the arches down!
Down with the walls, let not a stone remain

MASON. Come, comrades, come !   We built it, and we know
How best to hurl it down

ALL.   Come! Down with it!
                    [*They fall upon the building at every side*
FURST   The floodgate's burst   They're not to be restrained.
                    [*Enter* MELCHTHAL *and* BAUMGARTEN.
MELCH.   What! Stands the fortress still, when Sarnen lies
         In ashes, and when Rossberg is a ruin?
FURST.   You, Melchthal, here?   D'ye bring us liberty?
         Say, have you freed the country of the foe?
MELCH.   We've swept them from the soil.   Rejoice, my friend;
         Now, at this very moment, while we speak,
         There's not a tyrant left in Switzerland!
FURST.   How did you get the forts into your power?
MELCH.   Rudenz it was who with a gallant arm,
         And manly daring, took the keep at Sarnen.
         The Rossberg I had storm'd the night before.
         But hear, what chanced.   Scarce had we driven the foe
         Forth from the keep, and given it to the flames,
         That now rose crackling upwards to the skies,
         When from the blaze rush'd Diethelm, Gessler's page,
         Exclaiming, "Lady Bertha will be burnt!"
FURST.   Good heavens!
                    [*The beams of the scaffold are heard falling*
MELCH.   'Twas she herself.   Here had she been
         Immured in secret by the Viceroy's orders.
         Rudenz sprang up in frenzy.   For we heard
         The beams and massive pillars crashing down,
         And through the volumed smoke the piteous shrieks
         Of the unhappy lady.
FURST.   Is she saved?
MELCH.   Here was a time for promptness and decision!
         Had he been nothing but our baron, then
         We should have been most chary of our lives;
         But he was our confederate, and Bertha
         Honour'd the people.   So, without a thought.
         We risk'd the worst, and rush'd into the flames.
FURST.   But is she saved?
MELCH   She is   Rudenz and I
         Bore her between us from the blazing pile,
         With crashing timbers toppling all around.
         And when she had revived, the danger past,
         And raised her eyes to meet the light of heaven,

The baron fell upon my breast; and then
A silent vow of friendship pass'd between us—
A vow that, temper'd in yon furnace heat,
Will last through ev'ry shock of time and fate.

FURST. Where is the Landenberg?

MELCH.   Across the Brünig.
No fault of mine it was, that he, who quench'd
My father's eyesight, should go hence unharm'd.
He fled—I followed—overtook and seized him.
And dragg'd him to my father's feet. The sword
Already quiver'd o'er the caitiff's head.
When at the entreaty of the blind old man,
I spared the life for which he basely pray'd.
He swore URPHEDE *, never to return:
He'll keep his oath, for he has felt our arm.

FURST. Thank God, our victory's unstain'd by blood!

CHILDREN (*running across the stage with fragments of wood*)
Liberty! Liberty! Hurrah, we're free!

FURST. Oh! what a joyous scene! These children will,
E'en to their latest day, remember it.

[*Girls bring in the cap upon a pole. The whole
stage is filled with people.*

RUODI. Here is the cap, to which we were to bow!

BAUM. . Command us, how we shall dispose of it.

FURST Heavens! 'Twas beneath this cap my grandson stood!

SEVERAL VOICES.
Destroy the emblem of the tyrant's power!
Let it be burnt!

FURST   No. Rather be preserved!
'Twas once the instrument of despots—now ·
'Twill be a lasting symbol of our freedom.

[*Peasants, men, women, and children, some standing, others sitting upon the beams of the shat-
tered scaffold, all picturesquely grouped, in a
large semicircle.*

MELCH. Thus now, my friends, with light and merry hearts,

* The URPHEDE was an oath of peculiar force. When a man, who was at feud with another, invaded his lands and was worsted, he often made terms with his enemy by swearing the *Urphede*, by which he bound himself to depart, and never to return with a hostile intention.

We stand upon the wreck of tyranny;
And gallantly have we fulfill'd the oath,
Which we at Rootli swore, Confederates!

FURST   The work is but begun.   We must be firm.
For, be assured, the king will make all speed,
To avenge his Viceroy's death, and reinstate,
By force of arms, the tyrant we've expell'd.

MELCH.   Why let him come, with all his armaments!
The foe within has fled before our arms;
We'll give him welcome warmly from without!

RUODI.   The passes to the country are but few;
And these we'll boldly cover with our bodies.

BAUM.   We are bound by an indissoluble league,
And all his armies shall not make us quail.

[*Enter* ROSSELMANN *and* STAUFFACHER.

ROSSELMANN (*speaking as he enters*).
These are the awful judgments of the Lord!

PEAS. . What is the matter?

ROSSELMANN.   In what times we live!

FURST.   Say on, what is't?   Ha, Werner, is it you?
What tidings?

PEASANT.   What's the matter?

ROSSELMANN.   Hear and wonder!

STAUFF. We are released from one great cause of dread.

ROSSEL. The Emperor is murdered.

FURST.   Gracious Heaven!

[PEASANTS *rise up and throng round* STAUFFACHER

ALL.   Murder'd the Emp'ror? What! The Emp'ror! Hear!

MELCH.   Impossible! How came you by the news?

STAUFF. 'Tis true! Near Bruck, by the assassin's hand,
King Albert fell.   A most trustworthy man,
John Müller, from Schaffhausen, brought the news.

FURST.   Who dared commit so horrible a deed?

STAUFF. The doer makes the deed more dreadful still;
It was his nephew, his own brother's child,
Duke John of Austria, who struck the blow.

MELCH.   What drove him to so dire a parricide?

STAUFF. The Emp'ror kept his patrimony back,
Despite his urgent importunities;

'Twas said, indeed, he never meant to give it,
But with a mitre to appease the duke.
However this may be, the duke gave ear
To the ill counsel of his friends in arms;
And with the noble lords, Von Eschenbach,
Von Tegerfeld, Von Wart and Palm, resolved,
Since his demands for justice were despised,
With his own hands to take revenge at least.

FURST. But say, how compass'd he the dreadful deed?
STAUFF The king was riding down from Stein to Baden,
Upon his way to join the court at Rheinfeld.—
With him a train of Ligh-born gentlemen,
And the young Princes John and Leopold.
And when they'd reach'd the ferry of the Reuss,
The assassins forced their way into the boat,
To separate the Emperor from his suite.
His highness landed, and was riding on
Across a fresh plough'd field—where once, they say,
A mighty city stood in Pagan times—
With Habsburg's ancient turrets full in sight,
Where all the grandeur of his line had birth—
When Duke John plunged a dagger in his throat,
Palm ran him thro' the body with his lance,
Eschenbach cleft his skull at one fell blow,
And down he sank, all weltering in his blood,
On his own soil, by his own kinsmen slain.
Those on the opposite bank, who saw the deed,
Being parted by the stream, could only raise
An unavailing cry of loud lament
But a poor woman, sitting by the way,
Raised him, and on her breast he bled to death.

MELCH. Thus has he dug his own untimely grave,
Who sought insatiably to grasp at all.

STAUFF. The country round is fill'd with dire alarm.
The mountain passes are blockaded all,
And sentinels on ev'ry frontier set;
E'en ancient Zurich barricades her gates,
That for these thirty years have open stood,
Dreading the murd'rers, and th' avengers more.
For cruel Agnes comes, the Hungarian queen,

To all her sex's tenderness a stranger,
Arm'd with the thunders of the church, to wreak
Dire vengeance for her parent's royal blood,
On the whole race of those that murder'd him,—
Upon their servants, children, children's children,—
Nay, on the stones that build their castle walls.
Deep has she sworn a vow to immolate
Whole generations on her father's tomb,
And bathe in blood as in the dew of May

MELCH Know you which way the murderers have fled?

STAUFF. No sooner had they done the deed, than they
Took flight, each following a different route,
And parted, ne'er to see each other more.
Duke John must still be wand'ring in the mountains

FURST. And thus their crime has yielded them no fruits
Revenge is barren. Of itself it makes
The dreadful food it feeds on; its delight
Is murder—its satiety despair.

STAUFF. The assassins reap no profit by their crime;
But we shall pluck with unpolluted hands
The teeming fruits of their most bloody deed.
For we are ransomed from our heaviest fear;
The direst foe of liberty has fallen,
And, 'tis reported, that the crown will pass
From Habsburg's house into another line;
The Empire is determined to assert
Its old prerogative of choice, I hear

FURST and several others.
Has any one been named to you?

STAUFFACHER.   The Count
Of Luxembourg is widely named already.—

FURST. 'Tis well we stood so staunchly by the Empire!
Now we may hope for justice, and with cause

STAUFF. The Emperor will need some valiant friends.
And he will shelter us from Austria's vengeance.
        [The peasantry embrace. Enter SACRIST with
        perial messenger.

SACRIS. Here are the worthy chiefs of Switzerland!

ROSSELMANN and several others.
        Sacrist, what news?

SACRISTAN.   A courier brings this letter.
ALL (*to* WALTER FURST).
    Open and read it.
FURST (*reading*).   " To the worthy men
    Of Uri, Schwytz, and Unterwald, the Queen
    Elizabeth sends grace and all good wishes ! ·
MANY VOICES.
    What wants the queen with us ? Her reign is done.
FURST (*reads*).
    " In the great grief and doleful widowhood,
    In which the bloody exit of her lord
    Has plunged her majesty, she still remembers
    The ancient faith and love of Switzerland "
MELCH. She ne'er did that, in her prosperity.
ROSSEL. Hush, let us hear !
FURST (*reads*).   "And she is well assured,
    Her people will in due abhorrence hold
    The perpetrators of this damned deed.
    On the three Cantons, therefore, she relies,
    That they in nowise lend the murderers aid ;
    But rather, that they loyally assist,
    To give them up to the avenger's hand,
    Remembering the love and grace which they
    Of old received from Rudolph's princely house."
    [*Symptoms of dissatisfaction among the peasantry*
MANY VOICES.
    The love and grace !
STAUFF Grace from the father we, indeed, received,
    But what have we to boast of from the son ?
    Did he confirm the charter of our freedom,
    As all preceding emperors had done ?
    Did he judge righteous judgment, or afford
    Shelter, or stay, to innocence oppress'd ?
    Nay, did he e'en give audience to the envoys
    We sent, to lay our grievances before him ?
    Not one of all these things e'er did the king.
    And had we not ourselves achieved our rights
    By resolute valour, our necessities
    Had never touch'd him.   Gratitude to him !
    Within these vales he sowed not gratitude
    He stood upon an eminence—he might

Have been a very father to his people,
But all his aim and pleasure was to raise
Himself and his own house : and now may those
Whom he has aggrandized, lament for him !

FÜRST   We will not triumph in his fall, nor now
Recall to mind the wrongs we have endured.
Far be't from us ! Yet, that we should avenge
The sovereign's death, who never did us good,
And hunt down those who ne'er molested us,
Becomes us not, nor is our duty.   Love
Must bring its offerings free, and unconstrain'd;
From all enforced duties death absolves —
And unto him we are no longer bound.

MELCH.   And if the queen laments within her bower,
Accusing Heaven in sorrow's wild despair ;
Here see a people, from its anguish freed,
To that same Heav'n send up its thankful praise.
For who would reap regrets, must sow affection.

                              [*Exit the Imperial Courier*

STAUFFACHER (*to the people*).
But where is Tell ? Shall he, our freedom's founder,
Alone be absent from our festival ?
He did the most—endured the worst of all.
Come—to his dwelling let us all repair,
And bid the Saviour of our country hail !

                              [*Exeunt omnes*

Scene II

Interior of TELL's *cottage.   A fire burning on the hearth
The open door shows the scene outside.*

HEDWIG, WALTER, *and* WILHELM.

HEDW.   Boys, dearest boys ! your father comes to-day
He lives, is free, and we, and all are free !
The country owes its liberty to him !

WALT.   And I, too, mother, bore my part in it ;
I shall be named with him.   My father's shaft
Went closely by my life, but yet I shook not!

HEDWIG (*embracing him*).
Yes, yes, thou art restored to me again !

Twice have I given thee birth,—twice suffer'd all
A mother's agonies for thee, my child!
But this is past—I have you both, boys, both!
And your dear father will be back to-day.

[A monk appears at the door

WILH. See, mother, yonder stands a holy friar ;
He's asking alms, no doubt.

HEDWIG.   Go lead him in,
That we may give him cheer, and make him feel
That he has come into the house of joy.

[Exit, and returns immediately with a cup

WILHELM *(to the monk)*.
Come in, good man.   Mother will give you food!

WALT. Come in and rest, then go refresh'd away!

MONK *(glancing round in terror, with unquiet looks)*.
Where am I ? In what country ?

WALTER.   Have you lost
Your way, that you are ignorant of this ?
You are at Bürglen, in the land of Uri.
Just at the entrance of the Sheckenthal

MONK *(to HEDWIG)*.
Are you alone ? Your husband, is he here ?

HEDW. I momently expect him.   But what ails you?
You look as one whose soul is ill at ease.
Whoe'er you be, you are in want—take that

[Offers him the cup

MONK. Howe'er my sinking heart may yearn for food,
I will taste nothing till you've promised me —

HEDW. Touch not my dress, nor yet advance one step.
Stand off, I say, if you would have me hear you.

MONK. Oh, by this hearth's bright hospitable blaze,
By your dear children's heads, which I embrace—

[Grasps the boys

HEDW. Stand back, I say! What is your purpose, man ?
Back from my boys! You are no monk,—no, no.
Beneath that robe content and peace should dwell,
But neither lives within that face of thine.

MONK. I am the veriest wretch that breathes on earth

HEDW. The heart is never deaf to wretchedness ;
But thy look freezes up my inmost soul

WALTER (*springs up*).
    Mother, my father!
HEDWIG.   Oh, my God!
         [*Is about to follow, trembles and stops*
WILHELM (*running after his brother*).   My father!
WALTER (*without*).   Thou'rt here once more!
WILHELM (*without*).   My father, my dear father.
TELL (*without*).
    Yes, here I am once more! Where is your mother?
                 [*They enter*
WALT.   There at the door she stands, and can no further,
    She trembles so with terror and with joy.
TELL   Oh Hedwig, Hedwig, mother of my children!
    God has been kind and helpful in our woes.
    No tyrant's hand shall e'er divide us more.
HEDWIG (*falling on his neck*).
    Oh, Tell, what have I suffer'd for thy sake!
            [*Monk becomes attentive*
TELL.   Forget it now, and live for joy alone!
    I'm here again with you! This is my cot!
    I stand again on mine own hearth!
WILHELM.   But, father,
    Where is your crossbow left? I see it not
TELL.   Nor shalt thou ever see it more, my boy.
    It is suspended in a holy place,
    And in the chase shall ne'er be used again
HEDW. Oh, Tell! Tell!
             .[*Steps back, dropping his hand*
TELL.   What alarms thee, dearest wife?
HEDW. How—how dost thou return to me? This hand—
    Dare I take hold of it? This hand—Oh God!
TELL (*with firmness and animation*).
    Has shielded you and set my country free;
    Freely I raise it in the face of Heaven.
        [*Monk gives a sudden start—he looks at him*
    Who is this friar here?
HEDWIG.   Ah, I forgot him
    Speak thou with him; I shudder at his presence
MONK (*stepping nearer*).
    Are you that Tell that slew the governor?

TELL　Yes, I am he.　I hide the fact from no man.

MONK　You are that Tell!　Ah! it is God's own hand
That hath conducted me beneath your roof.

TELL (*examining him closely*).
You are no monk.　Who are you?

MONK　　　　　　　　　　　　　You have slain
The governor, who did you wrong.　I, too,
Have slain a foe, who late denied me justice.
He was no less your enemy than mine.
I've rid the land of him.

TELL (*drawing back*).　　　　Thou art—oh, horror!
In—children, children—in without a word
Go, my dear wife! Go! Go! Unhappy man,
Thou shouldst be——

HEDWIG.　　　　　　　Heav'ns, who is it?

TELL.　　　　　　　　　　　　　Do not ask
Away! away! the children must not hear it.
Out of the house—away!　Thou must not rest
'Neath the same roof with this unhappy man!

HEDW. Alas! What is it? Come!　[*Exit with the children*

TELL (*to the* MONK).　　　　Thou art the Duke
Of Austria—I know it.　Thou hast slain
The Emperor, thy uncle, and liege lord

JOHN　He robb'd me of my patrimony.

TELL.　　　　　　　　　　　　How!
Slain him—thy king, thy uncle!　And the earth
Still bears thee!　And the sun still shines on thee

JOHN.　Tell, hear me, ere you——

TELL.　　　　　　　　　　Reeking with the blood
Of him that was thy Emperor, and kinsman,
Durst thou set foot within my spotless house?
Show thy fell visage to a virtuous man,
And claim the rites of hospitality?

JOHN　I hoped to find compassion at your hands.
You also took revenge upon your foe!

TELL　Unhappy man! And dar'st thou thus confound
Ambition's bloody crime, with the dread act
To which a father's direful need impell'd him?
Hadst thou to shield thy children's darling heads,
To guard thy fireside's sanctuary—ward off
The last, worst doom from all that thou didst love?

To Heaven I raise my unpolluted hands,
To curse thine act and thee! I have avenged
That holy nature which thou hast profaned.
I have no part with thee. Thou art a murderer;
I've shielded all that was most dear to me.

JOHN.   You cast me off to comfortless despair!

TELL   My blood runs cold ev'n while I talk with thee.
Away! Pursue thine awful course! Nor longer
Pollute the cot where innocence abides!

                       [JOHN *turns to depart*

JOHN   I cannot live, and will no longer thus!

TELL   And yet my soul bleeds for thee—gracious Heaven
So young, of such a noble line, the grandson
Of Rudolph, once my lord and emperor,
An outcast—murderer—standing at my door,
The poor man's door—a suppliant, in despair!

                       [*Covers his face*

JOHN.   If thou hast power to weep, oh let my fate
Move your compassion—it is horrible.
I am—say, rather was—a prince. I might
Have been most happy, had I only curb'd
Th' impatience of my passionate desires
But envy gnaw'd my heart—I saw the youth
Of mine own cousin Leopold endow'd
With honour, and enrich'd with broad domains,
The while myself, that was in years his equal,
Was kept in abject and disgraceful nonage.

TELL.   Unhappy man, thy uncle knew thee well,
When he withheld both land and subjects from thee
Thou, by thy mad and desperate act hast set
A fearful seal upon his sage resolve.
Where are the bloody partners of thy crime?

JOHN   Where'er the demon of revenge has borne them;
I have not seen them since the luckless deed.

TELL   Know'st thou the Empire's ban is out,—that thou
Art interdicted to thy friends, and given
An outlaw'd victim to thine enemies!

JOHN   Therefore I shun all public thoroughfares,
And venture not to knock at any door—
I turn my footsteps to the wilds, and through
The mountains roam, a terror to myself.

From mine own self I shrink with horror back,
Should a chance brook reflect my ill-starr'd form
If thou hast pity for a fellow mortal——
                              [*Falls down before him.*

TELL   Stand up, stand up!
JOHN.   Not till thou shalt extend
        Thy hand in promise of assistance to me.
TELL.   Can I assist thee? Can a sinful man?
        Yet get thee up—how black soe'er thy crime,—
        Thou art a man. I, too, am one. From Tell
        Shall no one part uncomforted. I will
        Do all that lies within my power.
DUKE JOHN (*springs up and grasps him ardently by the hand,*
                                Oh, Tell,
        You save me from the terrors of despair.
TELL.   Let go my hand! Thou must away. Thou canst not
        Remain here undiscover'd, and discover'd,
        Thou canst not count on succour. Which way, then,
        Wilt bend thy steps? Where dost thou hope to find
        A place of rest?
DUKE JOHN.   Alas! alas! I know not.
TELL.   Hear, then, what Heaven suggesteth to my heart,
        Thou must to Italy,—to Saint Peter's City—
        There cast thyself at the Pope's feet,—confess
        Thy guilt to him, and ease thy laden soul!
JOHN   But will he not surrender me to vengeance?
TELL   Whate'er he does, receive as God's decree.
JOHN   But how am I to reach that unknown land?
        I have no knowledge of the way, and dare not
        Attach myself to other travellers.
TELL.   I will describe the road, and mark me well!
        You must ascend, keeping along the Reuss,
        Which from the mountains dashes wildly down
DUKE JOHN (*in alarm*).
        What! See the Reuss? The witness of my deed!
TELL.   The road you take lies through the river's gorge,
        And many a cross proclaims where travellers
        Have perish'd 'neath the avalanche's fall.
JOHN   I have no fear for nature's terrors, so
        I can appease the torments of my soul.
TELL   At every cross, kneel down and expiate

                                        2 E

Your crime with burning penitential tears—
And if you 'scape the perils of the pass,
And are not whelm'd beneath the drifted snows.
That from the frozen peaks come sweeping down,
You'll reach the bridge, that hangs in drizzling spray
Then if it yield not 'neath your heavy guilt,
When you have left it safely in your rear,
Before you frowns the gloomy Gate of Rocks,
Where never sun did shine   Proceed through this
And you will reach a bright and gladsome vale.
Yet must you hurry on with hasty steps,
For in the haunts of peace you must not linger

JOHN O Rudolph, Rudolph, royal grandsire! thus
Thy grandson first sets foot within thy realms!

TELL Ascending still, you gain the Gotthardt's heights
On which the everlasting lakes repose,
That from the streams of Heaven itself are fed,
There to the German soil you bid farewell;
And thence, with rapid course, another stream
Leads you to Italy, your promised land.

   [*Ranz des Vaches sounded on Alp-horns is heard
    without*

But I hear voices! Hence!

HEDWIG (*hurrying in*)   Where art thou, Tell?
Our father comes, and in exulting bands
All the confederates approach.

DUKE JOHN (*covering himself*). Woe's me!
I dare not tarry 'mid this happiness!

TELL Go, dearest wife, and give this man to eat.
Spare not your bounty. For his road is long,
And one where shelter will be hard to find
Quick! they approach.

HEDWIG.   Who is he?

TELL.   Do not ask!
And when he quits thee, turn thine eyes away,
That they may not behold the road he takes

   [DUKE JOHN *advances hastily towards* TELL, *but
   he beckons him aside and exit. When both
   have left the stage, the scene changes, and discloses in*

Scene III.

The whole valley before TELL'S *house, the heights which enclose it occupied by peasants, grouped into tableaux. Some are seen crossing a lofty bridge, which crosses the Shechen.* WALTER FURST *with the two boys.* WERNER *and* STAUF FACHER *come forward. Others throng after them. When* TELL *appears, all receive him with loud cheers.*

ALL.   Long live brave Tell, our shield, our liberator.
             [*While those in front are crowding round* TELL,
             and embracing him, RUDENZ *and* BERTHA *ap*
             pear. The former salutes the peasantry, the
             latter embraces HEDWIG. *The music from the*
             mountains continues to play. When it has
             stopped, BERTHA *steps into the centre of the*
             crowd.

BERTH   Peasants ! Confederates ! Into your league
             Receive me here, that happily am the first
             To find protection in the land of freedom.
             To your brave hands I now entrust my rights.
             Will you protect me as your citizen ?

PEAS.   Ay, that we will, with life and fortune both !

BERTH.   'Tis well ! And to this youth I give my hand.
             A free Swiss maiden to a free Swiss man !

RUD.   And from this moment all my serfs are free !
                         [*Music and the curtain falls*

THE END.

LONDON :

PRINTED BY WILLIAM CLOWES AND SONS, LIMITED,
STAMFORD STREET AND CHARING CROSS.

CATALOGUE OF
BOHN'S LIBRARIES.

740 *Volumes*, £158 19s. 6d.

The Publishers are now issuing the Libraries in a NEW AND MORE ATTRACTIVE STYLE OF BINDING. The original bindings endeared to many book-lovers by association will still be kept in stock, but henceforth all orders will be executed in the New Binding, unless the contrary is expressly stated.

New Volumes of Standard Works in the various branches of Literature are constantly being added to this Series, which is already unsurpassed in respect to the number, variety, and cheapness of the Works contained in it. The Publishers beg to announce the following Volumes as recently issued or now in preparation:—

Goethe's Faust. Part I. The Original Text, with Hayward's Translation and Notes, carefully revised, with an Introduction and Bibliography, by C. A. Buchheim, Ph.D., Professor of German Language and Literature at King's College, London. *[In the Press.*

Arthur Young's Tour in Ireland. Edited by A. W. Hutton, Librarian, National Liberal Club. *[Preparing.*

Ricardo on the Principles of Political Economy and Taxation. Edited with Notes by E. C. K. Gonner, M.A., Lecturer, University College, Liverpool. *[See p. 19.*

Schopenhauer's Essays. Selected and Translated. By E. Belfort Bax. *[See p. 9.*

Voltaire's Tales. Translated by R. B. Boswell. Vol. I. 3s. 6d. *[See p. 8.*

Count Grammont's Memoirs of the Court of Charles II. With the Boscobel Tracts, &c. New Edition. 3s. 6d. *[See p. 5.*

Gray's Letters. New Edition. Edited by the Rev. D. C. Tovey, M.A. *[In the press.*

Schools and Masters of Fence. By C. Egerton Castle. New Edition. With numerous Illustrations. *[In the press.*

Montaigne's Essays. Cotton's Translation, revised by W. C. Hazlitt. New Edition. 3 Vols. *[In the press.*

Descartes' Principal Works. Edited by Professor G. Croom Robertson and Thomas Whittaker. 2 Vols.

Hartley Coleridge's Essays and Marginalia. Edited by the Lord Chief Justice. *[Preparing.*

Hoffmann's Works. Translated by Lieut.-Colonel Ewing. Vol. II. *[In the press.*

Bohn's Handbooks of Games. New enlarged edition. In 2 vols. *[See p. 21.*

Vol. I.—Table Games, by Major-General Drayson, R.A., R. F. Green, and 'Berkeley.'
II.—Card Games, by Dr. W. Pole, F.R.S., R. F. Green, 'Berkeley,' and Baxter-Wray.

Bohn's Handbooks of Athletic Sports. 8 Vols. *[See p. 21.*

For BOHN'S SELECT LIBRARY, see p. 23.

BOHN'S LIBRARIES.

STANDARD LIBRARY.

338 *Vols. at* 3s. 6d. *each, excepting those marked otherwise.* (59*l*. 17s. 6*l*.)

ADDISON'S Works. Notes of Bishop Hurd. Short Memoir, Portrait, and 8 Plates of Medals. 6 vols.
This is the most complete edition of Addison's Works issued.

ALFIERI'S Tragedies. In English Verse. With Notes, Arguments, and Introduction, by E. A. Bowring, C.B. 2 vols.

AMERICAN POETRY. — *See Poetry of America.*

BACON'S Moral and Historical Works, including Essays, Apophthegms, Wisdom of the Ancients, New Atlantis, Henry VII., Henry VIII., Elizabeth, Henry Prince of Wales, History of Great Britain, Julius Cæsar, and Augustus Cæsar. With Critical and Biographical Introduction and Notes by J. Devey, M.A. Portrait.

—— *See also Philosophical Library.*

BALLADS AND SONGS of the Peasantry of England, from Oral Recitation, private MSS., Broadsides, &c. Edit. by R. Bell.

BEAUMONT AND FLETCHER. Selections. With Notes and Introduction by Leigh Hunt.

BECKMANN (J.) History of Inventions, Discoveries, and Origins. With Portraits of Beckmann and James Watt. 2 vols.

BELL (Robert).—*See Ballads, Chaucer, Green.*

BOSWELL'S Life of Johnson, with the TOUR in the HEBRIDES and JOHNSONIANA. New Edition, with Notes and Appendices, by the Rev. A. Napier, M.A., Trinity College, Cambridge, Vicar of Holkham, Editor of the Cambridge Edition of the 'Theological Works of Barrow.' With Frontispiece to each vol. 6 vols.

BREMER'S (Frederika) Works. Trans. by M. Howitt. Portrait. 4 vo's.

BRINK (B. ten). Early English Literature (to Wiclif). By Bernhard ten Brink. Trans. by Prof. H. M. Kennedy.

BROWNE'S (Sir Thomas) Works. Edit. by S. Wilkin, with Dr. Johnson's Life of Browne. Portrait. 3 vols.

BURKE'S Works. 6 vols.

—— **Speeches on the Impeachment** of Warren Hastings ; and Letters. 2 vols.

—— **Life.** By Sir J. Prior. Portrait.

BURNS (Robert). Life of. By J. G. Lockhart, D.C.L. A new and enlarged edition. With Notes and Appendices by W. Scott Douglas. Portrait.

BUTLER'S (Bp.) Analogy of Religion, Natural and Revealed, to the Constitution and Course of Nature : with Two Dissertations on Identity and Virtue, and Fifteen Sermons. With Introductions, Notes, and Memoir. Portrait.

CAMOËN'S Lusiad, or the Discovery of India. An Epic Poem. Trans. from the Portuguese, with Dissertation, Historical Sketch, and Life, by W. J. Mickle. 5th edition.

CARAFAS (The) of Maddaloni. Naples under Spanish Dominion. Trans. from the German of Alfred de Reumont. Portrait of Massaniello.

CARREL. The Counter-Revolution in England for the Re-establishment of Popery under Charles II. and James II., by Armand Carrel ; with Fox's History of James II. and Lord Lonsdale's Memoir of James II. Portrait of Carrel.

CARRUTHERS. — *See Pope, in Illustrated Library.*

CARY'S Dante. The Vision of Hell, Purgatory, and Paradise. Trans. by Rev. H. F. Cary, M.A. With Life, Chronological View of his Age, Notes, and Index of Proper Names. Portrait.
This is the authentic edition, containing Mr. Cary's last corrections, with additional notes.

HUGO'S (Victor) Dramatic Works: Hernani—Ruy Blas—The King's Diversion. Translated by Mrs. Newton Crosland and F. L. Slous.

—— **Poems,** chiefly Lyrical. Collected by H. L. Williams.

HUNGARY: Its History and Revolution, with Memoir of Kossuth. Portrait.

HUTCHINSON (Colonel). Memoirs of. By his Widow, with her Autobiography, and the Siege of Lathom House. Portrait.

IRVING'S (Washington) Complete Works. 15 vols.

—— **Life and Letters.** By his Nephew, Pierre E. Irving. With Index and a Portrait. 2 vols.

JAMES'S (G. P. R.) Life of Richard Cœur de Lion. Portraits of Richard and Philip Augustus. 2 vols.

—— **Louis XIV.** Portraits. 2 vols.

JAMESON (Mrs.) Shakespeare's Heroines. Characteristics of Women. By Mrs. Jameson.

JEAN PAUL.—*See Richter.*

JOHNSON'S Lives of the Poets. Edited, with Notes, by Mrs. Alexander Napier. And an Introduction by Professor J. W. Hales, M.A. 3 vols.

JONSON (Ben). Poems of.—*See Greene.*

JOSEPHUS (Flavius), The Works of. Whiston's Translation. Revised by Rev. A. R. Shilleto, M.A. With Topographical and Geographical Notes by Colonel Sir C. W. Wilson, K.C.B. 5 vols.

JUNIUS'S Letters. With Woodfall's Notes. An Essay on the Authorship. Facsimiles of Handwriting. 2 vols.

LA FONTAINE'S Fables. In English Verse, with Essay on the Fabulists. By Elizur Wright.

LAMARTINE'S The Girondists, or Personal Memoirs of the Patriots of the French Revolution. Trans. by H. T. Ryde. Portraits of Robespierre, Madame Roland, and Charlotte Corday. 3 vols.

—— **The Restoration of Monarchy** in France (a Sequel to The Girondists). 5 Portraits. 4 vols.

—— **The French Revolution of 1848.** Portraits.

LAMB'S (Charles) Elia and Eliana. Complete Edition. Portrait.

LAMB'S (Charles) Specimens of English Dramatic Poets of the time of Elizabeth. With Notes and the Extracts from the Garrick Plays.

—— **Talfourd's Letters of Charles** Lamb. New Edition, by W. Carew Hazlitt. 2 vols.

LANZI'S History of Painting in Italy, from the Period of the Revival of the Fine Arts to the End of the 18th Century. With Memoir and Portraits. Trans. by T. Roscoe. 3 vols.

LAPPENBERG'S England under the Anglo-Saxon Kings. Trans. by B. Thorpe, F.S.A. 2 vols.

LESSING'S Dramatic Works. Complete. By E. Bell, M.A. With Memoir by H. Zimmern. Portrait. 2 vols.

—— **Laokoon, Dramatic Notes, and** Representation of Death by the Ancients. Trans. by E. C. Beasley and Helen Zimmern. Frontispiece.

LOCKE'S Philosophical Works, containing Human Understanding, Controversy with Bishop of Worcester, Malebranche's Opinions, Natural Philosophy, Reading and Study. With Introduction, Analysis, and Notes, by J. A. St. John. Portrait. 2 vols.

—— **Life and Letters,** with Extracts from his Common-place Books. By Lord King.

LOCKHART (J. G.)—*See Burns.*

LUTHER'S Table-Talk. Trans. by W. Hazlitt. With Life by A. Chalmers, and LUTHER'S CATECHISM. Portrait after Cranach.

—— **Autobiography.**—*See Michelet.*

MACHIAVELLI'S History of Florence, THE PRINCE, Savonarola, Historical Tracts, and Memoir. Portrait.

MARLOWE. Poems of.—*See Greene.*

MARTINEAU'S (Harriet) History of England (including History of the Peace) from 1800-1846. 5 vols.

MENZEL'S History of Germany, from the Earliest Period to the Crimean War. Portraits. 3 vols.

MICHELET'S Autobiography of Luther. Trans. by W. Hazlitt. With Notes.

—— **The French Revolution** to the Flight of the King in 1791. Frontispiece.

MIGNET'S The French Revolution, from 1789 to 1814. Portrait of Napoleon.

MILTON'S Prose Works. With Preface, Preliminary Remarks by J. A. St. John, and Index. 5 vols. Portraits.

—— **Poetical Works.** With 120 Wood Engravings. 2 vols.

MITFORD'S (Miss) Our Village. Sketches of Rural Character and Scenery. 2 Engravings. 2 vols.

MOLIÈRE'S Dramatic Works. In English Prose, by C. H. Wall. With a Life and a Portrait. 3 vols.
' It is not too much to say that we have here probably as good a translation of Molière as can be given.'—*Academy.*

MONTAGU. Letters and Works of Lady Mary Wortley Montagu. Lord Wharncliffe's Third Edition. Edited by W. Moy Thomas. New and revised edition. With steel plates. 2 vols. 5*s.* each.

MONTESQUIEU'S Spirit of Laws. Revised Edition, with D'Alembert's Analysis, Notes, and Memoir. 2 vols.

NEANDER (Dr. A.) History of the Christian Religion and Church. Trans. by J. Torrey. With Short Memoir. 10 vols.

—— **Life of Jesus Christ, in its Historical Connexion and Development.**

—— **The Planting and Training of** the Christian Church by the Apostles. With the Antignosticus, or Spirit of Tertullian. Trans. by J. E. Ryland. 2 vols.

—— **Lectures on the History of** Christian Dogmas. Trans. by J. E. Ryland. 2 vols.

—— **Memorials of Christian Life in** the Early and Middle Ages; including Light in Dark Places. Trans. by J. E. Ryland.

NORTH'S Lives of the Right Hon. Francis North, Baron Guildford, the Hon. Sir Dudley North, and the Hon. and Rev. Dr. John North. By the Hon. Roger North. Edited by A. Jessopp, D.D. With 3 Portraits. 3 vols. 3*s.* 6*d.* each.
' Lovers of good literature will rejoice at the appearance of a new, handy, and complete edition of so justly famous a book, and will congratulate themselves that it has found so competent and skilful an editor as Dr. Jessopp.'—*Times.*

OCKLEY (S.) History of the Sara- cens and their Conquests in Syria, Persia, and Egypt. Comprising the Lives of Mohammed and his Successors to the Death of Abdalmelik, the Eleventh Caliph. By Simon Ockley, B.D., Portrait of Mohammed.

PASCAL'S Thoughts. Translated from the Text of M. Auguste Molinier by C. Kegan Paul. 3rd edition.

PERCY'S Reliques of Ancient Eng- lish Poetry, consisting of Ballads, Songs, and other Pieces of our earlier Poets, with some few of later date. With Essay on Ancient Minstrels, and Glossary. 2 vols.

PHILIP DE COMMINES. Memoirs of. Containing the Histories of Louis XI. and Charles VIII., and Charles the Bold, Duke of Burgundy. With the History of Louis XI., by Jean de Troyes. Translated, with a Life and Notes, by A. R. Scoble. Portraits. 2 vols.

PLUTARCH'S LIVES. Translated, with Notes and Life, by A. Stewart, M.A., late Fellow of Trinity College, Cambridge, and G. Long, M.A. 4 vols.

POETRY OF AMERICA. Selections from One Hundred Poets, from 1776 to 1876. With Introductory Review, and Specimens of Negro Melody, by W. J. Linton. Portrait of W. Whitman.

RACINE'S (Jean) Dramatic Works. A metrical English version, with Biographical notice. By R. Bruce Boswell, M.A. Oxon. 2 vols.

RANKE (L.) History of the Popes, their Church and State, and their Conflicts with Protestantism in the 16th and 17th Centuries. Trans. by E. Foster. Portraits. 3 vols.

—— **History of Servia.** Trans. by Mrs. Kerr. To which is added, The Slave Provinces of Turkey, by Cyprien Robert.

—— **History of the Latin and Teu-** tonic Nations. 1494-1514. Trans. by P. A. Ashworth, translator of Dr. Gneist's ' History' of the English Constitution.'

REUMONT (Alfred de).—*See Carafas.*

REYNOLDS' (Sir J.) Literary Works. With Memoir and Remarks by H. W. Beechy. 2 vols.

RICHTER (Jean Paul). Levana, a Treatise on Education ; together with the Autobiography, and a short Memoir.

—— **Flower, Fruit, and Thorn Pieces,** or the Wedded Life, Death, and Marriage of Siebenkaes. Translated by Alex. Ewing. The only complete English translation.

ROSCOE'S (W.) Life of Leo X., with Notes, Historical Documents, and Dissertation on Lucretia Borgia. 3 Portraits. 2 vols.

—— **Lorenzo de' Medici,** called ' The Magnificent,' with Copyright Notes, Poems, Letters, &c. With Memoir of Roscoe and Portrait of Lorenzo.

RUSSIA, History of, from the earliest Period to the Crimean War. By W. K. Kelly. 3 Portraits. 2 vols.

SCHILLER'S Works. 7 vols.

Vol. I.—History of the Thirty Years' War. Rev. A. J. W. Morrison, M.A. Portrait.

Vol. II.—History of the Revolt in the Netherlands, the Trials of Counts Egmont and Horn, the Siege of Antwerp, and the Disturbance of France preceding the Reign of Henry IV. Translated by Rev. A. J. W. Morrison and L. Dora Schmitz.

Vol. III.—Don Carlos. R. D. Boylan —Mary Stuart. Mellish — Maid of Orleans. Anna Swanwick—Bride of Messina. A. Lodge, M.A. Together with the Use of the Chorus in Tragedy (a short Essay). Engravings.

These Dramas are all translated in metre.

Vol. IV.—Robbers—Fiesco—Love and Intrigue—Demetrius—Ghost Seer—Sport of Divinity.

The Dramas in this volume are in prose.

Vol. V.—Poems. E. A. Bowring, C.B.

Vol. VI.—Essays, Æsthetical and Philosophical, including the Dissertation on the Connexion between the Animal and Spiritual in Man.

Vol. VII. — Wallenstein's Camp. J. Churchill. — Piccolomini and Death of Wallenstein. S. T. Coleridge.—William Tell. Sir Theodore Martin, K.C.B., LL.D.

SCHILLER and GOETHE. Correspondence between, from A.D. 1794-1805. Trans. by L. Dora Schmitz. 2 vols.

SCHLEGEL (F.) Lectures on the Philosophy of Life and the Philosophy of Language. Trans. by A. J. W. Morrison.

—— The History of Literature, Ancient and Modern.

—— The Philosophy of History. With Memoir and Portrait. Trans. by J. B. Robertson.

—— Modern History, with the Lectures entitled Cæsar and Alexander, and The Beginning of our History. Translated by L. Purcell and R. H. Whitelock.

—— Æsthetic and Miscellaneous Works, containing Letters on Christian Art, Essay on Gothic Architecture, Remarks on the Romance Poetry of the Middle Ages, on Shakspeare, the Limits of the Beautiful, and on the Language and Wisdom of the Indians. By E. J. Millington.

SCHLEGEL (A. W.) Dramatic Art and Literature. By J. Black. With Memoir by Rev. A. J. W. Morrison. Portrait.

SCHUMANN (Robert), His Life and Works. By A. Reissmann. Trans. by A. L. Alger.

—— Early Letters. Translated by May Herbert. With Preface by Sir G. Grove.

SHAKESPEARE'S Dramatic Art. The History and Character of Shakspeare's Plays. By Dr. H. Ulrici. Trans. by L. Dora Schmitz. 2 vols.

SHAKESPEARE (William). A Literary Biography by Karl Elze, Ph.D., LL.D. Translated by L. Dora Schmitz. 5s.

SHERIDAN'S Dramatic Works. With Memoir. Portrait (after Reynolds).

SISMONDI'S History of the Litera- ture of the South of Europe. Trans. by T. Roscoe. Portraits. 2 vols.

SMITH'S (Adam) Theory of Moral Sentiments; with Essay on the First Formation of Languages, and Critical Memoir by Dugald Stewart.

—— *See Economic Library.*

SMYTH'S (Professor) Lectures on Modern History; from the Irruption of the Northern Nations to the close of the American Revolution. 2 vols.

—— Lectures on the French Revolution. With Index. 2 vols.

SOUTHEY.—*See Cowper, Wesley, and (Illustrated Library) Nelson.*

STURM'S Morning Communings with God, or Devotional Meditations for Every Day. Trans. by W. Johnstone, M.A.

SULLY. Memoirs of the Duke of, Prime Minister to Henry the Great. With Notes and Historical Introduction. 4 Portraits. 4 vols.

TAYLOR'S (Bishop Jeremy) Holy Living and Dying, with Prayers, containing the Whole Duty of a Christian and the parts of Devotion fitted to all Occasions. Portrait.

TEN BRINK.—*See Brink.*

THIERRY'S Conquest of England by the Normans; its Causes, and its Consequences in England and the Continent. By W. Hazlitt. With short Memoir. 2 Portraits. 2 vols.

ULRICI (Dr.)—*See Shakespeare.*

VASARI. Lives of the most Eminent Painters, Sculptors, and Architects. By Mrs. J. Foster, with selected Notes. Portrait. 6 vols., Vol. VI. being an additional Volume of Notes by Dr. J. P. Richter.

VOLTAIRE'S Tales. Translated by R. B. Boswell. Vol. I., containing 'Babouc,' Memnon, Candide, L'Ingénu, and other Tales.

WERNER'S Templars in Cyprus. Trans. by E. A. M. Lewis.

WESLEY, the Life of, and the Rise and Progress of Methodism. By Robert Southey. Portrait. 5s.

WHEATLEY. A Rational Illustra- tion of the Book of Common Prayer.

YOUNG (Arthur) Travels in France. Edited by Miss Betham Edwards. With a Portrait.

HISTORICAL LIBRARY.

22 Volumes at 5s. each.   (*5l. 10s. per set.*)

EVELYN'S Diary and Correspondence, with the Private Correspondence of Charles I. and Sir Edward Nicholas, and between Sir Edward Hyde (Earl of Clarendon) and Sir Richard Browne. Edited from the Original MSS. by W. Bray, F.A.S. 4 vols. 45 Engravings (after Vandyke, Lely, Kneller, and Jamieson, &c.).

N.B.—This edition contains 130 letters from Evelyn and his wife, printed by permission, and contained in no other edition.

PEPYS' Diary and Correspondence. With Life and Notes, by Lord Braybrooke. With Appendix containing additional Letters and Index. 4 vols., with 31 Engravings (after Vandyke, Sir P. Lely, Holbein, Kneller, &c.).

N.B.—This is a reprint of Lord Braybrooke's fourth and last edition, containing all his latest notes and corrections, the copyright of the publishers.

JESSE'S Memoirs of the Court of England under the Stuarts, including the Protectorate. 3 vols. With Index and 42 Portraits (after Vandyke, Lely, &c.).

—— **Memoirs of the Pretenders and** their Adherents. 6 Portraits.

NUGENT'S (Lord) Memorials of Hampden, his Party and Times. With Memoir. 12 Portraits (after Vandyke and others).

STRICKLAND'S (Agnes) Lives of the Queens of England from the Norman Conquest. From authentic Documents, public and private. 6 Portraits. 6 vols.

—— **Life of Mary Queen of Scots.** 2 Portraits. 2 vols.

—— **Lives of the Tudor and Stuart** Princesses. With 2 Portraits.

PHILOSOPHICAL LIBRARY.

17 Vols. at 5s. each, excepting those marked otherwise. (*3l. 19s. per set.*)

BACON'S Novum Organum and Advancement of Learning. With Notes by J. Devey, M.A.

BAX. A Handbook of the History of Philosophy, for the use of Students. By E. Belfort Bax, Editor of Kant's 'Prolegomena.'

COMTE'S Philosophy of the Sciences. An Exposition of the Principles of the *Cours de Philosophie Positive.* By G. H. Lewes, Author of 'The Life of Goethe.'

DRAPER (Dr. J. W.) A History of the Intellectual Development of Europe. 2 vols.

HEGEL'S Philosophy of History. By J. Sibree, M.A.

KANT'S Critique of Pure Reason. By J. M. D. Meiklejohn.

—— **Prolegomena and Metaphysical** Foundations of Natural Science, with Biography and Memoir by E. Belfort Bax. Portrait.

LOGIC, or the Science of Inference. A Popular Manual. By J. Devey.

MILLER (Professor). History Philosophically Illustrated, from the Fall of the Roman Empire to the French Revolution. With Memoir. 4 vols. 3s. 6d. each.

SCHOPENHAUER on the Fourfold Root of the Principle of Sufficient Reason, and on the Will in Nature. Trans. from the German.

—— **Essays.** Selected and Translated by E. Belfort Bax.

SPINOZA'S Chief Works. Trans. with Introduction by R. H. M. Elwes. 2 vols.

Vol. I.—Tractatus Theologico-Politicus —Political Treatise.

Vol. II.—Improvement of the Understanding—Ethics—Letters.

THEOLOGICAL LIBRARY.

15 *Vols. at* 5s. *each* (*except Chillingworth*, 3s. 6d.). (3l. 13s. 6d. *per set.*)

BLEEK. Introduction to the Old Testament. By Friedrich Bleek. Trans. under the supervision of Rev. E. Venables, Residentiary Canon of Lincoln. 2 vols.

CHILLINGWORTH'S Religion of Protestants. 3s. 6d.

EUSEBIUS. Ecclesiastical History of Eusebius Pamphilus, Bishop of Cæsarea. Trans. by Rev. C. F. Cruse, M.A. With Notes, Life, and Chronological Tables.

EVAGRIUS. History of the Church. —*See Theodoret.*

HARDWICK. History of the Articles of Religion; to which is added a Series of Documents from A.D. 1536 to A.D. 1615. Ed. by Rev. F. Proctor.

HENRY'S (Matthew) Exposition of the Book of Psalms. Numerous Woodcuts.

PEARSON (John, D.D.) Exposition of the Creed. Edit. by E. Walford, M.A. With Notes, Analysis, and Indexes.

PHILO-JUDÆUS, Works of. The Contemporary of Josephus. Trans. by C. D. Yonge. 4 vols.

PHILOSTORGIUS. Ecclesiastical History of.—*See Sozomen.*

SOCRATES' Ecclesiastical History. Comprising a History of the Church from Constantine, A.D. 305, to the 38th year of Theodosius II. With Short Account of the Author, and selected Notes.

SOZOMEN'S Ecclesiastical History. A.D. 324-440. With Notes, Prefatory Remarks by Valesius, and Short Memoir. Together with the ECCLESIASTICAL HISTORY OF PHILOSTORGIUS, as epitomised by Photius. Trans. by Rev. E. Walford, M.A. With Notes and brief Life.

THEODORET and EVAGRIUS. Histories of the Church from A.D. 332 to the Death of Theodore of Mopsuestia, A.D. 427; and from A.D. 431 to A.D. 544. With Memoirs.

WIESELER'S (Karl) Chronological Synopsis of the Four Gospels. Trans. by Rev. Canon Venables.

ANTIQUARIAN LIBRARY.

35 *Vols. at* 5s. *each.* (8l. 15s. *per set.*)

ANGLO-SAXON CHRONICLE. — *See Bede.*

ASSER'S Life of Alfred.—*See Six O. E. Chronicles.*

BEDE'S (Venerable) Ecclesiastical History of England. Together with the ANGLO-SAXON CHRONICLE. With Notes, Short Life, Analysis, and Map. Edit. by J. A. Giles, D.C.L.

BOETHIUS'S Consolation of Philosophy. King Alfred's Anglo-Saxon Version of. With an English Translation on opposite pages, Notes, Introduction, and Glossary, by Rev. S. Fox, M.A. To which is added the Anglo-Saxon Version of the METRES OF BOETHIUS, with a free Translation by Martin F. Tupper, D.C.L.

BRAND'S Popular Antiquities of England, Scotland, and Ireland. Illustrating the Origin of our Vulgar and Provincial Customs, Ceremonies, and Superstitions. By Sir Henry Ellis, K.H., F.R.S. Frontispiece. 3 vols.

CHRONICLES of the CRUSADES. Contemporary Narratives of Richard Cœur de Lion, by Richard of Devizes and Geoffrey de Vinsauf; and of the Crusade at Saint Louis, by Lord John de Joinville. With Short Notes. Illuminated Frontispiece from an old MS.

DYER'S (T. F. T.) British Popular Customs, Present and Past. An Account of the various Games and Customs associated with different Days of the Year in the British Isles, arranged according to the Calendar. By the Rev. T. F. Thiselton Dyer, M.A.

EARLY TRAVELS IN PALESTINE. Comprising the Narratives of Arculf, Willibald, Bernard, Sæwulf, Sigurd, Benjamin of Tudela, Sir John Maundeville, De la Brocquière, and Maundrell; all unabridged. With Introduction and Notes by Thomas Wright. Map of Jerusalem.

ELLIS (G.) Specimens of Early English Metrical Romances, relating to Arthur, Merlin, Guy of Warwick, Richard Cœur de Lion, Charlemagne, Roland, &c. &c. With Historical Introduction by J. O. Halliwell, F.R.S. Illuminated Frontispiece from an old MS.

ETHELWERD, Chronicle of.—*See Six O. E. Chronicles.*

FLORENCE OF WORCESTER'S Chronicle, with the Two Continuations: comprising Annals of English History from the Departure of the Romans to the Reign of Edward I. Trans., with Notes, by Thomas Forester, M.A.

GEOFFREY OF MONMOUTH. Chronicle of.—*See Six O. E. Chronicles.*

GESTA ROMANORUM, or Entertaining Moral Stories invented by the Monks. Trans. with Notes by the Rev. Charles Swan. Edit. by W. Hooper, M.A.

GILDAS. Chronicle of.—*See Six O. E. Chronicles.*

GIRALDUS CAMBRENSIS' Historical Works. Containing Topography of Ireland, and History of the Conquest of Ireland, by Th. Forester, M.A. Itinerary through Wales, and Description of Wales, by Sir R. Colt Hoare.

HENRY OF HUNTINGDON'S History of the English, from the Roman Invasion to the Accession of Henry II.; with the Acts of King Stephen, and the Letter to Walter. By T. Forester, M.A. Frontispiece from an old MS.

INGULPH'S Chronicles of the Abbey of Croyland, with the CONTINUATION by Peter of Blois and others. Trans. with Notes by H. T. Riley, B.A.

KEIGHTLEY'S (Thomas) Fairy Mythology, illustrative of the Romance and Superstition of Various Countries. Frontispiece by Cruikshank.

LEPSIUS'S Letters from Egypt, Ethiopia, and the Peninsula of Sinai; to which are added, Extracts from his Chronology of the Egyptians, with reference to the Exodus of the Israelites. By L. and J. B. Horner. Maps and Coloured View of Mount Barkal.

MALLET'S Northern Antiquities, or an Historical Account of the Manners, Customs, Religions, and Literature of the Ancient Scandinavians. Trans. by Bishop Percy. With Translation of the PROSE EDDA, and Notes by J. A. Blackwell. Also an Abstract of the 'Eyrbyggia Saga' by Sir Walter Scott. With Glossary and Coloured Frontispiece.

MARCO POLO'S Travels; with Notes and Introduction. Edit. by T. Wright.

MATTHEW PARIS'S English History, from 1235 to 1273. By Rev. J. A. Giles, D.C.L. With Frontispiece. 3 vols.— *See also Roger of Wendover.*

MATTHEW OF WESTMINSTER'S Flowers of History, especially such as relate to the affairs of Britain, from the beginning of the World to A.D. 1307. By C. D. Yonge. 2 vols.

NENNIUS. Chronicle of.—*See Six O. E. Chronicles.*

ORDERICUS VITALIS' Ecclesiastical History of England and Normandy. With Notes, Introduction of Guizot, and the Critical Notice of M. Delille, by T. Forester, M.A. To which is added the CHRONICLE OF St. EVROULT. With General and Chronological Indexes. 4 vols.

PAULI'S (Dr. R.) Life of Alfred the Great. To which is appended Alfred's ANGLO-SAXON VERSION OF OROSIUS. With literal Translation interpaged, Notes, and an ANGLO-SAXON GRAMMAR and Glossary, by B. Thorpe. Frontispiece.

RICHARD OF CIRENCESTER. Chronicle of.—*See Six O. E. Chronicles.*

ROGER DE HOVEDEN'S Annals of English History, comprising the History of England and of other Countries of Europe from A.D. 732 to A.D. 1201. With Notes by H. T. Riley, B.A. 2 vols.

ROGER OF WENDOVER'S Flowers of History, comprising the History of England from the Descent of the Saxons to A.D. 1235, formerly ascribed to Matthew Paris. With Notes and Index by J. A. Giles, D.C.L. 2 vols.

SIX OLD ENGLISH CHRONICLES: viz., Asser's Life of Alfred and the Chronicles of Ethelwerd, Gildas, Nennius, Geoffrey of Monmouth, and Richard of Cirencester. Edit., with Notes, by J. A. Giles, D.C.L. Portrait of Alfred.

WILLIAM OF MALMESBURY'S Chronicle of the Kings of England, from the Earliest Period to King Stephen. By Rev. J. Sharpe. With Notes by J. A. Giles, D.C.L. Frontispiece.

YULE-TIDE STORIES. A Collection of Scandinavian and North-German Popular Tales and Traditions, from the Swedish, Danish, and German. Edit. by B. Thorpe.

ILLUSTRATED LIBRARY.

73 Vols. at 5s. each, excepting those marked otherwise. (19*l.* 7*s.* 6*d.* *per set.*)

ALLEN'S (Joseph, R.N.) Battles of the British Navy. Revised edition, with Indexes of Names and Events, and 57 Portraits and Plans. 2 vols.

ANDERSEN'S Danish Fairy Tales. By Caroline Peachey. With Short Life and 120 Wood Engravings.

ARIOSTO'S Orlando Furioso. In English Verse by W. S. Rose. With Notes and Short Memoir. Portrait after Titian, and 24 Steel Engravings. 2 vols.

BECHSTEIN'S Cage and Chamber Birds: their Natural History, Habits, &c. Together with SWEET'S BRITISH WARBLERS. 43 Coloured Plates and Woodcuts.

BONOMI'S Nineveh and its Palaces. The Discoveries of Botta and Layard applied to the Elucidation of Holy Writ. 7 Plates and 294 Woodcuts.

BUTLER'S Hudibras, with Variorum Notes and Biography. Portrait and 28 Illustrations.

CATTERMOLE'S Evenings at Had- don Hall. Romantic Tales of the Olden Times. With 24 Steel Engravings after Cattermole.

CHINA, Pictorial, Descriptive, and Historical, with some account of Ava and the Burmese, Siam, and Anam. Map, and nearly 100 Illustrations.

CRAIK'S (G. L.) Pursuit of Know- ledge under Difficulties. Illustrated by Anecdotes and Memoirs. Numerous Woodcut Portraits.

CRUIKSHANK'S Three Courses and a Dessert; comprising three Sets of Tales, West Country, Irish, and Legal; and a Mélange. With 50 Illustrations by Cruikshank.

—— **Punch and Judy.** The Dialogue of the Puppet Show; an Account of its Origin, &c. 24 Illustrations and Coloured Plates by Cruikshank.

DANTE, in English Verse, by I. C. Wright, M.A. With Introduction and Memoir. Portrait and 34 Steel Engravings after Flaxman.

DIDRON'S Christian Iconography; a History of Christian Art in the Middle Ages. By the late A. N. Didron. Trans. by E. J. Millington, and completed, with Additions and Appendices, by Margaret Stokes. 2 vols. With numerous Illustrations.

Vol. I. The History of the Nimbus, the Aureole, and the Glory; Representations of the Persons of the Trinity.

Vol. II. The Trinity; Angels; Devils; The Soul; The Christian Scheme. Appendices.

DYER (Dr. T. H.) Pompeii: its Buildings and Antiquities. An Account of the City, with full Description of the Remains and Recent Excavations, and an Itinerary for Visitors. By T. H. Dyer, LL.D. Nearly 300 Wood Engravings, Map, and Plan. 7*s.* 6*d.*

—— **Rome:** History of the City, with Introduction on recent Excavations. 8 Engravings, Frontispiece, and 2 Maps.

GIL BLAS. The Adventures of. From the French of Lesage by Smollett. 24 Engravings after Smirke, and 10 Etchings by Cruikshank. 612 pages. 6*s.*

GRIMM'S Gammer Grethel; or, German Fairy Tales and Popular Stories, containing 42 Fairy Tales. By Edgar Taylor. Numerous Woodcuts after Cruikshank and Ludwig Grimm. 3*s.* 6*d.*

HOLBEIN'S Dance of Death and Bible Cuts. Upwards of 150 Subjects, engraved in facsimile, with Introduction and Descriptions by the late Francis Douce and Dr. Dibdin.

INDIA, Pictorial, Descriptive, and Historical, from the Earliest Times. 100 Engravings on Wood and Map.

JESSE'S Anecdotes of Dogs. With 40 Woodcuts after Harvey, Bewick, and others; and 34 Steel Engravings after Cooper and Landseer.

KING'S (C. W.) Natural History of Precious Stones and Metals. Illustrations. 6*s.*

LODGE'S Portraits of Illustrious Personages of Great Britain, with Biographical and Historical Memoirs. 240 Portraits engraved on Steel, with the respective Biographies unabridged. Complete in 8 vols.

LONGFELLOW'S Poetical Works, including his Translations and Notes. 24 full-page Woodcuts by Birket Foster and others, and a Portrait.

—— Without the Illustrations, 3*s.* 6*d.*

—— **Prose Works.** With 16 full-page Woodcuts by Birket Foster and others.

LOUDON'S (Mrs.) Entertaining Naturalist. Popular Descriptions, Tales, and Anecdotes, of more than 500 Animals. Numerous Woodcuts.

MARRYAT'S (Capt., R.N.) Masterman Ready; or, the Wreck of the *Pacific.* (Written for Young People.) With 93 Woodcuts. 3*s.* 6*d.*

—— **Mission; or, Scenes in Africa.** (Written for Young People.) Illustrated by Gilbert and Dalziel. 3*s.* 6*d.*

—— **Pirate and Three Cutters.** (Written for Young People.) With a Memoir. 8 Steel Engravings after Clarkson Stanfield, R.A. 3*s.* 6*d.*

—— **Privateersman.** Adventures by Sea and Land One Hundred Years Ago. (Written for Young People.) 8 Steel Engravings. 3*s.* 6*d.*

—— **Settlers in Canada.** (Written for Young People.) 10 Engravings by Gilbert and Dalziel. 3*s.* 6*d.*

—— **Poor Jack.** (Written for Young People.) With 16 Illustrations after Clarkson Stanfield, R.A. 3*s.* 6*d.*

—— **Midshipman Easy.** With 8 full-page Illustrations. Small post 8vo. 3*s.* 6*d.*

—— **Peter Simple.** With 8 full-page Illustrations. Small post 8vo. 3*s.* 6*d.*

MAXWELL'S Victories of Wellington and the British Armies. Frontispiece and 4 Portraits.

MICHAEL ANGELO and RAPHAEL, Their Lives and Works. By Duppa and Quatremère de Quincy. Portraits and Engravings, including the Last Judgment, and Cartoons.

MUDIE'S History of British Birds. Revised by W. C. L. Martin. 52 Figures of Birds and 7 coloured Plates of Eggs. 2 vols.

NAVAL and MILITARY HEROES of Great Britain; a Record of British Valour on every Day in the year, from William the Conqueror to the Battle of Inkermann. By Major Johns, R.M., and Lieut. P. H. Nicolas, R.M. Indexes. 24 Portraits after Holbein, Reynolds, &c. 6*s.*

NICOLINI'S History of the Jesuits: their Origin, Progress, Doctrines, and Designs. 8 Portraits.

PETRARCH'S Sonnets, Triumphs, and other Poems, in English Verse. With Life by Thomas Campbell. Portrait and 15 Steel Engravings.

PICKERING'S History of the Races of Man, and their Geographical Distribution; with AN ANALYTICAL SYNOPSIS OF THE NATURAL HISTORY OF MAN. By Dr. Hall. Map of the World and 12 coloured Plates.

PICTORIAL HANDBOOK OF Modern Geography on a Popular Plan. Compiled from the best Authorities, English and Foreign, by H. G. Bohn. 150 Woodcuts and 51 coloured Maps.

—— Without the Maps, 3*s.* 6*d.*

POPE'S Poetical Works, including Translations. Edit., with Notes, by R. Carruthers. 2 vols. With numerous Illustrations.

—— **Homer's Iliad,** with Introduction and Notes by Rev. J. S. Watson, M.A. With Flaxman's Designs.

—— **Homer's Odyssey,** with the BATTLE OF FROGS AND MICE, Hymns, &c., by other translators including Chapman. Introduction and Notes by J. S. Watson, M.A. With Flaxman's Designs.

—— **Life,** including many of his Letters. By R. Carruthers. Numerous Illustrations.

POTTERY AND PORCELAIN, and other objects of Vertu. Comprising an Illustrated Catalogue of the Bernal Collection, with the prices and names of the Possessors. Also an Introductory Lecture on Pottery and Porcelain, and an Engraved List of all Marks and Monograms. By H. G. Bohn. Numerous Woodcuts.

—— With coloured Illustrations, 10*s.* 6*d.*

PROUT'S (Father) Reliques. Edited by Rev. F. Mahony. Copyright edition, with the Author's last corrections and additions. 21 Etchings by D. Maclise, R.A. Nearly 600 pages.

RECREATIONS IN SHOOTING. With some Account of the Game found in the British Isles, and Directions for the Management of Dog and Gun. By 'Craven.' 62 Woodcuts and 9 Steel Engravings after A. Cooper, R.A.

RENNIE. Insect Architecture. Revised by Rev. J. G. Wood, M.A. 186 Woodcuts.

ROBINSON CRUSOE. With Memoir of Defoe, 12 Steel Engravings and 74 Woodcuts after Stothard and Harvey.

—— Without the Engravings, 3s. 6d.

ROME IN THE NINETEENTH CENtury. An Account in 1817 of the Ruins of the Ancient City, and Monuments of Modern Times. By C. A. Eaton. 34 Steel Engravings. 2 vols.

SHARPE (S.) The History of Egypt, from the Earliest Times till the Conquest by the Arabs, A.D. 640. 2 Maps and upwards of 400 Woodcuts. 2 vols.

SOUTHEY'S Life of Nelson. With Additional Notes, Facsimiles of Nelson's Writing, Portraits, Plans, and 50 Engravings, after Birket Foster, &c.

STARLING'S (Miss) Noble Deeds of Women; or, Examples of Female Courage, Fortitude, and Virtue. With 14 Steel Portraits.

STUART and REVETT'S Antiquities of Athens, and other Monuments of Greece; with Glossary of Terms used in Grecian Architecture. 71 Steel Plates and numerous Woodcuts.

SWEET'S British Warblers. 5s.—*See Bechstein.*

TALES OF THE GENII; or, the Delightful Lessons of Horam, the Son of Asmar. Trans. by Sir C. Morrell. Numerous Woodcuts.

TASSO'S Jerusalem Delivered. In English Spenserian Verse, with Life, by J. H. Wiffen. With 8 Engravings and 24 Woodcuts.

WALKER'S Manly Exercises; containing Skating, Riding, Driving, Hunting, Shooting, Sailing, Rowing, Swimming, &c. 44 Engravings and numerous Woodcuts.

WALTON'S Complete Angler, or the Contemplative Man's Recreation, by Izaak Walton and Charles Cotton. With Memoirs and Notes by E. Jesse. Also an Account of Fishing Stations, Tackle, &c., by H. G. Bohn. Portrait and 203 Woodcuts, and 26 Engravings on Steel.

—— **Lives of Donne, Wotton, Hooker,** &c., with Notes. A New Edition, revised by A. H. Bullen, with a Memoir of Izaak Walton by William Dowling. 6 Portraits, 6 Autograph Signatures, &c.

WELLINGTON, Life of. From the Materials of Maxwell. 18 Steel Engravings.

—— **Victories of.**—*See Maxwell.*

WESTROPP (H. M.) A Handbook of Archæology, Egyptian, Greek, Etruscan, Roman. By H. M. Westropp. Numerous Illustrations.

WHITE'S Natural History of Selborne, with Observations on various Parts of Nature, and the Naturalists' Calendar. Sir W. Jardine. Edit., with Notes and Memoir, by E. Jesse. 40 Portraits and coloured Plates.

CLASSICAL LIBRARY.

TRANSLATIONS FROM THE GREEK AND LATIN.

103 Vols. at 5s. each, excepting those marked otherwise. (25l. 3s. per set.)

ACHILLES TATIUS. — *See Greek Romances.*

ÆSCHYLUS, The Dramas of. In English Verse by Anna Swanwick. 4th edition.

—— **The Tragedies of.** In Prose, with Notes and Introduction, by T. A. Buckley, B.A. Portrait. 3s. 6d.

AMMIANUS MARCELLINUS. History of Rome during the Reigns of Constantius, Julian, Jovianus, Valentinian, and Valens, by C. D. Yonge, B.A. Double volume. 7s. 6d.

ANTONINUS (M. Aurelius), The Thoughts of. Translated, with Notes. Biographical Sketch, and Essay on the Philosophy, by George Long, M.A. 3s. 6d. Fine Paper edition on hand-made paper. 6s.

APOLLONIUS RHODIUS. 'The Argonautica.' Translated by E. P. Coleridge.

APULEIUS, The Works of. Comprising the Golden Ass, God of Socrates, Florida, and Discourse of Magic, &c. Frontispiece.

ARISTOPHANES' Comedies. Trans., with Notes and Extracts from Frere's and other Metrical Versions, by W. J. Hickie. Portrait. 2 vols.

ARISTOTLE'S Nicomachean Ethics. Trans., with Notes, Analytical Introduction, and Questions for Students, by Ven. Archdn. Browne.

— **Politics and Economics.** Trans., with Notes, Analyses, and Index, by E. Walford, M.A., and an Essay and Life by Dr. Gillies.

— **Metaphysics.** Trans., with Notes, Analysis, and Examination Questions, by Rev. John H. M'Mahon, M.A.

— **History of Animals.** In Ten Books. Trans., with Notes and Index, by R. Cresswell, M.A.

— **Organon**; or, Logical Treatises, and the Introduction of Porphyry. With Notes, Analysis, and Introduction, by Rev. O. F. Owen, M.A. 2 vols. 3s. 6d. each.

— **Rhetoric and Poetics.** Trans., with Hobbes' Analysis, Exam. Questions, and Notes, by T. Buckley, B.A. Portrait.

ATHENÆUS. The Deipnosophists. Trans. by C. D. Yonge, B.A. With an Appendix of Poetical Fragments. 3 vols.

ATLAS of Classical Geography. 22 large Coloured Maps. With a complete Index. Imp. 8vo. 7s. 6d.

BION.—*See Theocritus.*

CÆSAR. Commentaries on the Gallic and Civil Wars, with the Supplementary Books attributed to Hirtius, including the complete Alexandrian, African, and Spanish Wars. Portrait.

CATULLUS, Tibullus, and the Vigil of Venus. Trans. with Notes and Biographical Introduction. To which are added, Metrical Versions by Lamb, Grainger, and others. Frontispiece.

CICERO'S Orations. Trans. by C. D. Yonge, B.A. 4 vols.

— **On Oratory and Orators.** With Letters to Quintus and Brutus. Trans., with Notes, by Rev. J. S. Watson, M.A.

— **On the Nature of the Gods,** Divination, Fate, Laws, a Republic, Consulship. Trans. by C. D. Yonge, B.A.

— **Academics,** De Finibus, and Tusculan Questions. By C. D. Yonge, B.A. With Sketch of the Greek Philosophers mentioned by Cicero.

CICERO'S Works.—*Continued.*

— **Offices**; or, Moral Duties. Cato Major, an Essay on Old Age; Lælius, an Essay on Friendship; Scipio's Dream; Paradoxes; Letter to Quintus on Magistrates. Trans., with Notes, by C. R. Edmonds. Portrait. 3s. 6d.

DEMOSTHENES' Orations. Trans., with Notes, Arguments, a Chronological Abstract, and Appendices, by C. Rann Kennedy. 5 vols. (One, 3s. 6d.; four, 5s.)

DICTIONARY of LATIN and GREEK Quotations; including Proverbs, Maxims, Mottoes, Law Terms and Phrases. With the Quantities marked, and English Translations. With Index Verborum (622 pages).

— Index Verborum to the above, with the *Quantities* and Accents marked (56 pages), limp cloth. 1s.

DIOGENES LAERTIUS. Lives and Opinions of the Ancient Philosophers. Trans., with Notes, by C. D. Yonge, B.A.

EPICTETUS. The Discourses of. With the Encheiridion and Fragments. With Notes, Life, and View of his Philosophy, by George Long, M.A.

EURIPIDES. Trans. by T. A. Buckley, B.A. Portrait. 2 vols.

GREEK ANTHOLOGY. In English Prose by G. Burges, M.A. With Metrical Versions by Bland, Merivale, and others.

GREEK ROMANCES of Heliodorus, Longus, and Achilles Tatius; viz., The Adventures of Theagenes and Chariclea; Amours of Daphnis and Chloe; and Loves of Clitopho and Leucippe. Trans., with Notes, by Rev. R. Smith, M.A.

HELIODORUS.—*See Greek Romances.*

HERODOTUS. Literally trans. by Rev. Henry Cary, M.A. Portrait. 3s. 6d.

HESIOD, CALLIMACHUS, and Theognis. In Prose, with Notes and Biographical Notices by Rev. J. Banks, M.A. Together with the Metrical Versions of Hesiod, by Elton; Callimachus by Tytler; and Theognis, by Frere.

HOMER'S Iliad. In English Prose, with Notes by T. A. Buckley, B.A. Portrait.

— **Odyssey,** Hymns, Epigrams, and Battle of the Frogs and Mice. In English Prose, with Notes and Memoir by T. A. Buckley, B.A.

HORACE. In Prose by Smart, with Notes selected by T. A. Buckley, B.A. Portrait. 3s. 6d.

JULIAN THE EMPEROR. Containing Gregory Mazianzen's Two Invectives and Libanus' Monody, with Julian's Theosophical Works. By the Rev. C. W. King, M.A

JUSTIN, CORNELIUS NEPOS, and Eutropius. Trans., with Notes, by Rev. J. S. Watson, M.A.

JUVENAL, PERSIUS, SULPICIA, and Lucilius. In Prose, with Notes, Chronological Tables, Arguments, by L. Evans, M.A. To which is added the Metrical Version of Juvenal and Persius by Gifford. Frontispiece.

LIVY. The History of Rome. Trans. by Dr. Spillan and others. 4 vols. Portrait.

LONGUS. Daphnis and Chloe.—*See Greek Romances.*

LUCAN'S Pharsalia. In Prose, with Notes by H. T. Riley.

LUCIAN'S Dialogues of the Gods, of the Sea Gods, and of the Dead. Trans. by Howard Williams, M.A.

LUCRETIUS. In Prose, with Notes and Biographical Introduction by Rev. J. S. Watson, M.A. To which is added the Metrical Version by J. M. Good.

MARTIAL'S Epigrams, complete. In Prose, with Verse Translations selected from English Poets, and other sources. Dble. vol. (670 pages). 7s. 6d.

MOSCHUS.—*See Theocritus.*

OVID'S Works, complete. In Prose, with Notes and Introduction. 3 vols.

PAUSANIAS' Description of Greece. Trans., with Notes and Index, by Rev. A. R. Shilleto, M.A., sometime Scholar of Trinity College, Cambridge. 2 vols.

PHALARIS. Bentley's Dissertations upon the Epistles of Phalaris, Themistocles, Socrates, Euripides, and the Fables of Æsop. With Introduction and Notes by Prof. W. Wagner, Ph.D.

PINDAR. In Prose, with Introduction and Notes by Dawson W. Turner. Together with the Metrical Version by Abraham Moore. Portrait.

PLATO'S Works. Trans. by Rev. H. Cary, H. Davis, and G. Burges. 6 vols.

—— **Dialogues.** A Summary and Analysis of. With Analytical Index to the Greek text of modern editions and to the above translations, by A. Day, LL.D.

PLAUTUS'S Comedies. In Prose, with Notes by H. T. Riley, B.A. 2 vols.

PLINY'S Natural History. Trans., with Notes, by J. Bostock, M.D., F.R.S., and H. T. Riley, B.A. 6 vols.

PLINY. The Letters of Pliny the Younger. Melmoth's Translation, revised, with Notes and short Life, by Rev. F. C. Bosanquet, M.A.

PLUTARCH'S Morals. Theosophical Essays. Trans. by Rev. C. W. King, M.A.

—— **Ethical Essays.** Trans. by Rev. A. R. Shilleto, M.A.

—— **Lives.** *See page 7.*

PROPERTIUS, The Elegies of. With Notes, translated by Rev. P. J. F. Gantillon, M.A., with metrical versions of Select Elegies by Nott and Elton. 3s. 6d.

QUINTILIAN'S Institutes of Oratory. Trans., by Rev. J. S. Watson, M.A. 2 vols.

SALLUST, FLORUS, and VELLEIUS Paterculus. Trans., with Notes and Biographical Notices, by J. S. Watson, M.A.

SENECA DE BENEFICIIS. Translated by Aubrey Stewart, M.A. 3s. 6d.

SENECA'S Minor Essays. Translated by A. Stewart, M.A.

SOPHOCLES. The Tragedies of. In Prose, with Notes, Arguments, and Introduction. Portrait.

STRABO'S Geography. Trans., with Notes, by W. Falconer, M.A., and H. C. Hamilton. Copious Index, giving Ancient and Modern Names. 3 vols.

SUETONIUS' Lives of the Twelve Cæsars and Lives of the Grammarians. The Translation of Thomson, revised, with Notes, by T. Forester.

TACITUS. The Works of. Trans., with Notes. 2 vols.

TERENCE and PHÆDRUS. In English Prose, with Notes and Arguments, by H. T. Riley, B.A. To which is added Smart's Metrical Version of Phædrus. With Frontispiece.

THEOCRITUS, BION, MOSCHUS, and Tyrtæus. In Prose, with Notes and Arguments, by Rev. J. Banks, M.A. To which are appended the METRICAL VERSIONS of Chapman. Portrait of Theocritus.

THUCYDIDES. The Peloponnesian War. Trans., with Notes, by Rev. H. Dale. Portrait. 2 vols. 3s. 6d. each.

TYRTÆUS.—*See Theocritus.*

VIRGIL. The Works of. In Prose, with Notes by Davidson. Revised, with additional Notes and Biographical Notice, by T. A. Buckley, B.A. Portrait. 3s. 6d.

XENOPHON'S Works. Trans., with Notes, by J. S. Watson, M.A., and Rev. H. Dale. Portrait. In 3 vols.

COLLEGIATE SERIES.

11 *Vols. at* 5s. *each.* (2l. 15s. *per set.*)

DANTE. The Inferno. Prose Trans., with the Text of the Original on the same page, and Explanatory Notes, by John A. Carlyle, M.D. Portrait.

—— **The Purgatorio.** Prose Trans., with the Original on the same page, and Explanatory Notes, by W. S. Dugdale.

DOBREE'S Adversaria. (Notes on the Greek and Latin Classics.) Edited by the late Prof. Wagner. 2 vols.

DONALDSON (Dr.) The Theatre of the Greeks. With Supplementary Treatise on the Language, Metres, and Prosody of the Greek Dramatists. Numerous Illustrations and 3 Plans. By J. W. Donaldson, D.D.

GOETHE'S Faust. Part I. German Text, with Hayward's Prose Translation and Notes. Revised, with Introduction and Bibliography, by Dr. C. A. Buchheim. 5s.

KEIGHTLEY'S (Thomas) Mythology of Ancient Greece and Italy. Revised by Dr. Leonhard Schmitz. 12 Plates.

HERODOTUS, Notes on. Original and Selected from the best Commentators. By D. W. Turner, M.A. Coloured Map.

—— **Analysis and Summary of,** with a Synchronistical Table of Events—Tables of Weights, Measures, Money, and Distances — an Outline of the History and Geography—and the Dates completed from Gaisford, Bachr, &c. By J. T. Wheeler.

NEW TESTAMENT (The) in Greek. Griesbach's Text, with the Readings of Mill and Scholz, and Parallel References. Also a Critical Introduction and Chronological Tables. Two Fac-similes of Greek Manuscripts. 650 pages. 3s. 6d.

—— or bound up with a Greek and English Lexicon to the New Testament (250 pages additional, making in all 900). 5s.

The Lexicon separately, 2s.

THUCYDIDES. An Analysis and Summary of. With Chronological Table of Events, &c., by J. T. Wheeler.

SCIENTIFIC LIBRARY.

48 *Vols. at* 5s. *each, excepting those marked otherwise.* (12l. 19s. *per set.*)

AGASSIZ and GOULD. Outline of Comparative Physiology. Enlarged by Dr. Wright. With Index and 300 Illustrative Woodcuts.

BOLLEY'S Manual of Technical Analysis; a Guide for the Testing and Valuation of the various Natural and Artificial Substances employed in the Arts and Domestic Economy, founded on the work of Dr. Bolley. Edit. by Dr. Paul. 100 Woodcuts.

BRIDGEWATER TREATISES.

—— **Bell (Sir Charles) on the Hand;** its Mechanism and Vital Endowments, as evincing Design. Preceded by an Account of the Author's Discoveries in the Nervous System by A. Shaw. Numerous Woodcuts.

—— **Kirby on the History, Habits,** and Instincts of Animals. With Notes by T. Rymer Jones. 100 Woodcuts. 2 vols.

—— **Buckland's Geology and Mineralogy.** With Additions by Prof. Owen, Prof. Phillips, and R. Brown. Memoir of Buckland. Portrait. 2 vols. 15s. Vol. I. Text. Vol. II. 90 large plates with letterpress.

BRIDGEWATER TREATISES. *Continued.*

—— **Chalmers on the Adaptation of** External Nature to the Moral and Intellectual Constitution of Man. With Memoir by Rev. Dr. Cumming. Portrait.

—— **Prout's Treatise on Chemistry,** Meteorology, and the Function of Digestion, with reference to Natural Theology. Edit. by Dr. J. W. Griffith. 2 Maps.

—— **Roget's Animal and Vegetable** Physiology. 463 Woodcuts. 2 vols. 6s. each.

—— **Kidd on the Adaptation of Ex-** ternal Nature to the Physical Condition of Man. 3s. 6d.

CARPENTER'S (Dr. W. B.) Zoology. A Systematic View of the Structure, Habits, Instincts, and Uses of the principal Families of the Animal Kingdom, and of the chief Forms of Fossil Remains. Revised by W. S. Dallas, F.L.S. Numerous Woodcuts. 2 vols. 6s. each.

—— **Mechanical Philosophy, Astro-** nomy, and Horology. A Popular Exposition. 181 Woodcuts.

CARPENTER'S Works.—*Continued.*

—— **Vegetable Physiology and Systematic Botany.** A complete Introduction to the Knowledge of Plants. Revised by E. Lankester, M.D., &c. Numerous Woodcuts. 6s.

—— **Animal Physiology.** Revised Edition. 300 Woodcuts. 6s.

CHEVREUL on Colour. Containing the Principles of Harmony and Contrast of Colours, and their Application to the Arts ; including Painting, Decoration, Tapestries, Carpets, Mosaics, Glazing, Staining, Calico Printing, Letterpress Printing, Map Colouring, Dress, Landscape and Flower Gardening, &c. Trans. by C. Martel. Several Plates.

—— With an additional series of 16 Plates in Colours, 7s. 6d.

ENNEMOSER'S History of Magic. Trans. by W. Howitt. With an Appendix of the most remarkable and best authenticated Stories of Apparitions, Dreams, Second Sight, Table-Turning, and Spirit-Rapping, &c. 2 vols.

HOGG'S (Jabez) Elements of Experimental and Natural Philosophy. Being an Easy Introduction to the Study of Mechanics, Pneumatics, Hydrostatics, Hydraulics, Acoustics, Optics, Caloric, Electricity, Voltaism, and Magnetism. 400 Woodcuts.

HUMBOLDT'S Cosmos ; or, Sketch of a Physical Description of the Universe. Trans. by E. C. Otté, B. H. Paul, and W. S. Dallas, F.L.S. Portrait. 5 vols. 3s. 6d. each, excepting vol. v., 5s.

—— **Personal Narrative of his Travels** in America during the years 1799-1804. Trans., with Notes, by T. Ross. 3 vols.

—— **Views of Nature ; or, Contemplations** of the Sublime Phenomena of Creation, with Scientific Illustrations. Trans. by E. C. Otté.

HUNT'S (Robert) Poetry of Science ; or, Studies of the Physical Phenomena of Nature. By Robert Hunt, Professor at the School of Mines.

JOYCE'S Scientific Dialogues. A Familiar Introduction to the Arts and Sciences. For Schools and Young People. Numerous Woodcuts.

JUKES-BROWNE'S Student's Handbook of Physical Geology. By A. J. Jukes-Browne, of the Geological Survey of England. With numerous Diagrams and Illustrations, 6s.

JUKES-BROWNE'S Works.—*Cont.*

—— **The Student's Handbook of** Historical Geology. By A. J. Jukes-Brown, B.A., F.G.S., of the Geological Survey of England and Wales. With numerous Diagrams and Illustrations. 6s.

—— **The Building of the British** Islands. A Study in Geographical Evolution. By A J. Jukes-Browne, F.G.S. 7s. 6d.

KNIGHT'S (Charles) Knowledge is Power. A Popular Manual of Political Economy.

LILLY. Introduction to Astrology. With a Grammar of Astrology and Tables for calculating Nativities, by Zadkiel.

MANTELL'S (Dr.) Geological Excursions through the Isle of Wight and along the Dorset Coast. Numerous Woodcuts and Geological Map.

—— **Petrifactions and their Teachings.** Handbook to the Organic Remains in the British Museum. Numerous Woodcuts. 6s.

—— **Wonders of Geology ; or, a** Familiar Exposition of Geological Phenomena. A coloured Geological Map of England, Plates, and 200 Woodcuts. 2 vols. 7s. 6d. each.

SCHOUW'S Earth, Plants, and Man. Popular Pictures of Nature. And Kobell's Sketches from the Mineral Kingdom. Trans. by A. Henfrey, F.R.S. Coloured Map of the Geography of Plants.

SMITH'S (Pye) Geology and Scripture ; or, the Relation between the Scriptures and Geological Science. With Memoir.

STANLEY'S Classified Synopsis of the Principal Painters of the Dutch and Flemish Schools, including an Account of some of the early German Masters. By George Stanley.

STAUNTON'S Chess Works. — *See page 21.*

STÖCKHARDT'S Experimental Chemistry. A Handbook for the Study of the Science by simple Experiments. Edit. by C. W. Heaton, F.C.S. Numerous Woodcuts.

URE'S (Dr. A.) Cotton Manufacture of Great Britain, systematically investigated ; with an Introductory View of its Comparative State in Foreign Countries. Revised by P. L. Simmonds. 150 Illustrations. 2 vols.

—— **Philosophy of Manufactures,** or an Exposition of the Scientific, Moral, and Commercial Economy of the Factory System of Great Britain. Revised by P. L. Simmonds. Numerous Figures. 800 pages. 7s. 6d.

ECONOMICS AND FINANCE.

GILBART'S History, Principles, and Practice of Banking. Revised to 1881 by A. S. Michie, of the Royal Bank of Scotland. Portrait of Gilbart. 2 vols. 10s.

RICARDO on the Principles of Political Economy and Taxation. Edited by E. C. K. Gonner, M.A., Lecturer, University College, Liverpool. 5s.

SMITH (Adam). The Wealth of Nations. An Inquiry into the Nature and Causes of. Edited by E. Belfort Bax. 2 vols. 7s.

REFERENCE LIBRARY.

32 Volumes at Various Prices. (8l. 3s. per set.)

BLAIR'S Chronological Tables. Comprehending the Chronology and History of the World, from the Earliest Times to the Russian Treaty of Peace, April 1856. By J. W. Rosse. 800 pages. 10s.

—— **Index of Dates.** Comprehending the principal Facts in the Chronology and History of the World, from the Earliest to the Present, alphabetically arranged; being a complete Index to the foregoing. By J. W. Rosse. 2 vols. 5s. each.

BOHN'S Dictionary of Quotations from the English Poets. 4th and cheaper Edition. 6s.

BOND'S Handy-book of Rules and Tables for Verifying Dates with the Christian Era. 4th Edition. 5s.

BUCHANAN'S Dictionary of Science and Technical Terms used in Philosophy, Literature, Professions, Commerce, Arts, and Trades. By W. H. Buchanan, with Supplement. Edited by Jas. A. Smith. 6s.

CHRONICLES OF THE TOMBS. A Select Collection of Epitaphs, with Essay on Epitaphs and Observations on Sepulchral Antiquities. By T. J. Pettigrew, F.R.S., F.S.A. 5s.

CLARK'S (Hugh) Introduction to Heraldry. Revised by J. R. Planché. 5s. 950 Illustrations.

—— *With the Illustrations coloured,* 15s.

COINS, Manual of.—*See Humphreys.*

COOPER'S Biographical Dictionary. Containing concise notices of upwards of 15,000 eminent persons of all ages and countries. 2 vols. 5s. each.

DATES, Index of.—*See Blair.*

DICTIONARY of Obsolete and Provincial English. Containing Words from English Writers previous to the 19th Century. By Thomas Wright, M.A., F.S.A., &c. 2 vols. 5s. each.

EPIGRAMMATISTS (The). A Selection from the Epigrammatic Literature of Ancient, Mediæval, and Modern Times. With Introduction, Notes, Observations, Illustrations, an Appendix on Works connected with Epigrammatic Literature, by Rev. H. Dodd, M.A. 6s.

GAMES, Handbook of. Edited by Henry G. Bohn. Numerous Diagrams. 5s. (*See also page 21.*)

HENFREY'S Guide to English Coins. Revised Edition, by C. F. Keary, M.A., F.S.A. With an Historical Introduction. 6s.

HUMPHREYS' Coin Collectors' Manual. An Historical Account of the Progress of Coinage from the Earliest Time, by H. N. Humphreys. 140 Illustrations. 2 vols. 5s. each.

LOWNDES' Bibliographer's Manual of English Literature. Containing an Account of Rare and Curious Books published in or relating to Great Britain and Ireland, from the Invention of Printing, with Biographical Notices and Prices, by W. T. Lowndes. Revised Edition by H. G. Bohn. 6 vols. cloth, 5s. each, or in 4 vols., half morocco, 2l. 2s.

MEDICINE, Handbook of Domestic, Popularly Arranged. By Dr. H. Davies. 700 pages. 5s.

NOTED NAMES OF FICTION. Dictionary of. Including also Familiar Pseudonyms, Surnames bestowed on Eminent Men, &c. By W. A. Wheeler, M.A. 5s.

POLITICAL CYCLOPÆDIA. A Dictionary of Political, Constitutional, Statistical, and Forensic Knowledge; forming a Work of Reference on subjects of Civil Administration, Political Economy, Finance, Commerce, Laws, and Social Relations. 4 vols. 3s. 6d. each.

PROVERBS, Handbook of. Containing an entire Republication of Ray's Collection, with Additions from Foreign Languages and Sayings, Sentences, Maxims, and Phrases. 5s.
—— **A Polyglot of Foreign.** Comprising French, Italian, German, Dutch, Spanish, Portuguese, and Danish. With English Translations. 5s.

SYNONYMS and ANTONYMS; or, Kindred Words and their Opposites, Collected and Contrasted by Ven. C. J. Smith, M.A. 5s.

WRIGHT (Th.)—*See Dictionary.*

NOVELISTS' LIBRARY.

13 Volumes at 3s. 6d. each, excepting those marked otherwise. (2l. 8s. 6d. per set.)

BJÖRNSON'S Arne and the Fisher Lassie. Translated from the Norse with an Introduction by W. H. Low, M.A.

BURNEY'S Evelina; or, a Young Lady's Entrance into the World. By F. Burney (Mme. D'Arblay). With Introduction and Notes by A. R. Ellis, Author of 'Sylvestra,' &c.
—— **Cecilia.** With Introduction and Notes by A. R. Ellis. 2 vols.

DE STAËL. Corinne or Italy. By Madame de Staël. Translated by Emily Baldwin and Paulina Driver.

EBERS' Egyptian Princess. Trans. by Emma Buchheim.

FIELDING'S Joseph Andrews and his Friend Mr. Abraham Adams. With Roscoe's Biography. *Cruikshank's Illustrations.*
—— **Amelia.** Roscoe's Edition, revised. *Cruikshank's Illustrations.* 5s.
—— **History of Tom Jones, a Found**ling. Roscoe's Edition. *Cruikshank's Illustrations.* 2 vols.

GROSSI'S Marco Visconti. Trans. by A. F. D.

MANZONI. The Betrothed: being a Translation of 'I Promessi Sposi.' Numerous Woodcuts. 1 vol. 5s.

STOWE (Mrs. H. B.) Uncle Tom's Cabin; or, Life among the Lowly. 8 full-page Illustrations.

ARTISTS' LIBRARY.

9 Volumes at Various Prices. (2l. 8s. 6d. per set.)

BELL (Sir Charles). The Anatomy and Philosophy of Expression, as Connected with the Fine Arts. 5s. Illustrated.

DEMMIN. History of Arms and Armour from the Earliest Period. By Auguste Demmin. Trans. by C. C. Black, M.A., Assistant Keeper, S. K. Museum. 1900 Illustrations. 7s. 6d.

FAIRHOLT'S Costume in England. Third Edition. Enlarged and Revised by the Hon. H. A. Dillon, F.S.A. With more than 700 Engravings. 2 vols. 5s. each.
Vol. I. History. Vol. II. Glossary.

FLAXMAN. Lectures on Sculpture. With Three Addresses to the R.A. by Sir R. Westmacott, R.A., and Memoir of Flaxman. Portrait and 53 Plates. 6s.

HEATON'S Concise History of Painting. New Edition, revised by W. Cosmo Monkhouse. 5s.

LECTURES ON PAINTING by the Royal Academicians, Barry, Opie, Fuseli. With Introductory Essay and Notes by R. Wornum. Portrait of Fuseli. 5s.

LEONARDO DA VINCI'S Treatise on Painting. Trans. by J. F. Rigaud, R.A. With a Life and an Account of his Works by J. W. Brown. Numerous Plates. 5s.

PLANCHÉ'S History of British Costume, from the Earliest Time to the 10th Century. By J. R. Planché. 400 Illustrations. 5s.

LIBRARY OF SPORTS AND GAMES.

14 Volumes at 3s. 6d. and 5s. each. (2l. 18s. per set.)

BOHN'S Handbooks of Athletic Sports. With numerous Illustrations. In 8 vols. 3s. 6d. each.

Vol. I.—Cricket, by Hon. and Rev. E. Lyttelton; Lawn Tennis, by H. W. W. Wilberforce; Tennis, Rackets, and Fives, by Julian Marshall, Major Spens, and J. A. Tait; Golf, by W. T. Linskill; Hockey, by F. S. Creswell.

Vol. II.—Rowing and Sculling, by W. B. Woodgate; Sailing, by E. F. Knight; Swimming, by M. and J. R. Cobbett.

Vol. III.—Boxing, by R. G. Allanson-Winn; Single Stick and Sword Exercise, by R. G. Allanson-Winn and C. Phillipps-Wolley; Wrestling, by Walter Armstrong; Fencing, by H. A. Colmore Dunn.

Vol. IV.—Rugby Football, by Harry Vassall; Association Football, by C. W. Alcock; Baseball, by Newton Crane; Rounders, Field Ball, Bowls, Quoits, Curling, Skittles, &c., by J. M. Walker, M.A., and C. C. Mott.

Vol. V.—Cycling and Athletics, by H. H. Griffin; Skating, by Douglas Adams.

Vol. VI.—Practical Horsemanship, including Riding for Ladies. By W. A. Kerr, V.C.

Vol. VII.—Driving, and Stable Management. By W. A. Kerr, V.C. [*Preparing.*

Vol. VIII.—Gymnastics, by A. F. Jenkin; Clubs and Dumb-bells, by G. T. B. Cobbett and A. F. Jenkin. [*In the press.*

BOHN'S Handbooks of Games. New Edition, entirely rewritten. 2 volumes. 3s. 6d. each.

Vol. I. TABLE GAMES.

Contents:—Billiards, with Pool, Pyramids, and Snooker, by Major-Gen. A. W. Drayson, F.R.A.S., with a preface by W. J. Peall—Bagatelle, by 'Berkeley'—

Chess, by R. F. Green—Draughts, Backgammon, Dominoes, Solitaire, Reversi, Go Bang, Rouge et noir, Roulette, E.O., Hazard, Faro, by 'Berkeley.'

Vol. II. CARD GAMES.

Contents:—Whist, by Dr. William Pole, F.R.S., Author of 'The Philosophy of Whist, &c.'—Solo Whist, by R. F. Green; Piquet, Ecarté, Euchre, Bézique, and Cribbage, by 'Berkeley;' Poker, Loo, Vingt-et-un, Napoleon, Newmarket, Rouge et Noir, Pope Joan, Speculation, &c. &c., by Baxter-Wray.

CHESS CONGRESS of 1862. A collection of the games played. Edited by J. Löwenthal. New edition, 5s.

MORPHY'S Games of Chess, being the Matches and best Games played by the American Champion, with explanatory and analytical Notes by J. Löwenthal. With short Memoir and Portrait of Morphy. 5s.

STAUNTON'S Chess-Player's Handbook. A Popular and Scientific Introduction to the Game, with numerous Diagrams. 5s.

—— **Chess Praxis.** A Supplement to the Chess-player's Handbook. Containing the most important modern Improvements in the Openings; Code of Chess Laws; and a Selection of Morphy's Games. Annotated. 636 pages. Diagrams. 5s.

—— **Chess-Player's Companion.** Comprising a Treatise on Odds, Collection of Match Games, including the French Match with M. St. Amant, and a Selection of Original Problems. Diagrams and Coloured Frontispiece. 5s.

—— **Chess Tournament of 1851.** A Collection of Games played at this celebrated assemblage. With Introduction and Notes. Numerous Diagrams. 5s.

BOHN'S CHEAP SERIES.

Price 1s. *each.*

A Series of Complete Stories or Essays, mostly reprinted from Vols. in Bohn's Libraries, and neatly bound in stiff paper cover, with cut edges, suitable for Railway Reading.

Bohn's Select Library of Standard Works.

WEBSTER'S INTERNATIONAL DICTIONARY.

An entirely New Edition of WEBSTER'S DICTIONARY, thoroughly Revised, considerably Enlarged, and reset in New Type from beginning to end.

Demy 4to. 2118 *pages,* 3500 *illustrations.*

Prices: Cloth, £1 11s. 6d.; half-calf, £2 2s.; half-russia, £2 5s.; calf, £2 8s. Also in 2 vols. cloth, £1 14s.

In addition to the Dictionary of Words, with their pronunciation, etymology, alternative spellings, and various meanings, illustrated by quotations and numerous woodcuts, there are several valuable appendices, comprising a Pronouncing Gazetteer of the World; Vocabularies of Scripture, Greek, Latin, and English Proper Names; a Dictionary of the noted Names of Fiction; a Brief History of the English Language; a Dictionary of Foreign Quotations, Words, Phrases, Proverbs, &c.; a Biographical Dictionary with 10,000 Names, &c.

This last revision, comprising and superseding the issues of 1847, 1864, and 1880, is by far the most complete that the Work has undergone during the sixty-two years that it has been before the public. Every page has been treated as if the book were now published for the first time.

SOME PRESS OPINIONS ON THE NEW EDITION.

'We believe that, all things considered, this will be found to be the best existing English dictionary in one volume. We do not know of any work similar in size and price which can approach it in completeness of vocabulary, variety of information, and general usefulness.'—*Guardian.*

'The most comprehensive and the most useful of its kind.'—*National Observer.*

'A magnificent edition of Webster's immortal Dictionary.'—*Daily Telegraph.*

'A thoroughly practical and useful dictionary.'—*Standard.*

'A special feature of the present book is the lavish use of engravings, which at once illustrate the verbal explanations of technical and scientific terms, and permit them to remain readably brief. It may be enough to refer to the article on "Cross." By the use of the little numbered diagrams we are spared what would have become a treatise, and not a very clear one. . . . We recommend the new Webster to every man of business, every father of a family, every teacher, and almost every student—to everybody, in fact, who is likely to be posed at an unfamiliar or half-understood word or phrase.'— *St. James's Gazette.*

Prospectuses, with Specimen Pages, on application.

London: GEORGE BELL & SONS, York Street, Covent Garden.

www.ingramcontent.com/pod-product-compliance
Lightning Source LLC
Chambersburg PA
CBHW031827270326
41932CB00008B/575